THE SECRET DIARY OF
ARNOLD DOUWES

THE SECRET DIARY OF ARNOLD DOUWES

Rescue in the Occupied Netherlands

ARNOLD DOUWES

*Edited by Bob Moore
and Johannes Houwink ten Cate*

INDIANA UNIVERSITY PRESS

This book is a publication of

Indiana University Press
Office of Scholarly Publishing
Herman B Wells Library 350
1320 East 10th Street
Bloomington, Indiana 47405 USA

iupress.indiana.edu

© 2019 by Bob Moore and Johannes Houwink ten Cate

All rights reserved
No part of this book may be reproduced or utilized in any form or by any means, electronic or mechanical, including photocopying and recording, or by any information storage and retrieval system, without permission in writing from the publisher. The paper used in this publication meets the minimum requirements of the American National Standard for Information Sciences—Permanence of Paper for Printed Library Materials, ANSI Z39.48-1992.

Manufactured in the United States of America

Cataloging information is available from the Library of Congress.

ISBN 978-0-253-04418-1 (cloth)
ISBN 978-0-253-04420-4 (ebook)

1 2 3 4 5 24 23 22 21 20 19

Contents

Prologue vii
Editors' Preface xi
Acknowledgments xiii
Translator's Note xv

The Diary and Its Context 7

The Diary 47

Aftermath 287

Epilogue 295

Glossary 299
Biographical Sketches 305
Index 331

Prologue

In 1983, I had been barely one year at my job at Yad Vashem as head of the Righteous Among the Nations Department, when I was approached by Haim Roet. Born in the Netherlands in 1932, he was hidden in several places in the Nieuwlande region (Drenthe province) with the help of Arnold Douwes and his Jewish colleague Max "Nico" Léons. Douwes had already earned the Yad Vashem honor of "Righteous Among the Nations" in 1965 and was living in Israel, not far from Tel Aviv. Roet discussed with me the debate in the Yad Vashem Commission for the Righteous with regard to Douwes's request to include among the Righteous several hundred Nieuwlande residents who, he claimed, answered his and Léons's call for sheltering Jews during the German occupation of the Netherlands and thus saved their lives. In fact, Douwes had kept notes in a diary during the war years carefully listing all the locations he secretly visited in the Nieuwlande countryside to find places where Jews, coming mainly from Amsterdam, would be afforded safe shelter. These notes were hidden in a secret place, but Douwes was able to recover them after the war. The notes gave the details in coded language, the names and acts of the people in the Nieuwlande region who had aided him in hiding Jews from the Germans. He then insisted that all these rescuers also be accorded the Righteous title. He was quite adamant about it, once going so far as threatening that if these rescuer colleagues of his were not recognized, he would request to have his tree, planted years earlier, removed from Yad Vashem.

Born in 1906, the son of a pastor, Douwes was recruited for the underground by Johannes Post, a farmer and town councilor in the village of Nieuwlande, and immediately dedicated himself to saving Jews. Assisted by Max Léons, a Jew posing as a Protestant, Douwes systematically traversed great stretches of the Nieuwlande countryside on his bicycle, stopping at every house and farm to ask whether they would be willing to lodge a Jewish child. When convincing failed, Douwes was not beyond, in some instances, forcing people to admit Jews for shelter, using all kinds of excuses and addressing the reluctant hosts in their own dialect (which he would take the time to learn). Haim Roet, as an 11-year-old boy, was himself one of the beneficiaries of Douwes's help. Fetched by train from Amsterdam to Zwolle, in eastern Holland, and then taken by Douwes on his bicycle to Dedemsvaart, Roet was hidden in several places. Lou Gans, one of Douwes's other many beneficiaries, described him in the following glowing terms: "You met him. Look in his eyes; look at his tight-lipped face. Then you will understand that no brute in the whole world could resist his will. . . . Did he save

50 Jews, 100, 200, or 500? Heaven knows! He himself could hardly say, because there were so many Jews he helped!"

An operation of such magnitude could not go long unnoticed, and the Gestapo was on the lookout for him. To avoid arrest, he changed his appearance, sporting a moustache and wearing a hat and eyeglasses to hide his face as much as possible. Despite all these precautions, Douwes was arrested on October 19, 1944. Luckily for him, while he was imprisoned in the Assen prison, fearing execution or deportation with fatal consequences, the underground rescued him in a daring operation on December 11, 1944. He then went into hiding until the country's liberation. It is estimated that Douwes was responsible for saving some 350 Jews, including around 100 children. In 1965, Yad Vashem awarded him the title of Righteous Among the Nations.

Subsequently, Douwes championed the cause of honoring many other rescuers in Nieuwlande, but the issue before the Commission for the Righteous in 1983—which at the time was headed by Dr. Moshe Bejski, one of the *Schindlerjuden* (Schindler Jews), and also then a sitting justice on Israel's Supreme Court—was that by the commission's own criteria, each nomination to the Righteous title had to be supported by evidence from the beneficiary party—in other words, the Jewish persons saved by his/her rescuers. In the Nieuwlande case, this was lacking as neither the names of all the people sheltered there nor their current addresses were known. In fact, nearly all the evidence presented was based on Arnold Douwes's writings during the war years, save for testimonies from his rescuer colleague Léons and people such as Haim Roet, who had been aided by the Nieuwlande region residents. Would that be sufficient to recognize the several hundred persons as Righteous Among the Nations, as requested by Douwes? There was no precedent for this in the commission's history. At the same time, the case's rapporteur, Dr. Jozeph Michman (formerly Melkman), strongly supported Douwes's request, and the commission chairman, Justice Bejski, also leaned in that direction.

In the meantime, Haim Roet sat for hours with me, going over the full names of all those on Douwes's list of Nieuwlande rescuers (originally numbering 270, including husbands and wives), to verify their correct full names. Roet also took me on a trip to Douwes's home, then at Kiryat Ekron, near Rehovot, to meet the man and clarify certain points in his story. Finally, that same year, after several sessions, the Commission for the Righteous voted to award the Righteous title to 202 of the Nieuwlande rescuers. Ceremonies then took place both at Yad Vashem, where a special commemorative stone was dedicated on which were engraved the names of all the 202 recognized rescuers, and in Nieuwlande, where the community received a specially worded certificate of honor on behalf of Yad Vashem. Upon my request, Arnold Douwes, who in the meantime had moved back to the Netherlands, sent me a copy of his wartime diary, which he had rewritten, and which I kept with me, waiting for an opportunity to have it published. I managed to visit him in Amsterdam, shortly before his passing in 1999. I am presently happy that Douwes's longtime wish to have his diary, originally written in Dutch, will appear both in the original Dutch and a new English version in a scholarly project conceived by Professor Bob Moore. Hopefully, it will also one day appear in the Hebrew language, for the benefit of Israeli readers.

I wish also to underline that Nieuwlande was the first large-scale community that was honored by Yad Vashem in toto, coupled with over two hundred individual local rescuers. This created a precedent that made it possible in 1990 to honor a similar community, in France, that rescued many Jews, running into the hundreds and perhaps even more: Le Chambon-sur-Lignon. This, too, was in the form of a special certificate that I had the privilege to personally present on behalf of Yad Vashem to the Le Chambon-sur-Lignon community, coupled with honors to individual rescuers of that town and immediate vicinity.

Dr. Mordecai Paldiel
Former Director, Righteous Among the
Nations Department, Yad Vashem (1982–2007).

History Professor, Yeshiva University–Stern College
and Touro College, New York.

March 2017

Editors' Preface

THE DIARY OF Arnold Douwes is in many ways a remarkable document. During the German occupation of the Netherlands, he was an itinerant gardener who in late 1942 became a member of an active resistance group in the eastern Netherlands organized by Johannes Post in and around the village of Nieuwlande. This was a village in the eastern Dutch province of Drenthe, well away from the big cities in the west and close to the German border. The group was involved in direct actions against the German and their Dutch collaborators but also engaged in sheltering those on the run, either from political or racial persecution or in order to avoid being conscripted for labor service in Germany. While there were many networks helping labor draft evaders, the work done by Post's group was unusual in that it was largely devoted to the rescue of adult Jews. When Post was targeted by the authorities and had to leave the district in July 1943, Douwes took over leadership of this aspect of his work; for the next fifteen months, he took sole responsibility for those in hiding and is credited with helping several hundred Jews remain underground during the occupation. Rescue networks of this size were rare in the Netherlands, and in the rest of occupied Europe, but what makes Douwes unique is that he kept a record of all his activities, writing extensive notes and then burying them in jam jars in various safe places. This ran contrary to all the precepts of clandestine work and although there are instances of other men and women engaged in illegal actions who kept some limited notes on their work, this is probably the only example of a comprehensive contemporary record kept by a network organizer.

His writings provide a highly detailed description of his travels and his day-to-day activities. While working with Post, he was involved in direct actions, including arson and raids on government offices, but once in sole charge of the rescue operation, he left the armed resistance largely to others and concentrated on negotiating hiding places for Jews and others fleeing from the big cities, as well as finding the money, identity documents, and ration cards that were essential to maintain people in hiding. Also remarkable is the fact that at least three of his closest collaborators were themselves Jews in hiding. Max Léons (Nico) often traveled with him in the second half of 1943, visiting likely hosts and negotiating for hiding places—a task that the cantankerous Douwes found hard to accomplish. Isidoor Davids (Peter) was underground in the village and was a talented graphic artist who turned his hand to forgery for the benefit of the network. Likewise Lou Gans (Herman), whose accomplishments as an artist were put to good

xi

use in producing drawings and postcards that were then reproduced and sold to raise funds.

As Douwes survived the occupation, he was able to retrieve the jam jars after the liberation and compiled a manuscript of approximately 250 pages from the notes he had made. This was deposited in the archives of the then Rijksinstituut voor Oorlogsdocumentatie (now Nederlands Instituut voor Oorlogs- Holocaust- en Genocide Studies, NIOD) where it remains to this day. Arnold Douwes always wanted his diary published and commissioned an English translation that he then enhanced with further details and observations, but for various reasons the work was not published during his lifetime. The edition presented here is essentially the original Dutch version, which is largely untrammeled by any postwar reflections on the part of the author and retains the narrative tension of a diarist who did not know what the following days or weeks might bring.

The introduction is an attempt to contextualize the diary for readers who may be unfamiliar with the circumstances or the locality in which these events took place. It begins by expanding on the unique nature of the diary as a document before discussing in general terms the plight of Jews in the Netherlands during the German occupation. From there, it focuses on the development of civil resistance to increasing Nazi terror and then on the specifics of Nieuwlande as a locality and the roles of Johannes Post and Arnold Douwes.

The diary itself has three distinct parts. The first is a preamble written by Douwes as an introduction to his notes that deals with his career between the outbreak of war in 1940 and the beginnings of his diary in July 1943. What follows is the day-to-day diary compiled from the notes in jam jars until his arrest in October 1944 and then a postscript where he describes what happened to him after his arrest and subsequent escape from police custody. In the course of his writing, Douwes mentions many different people, and the editors have made every attempt to identify those involved and include them in the biographical sketches. Likewise, he has references to all manner of events, organizations, local customs, and even local foodstuffs, and here again the annotations and the glossary are an attempt to make sense of these for the general reader.

Acknowledgments

No project of this nature could be completed without considerable help, and here we would like to begin by thanking Arnold Douwes's three daughters for permission to publish the diary and fulfill their father's wishes that it be read by a wider public. His niece Joke Stegeman was also instrumental in bringing the Dutch and English versions of this book to fruition, and it was largely through their collective testimonies that we were able to write about Douwes's postwar life. Enormous thanks are also due to Ds. Geert Hovingh, who read through the entire translation, correcting many inaccuracies and providing invaluable additional details on many of the people mentioned as well as many of the photographs included in the book. Likewise, the expertise on Hoogeveen and the surrounding area provided indirectly by local historian Albert Metselaar has enhanced our understanding of both the region and the period. Bert Jan Flim, the historian of rescued children in the Netherlands gave freely of his time and advice, as did Wim Berkelaar who helped with an understanding of terms used within the Protestant churches. We would also like to record our thanks to Jan van der Sleen and the Stichting "De Duikelaar" in Nieuwlande for permission to publish photographs and other artworks in their possession, as well as to Yad Vashem for the photograph of Arnold Douwes in Israel.

In addition, Johannes Houwink ten Cate would like to thank Monique van Kessel, his colleagues at NIOD, Marjan Schwegman, Frank van Vree, Nanci Adler, and Peter Romijn, as well as André Boers for his hospitality and his facilitating contact with Arnold's daughters in Israel and Hans Warendorf for his advice and friendship. Bob Moore would like to thank seminar audiences at the Lichtenberg-Kolleg in Göttingen, the University of Sheffield, and the Grenoside Local History Society in Sheffield for their collective comments, which have informed the annotations to the text; his colleagues in the Department of History at the University of Sheffield; and the Lichtenberg-Kolleg and Institut für Zeitgeschichte in Munich for fellowships that have provided the time and space to bring this project to fruition.

Finally, we would both like to acknowledge our debt to Dr. Mordecai Paldiel for his advice and for contributing the prologue.

Bob Moore
Johannes Houwink ten Cate
Göttingen/Munich/Amsterdam
January 2018

Translator's Note

IN THE MONTHS after the liberation of the Netherlands in 1945, Arnold Douwes was able to collect together the extensive notes he had so carefully hidden in jam jars in the ground while undertaking illegal work in and around the village of Nieuwlande. Although a few jam jars were never recovered and some of the notes had suffered from water damage, he was nonetheless able to compile a typescript that is now held by NIOD.

In the 1980s, Arnold Douwes's ambition to see his diary published led to a translation of the original Dutch typescript by Mirjam Bolle-Levie, and I would like to acknowledge the role that her work has played in this new translation of his text. Arnold himself then embellished her translation with observations and further remembrances, but for this project, it seemed more appropriate to go back to the original Dutch version without the insertions—except where they added to the reader's understanding of the events being described. Such insertions appear in square brackets. Anything in parentheses has been faithfully transcribed from the original text.

As the text was pieced together from the notebooks and notes compiled by Douwes at the time, it is often rendered in very short sentences and paragraphs, and this has been retained in the English version. Names and aliases are not always rendered consistently, and while some attempts have been made to rationalize this, inconsistencies remain. Insofar as it has been possible to identify those mentioned, they are appended in the biographical sketches. In some cases, Douwes himself admits to not knowing the context of specific entries and these have had to be left unresolved. Douwes invariably refers to any Germans using the Dutch derogatory term *mof/moffen*, and this has been rendered as *Krauts* throughout. Some Dutch words are also difficult to render in English. For example, the Dutch word used to describe someone who went into hiding or went underground is *onderduiker* (m) or *onderduikster* (f), literally someone who dives under, and such a person might also be referred to as a *duikelaar*, a diver. All these terms have been left in the original Dutch, as have some technical terms, for example those related to the system of ration cards and food distribution used in the Netherlands during the war. In every case, there is an explanatory note where such a term is first used. The role of religion has often been seen as a central issue when it comes to the rescue of Jews in the Netherlands, and especially in this part of the country where Calvinism had a strong hold on sections of the population. Unfortunately, when referring to clergymen, Douwes does not always make it clear whether they were Dutch Reformed or Orthodox Calvinist. In many cases, we have been able to resolve this with the invaluable help of Geert Hovingh, but firm conclusions about the respective roles played by these denominations in this particular network still need to be treated with some caution.

Bob Moore
Göttingen

THE SECRET DIARY OF
ARNOLD DOUWES

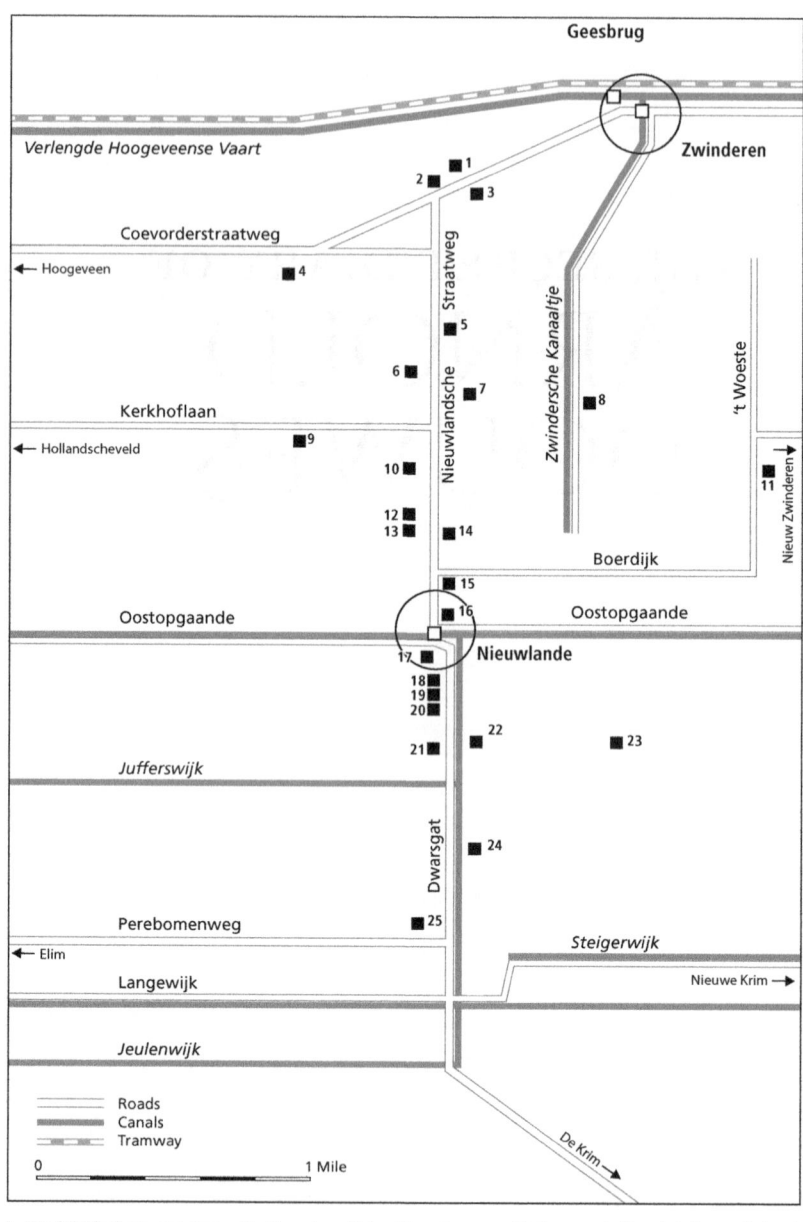

1 Hendrik Bleeker's workshop	10 Nieuwboer Sisters/Veenstra
2 Hendrik Veenstra	11 Klaas Nienhuis
3 Geesbrug school	12 Gereformeerde (calvinist) church
4 Hendrik Blok	13 Koffiehuis Van der Vinne
5 Johannes Lanting	14 Meester Bos
6 Hendrik Schonewille	15 Jacob Kamphuis
7 Johannes Post	16 Café Klijnsma
8 Hemke van der Zwaag	17 Simon Dijk
9 Boele Meier	
18 Hervormde (Dutch Reformed) church	
19 Christian school	
20 Meester Otten	
21 Post Office	
22 Jan Post	
23 Jan Schonewille	
24 Dirk van Dijken	
25 Dutch Reformed school	

Nieuwlande Village

The Netherlands 1940–1945

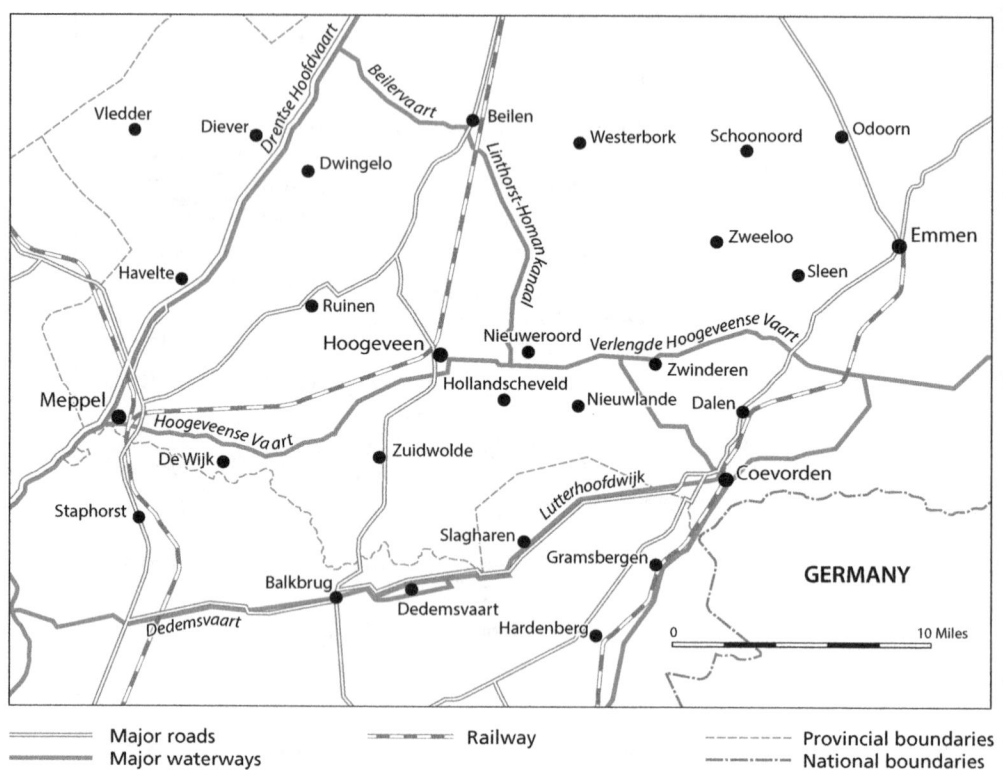

Southern Drenthe

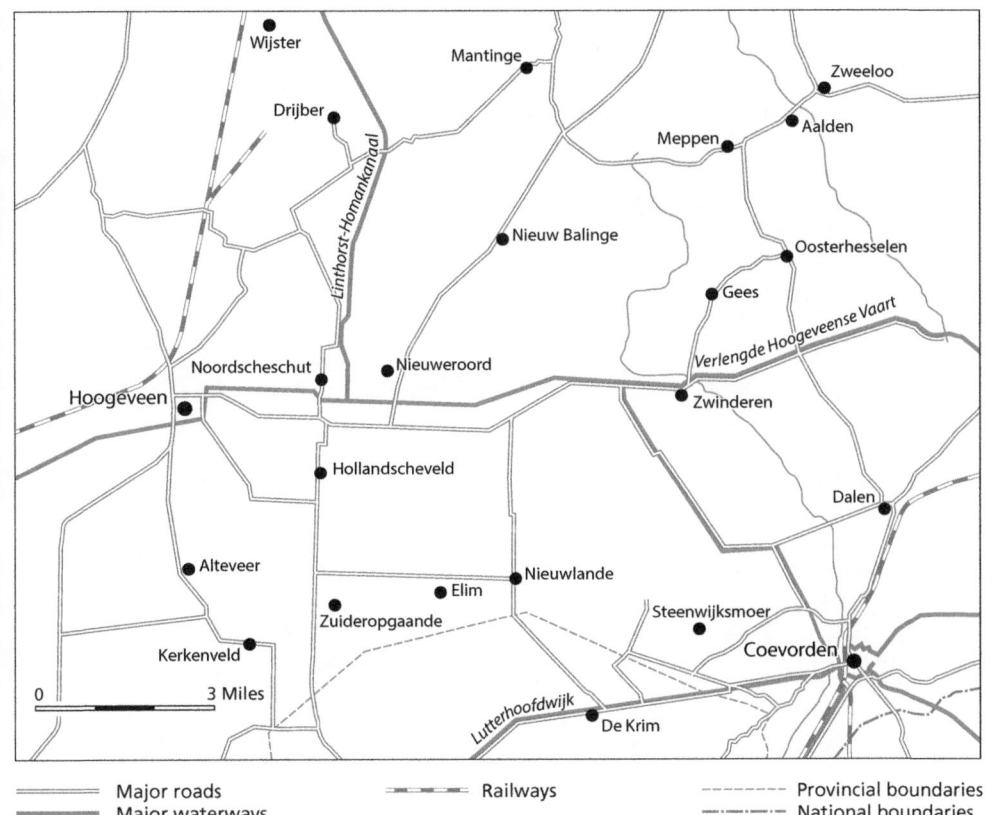

Nieuwlande and surrounding villages

The Diary and Its Context

THE IMPORTANCE OF THE DIARY

Between July 1943 and October 1944, at the height of the German occupation of the Netherlands, the itinerant gardener and nurseryman Arnold Douwes led a network dedicated to hiding Jews and others persecuted by the Nazis centered on the community of Nieuwlande in the eastern province of Drenthe. During that time, he kept notes on his day-to-day activities that provide a unique insight on the rescue activities carried out to shelter Jews in and around Nieuwlande. Ultimately, his leadership helped several hundred Jews survive the occupation, and more than 200 people from the district being honored by Yad Vashem as Righteous Among the Nations. Remarkable in its own right as an example of community mobilization and certainly comparable with the histories of Le Chambon and Dieulefit in France, the events at Nieuwlande and the surrounding villages have to be seen in the context of the tragedy that befell the Jewish communities in the Netherlands during the course of the German occupation. With so many Jews succumbing to deportation and annihilation in the camps of Eastern Europe, the work done by a small number of committed individuals takes on an added significance, not only for our understanding of conditions in the Netherlands, but also for a wider perspective on rescue across Western Europe.

Douwes was already wanted by the police for anti-German activities before arriving in Nieuwlande in 1942, but here he fell under the spell of the Orthodox Calvinist (Gereformeerde) and charismatic Johannes Post, a prosperous and well-known local farmer who had spearheaded the earliest resistance in the district.[1] When Post had to leave the area, ultimately to take on a national role as a leader of the Landelijke Knokploegen (LKP, armed resistance squads), it was Douwes who took over the work started by his mentor in finding hiding places and supporting those forced to go underground. For more than 16 months, he almost single-handedly masterminded the movement, hiding and caring for an increasing number of fugitives, most of whom were Jews who had avoided the round-ups in the major Dutch cities in the West that had begun in July 1942. In spite of being constantly on the move, and against all the precepts of illegal work, he kept a detailed record of everything he did during that period. Every day, or whenever the opportunity presented itself, he would write down reflections on the work he was doing, the people he worked with, and the war situation in general. These notes on scraps of paper would then be consigned to jam jars and hidden in the gardens of the houses where he was based. Surviving arrest and interrogation by the Gestapo, he was released from prison by a resistance raid and spent the rest of the war in hiding himself. After the liberation, he recovered the jam jars from their hiding places and consolidated the notes into a chronological typescript form before handing them to the editors of a book on the resistance work of the LO and LKP.[2] Once this book was published, the diary was then handed to the then Rijksinstituut voor Ooorlogsdocumentatie (RIOD) in Amsterdam.[3]

Accounts of rescue work in the level of detail that Douwes provides are a great rarity, and the text retains a narrative tension as the author himself had no idea what would happen before he wrote his next entry. This is an unashamedly frank account of his day-to-day life that provides a vivid description of what underground life was like for him and the day-to-day tribulations and crises he experienced. It is also unstinting, both in its praise and its criticism of his coworkers and the people they were helping. To his great credit, Douwes chose not to allow hindsight to color his account when piecing together his notes into a manuscript edition of the diary but merely added a preface that described his career between the outbreak of war and his arrival in Nieuwlande, as well as a postscript that detailed what happened to him after his arrest in October 1944.

Douwes himself was an unlikely rescuer. The son of a pastor born in Laag-Keppel in Gelderland in 1906, he went through the highly unusual childhood experience of having his father divorce his mother when she left the family and went to live with the local doctor. Most of his siblings went on to have respectable, middle-class careers, but Arnold opted out of a formal classical education and instead enrolled at a horticultural college. Failing to complete his training, he then immigrated to Canada, arriving in Halifax, Nova Scotia, on the SS *Veendam* on June 3, 1926. Initially he stayed with a relation but then spent the next 10 years as an itinerant in Canada and the United States, sometimes working in the logging industry, but by his own admission, sometimes having to sort through dustbins for food. He returned to the Netherlands in 1936 as, by his own account, he had been deported as a subversive and a Communist after an altercation with a restaurant owner in Chicago, although this has not been verified from US sources. By this stage, both his parents had died and his inheritance allowed him to resume his horticultural studies. After graduating, he moved to Italy and then to France, returning only when the latter country declared war on Germany on September 3, 1939.[4] He then worked as a nurseryman in Boskoop and then in his home village of Laag-Keppel.[5] Already wanted for anti-German activities, he was further radicalized when the German Green Police (Ordnungspolizei) arrested his Jewish childhood friend Sam Jacobs sometime in 1941. He was himself arrested on September 19, 1941, and after a few weeks in jail effectively went on the run. For the next year, he traveled around the country, staying with friends and family, before arriving in Nieuwlande and encountering Johannes Post.

Only in the winter of 1942–43 did Douwes commit to helping Post, initially traveling the country acquiring, buying, or stealing identity cards and collecting money to finance the illegal work, a task that, by his own admission, Douwes hated. Soon he was also involved in direct actions, including a raid on four different municipal offices in one night and setting fire to the farmhouses of well-known local Dutch National Socialist sympathizers. Working alongside Post gradually drew him into direct contact with the work of sheltering those underground, and this set the tone for his future activities when "the big shot" (as Post was known) left the neighborhood and went underground. By the time the diary's daily entries begin, on July 3, 1943, some six months after Douwes had joined Post's network, he was wholly concerned with all aspects of rescue and had backed away from involvement in armed actions. These were taken over by other people within Post's wider network.

What new insights does the diary give us? First and foremost, it gives a very clear picture about how such a network was created and then maintained. Networks of this size and scale were a relative rarity in the Netherlands as most sheltering was negotiated on an individual basis—at least initially. Reliance on, and support from, family members is very much to the fore, both for Johannes Post as well as for Douwes, with brothers and sisters being directly involved or providing sanctuary and succor for "front line" illegal workers. Some of Post's brothers were themselves armed resisters but others who were clergymen also actively helped the cause. Douwes was similarly able to seek help from his siblings, and one of his most important early contacts in Dedemsvaart was Frederik Stegeman, the brother of his sister's husband. His house, "De Flochte," would become Douwes's first safe house and the garden the repository for many of his diary jam jars. Beyond immediate family ties, the diary shows how others were brought into the network through personal contacts or recommendations. In Dedemsvaart, these included Sister Scholten, the district nurse, and Kats, the bicycle repair man, and in Nieuwlande there was schoolteacher Seine Otten and Pastor Volger in nearby Hollandscheveld. Over time, the key personnel in the network changed as circumstances altered or as individuals and families came under threat and had to move or go underground themselves. Also of note was the role played by numerous Dutch Reformed and Orthodox Calvinist pastors and schoolteachers in the district. Douwes used them extensively, as the diary makes clear. Some took Jews into their houses while others helped with addresses, mediation, and money.

Likewise, sympathetic municipal officials and local doctors who ignored the risks involved in helping Jews were also an invaluable resource.

In his first months, Douwes worked alongside "Nico," the underground name of Max Léons, a Jew who had been in hiding since the beginnings of the deportations in July 1942 and who had found his way to Nieuwlande. Not content with being passive, Léons undertook an active role, including accompanying Douwes on many of his journeys looking for hiding places. If anything, Nico took far greater risks than Douwes in going out in public, as he had a very Jewish appearance and would feign having a cold to explain the handkerchief hiding his face if he was stopped at a checkpoint. At much the same time, Douwes acquired the help of two other Jews in hiding—"Peter," real name Ish (Isidoor) Davids, and "Herman" (Lou Gans)—who both provided long-term support, in the case of Peter, a talented forger, transforming documentation to fit the needs of illegal workers and those in hiding.[6] These two were also heavily engaged in producing underground newssheets, postcards, and illustrations, the latter being sold to help fund the network's activities. The diary therefore bears witness to the commitment of these Jewish rescuers who have been marginalized and ignored in the literature that focuses exclusively on the roles played by gentiles.

Douwes's motto of "never turning anyone away" created its own pressures and meant he was constantly searching for reliable people prepared to take on the inherent risks in harboring Jews. He used personal contacts and could sometimes be found accompanied by a clergyman from the local parish approaching families or individuals whom they had recommended. Even Douwes acknowledged that he had no negotiating skills and often relied on Nico to smooth the way toward getting agreements:

> Arnold's methods were not always tactful. He would often ask for a place for one fugitive, yet bring two. He sometimes requested shelter for a small child, but would bring an older one. Arnold often got carried away with emotion and it was not uncommon for him to resort to shouts and insults. His confrontational methods, which reflected the extreme urgency of the situation and the danger posed to both fugitives and hosts, earned him widespread criticism. He was accused of bringing too many Jews to Nieuwlande, of being reckless and irresponsible, of placing everyone at risk. However, Arnold persisted with his efforts and remarked in his diary that his method "worked."[7]

His belief in the rectitude and necessity of what he was doing comes across clearly in his writings, and this led to many frustrations when he believed others could be doing more to help. The diary shows how his network expanded over time as the numbers who needed shelter grew, and the desperation of Douwes and his fellow workers in trying to find more hiding places increased. This imperative was driven not just by new arrivals but also by the need to move existing guests, either to prevent burgeoning tensions between them and their hosts or because the hiding places had become unsafe or compromised. This could be temporary, as when rescuers had family visiting, but hosts could and did opt out altogether if they thought the risks had become too great or their circumstances changed. Neighbors could become suspicious, other members of the family might be sought by the authorities, or locations could become inherently unsafe through repeated raids.

Another key element highlighted here is the importance of fundraising. There was a trade in identity cards that had to be financed and travel costs to be considered, but hosts also needed to be compensated for feeding and housing their "guests" over long periods of time. Although Douwes hated collecting money, it was an essential part of the work. He also resented the fact that he could sometimes be offered money in lieu of a promise of accommodation, almost as though he was being paid to go away. Money remained a major issue throughout the occupation, and the sums collected had to be substantial. The same was true of identity cards and ration cards. These were essential for everyday life, even if the holders never used them personally, as they allowed hosts to buy additional food to feed their guests. The network was confronted by a constantly changing landscape of regulations for identity and ration cards, a process designed by the authorities primarily to flush out the increasing numbers of labor draft evaders as well as the Jews in hiding.

The crucial role of transport and communication also comes out very clearly. The station in nearby Hoogeveen became the main artery bringing couriers and fugitives from the western cities and also a route to Groningen and Friesland to the north. While it was by far the quickest route, it was also the most dangerous, with regular identity checks at stations and sometimes also on the trains themselves. As the war progressed, train services became increasingly unreliable, leading to further problems and anxieties for Douwes and his compatriots, not least when trains arrived long after curfew time. In the last month before his arrest, the trains had stopped altogether in the wake of the failed Allied landings at Arnhem.[8] Traveling between villages, Douwes frequently rode a bicycle and also used bicycles to move fugitives. Without a reliable machine with proper tires, he would have been lost. Children were carried on panniers, but it was assumed that adults could all ride bicycles—although there were occasions where this assumption was severely tested. Knowledge of the local byways was equally crucial in avoiding checkpoints on the main roads, and the diary has many examples of Douwes using alternative and circuitous routes when warned about such hazards. Coded letters and messages were the staple form of local communication, although the few local telephones were also pressed into service as a means of reaching contacts elsewhere in the country or for sending out warnings of impending raids. Over time, this became more and more difficult, and finally, the occupiers shut down the telephone network for civilian use altogether.

Ultimately, Douwes became the victim of his own success. Having expanded the network to involve more rescuers and take in more fugitives, the risks of betrayal and discovery multiplied. No system was completely watertight, and even the most innocent of communications had the potential to lead to disaster. Likewise, the expectations both of hosts and fugitives could be totally at odds with reality, to the point where they attempted to circumvent the controls placed on them. The network organizers insisted on censoring all the mail they delivered or posted—objecting vehemently to those written in Yiddish—but became even more worried, and indeed angry, when discovering those in hiding had smuggled letters unseen into the postal system. Similarly, hosts had expectations of their guests that were not always met, especially when they had been misled by network organizers. For example, there were cases of women who were assumed to have household skills but who were unable or unwilling to carry out even the most basic of tasks. Class and social distinctions between hosts and guests also created inevitable tensions that necessitated moving people regularly. In the latter stages of the diary, it becomes clear that the net is closing in around Douwes. The hoped-for liberation in the autumn of 1944 had failed to materialize, and the Germans and local Dutch Nazis had stepped up their efforts to locate the Jews. Reliable hiding places became insecure and key members of the network were compromised or even arrested in the weeks prior to his own arrest. By this stage, he tried to avoid the hosts as his power to organize and provide resources for all the people supported by his network had all but gone. He had essentially become trapped by his obligations to those he sheltered—a prisoner of the very network he had created.

CONTEXT: THE PERSECUTION OF THE JEWS IN THE NETHERLANDS

The wider context of Douwes's activities was the Nazi persecution of the Jews in the Netherlands during the occupation period. Of the country's Jewish population, more than 107,000 were arrested and deported to the East, and only around 5,000 returned from the camps. Of the remainder, a small number escaped to neutral territories, some were temporarily protected by marriage to non-Jews or by bureaucratic subterfuge, and some went into hiding. Yet even taken together, the total of survivors was pitifully small and constituted no more than 20 to 25 percent of the prewar community.[9] Measures specifically targeted against the Jews did not begin immediately after the surrender on May 15, 1940, although they were quickly banned from the air raid precaution service in early July 1940 and excluded from appointments or promotion within the civil service from September of that year.[10] During the autumn, further administrative measures were introduced to identify Jews, including a so-called Aryan attestation (*Ariërverklaring*) whereby all those in government service had to sign a declaration about their parentage. This was followed in early January 1941 by a German ordinance, VO6/1941, that made registration for all Jews compulsory. Most complied, believing that the information they were giving already existed in the comprehensive population registration system held by each municipality and that attempts at evasion would be immediately evident and lead to severe punishment.[11] The following month saw a watershed moment in the history of the occupation and in the persecution of the Jews in the Netherlands. The February Strike (*Februaristaking*) has gone down in history as a unique example of popular resistance to Nazi policies against the Jews. After a series of Dutch National Socialist provocations and civil resistance in Jewish neighborhoods in Amsterdam, German repression and the arrest of 425 young Jewish men led to a national strike initiated by the Communists and other anti-Nazi groups that lasted for two days before it was suppressed.[12]

This showed the Dutch population that German reprisals could be severe and also demonstrated to the Germans that they would need to tread carefully in framing and executing future policies against the Jews. The Jewish communities in Amsterdam were required to establish a Jewish Council, a single representative body that came to dominate all aspects of Jewish life across the country. As Jews were increasingly isolated from the rest of society, the council created a whole range of subsidiary organizations to provide for welfare, housing, education, and the like. Both its leadership and the wider Jewish community were heavily influenced in their behavior by the fate of the 425 young men arrested in the aftermath of the *Februaristaking*, who were sent, first to a camp at Schoorl in the Netherlands, then to Konzentrationslager (KZ) Buchenwald, and later to KZ Mauthausen in Austria, where all were reported as dead within six weeks. Without knowing the circumstances, the Jewish population equated the threat of Mauthausen with death, and this acted as a disincentive for any form of future disobedience to German measures.

The Nuremberg Laws were imposed on the country, and the statutes were published exclusively in the one remaining Jewish newspaper, *Het Joodsche Weekblad*. By mid-September 1941, signs saying "forbidden for Jews" were appearing in Amsterdam and elsewhere, a visible manifestation of their complete exclusion from public places, including parks, cafés, cinemas, theaters, concert halls, swimming pools, and libraries. Jewish children were henceforward also restricted to Jewish schools. Slowly but surely, Jews were removed from every aspect of economic life and banned from providing any services for non-Jews. Their wealth was registered and ultimately compulsorily lodged with the Lippmann-Rosenthal Bank, a device by which the Germans gained access to Jewish wealth without engaging in formal sequestration.[13] By early 1942, the process of identification, registration, pauperization, and isolation was all but complete and reinforced by identity cards being marked with a red letter J and subsequently by the introduction of the Jewish star on May 3 for both people and houses.[14] On June 26, the Jewish Council was notified that Jews were liable for "labor service" in the East and that lists were to be drawn up immediately. This led inexorably to the first raids on Jewish neighborhoods in Amsterdam on July 14 (after insufficient numbers reported for transport in Amsterdam voluntarily), and the first deportation trains left from the transit camp at Westerbork to KZ Auschwitz on July 15. From then until the summer of 1943, the process of rounding up Jews in Amsterdam and their regular shipment to the camps in the East via Westerbork served to remove the vast majority of the Jews from the country.[15]

The operation of this apparently seamless process begs a series of questions. Why did more Jews not try to escape or evade arrest and deportation? Why did they continue to adhere to the advice given by the Jewish Council and allow themselves to be rounded up? This image of a Jewish population either wedded to a concept of obedience to authority (*gezagsgetrouwheid*) or cowed into submission by the possibility of disobeying German ordinances and being treated as punishment cases (*strafgevallen*) and sent to Mauthausen and certain death has dominated traditional explanations of its behavior, a conclusion supported by the assumption that only a minority of around 25,000–30,000 Jews even considered trying to evade arrest and deportation after the occupation regime had been established.[16]

Part of the explanation for this apparent passivity stems from the circumstances in which the Jews found themselves by the summer of 1942. Their judicial and social isolation had been compounded by an existing feature of Dutch society where a series of ideological or religious communities existed side by side but were separated socially, culturally, and politically. This pillarization (*verzuiling*) of Dutch society involved Roman Catholicism, (Orthodox) Calvinism, Social Democracy, and Liberalism, but although some Jews existed in the latter two *zuilen*, it could be argued that the Jews formed a separate small *zuil*—especially in Amsterdam. This propensity toward social and cultural separation between the groups made it harder for the Jews to find help from their non-Jewish neighbors.[17] Moreover, most Jews in that city were numbered among the proletariat with no access to resources, but even the middle classes could no longer access their wealth and were thus little better served than their poorer counterparts. Only the minority of well-off Jewish families who had been able to cloak some of their assets had any residual independence. Movement was also fraught with difficulties. All citizens had to be registered at an address and could not move without permission from the local authorities. They were likewise required to carry an identity card that included both their picture and fingerprint. Police controls on transport and even on street corners were commonplace, and Jews' identity cards became instantly identifiable. Under these circumstances, leaving the city or hiding was beyond the scope of what most Jews could realistically consider even before their family circumstances were taken into consideration—where children and aged relatives could hamper plans for escape or going "underground."

There is no doubt that the German authorities charged with making the Netherlands *Judenrein* were very successful. Their harnessing of the Jewish Council and the local Dutch police was a major contributory factor in the speed of the process, as was the untrammeled use of information from the population registry and the censuses of Jews compiled in the early months of the occupation. In general, Jews were arrested and taken to the Hollandsche Schouwburg (a theater rechristened the Joodsche Schouwburg by the Germans), but during the first six weeks of the action, deportees were taken directly to the Central Station, as were the sick and elderly rounded up in the first weeks of 1943 and the victims of the large street raids in the same year. Those arrested were moved at night and transported by train to the Westerbork transit camp in Drenthe in the eastern Netherlands.[18]

While this became the pattern for the majority of the Jews deported from the Netherlands, some were held in other places, most notably KZ Vught, where skilled workers were employed on war work, and at the Police Camp in Amersfoort, which held men suspected of, or convicted of political offences.[19] In order to facilitate their work, the Germans ordered the removal of all Jews from the provinces, either to Amsterdam or to Vught. This process had supposedly been completed by April 1943, when the entire country, save Amsterdam, was declared free of Jews. By that time, the German administration was concentrating on arranging the removal of the remaining Jews from the city. By the end of September 1943, all the Jews—including even the leadership of the Jewish Council—had been taken to Westerbork, leaving only a very small number of exempted Jews still living in Amsterdam to fulfill very specific tasks.[20]

As the number of Jews living legally decreased, the German authorities turned their attention to the Jews they suspected of having gone into hiding—those who could not be found at the addresses where they were registered. This process involved elements of the Dutch and German police, almost always working at the behest of the IVB4 branch office of the Reichssicherheitshauptamt (RSHA) and the Zentralstelle für jüdische Auswanderung (Central Office for Jewish Emigration).[21] Working from information received, they would raid neighborhoods and specific locations in Amsterdam and elsewhere looking for Jews in hiding. More dangerous still for the fugitives were a new breed of bounty hunters who tracked down Jews in exchange for monetary payments.[22]

RESISTANCE AND RESCUE

While the German authorities were preparing the way for the eventual deportation of the Jews, the Dutch public was coming to terms with the implications of long-term occupation. Initially, what few acts of civil disobedience occurred were at an individual level. Like its German counterpart, Dutch civil society became atomized by the abolition or Nazification of most civic organizations and institutions, although again, as in Germany, the various Christian churches were allowed to continue. However, their newssheets were banned, and their behavior and freedom of action was tempered by the arrests of known anti-Nazi clerics, an assumption that they were being closely monitored, and by the knowledge of what had taken place in Poland. This led to the churches' leadership adopting a fairly circumspect approach to their dealings with the Germans—seeing the protection of church institutions and the continued freedom of worship as more important than most individual issues. Although there was a collective protest about the introduction of the "Aryan attestation" in the autumn of 1940, a further protest by the Catholic Church against the deportations in July 1942 was countered by the Germans arresting its Jewish converts.[23] Other forms of dissent were also quickly stifled, for example with the demonstrations against the exclusion of Jewish staff from the Universities, which ultimately resulted in further restrictions and closures.[24]

The totality of German control over the country and the overwhelming success of the Nazi war machine made any form of resistance in the first years of occupation a rare occurrence. The first manifestations came from the political extremes, with the Communists continuing their clandestine operations from the prewar period, but under increasing threat from both Dutch and now also German agencies. As such, most of their activities were defensive and designed to protect party members—especially at a time when the Nazi-Soviet Pact had made the Nazis de facto allies. Evident also in this period were embryonic organizations of the patriotic right—composed primarily of demobilized army officers, but active resistance was restricted to a miniscule proportion of the country's population before the summer of 1942. With the exception of the Communists, clandestine work was alien in a society used to order and obedience to the laws, and thus the survival of any underground organizations started by well-meaning groups and individuals was essentially determined by trial and error. Ranged against the police, the German security agencies, and a proportion of the population wedded to National Socialist ideals, any naivety, lapses in security, or words in the wrong place or to the wrong person could spell disaster.[25]

While there were isolated acts of sabotage and other forms of direct action in the first years of occupation, most energy was expended in the creation of an illegal press. For example, the existing Communist newspaper *De Waarheid* continued publication clandestinely throughout the occupation, but others were a product of the occupation itself. Many started out as little more than handbills, distributed locally through letterboxes or from person to person, often emanating from existing confessional or political groups. Over time, a few became more widely disseminated, such as *Vrij Nederland* and later *Trouw*, which emerged from the Orthodox Calvinist community, or had their content adopted by similar publications in other regions. As we shall see, the networks created to distribute illegal newspapers often became the basis for other forms of illegal work later in the occupation.[26]

From the outset, the Dutch economy was geared to serve the interests of German war effort, with foodstuffs, industrial production, and surplus manpower being sent to the Reich. However, this became even more onerous during the course of 1942 as the war of attrition on the Eastern Front placed increasing demands on the German economy and forced its planners to look for additional resources and manpower.[27] What had previously been a voluntary system of attracting labor into Germany now took on a more coercive aspect, with compulsory labor service replacing the previous incentive-based systems. In addition, localized measures had a disproportionate effect on the population. The German need for additional transport led them to confiscate bicycles across the Netherlands, something that was seen as a direct attack on civilian mobility, the ability to earn a living, and a central feature of everyday existence. These two German measures together served to spark the first incidence of mass civil disobedience, with labor conscripts going into hiding and people burying their bicycles or handing in derelict models as substitutes.[28]

This shift toward increasing civil disobedience prompted the creation of more organized resistance groups whose main purpose was to help those on the run for political reasons or evading the labor draft. Although localized in the beginning, the networks created to help labor draft evaders were ultimately coordinated into a single national organization, the Landelijke Organisatie voor Hulp aan Onderduikers (LO).[29] Instigated in the autumn of 1942, the LO took time to develop by linking local groups one by one, and thus had little impact on Jews attempting to avoid deportation in the second half of 1942 and the first months of 1943. The demands of this type of work also gave rise to the so-called Landelijke Knokploegen, which were primarily created to carry out raids on government buildings to steal ration and identity cards, as well as to destroy records that might betray the whereabouts of those called up for labor service. Their activities also sometimes extended to include other forms of direct action, including assassinations, against the Germans and their Dutch fellow travelers, with a small number groups taking this on as a primary task.[30] Over time, the Germans became increasingly desperate and by the latter stages of 1944, and with the Allies already occupying the southern parts of the country, any pretense of selection was abandoned in favor of wholesale roundups of every able-bodied person in specific neighborhoods, for example in the raids on Rotterdam in November of that year.[31]

When the first roundups and deportations from Amsterdam began in July 1942, very few Jews had made any preparations for escape or going into hiding. There was little understanding of what it might entail, except that it would criminalize them and make them subject to summary punishments if caught. Crucially, going underground was an open-ended commitment as there was no sign that Germany was likely to be defeated or that the persecution would be brought to an end. Resources were finite, if they existed at all, and this brought into question how long anyone might remain in hiding. The majority were undoubtedly overwhelmed by their plight and waited, bags packed, for the police to arrive and take them away. This image of passivity is difficult to interrogate as the majority never returned to tell of their experiences, but the limited evidence suggests that their acceptance of their fate was largely determined by advice emanating from the Jewish Council to comply with German demands and their own perceived lack of viable alternatives.

This throws into stark relief the exceptionality of Otto Frank's preparations for evasion. The iconic status of his daughter has thrown the spotlight on his family's experiences, but they were far from typical. Long before the deportations for "labor service in the East" had been made public, Otto had contrived to prepare a hiding place for himself, his family, and others. Helped by his non-Jewish business partners and using their premises, he had built a permanent hiding place in the *achterhuis* of Prinsengracht 263. His perspicacity was not shared by many others, but few Jews enjoyed the same level of cooperation and ongoing help from non-Jewish business partners who could act as a front and provide food and other essentials for those in hiding. He and his family were also atypical insofar as they stayed together and in one place as it was more common for families to have been split up and to have been hidden in more than one location.

That said, the ways in which Jews in the Netherlands attempted to go underground were many and various. There were cases of self-help, where individuals or families attempted to cloak their identities by moving to another district using false papers. This required both substantial resources—something that most Jews could only dream about—and confidence that their identity documents would stand the closest scrutiny. A variant of this was of a family who had moved to The Hague as late as 1943 and passed themselves off as evacuees from another part of the country and then lived openly—even sending their children to local schools "because none of them looked particularly Jewish."[32] Living "legally" in this way would give them access to the all-important ration stamps and the ability to buy food on the open market. While such examples do exist, they are the exception rather than the rule. Some foreign Jews had also managed to avoid, or had been omitted from, the registration process in 1941, which meant that there was no evidence of their religion or racial origins anywhere in official records. For example, a German Jewish woman who had arrived in the country before the war had obtained employment as a domestic servant in a sanatorium and was never asked about her background or asked to fill in any forms, so she remained there undetected throughout the occupation.[33]

However, most Jews did not have the luck, foresight, or contacts to evade the deportations in this way. More commonplace was the help asked for or volunteered at the moment when the call-ups and deportations began. Friends, neighbors, acquaintances, landlords, business partners, and work colleagues were obvious points of contact when danger threatened. There are some cases of help being volunteered as early as 1939 and 1940, but other relationships began with offers to hide material assets when Jewish property was being registered and sequestered during 1941. Limited schemes could then escalate into help with going into hiding—either directly with the person or family concerned—or with them brokering safe places elsewhere. Business contacts could also act as a catalyst or prompt for assistance, as with the case of Otto Frank, but there were also examples of landlords offering to hide their tenants when they were sought by the authorities. A family in Zwolle had a Jewish radio engineer tenant whom they allowed to continue working in the house when Jews were prohibited from owning or having radios. Later, they also sheltered him when the deportations began and took in others, with the husband even acquiring an allotment to grow more food to help feed their guests.[34] Some assistance was offered completely unsolicited, for example the family who received a note through the letterbox—"If you ever find yourself in difficulties, remember you can always rely on us"—and on taking up the offer, the hosts' first words when his guests arrived: "You are not going to Poland under any circumstances."[35] One further form of help could come through families where there had been mixed marriages between Jewish and gentile partners. In such cases, the non-Jewish side of the family could provide an obvious point of contact and help for their Jewish in-laws.

These instances of unsolicited gentile help for the Jews should not be taken as the norm but merely as specific examples of individual acts of kindness and self-sacrifice at a time when there was no end to the occupation in sight and helpers might be putting themselves and their families in mortal danger from German reprisals. Popular perceptions of the penalties imposed on those caught helping Jews were often more severe than the actuality. The national daily newspaper *De Telegraaf* had printed a story that gentiles who helped Jews would be treated as Jews, but with hindsight it appears that the most severe punishment meted out was six months in imprisonment in KZ Vught. For every offer of help, there were undoubtedly many more refusals, although such generalizations have to be treated with caution. While most of the population appeared indifferent to the fate of the Jews or at least not wishing to take on the risks involved, a few refusals stemmed from the fact that the individuals concerned were already sheltering Jews or engaged in other forms of illegal work and did not want to compromise their activities by adding to their exposure. Thus, one woman involved in rescuing Jews in Friesland had met with a refusal when she asked her daughter living in a nearby village for help. Only after the war was it revealed that the daughter was already sheltering Jews and had no room for more. This story is exceptional, but many other would-be rescuers found themselves compromised when members of their family evaded the call-up for labor service (*arbeidsinzet*), which rendered their homes liable to raids by the authorities. A further and ever-present problem for some was the proximity and unwanted surveillance by Dutch National Socialist neighbors. Disentangling these as real threats as opposed to excuses is impossible at this distance but at least shows that responses to the plight of the Jews cannot be easily categorized or explained.

Hiding, whatever form it took, involved expenses in the form of rent, the purchase of food, and the provision of some form of identity documents, even before consideration of possible additional one-off costs to pay for doctors or dentists in the case of illness or injury. Most of the Jews who went into hiding had only limited and finite resources but nonetheless often entered into contractual relationships with their rescuers, agreeing to pay rents and costs of upkeep during their stay. This begs the question of what charges might have been considered reasonable to defray the costs involved. With individual arrangements, there were no controls on charges, and hosts could insist on sometimes exorbitant payments to take account of the risks they were undertaking. There were certainly recorded instances of guests paying off such debts years after the occupation was over.

Being hidden also took a multiplicity of different forms. At one end of the scale there were examples of Jews living more or less openly as house guests, "cloaked" as evacuated relatives from the coastal zones or from Rotterdam, but this required very secure identity papers and a credible cover story that included a family history. In complete contrast, there were guests confined to attic spaces with no outside contact save for the provision of food. One couple reportedly spent more than 900 days perched on the rafters of an attic while elsewhere a young boy was locked in an attic room and fed through a hatch. When he was finally released, he had lost the power of speech. Other stories tell of attics, spaces under floorboards, outhouses, haystacks, and even specially created outdoor bunkers being used as refuges when danger threatened, but not necessarily as permanent hiding places. To a large extent, the day-to-day living conditions were dictated by the hosts with some being more security-conscious than others and insisting on their lodgers staying hidden for most or all of the time. However, there were many other instances where guests were allowed to be part of the life of the house, for example by eating with the family and helping out with domestic chores.[36] This was often determined by location. Houses in towns and cities were far more likely to be visited and under scrutiny from neighbors than farms or smallholdings in the countryside, where a more liberal regime was possible. It is also worth noting that irrespective of location, the burden of having permanent house guests fell disproportionately on the women of the household, whose responsibility for provisioning, feeding, and general care was a constant pressure. One example of this was the need to shop in different places lest the use of additional ration coupons drew attention to the fact that more was being bought than could possibly be required for the known members of the household. More problematic still were fugitives who did not have ration coupons or hosts who could access them, in which the only alternative was recourse to the vagaries of the black market—with all the additional costs and risks that entailed.

Leaving aside the practicalities of everyday existence, there were also huge ramifications for strangers living in such proximity with all the stresses that clandestine living entailed. Some sort of modus vivendi was possible only if all parties adapted to the circumstances, but this was not always the case. There were examples of guests making completely unreasonable demands on their hosts, for example the man who arrived at his place of refuge with all his possessions, including a grand piano, packed in a furniture van.[37] More commonly there were clashes over standards of hygiene, where sophisticated urban dwellers were unused to the more rustic modes of living common in the farms where they were hidden. By the same token, guests could also alienate their hosts. One classic case was of a host complaining that he could not stand his guest—not because he was a Jew, but because he was a German![38] Nationalist prejudices could run very deep. More likely were complaints about guests not being security conscious—for example leaving the house to "test" their identity papers or just wandering off. More dangerous were the attempts made by those in hiding to contact family members elsewhere. In such circumstances, it was all too easy to give away locations in messages or letters that would compromise all concerned if they were intercepted or fell into the wrong hands.

It has been estimated that most of the Jews "rescued" by going into hiding in the Netherlands began with individual arrangements, although many rescuers subsequently found their way to resistance organizations for help with identity papers, ration coupons, and the like. Very few rescuers escalated their activities beyond one or two people, but there were some notable exceptions. Corrie ten Boom was the daughter of a watchmaker in Haarlem, and their family house above the shop had been a focus for all manner of philanthropy in the years before 1940. It was the son of the house and former minister, Willem, who had started helping first German Jews and later Dutch Jews, as well in placing them with farmers in rural areas where there was less of a German presence. The house soon became a known center where Jews could look for help and shelter. The family exploited its position in the town and its contacts to find hiding places but also came to accommodate in the house seven Jews who could not be found refuges elsewhere, either because they looked "too Jewish" or had illnesses that posed some form of threat. Ultimately the whole operation was uncovered by the Gestapo on February 28, 1944, when a series of raids were carried out that also caught many members of the local resistance. While the security precautions in the house worked well for two years, the single location, the sheer numbers of people who passed through, and the inevitably increasing local knowledge of what the family was doing all increased the likelihood of discovery, although the betrayal ultimately came from a Dutch National Socialist neighbor.[39]

A similar initiative occurred in the farmland on the Haarlemmermeer where Johannes Bogaard and his family instigated a rescue operation based on their deep anti-German sentiments and a strong commitment to helping God's chosen people in their hour of need. Their work began in July 1942 when the first Jewish family was brought to the farm from Amsterdam. They had been friends of the Bogaards, but it was through their circle of friends that others were persuaded not to report for deportation and then also given sanctuary on the farm. The intention was to find hiding places among Bogaard's friends and acquaintances in the local Calvinist communities, but this proved increasingly difficult as the demand increased. Johannes and his sons met with many refusals and, as a result, had to take many more onto the farms than they could reasonably accommodate—victims of a policy of never turning anyone away. It was estimated that, at the height of the operation, there were as many as 300 fugitives sheltered on their own farms or in the surrounding area, this all being achieved without any outside help. Like the ten Booms, their activities were well known in the locality and even among the bus drivers, who provided directions for fugitives looking for the farm. Inevitably, the premises were raided on more than one occasion, although even when Jews were initially discovered there, it only resulted in Bogaard Sr. spending a short time in custody. In spite of being known to the authorities and the dangers this entailed, the family continued its activities until a policeman was shot dead near the farm and a further raid on October 6, 1943, saw the arrests of 34 Jews and various members of the Bogaard family.[40] Most did not survive the war.

While these rescue attempts were instigated by individual families, they nonetheless grew to encompass helpers beyond the immediate community and harnessed assistance from friends, extended family, and their church communities as the scope of the work and the numbers they were hiding increased. In both these cases, the families concerned were devoutly religious, and it has been claimed that the Orthodox Calvinist minority played a disproportionate role in the rescue of Jews in the Netherlands because they saw parallels between their own perceived oppressed status and the plight of the modern-day successors of the Hebrews who were "God's chosen people" in the Old Testament. The idea that the Calvinists were proportionally more numerous among the rescuers than their Reformed Church and Roman Catholic counterparts does need some qualification. The fact that the initial motivation had come from a member of the Calvinist community would almost certainly mean that others from the same community would be drawn in. There were several instances in the rural provinces of the eastern Netherlands where whole congregations were mobilized at the behest of the local pastor. This was summed up neatly by one of those involved in Hoogeveen (Drenthe) when he said that if you didn't have someone hiding under your roof you couldn't be considered as a real member of the community.[41] Having said that, help was not always confessionally specific as one survivor noted about his devoutly Calvinist hosts: "[They] do not buy from the local grocer because he is too left wing, but do accept *onderduikers* from him as part of their joint struggle against the enemy."[42]

While organized help for adult Jews took time to emerge after July 1942, this was not the case for Jewish children, where a number of dedicated networks emerged with the sole purpose of saving them from deportation. The first of these organizations were founded by university students in Utrecht and Amsterdam. Restrictions and closures as a result of protests had served to radicalize previously apolitical students who stayed in contact via student societies that, although largely banned by the Germans, continued to function clandestinely. The Utrecht initiative began with Ad Groenendijk and Cor Bastiaanse when the latter was asked by a Jewish girl if she could hide the children of several families targeted in the first call-ups. Bastiaanse collected the children from Amsterdam and began by hiding them in her attic before arranging for their distribution to other addresses. The instigators relied initially on their parents, extended families, and those of other trusted students to provide what were thought to be no more than temporary foster homes.[43] Interestingly, one of the major personalities in the so-called Utrechtse Kinderkomité, Jan Meulenbelt, explained that the specialization in helping Jewish children came about because it was easier to find places for children and also that the Germans were not thought to view it as criminal activity, even though it involved many acts that were, in themselves, illegal.[44] However, from the outset, the students were very security-conscious and developed ways of working to minimize the potential risks involved, for example by not using any hiding places in Amsterdam itself as many areas of the city were subject to regular German raids.

Meulenbelt became the catalyst for recruiting what ultimately became almost a separate network among students in Amsterdam. Chief among these were Jur Haak, a mathematician, and Piet Meerburg, an antimilitarist law student who had been spurred into action by the arrest of a fellow Jewish student. The Amsterdam student group provided more activists and also more contacts for the work of finding hiding places for Jewish children across the country. However, they were not the only groups involved in this type of work. A third network, which became known as the Naamloze Venootschap (NV), came into being when an Austrian Calvinist couple who had fled to the Netherlands because of their Jewish ancestry contacted their pastor Constant Sikkel and asked for assistance. The pastor then used his next sermon to ask his congregation what might be done to help such people. Two brothers in his congregation, Jaap and Gerard Musch, took up the challenge and in a short space of time the couple were taken to a farm in Gelderland and their two children to addresses in Friesland. Lacking the necessary contacts to find many other hiding places, both brothers ultimately moved to the southern province of Limburg, where, armed with a letter of introduction from their pastor, they were able to enlist the help of one of his counterparts, Gerard Pontier, and through him members of his congregation.[45]

The last major network in this field came about as an offshoot from the so-called *Trouw groep*, a wider resistance network derived from the illegal newspaper of the same name. Its instigator in Amsterdam was Hester van Lennep, the daughter of a well-known and respected Dutch family. In late 1942, she was approached by a notary to see if she could help hide a Jewish child. At that time, she owned a skincare clinic in the city, and it soon became known in Jewish circles that one might go there to find hiding places for children. Her first hiding place was with her mother in Hilversum, and this became a catalyst for finding other addresses in that area among her mother's friends and acquaintances. Through her older sister, van Lennep was introduced to Gezina van der Molen, a remarkable woman from a highly orthodox Calvinist background who was part of the editorial group of the illegal newspaper *Vrij Nederland*. It transpired that the newspaper's circle had already talked about doing "something" for Jewish children, and this encounter provided access to a much wider circle of contacts and potential addresses among people who were already known and trusted by a resistance organization. Van der Molen fell out with the leadership of *Vrij Nederland* after being imprisoned for several weeks in the summer of 1942. Forced to go underground, she was invited by the leadership of the Calvinist Anti-Revolutionary Party to create and edit a new clandestine newspaper that would represent its interests, and the first editions of *Trouw* appeared in January 1943.[46]

All these networks had to work extremely hard to find addresses for their charges and often move them as circumstances changed. The supply of new addresses was therefore a never-ending struggle, but even demand had to be generated where organizations who were determined to do something found that they had no means of contacting their intended targets. Linking to the Jewish community and then persuading parents to give up their children into the hands of strangers was no easy matter. In several cases, doctors, pediatricians, protestant ministers, Roman Catholic priests, and social workers acted as go-betweens, facilitating contacts and the transfer of children to couriers who would take them from Amsterdam to destinations elsewhere in the country. A different, but no less fraught method, was the cooperation between the staff of the crèche attached to the Joodsche Schouwburg and outside resistance groups. Led by Walter Süsskind, the nurses in the crèche were able to take Jewish babies and toddlers for walks outside the building, from where they could be spirited away by rescuers. However, as Süsskind himself pointed out, only a few could be saved in this way as to remove too many would invite German suspicions. The majority had to be sacrificed to save the few.[47]

Understanding the mentality of the minority of Dutch men and women who engaged in this type of work is fraught with difficulties. When questioned, many merely pointed out that "something" had to be done or that it was "the right thing to do," and this religious and/or moral framework was undoubtedly the deciding factor in many instances. As we have seen, others were driven by personal friendships, direct experience of German actions against the Jews, or longer-standing anti-German feelings, where helping the Jews was perceived as a way of confounding the occupiers. In every case, the rescuers had an idea of the risks they were running, not least because the stated penalties for *Judenbegünstigung* were well advertised by the Germans even if the implementation of the laws was somewhat different. While the moral element was very much to the fore in rescuer behavior, there were other features that should not be ignored. Both adults and children in hiding sometimes recorded that their hosts made attempts to convert them to Christianity. There was at least one recorded case of a farmer offering Jews in hiding the chance to stay in the farmhouse—but only if they converted. As they refused, he insisted that they stayed in the barn with the animals. In the case of adults, the motivation was clear, but with children, they were often asked to learn the basic elements of their hosts' religion, such as the catechism or the Lord's Prayer, simply so that their cover story about being distant relations would be credible when they were taken to church on Sundays. That said, there were many instances after the liberation where foster families attempted to retain children if no relations survived to claim them, leading to a whole series of acrimonious postwar debates about custody.[48] Other, less philanthropic motives for sheltering Jews also emerged. Some hosts were undoubtedly venal and attracted by the idea of charging exorbitant amounts of money to hide their charges; others saw them as a source of unpaid labor—either as domestic servants or working on farms—and there were also isolated cases of attempted or actual sexual exploitation as well.[49]

The existence of networks and network organizers could act as a counter to the worst abuses and expedite finding alternative accommodation where those in hiding were exploited or where hosts found their guests impossible to live with or a downright danger to all concerned by their behavior and lack of security-consciousness. Over time, they came to encompass a larger number of Jews in hiding as even hosts who had initially entered into private or individual arrangements looked for outside help in the provision of identity papers, food, or other assistance. Exactly how those contacts were made in an era where secrecy was at a premium is not always easy to ascertain, but trusted individuals such as clergymen could usually be relied on not to betray confidences, even if they could not or would not help. Indeed, many of the networks had clergymen playing central roles, recommending parishioners as possible hosts and using their religious connections to seek out like-minded colleagues to help. While these pastors and priests were regularly implicated in network activities, they would often prioritize their spiritual role within the community while delegating the day-to-day tasks to their clerical subordinates as a means of protecting the church as an institution.

As with the activities of the students in hiding Jewish children, it was the personal contacts made by those who instigated the help for Jews that determined where those in hiding were sent. It led to a degree of concentration in hiding places, with one village or locality being a center for hiding Jews, while another, apparently similar one having no involvement whatsoever. Nieuwlande in Drenthe is one such example where the work of Johannes Post and then Arnold Douwes was central to its development, but there were others such as Heerenveen and Bontebok in Friesland, where perhaps 1,200 Jews and non-Jews were sheltered, and Sevenum and Grubbenvorst, both in Limburg, where two very small obilized by their clergymen played host to around 100 Jews.[50] This was increasingly blurred as more and more Dutch men and women went underground to avoid the labor draft, although even at this stage differentiations were made between labor draft evaders and Jews, and within the latter category between children and adults. Members of the LO reported huge difficulties in finding places for adult Jews as "even at the end they refused to take Jews," whereas Jewish children were almost invariably taken up with alacrity. In many parts of the country help for Jews within the LO remained separate from the larger task of helping non-Jewish *onderduikers*, ostensibly because of the difficulties and the greater risks involved.[51]

It should always be remembered that the sheltering of Jews was done by a very small proportion of the population, although larger numbers of people came to know where Jews were hidden and by whom. Yet even within this very small cohort, the work begun by Johannes Post and continued by Arnold Douwes was exceptional in its focus on adult Jews, and it is to the history of this particular region and to Post's network that we now turn.

THE SPECIFICS OF THE NAZI OCCUPATION IN DRENTHE

The network begun by Johannes Post (1906–1944) and continued by Arnold Douwes (1906–1999) saved the lives of an estimated 300 to 400 Jews in 1943 and 1944 and was based in the province of Drenthe in the Northeast Netherlands, close to the border with Germany.[52] The leading historian of this region, Michiel Gerding, has shown clearly that the experience of war and occupation in Drenthe was different from that in the Western Netherlands in many respects, and these differences may go some way to explaining the longevity of the network organized and run by Post and Douwes. As a region, Drenthe had a long history of relative isolation and underdevelopment, and the fact that many rural households did not have electrical power in the 1930s underscores this.[53] It was still possible to find agricultural laborers and their families living in turf huts with earthen floors. Drenthe was sparsely populated, and this in turn meant that contacts between towns and villages were limited. The province was also poor, with an economy based on digging peat and agriculture rather than on industry. Peat had been valuable as a fuel during the First World War, but had been almost entirely replaced by coal after 1918. The local farmers did relatively well during the first postwar decade but suffered dramatically from the international economic crisis of the thirties, that, as in other regions, started in Drenthe as a crisis of agricultural overproduction.

The province was also exceptional in being a stronghold of the Dutch Nazi Party, the Nationaal-Socialistische Beweging (NSB).[54] In the provincial elections of 1935, the NSB gained 11.2 percent of the vote in Drenthe when the national average was 8.0 percent,[55] which in itself was a huge success for a nonreligious newcomer in the conservative and very Christian political landscape of the

Netherlands. In only one other province, Limburg, was the NSB more successful, with 11.7 percent of the popular vote.[56] In some of the smaller towns in Drenthe—Rolde, Vries, and Anloo—the NSB garnered a stunning 28.0 percent, 27.0 percent, and 33.0 percent of the popular vote respectively.[57] Within Drenthe, the NSB was popular with the independent farmers who owned the larger farms and who had perhaps suffered most from the economic downturn, but there were plenty of small farmers and workers who were equally affected.[58] Many of them had joined a highly respectable organization in the 1930s called Landbouw and Maatschappij (Agriculture and Society), whose leadership had subsequently become associated with the NSB. This may help explain this remarkable electoral performance, based more on affection for Landbouw and Maatschappij than on the program of the NSB.[59] Thus many supporters came from those who were politically and religiously neutral but who hoped that voting for the NSB would provide benefits the farmers of the region.[60]

In the peateries, however, the district where Post and Douwes lived, the Dutch Nazi Party was far less successful. "The most orthodox religious communities were the least sensitive" to Nazi propaganda, and they were to be found primarily in the peateries. In Hoogeveen, the nearest large town to Post and Douwes's village of Nieuwlande, with its large devout Orthodox Calvinist community and a Reformed church that was strictly observant as well, the Dutch Nazi Party gained virtually no support whatsoever.[61] Here, a mere 1 percent of the electorate voted for the NSB.[62] Perhaps because of this particular religious structure in Hoogeveen around 20 percent of its Jews managed to survive the occupation in hiding.[63] This was in sharp contrast to the extremely low survival rate of Jewry elsewhere in Drenthe, which will be discussed later.

Drenthe was also special, because—after the short national strike in April–May 1943 against the reinternment of the Dutch armed forces for labor service in Germany—its resistance movement became larger than the national average.[64] While the strike had little effect in the cities of the west, in Drenthe it was perceived as a strike against Nazification, the NSB, the persecution of the Jews, and the restrictions on freedom.[65] Beginning in Overijssel, it soon spread to Drenthe, where the farmers in Zuidwolde refused to send their milk to the dairies and swathes of the rest of the province then followed. There were also strikes in the few existent factories although some towns, such as Assen, Hoogeveen, and Beilen, remained relatively untouched. The occupiers responded with summary justice and some local people were sentenced to death and executed. This merely escalated the tension, and farmhouses of known NSB members were attacked and set on fire. This was a typical expression of resistance in Drenthe. There were arson attacks in Elp, Gieten, Zuidwolde, De Wijk, and Hoogeveen—some of which involved Post and Douwes.[66]

The strikes and their aftermath resulted in a sharpening of the political divisions in the region. The members of the NSB and German sympathizers "associated themselves more openly with the occupiers," whose protection they now increasing required.[67] Moreover, there was good reason for their fears as resistance groups stepped up their activities. Seen with hindsight, the strikes of April–May 1943 were a watershed where any pretense of tact on the part of the occupying Germans was dropped. Henceforward, the regime was entirely coercive in driving the needs of the German war economy. That said, it is wrong to talk about the resistance as a single entity since the reality was of a series of separate organizations that were only united as the war came to an end. Drenthe boasted five separate armed Knokploegen (resistance groups). For example, Jan Gunnink (Ome Hein) had established a group in Meppel that specialized in the distribution of the illegal newspaper *Vrij Nederland*. Out of this came a separate organization led by Gerrit de Boer that included Gunnink's three sons as well as Albert Rozeman (who appears in Douwes's diary). It raided the police station in Den Bosch and stole a quantity of revolvers that were then used to mount raids on government offices and carry out other sabotage actions. In August 1944, Gunnink became head of the local LKP and in December that year mounted a raid on the local police station to free inmates arrested by the SD who were in danger of summary execution. They included Peter van den Hurk and his wife, who had been active with others in helping Allied pilots. De Boer was shot and killed during the raid. There was also a separate group based in Hoogeveen as well as the Knokploeg established by Johannes Post himself and later led by Hemke van der Zwaag. Beyond the armed groups there were also other organizations helping Allied pilots or Jews, as well as various branches of the LO. In total, it has been estimated that Drenthe had up to 45,000 active resisters, of whom 20,000 were arrested. Of the latter, many were either shot or sent to concentration camps in Germany and only around 50 percent survived the war.

The province also saw a number of "liquidations" of high-profile pro-German Dutch officials, collaborators, infiltrators, and even one or two problematic Jews in hiding. The collaborationist Dutch police inspector and informer from Assen, Hendrik De Kruyff, was targeted by a group led by Johannes Post. His home and movements were carefully studied, and it was discovered that he habitually walked his dogs at 10:30 p.m. each evening. Post entrusted Jan Naber and Albert Rozeman, who became the acknowledged leaders of the Knokploeg in Zuid-Drenthe, with the task of killing him, and on July 16, 1943, they confronted him in the street. Although wounded, De Kruyff survived the attack.[68] In Beilen on March 11, 1944, the local Marechaussee commandant Hendrik Huizing was assassinated by a group led by Johannes Post, the victim having been lured from his house and then shot in the street. This action led to severe restrictions on the people of the village and indirectly to the arrest of Albert Rozeman and his son. The murdering of Jews who posed a security risk was a rarity but did very occasionally take place, usually carried out by men from the Knokploegen. However, this was not always the case. In Zweeloo, the Dutch Reformed pastor poisoned a 22-year-old Jewish *onderduiker* who was extremely nervous and constantly threatened to leave the house, saying that he knew all about the illegal activity in the area. Attempts to move him failed, and he was murdered by his host.[69]

In total, the Knokploegen from Drenthe were reputedly responsible for some 40 major armed robberies and raids on municipal and distribution offices, primarily to supply the population with additional identity and ration cards.[70] They were helped by Allied parachute drops of arms especially after September 1944. In total, there were 12 sorties over Drenthe that delivered containers with machine guns, ammunition, and dynamite. Also notable was assistance given to Allied airmen who had been shot down over occupied territory and other prisoners of war who were on the run having escaped from captivity in Germany. Douwes refers to activities of this sort, including the spiriting away of an American airman and a longer-term association with two escaped French prisoners-of-war. Activities of this sort were easier to organize in the sparsely populated countryside than in the more urbanized provinces of the West and were also aided by an increased willingness on the part of the general population to help. So many more families were now affected by the attempted conscription of men for work in Germany that hiding places and material aid became easier to find, although as Douwes frequently points out, this charitable impulse did not always extend to Jews.

Nazi repression of resistance activity was therefore increasingly fierce from the second half of 1943 onward, when Douwes started working on his diary. The occupiers stepped up the Nazification of the civil administration so that eventually 30 of the 34 municipalities had NSB mayors who were also in charge of the local police and responsible for law and order. There was also the introduction of the Landwacht, a Dutch Nazi paramilitary formation armed with hunting rifles.[71] They tracked down Jews and members of the resistance and in some cases terrorized local communities with their violence and bloodshed.[72] In his diary, Douwes mentioned them frequently and was evidently extremely afraid of them. After September 1944, the resistance also had to contend with an increased German police presence that served to add still further to the climate of fear.[73]

This was the most difficult period of the occupation, when the Allies had liberated the southern half of the country but had failed to cross the major rivers at Arnhem. Chaos reigned in the north, fueled by uncertainty on all sides, with the resistance desperately hoping for an early liberation and the Germans and their Dutch sympathizers increasingly panicked by the course of events. Thousands of NSB members and their families moved eastward through Drenthe toward Germany, fearing the wrath of their countrymen when the liberation came. At the same time, the struggle against the resistance was stepped up. Bloedgroep Norg was a particularly sadistic group of Landwachters that operated in Drenthe at the end of 1944 against suspected resisters and usually carried out summary executions of those they captured.[74] This increased repression nevertheless failed to prevent the most spectacular of the raids waged by the armed resistance. This was the liberation of 29 arrested resistance fighters from the prison of Assen on December 11, 1944, an operation carried out by six young men and a young woman aged between 20 and 24 that took no more than 14 minutes.[75] Arnold Douwes was among those who escaped; if he had not been liberated, his diary would almost certainly have been lost forever.

The success of the rescue operation organized by Post and Douwes is exceptional because of its size and scope but also because Drenthe had the lowest survival rate of its resident Jews across all of the occupied Netherlands.[76] This came about because many Jewish men had been forced out of their jobs in the course of 1942 and were then called up by Dutch labor agencies for work in labor camps—clearing grounds and planting trees. These unguarded camps in desolate regions, consisting of wooden barracks, had been constructed before the war to house the unemployed used on work-creation projects, but these men had subsequently been sent to work in Germany. With the camps now empty, it was possible to use them for Jewish labor.[77] In September 1942, the Nazi authorities, after some careful preparations, ordered the local regular Dutch police forces all over occupied Holland to arrest all of the Jews in the labor camps and their families still at home. On the night of October 2, 1942, this unique national action and the largest single raid against the Jews during the entire Nazi occupation led to the arrest of most of the Jews living in the three northern provinces.[78] In Hoogeveen on that night, 165 Jewish citizens were collected in the café Het Centrum on the marketplace, leaving only 43 who avoided the roundup—little more than 20 percent of the total—but in many places, the proportion of victims was even higher.

The historian of the Jewish community in Meppel in Drenthe, Thijs Rinsema, has carefully documented how the Jews still living at home were arrested by the local Dutch, non-Nazi policemen, with the explicit consent of their commanding officer, the Dutch mayor of that city. This had been done on the orders of the provincial representative of the Nazi Reich commissar, Dr. Arthur Seyss-Inquart, who had told a meeting of approximately 20 mayors and Dutch police officials that all of the Jews were to be taken to the Westerbork transit camp.[79] The Jewish men in the labor camps, on the other hand, were arrested by German Order Police,[80] usually referred to as "Green Police" because of the color of their uniforms.[81] It seems plausible that this sudden deportation of all the Jews from the North may have increased the willingness of the gentile population to help Jews by hiding them illegally, as has been suggested by Bert Jan Flim, but this remains difficult if not impossible to prove.[82] What is certain is that only a few of Drenthe's Jews went into hiding prior to October 2, 1942, and most fell victim to the comprehensive raids that took place on that one night.[83] The majority of the Jews subsequently hidden by Post and Douwes were not local, but from other provinces and especially from Amsterdam, which had by far the largest Jewish community and where all Jews had been forced to live after January 1942, when the German authorities began removing them from the provinces.

NIEUWLANDE AND JOHANNES POST

To make better sense of the diary and the events it describes, it is essential to understand something of the social and economic structure of this particular district in Drenthe. Unlike most settlements in the province and in the country as a whole that had histories stretching back many centuries, Nieuwlande ("New Land") was in many ways unusual, because it was literally a "new" village built on the former peateries of no less than five existing municipalities: Hoogeveen, Coevorden, Oosterhesselen, Dalen, and Gramsbergen.[84] The name itself was coined by a certain J. Dijkema, one of the local farmers around 1909 who had the word *Nieuwlande* painted on the roof tiles of his farm.[85] At the end of the nineteenth century, it consisted of around 40 dwellings and boasted a wooden Bethel chapel built by a local evangelist society keen to bring the word of God to this new settlement.[86]

By 1910, the peat deposits in Hoogeveen were more or less exhausted and the land had been planted with trees as the soil was too poor for any other form of cultivation. As peat was replaced by coal as a fuel, the owners of the peateries switched to forestry (as the timber could be used in the mines).[87] The drainage systems developed to dry out the peat deposits created a network of waterways that could also be used to carry the wood. By 1900, Hoogeveen had become the most wooded municipality in Drenthe.[88] Thirty years later, the unmetalled roads in the district were still difficult to negotiate as many of them were so close to the top of the water table. To get from one neighborhood to another, men used so-called *vlonders* (logs or planks bound together) to cross the drainage ditches, and properly constructed lifting bridges were a rarity. In this respect, the area around Nieuwlande was very similar. In 1910, forestry still dominated, but by 1933, it was at the center of vast arable lands, where potatoes were grown commercially for the potato flour industry. This marked it out from the rest of Hoogeveen, where cattle breeding had dominated the agricultural landscape since the 1860s. In contrast to Drenthe, and indeed to the rest of the Netherlands, agriculture became more important in Hoogeveen municipality thanks largely to Nieuwlande, with employment in the sector increasing from 28 percent in 1889 to 41 percent in 1930.[89]

The land around Nieuwlande was not particularly fertile and needed a great deal of work but benefited from the fall in agricultural fertilizer prices. Most holdings in the region around Hoogeveen were small, amounting to less than five hectares, but some of them were sold to approximately 50 families of young and ambitious Gereformeerde farmers, whose origins were in the most northern province of Groningen and the east of Drenthe. They built large farmhouses and made good money from their crops of grain and potatoes. The first telephone

Postcard view of Nieuwlande from 1937. Collection v.d.Sleen.

connection in the village came in 1922, and electric power at the beginning of the 1930s. There were also social differences within the village. The local laborers, who had previously worked as peat cutters, originated from Hoogeveen or from the provinces of Overijssel and Gelderland and spoke a different dialect. They were as devout as the farmers but almost all Dutch Reformed rather than Calvinists. With neither the capital nor the skills to become farmers in their own right, they had become farmworkers and were viewed somewhat suspiciously by their employers, who saw them as inferiors and too fond of the local gin.[90] These two social groups did not mix. It was unthinkable that a farmer would invite a farmworker into his house; rather he would pay him his wages in the barn or the stables.[91]

Between these two groups there was a small group of both Dutch Reformed and orthodox Calvinist tenant farmers who—like Johannes Post—originated from the locality and finally a small middle class. However, these various groups needed each other during the "pioneer phase" between 1910 and 1930, especially when agricultural prices fell after 1918 and again after 1930. There were many business failures and farmers deciding to emigrate but none of this reduced the divisions in the community. There remained a social distinction between the larger farmers and the smallholders and agricultural laborers; a religious divide between the Dutch Reformed and Orthodox Calvinists; and a political division between the Calvinists who voted for the Anti-Revolutionaire Partij (ARP), the Dutch Reformed who voted for the Liberal Democrats or the Christian Historical

Union (CHU) and the agricultural workers who were increasingly adherent to the Dutch Labor Party (SDAP). Before the war, it was the social divisions that were the most marked, but these slowly broke down during the economic crisis of the 1930s and the beginnings of the occupation, something that happened more easily in Nieuwlande because there were no long-standing community traditions to prevent it. Everyone knew each other and trusted each other, especially when they were all confronted by a common enemy.[92]

The religious mix within the community is also important. The highly devout Orthodox Calvinist Church (Gereformeerde Kirk) had emerged as a reaction to the Dutch Reformed Church (Hervormde Kirk) that had itself been reestablished when the French occupation had ended in 1815. The Dutch Reformed Church was supposedly the "national" church that stood for an inclusive moderate Protestantism, but was essentially the church of the well-to-do middle classes. The Orthodox Calvinist movement mobilized the "little people" who were devout and wedded to a literal interpretation of the Bible. Devout Orthodox Calvinists broke with the Dutch Reformed Church in two schisms of 1834 and 1886 before uniting as the Gereformeerde Kerken in Nederland in 1892. They were led by Abraham Kuyper, a prominent Christian Reformed minister and theologian who had founded the national newspaper *De Standaard* in 1872. As the dominant leader of the Gereformeerden in the Netherlands during the last 20 years of the nineteenth century and the first 20 years of the twentieth century, he played a major role in Dutch politics as the conservative founder of the Anti-Revolutionaire Partij in 1897 and was Dutch minister president (prime minister) between 1901 and 1903.[93] While the Gereformeerden were a substantial group in Nieuwlande and the surrounding villages, they were by no means exclusive, either theologically or socially. As the diary makes clear, three years into the occupation there were many interactions between Orthodox Calvinist and Dutch Reformed pastors and their parishioners, all of whom who played a role in Douwes's network.

There is no doubt that Johannes Post ultimately became the most important resistance leader in Drenthe. He was a man of humble beginnings but nevertheless quite successful at an early age. Post's father had been one the very few men in the region who had started as a worker in the peateries but had saved enough to buy a small farm of his own, partly through trading in timber. His father also was the first literate person in his family and had converted from the Dutch Reformed Church to Orthodox Calvinism. [94] He fathered 11 children, of whom Johannes was his youngest, and within the small and closely knit community of Orthodox Calvinist farmers in Nieuwlande, the Post brothers and sisters with their in-laws formed a strong clan.[95] In many respects, Post was an archetype of this community: a principled, self-made man, intelligent and independent in both his thinking and his actions. For example, he was very much part of the group of larger farmers, but unlike his contemporaries, he associated with his workers.[96] In business terms he was very successful, growing potatoes as well as trading in horses and eggs. He also rented and bought land so that just before the war he was farming nearly 50 hectares.[97] This needs to be seen in context where only 2 percent of the holdings in Hoogeveen and 10 percent in the whole of Drenthe were on that scale.[98]

In 1935, the same year that the Dutch Nazi Party achieved its impressive election victory in Drenthe, Johannes Post—who was 28 at that time—was elected as a member of the town council of Oosterhesselen for the Anti-Revolutionaire Partij. A further indication of his status in the community was that Post was immediately elected as one of two aldermen, and in 1938, when the community mounted a pageant to celebrate Queen Wilhelmina's 40 years on the throne, it was Post who was chosen to play the lead role of William the Silent.[99] After his reelection for a second term in 1939, he was present at a meeting in October 1940 where the council decided to implement the requirement that all civil servants in municipal employment should sign official statements that they were not of Jewish descent. Those who could not make such a declaration were—it goes without saying—dismissed soon afterward. This episode makes it clear that, contrary to the assertions made by some biographers, Post was not involved in opposition or resistance from the very beginning of the Nazi occupation in May 1940.[100]

Only toward the end of 1942 did Johannes Post become involved in the rescue of Jews through his brother Marinus, who owned a farm near Kampen, one of the strongholds of what has become known as the Dutch Bible belt. It was also Marinus who gave Johannes his first revolver.[101] Post was also present at a meeting in the Christian Orthodox Calvinist church in Hoogeveen in December 1942 where Frits Slomp, one of the two founders of what was to become the LO, urged the various rescuers of Jews there to pool their efforts and to harmonize the needs of the persecuted with the wishes of those willing to give refuge.[102] Slomp, who had been born in the nearby village of Ruinerwold, was no stranger to Nieuwlande or to Johannes Post, having begun his Orthodox Calvinist ministry there in 1927 before leaving in 1930.[103] In spite of this personal connection, Post chose to stay at arm's length from Slomp's initiative, primarily because he saw the dangers inherent in large-scale resistance organizations and preferring to be in charge of a group where he knew and trusted everyone involved.[104] Post's network in Nieuwlande was based around his farmhouse, and this became the hub for all his various activities and a magnet for those seeking help with a seemingly constant stream of visitors. The day-to-day work on the farm continued but was supplemented by all the tasks that Douwes was later to take on: providing hiding places, money, and documents for those underground, as well as direct actions against the German occupiers and Dutch collaborators.

By the summer of 1943, Post was establishing a reputation as a well-known resistance leader associated with the *Trouw-groep*. In concert with Jan Wildschut; a former career soldier, Jan Naber; and Albert Rozeman (known as the NV after their aliases "Nico" and "Victor"), he masterminded a number of raids on town halls and distribution offices—raids designed to destroy records or to secure documentation and papers that would protect the increasing numbers of Dutchmen who had gone underground to avoid being conscripted for labor in Germany. This included raids on Dutch municipal offices in four towns on a single day, in Sleen, Zweelo, Oosterhesselen, and Nieuweroord. Obviously, this was a quite impressive feat. The group were also responsible for setting fire to buildings owned or used by the Dutch NSB. He, his family, and several close associates were forced to go underground after they were betrayed by an informer to whom they had given a hiding place. While on the run, Post continued to run the network from hiding places in the vicinity but was arrested in Ugchelen near Apeldoorn with one of his couriers, Celina Kuijper (referred to as "Thea" in the diary) on July 16, 1943. He was able to escape with the help of a sympathetic Dutch detective some two days later, but Thea remained in captivity, and as a Jewess was later sent to Westerbork and then deported to the East.

Now known to the police, Post was forced to leave the district, handing over the running of his Nieuwlande operations to Arnold Douwes and Hemke van der Zwaag. He spent several months underground, staying in Hoogeveen, Meppel, and Rijnsburg, where his brother Henk was a pastor and where Marinus had also fled after his home had been raided. Subsequently, he organized another armed group with Marinus, again associated with the *Trouw-groep* rather than the Knokploegen of the LO, carrying out raids in the west of the country. However, his knowledge of the northeast of the country made him the obvious choice to unite the various armed groups in the northern provinces of Friesland, Groningen, and Drenthe. With hindsight, this was his most successful period because, as other major resistance figures were killed, arrested, or forced into hiding, he became recognized as a national leader and shifted his operations to Amsterdam.[105] However, it was a heavy responsibility that he ultimately failed to handle.[106]

Back in Amsterdam, Post's health deteriorated because he developed an addiction to pervitine, a type of amphetamine, which he took to overcome fatigue.[107] As a result, he developed symptoms of paranoia and started making decisions that defied belief, such as his order to shoot all members of Dutch Nazi Landwacht on sight. Post was aware of the fact that he was rapidly losing control over his own organization and opted for a dramatic act that, if successful, would completely restore his credibility: a raid on the more important of the two prisons in Amsterdam with the aim of freeing other resistance fighters held there, including his longtime associate Jan Wildschut, who had been caught during an abortive raid on a distribution office in Haarlem.[108] Post participated personally in this very risky endeavor, accompanied by some close friends from the past, but against the advice of other resistance leaders, who warned him not trust the SS guard whose cooperation was an essential part of the plan.[109] When the men entered the prison on the night of July 15, 1944, they were immediately ambushed by German soldiers. Six were captured during the raid while Post and a few others were arrested the following day, and subsequently all were executed.[110]

After his untimely death at the hands of the Nazis and after the liberation, Post became something of a celebrity, not only because of his status as a leading resister (*verzetsstrijder*) but also because his life story was turned into a highly popular and rather romantic novel by the most important novelist of life in Drenthe, the primary school teacher Anne de Vries (1904–1964). His book, *De levensroman van Johannes Post* (The biographical novel of Johannes Post) was published in 1948 at the height of the literary trend that saw the Dutch as a nation of resisters and made Post into one of the most well-known of all the resistance fighters in The Netherlands.[111] Within six months the book sold 35,000 copies and had been reprinted fifteen times by 2018.[112] De Vries focused on Post's Christian belief as the source of his inspiration, and seen in this light, his biography is more about the many virtues of the Christian faith than it is an accurate portrait of the man himself.[113] Following the success of this novel, six schools, two bridges, and tens of streets now bear his name.[114] In his more recent and detailed biography of Post, Geert Hovingh has provided a much more balanced view of the man and his actions. The result is a very frank book, which describes in detail how Post, after a series of spectacular successes, went off the rails and lost sight of his mission as a resistance fighter. His raid on the German (and Dutch) prison on the Weteringschans in Amsterdam in July 1944 may have been prompted by the best of motives but has been remembered as one of the most disastrous failures of the Dutch resistance movement as a whole.[115]

THE LIFE OF ARNOLD DOUWES

The details of Arnold Douwes's early life are far from clear, mainly because he disliked discussing his life before the occupation, either with his three daughters or with friends.[116] He was born in 1906, the same year as Post, as the son of the Dutch Reformed minister Ds. Petrus Arnoldus Conradus Douwes (1871–1935) in Laag-Keppel, in the province of Gelderland. What Arnold did tell his daughters was that his mother, Johanna Adriana Douwes-Willeumier (1875–1939), left his father and their eight children in 1916, when he was 10 years old and almost immediately after his youngest sister, Guillette (1915–1996), had been born in 1915.[117] In what was an astonishing act for that period and in that community, his mother then moved in with the general practitioner of the village Hendrik Jan Bosch (1866–1933), who lived a few houses away,[118] and subsequently gave birth to their son Hendrik.[119] This must have created quite a scandal in such a small village, because indiscrete infidelity by a married woman carried as much of a social stigma as the official separation of a couple. It was simply unheard of. This seems to have traumatized Douwes.[120] Perhaps the departure of his mother increased the firmness of the bond between him and his siblings, all of whom remained with their father and were raised by him. His diary contains many references to the silent strength of these family ties. Later, there was a stepmother in the household, Cornelia Charlotta Knake (1888–1972), but no further siblings. Douwes said very little about this in his diary and the marriage took place the same year that he left the country for North America.

Douwes was trained as a manager and entrepreneur at the horticultural high school (Rijks Middelbare Tuinbouwschool) in Boskoop.[121] As the son of an academically educated father, such a career path made him something of a black sheep in the family. While his elder brothers, Jan (1900–1976) and Julius (1914–1991), for example, followed in their father's footsteps and became Orthodox Calvinist ministers,[122] his younger sister Juliana (1909–1999) was also something of a renegade, as she converted to Roman Catholicism and became a nun. Douwes's initial training in horticulture took place during the mid-1920s, but in a first sign of his problems with authority, he was expelled from the school in 1926 because of his bad behavior.[123] It was not only his lack of education that was unusual about Douwes but also the fact that he did not aspire to a steady job with good prospects, which was what was expected of young men by Dutch society and also by Dutch young women looking for husbands. His lack of a steady job reduced his chances of engagement and marriage to practically zero. Perhaps also, the traumatic history of his parents' marriage decreased his interest in having any permanent bond with a woman.

Revealing his nature as a happy-go-lucky adventurer, Douwes then decided to try his luck in Canada and the United States of America.[124] Arriving in Canada in June 1926, he soon went to the United States and may later have teamed up with his half brother Hendrik Bosch.[125] There he lived, not as an entrepreneur but, according to his daughters, "as a hippie,"[126] working as a laborer. To all intents and purposes, he became a "hobo," an itinerant and a victim of the crisis of agricultural overproduction that hit the American countryside as much as it did the European. Douwes later told a very close friend that he had, at times, searched garbage cans for discarded food and had eaten whatever he found.[127] He also often maintained that he was deported from the United States after he had strongly remonstrated with a Chicago restaurant owner who refused to serve an African-American. He spent a couple of nights in jail and then, obviously very much irritated by the American authorities, decided to join the Communist Party or one of its organizations.[128] He was then arrested and deported from the United States because of his affiliation, probably in 1936.[129] Douwes also claimed that, after his return to the Netherlands, the US Supreme Court admitted that he had been right all along.[130] Obviously, the last part of this story is less credible. Be that as it may, Douwes returned to his former school in Boskoop and this time behaved himself and graduated in 1938, as the oldest—he was 32—and the best of his class.[131] He then took up employment in the district, working for a company engaged in arboriculture.[132]

But the restless adventurer Douwes soon left the Netherlands again, this time for France, where he worked as a gardener close to the Italian border, until, as a foreigner, he was required to leave the area when France became embroiled in the war.[133] Returning again to the Netherlands, he resumed working in horticulture, and according to his prologue to the diary, he was arrested by the German police. This may have been his third arrest in five years—this time because of his criticism of the Nazis' anti-Jewish measures. As a result, he spent time behind bars in Arnhem for some weeks after September 19, 1941.[134] Released, he then returned to the bohemian lifestyle he had displayed while in the United States. With a bicycle as his only earthly possession, he roamed through the Dutch countryside for weeks or perhaps months in the summer of 1942. Ultimately, he found himself back in Drenthe, visiting the home of Frederik Stegeman, the brother of his brother-in-law Pastor Herman Stegeman, who was married to Arnold's sister Bertha. Via Frederik Stegeman, he was introduced to the reformed Protestant minister of Hollandscheveld, Pastor Volger—and then met Johannes Post via the Volgers' housemaid, Aaltje Boertje, who had earlier worked for Johannes and Dien Post and their eight children.[135]

As the son of a Protestant minister, Douwes was obviously well acquainted with the Orthodox Calvinist subculture represented by Post—a farmer, alderman, and father of eight—who was much more of a success in life than Douwes. He stayed with the Post family for some months, then left, returning only in the late autumn of 1942. After Post had tested Douwes's courage on a number of occasions, first by getting him to steal identity cards and then in helping set fire to a farm owned by a Dutch Nazi living nearby, Post decided to trust him with helping the Jews whom he had hidden.[136] What Post and Douwes shared, apart from their distaste for Nazism and empathy with the downtrodden, was a strong desire for adventure, which at times was hard to combine with their ambition to bear the burden of responsibility for the well-being of others. Post does not seem to have said this to Douwes in so many words, but the fact that Douwes was still a bachelor and very much unemployed, and therefore free of any social responsibilities, made him an ideal candidate for resistance work. Moreover, the fact that he had grown used to poverty and primitive living conditions now served him equally well—and because of his training, nobody was more qualified to construct secret hiding places in the woods than Douwes.

Some weeks before he took over Post's rescue activities, Douwes had begun his diary. Evidently, he was keenly aware of the fact that for the first time of his life, at the age of 36, he was doing something important, which he might later want to share with an audience. Ostensibly, his wish to record his activities superseded the numerous risks he was taking in writing and hiding his notes. Conversely, his self-confidence in his own ability to keep his mouth shut was ultimately well-justified. Even after his interrogation by the German security police and Gestapo, he did not betray his own networks.[137] This needs to be seen in the context of postwar statements made by the Nazi police chief Dr. Wilhelm Harster that 90 percent of the Dutch prisoners talked before they were tortured, just out of fear.[138]

THE ORIGINS OF THE DOUWES DIARY

The last topic that needs to be discussed here are the origins of the diary itself. Between July 1943 and October 1944, Douwes wrote short notes in some 35 small notebooks,[139] which he then hid in jam jars buried in the garden of Frederik Stegeman's house, De Flochte, in Oude Zuidwolderstraatweg in Dedemsvaart, which he sometimes used as a refuge and safe house.[140] However, he also worked on his diary when he was staying in Nieuwlande and hid notes in the garden of his friend Seine Otten.[141]

After the liberation, he dug up most of the jam jars and put together a text of 247 typed pages based on the 35 notebooks. He may have added clarifications at the time, but it does not appear that he made major changes to the text; indicated by the fact that he did not try to write new diary entries for the periods in which he had been too busy to make notes. When he wrote from his memory, rather than from his short notes, he explicitly mentioned this in his text.[142] After the liberation, he gave a copy of his typed diary to the Netherlands State Institute for War Documentation in Amsterdam (RIOD) but is not clear precisely why it was never published in Dutch. At the beginning of the 1990s, Douwes had plans for a publication in English and discussed this with Yad Vashem in Jerusalem,[143] and at much the same time, he rewrote a more expanded version. In so doing, he followed the guidance given by Dr. Mordechai Paldiel, then director of the Department of the Righteous at Yad Vashem,[144] in making sure that the original Dutch version was differentiated from the elements he added later for a non-Dutch audience.[145] However, this text also remained unpublished.

NOTES

1. See, Geert Hovingh, *Johannes Post, exponent van het verzet: een biografie* (Kampen: Kok, 1995), and G. Wijbenga, *Johannes Post de verzetsstrijder: zijn leven, de Knokploeg, verzetsdaden* (Emmen : Centrale Drukkerij en Publikatievoorziening, 1992).

2. Hendrik van Riessen et al., eds., *Het Grote Gebod: gedenkboek van het verzet in LO en LKP*, 2 vols. (Kam Kok, 1951).

3. Now NIOD: Institut voor Oorlogs- Holocaust- en Genocidestudies, Amsterdam.

4. Arnold Stegeman, *Arnold Douwes: Belevenissen van een verzetsman in de periode 1940–1945* (Heiloo: Stegeman, 2002), 9.

5. Stegeman, *Arnold Douwes*, 14–19, 27–34.

6. Stegeman, *Arnold Douwes*, 65–67.

7. Yad Vashem website: http://db.yadvashem.org/righteous/family.html?language=en&itemId=4043157; Mordechai Paldiel, *Saving One's Own: Jewish Rescuers during the Holocaust* (Philadelphia: Jewish Publication Society, 2017), 311.

8. In advance of the Allied landings at Arnhem, Dutch railway workers had been instructed to strike by the government-in-exile, but the failure of the Allied assault left the workers facing severe retribution and most went underground. In the meantime, the Germans shut down the railways to all civilian traffic, bringing in their own personnel to run military trains.

9. This was first mentioned by Abel Herzberg, "Kroniek der Jodenvervolging," in *Onderdrukking en Verzet*, vol. 3, ed. J. J. Bolhuis et al. (Arnhem: van Loghum Slaterus, 1950), 247–48.

10. Jacques Presser, *The Destruction of the Dutch Jews* (New York: Dutton, 1969), 18–19.
11. L. De Jong, *Het Koninkrijk der Nederlanden in de Tweede Wereldoorlog*, 13 vols. ('s-Gravenhage: Staatsuitgeverij, 1972), 4:875.
12. See, in this context, B. A. Sijes, *De Februari-staking: 25–26 Februari 1941* ('s-Gravenhage: Nijhoff, 1954), 90–91.
13. Presser, *Destruction*, 72–73.
14. Bob Moore, *Victims and Survivors: The Nazi Persecution of the Jews in the Netherlands, 1940–1945* (London: Arnold, 1997), 89–90.
15. For more detailed statistics, see Gerhard Hirschfeld, "Die Niederlande," in *Dimension des Volkermords: Die Zahl der jüdischen Opfer des Nazionalsozialismus*, ed. Wolfgang Benz (Munich: Oldenbourg, 1991), 137–65; Ad van Liempt, *Hitler's Bounty Hunters: The Betrayal of the Jews* (Oxford: Berg, 2005), 11; and Johannes Houwink ten Cate, "'Het jongere deel': Demografische en sociale kenmerken van het jodendom in Nederland tijdens de vervolging," *Oorlogsdocumentatie '40–45 Jaarboek van Het Rijksinstituut voor Oorlogsdocumentatie* 1 (1989): 9–66.
16. Houwink ten Cate, "Het jongere deel," 17; Moore, *Victims and Survivors*, 146. It was estimated that around 4,000 Jews had fled from the Netherlands to Belgium and France during the invasion, although some of them returned subsequently. There were also around 5,000 people who put their faith in other lists or in being so-called Calmeyer cases, where the racial origins of individuals were examined by Hans Calmeyer, a functionary in the (German) Commissariat for Administration and Justice.
17. For a detailed explanation of *verzuiling*, see Arend Lijphart, *The Politics of Accommodation: Pluralism and Democracy in the Netherlands* (Berkeley, CA: Stanford University Press, 1968), and for a recent critique, Piet de Rooy, *A Tiny Spot on the Earth: The Political Culture of the Netherlands in the Nineteenth and Twentieth Century* (Amsterdam: Amsterdam University Press, 2015), 221–27.
18. Eva Moraal, *Als ik morgen niet op transport ga . . . kamp Westerbork in beleving en herinnering* (Amsterdam: De Bezige Bij, 2014); Presser, *Destruction*, 406–64.
19. Presser, *Destruction*, 464–78; P. W. Klein and Justus van de Kamp, *Het Philips Kommando in Kamp Vught* (Amsterdam: Contact, 2003); Marieke Meeuwenoord, *Het hele leven is hier een wereld op zichzelf: de geschiedenis van kamp Vught* (Amsterdam: De Bezige Bij, 2014).
20. Coen Stuldreher, *De legale rest: gemengd gehuwde Joden onder de Duitse bezetting* (Amsterdam: Boom, 2007).
21. Anna Hájková, *The Making of a Zentralstelle: die Eichmann-Männer in Amsterdam* (Prague: Sefer/Institut Theresienstädter Initiativ, 2003).
22. Van Liempt, *Hitler's Bounty Hunters*, 24–28.
23. Moore, *Victims and Survivors*, 128.
24. See in this context, Jeroen Kemperman, *Oorlog in de collegebanken: studenten in verzet 1940–1945* (Amsterdam: Boom, 2018).
25. Richter Roegholt and Jacob Zwaan, *Het Verzet 1940–1945* (Weesp: Fibula van Dishoeck, 1985); Dick van Galen Last, "The Netherlands," in *Resistance in Western Europe*, ed. Bob Moore (Oxford: Berg, 2000) 189–219.
26. Hansje Galesloot, *Partij in het verzet: de CPN in de Tweede Wereldoorlog* (Amsterdam: Pegasus, 1986).
27. See Hein Klemann, *Nederland 1938–1948: economie en samenleving in jaren van oorlog en bezetting* (Amsterdam: Boom, 2002).
28. Bob Moore, "The Netherlands," in *The Civilian in War*, ed. Jeremy Noakes (Exeter: Exeter University Press, 1992), 138–39.

29. *Onderduikers* was the term used to describe all those in hiding including Jews, labor draft evaders, and political fugitives. Literally it means "those who dive under." H. van Riessen et al., *Het Grote Gebod*, 2 vols. (Kampen: Kok, 1951). One of the LO founders, Fredrik Slomp (Frits de Zwerver), was an Orthodox Calvinist pastor who had begun his ministry in Nieuwlande in 1927.

30. In this context, see Coen Hilbrink, *Knokploegen: religie en gewapend verzet, 1943–1944* (Amsterdam: Boom, 2015), and Coen van Tricht, *De ondergrondse: Landelijke Organisatie Onderduikers (LO), Knokploegen (KP)* (Soesterberg: Aspekt, 2008).

31. B. A. Sijes, *De Razzia van Rotterdam: 10–11 November 1944*, repr. ed. (Amsterdam: Sijthoff, 1984).

32. Bob Moore, *Survivors: Jewish Self-Help and Rescue in Nazi-Occupied Western Europe* (Oxford: Oxford University Press, 2010), 217–18.

33. Wiener Library, London, 1058/4, interview conducted by Bob Moore with Annie Hoek-Wallach, September 16, 1987.

34. Moore, *Survivors*, 221–22.

35. Moore, *Survivors*, 220.

36. See in this context, Presser, *Destruction*, 381–405.

37. Presser, *Destruction*, 397–98.

38. Moore, *Survivors*, 248; Douwes Diary, March 17, 1944.

39. Corrie ten Boom, *The Hiding Place* (New York: Chosen Books, 1971); Guus Hartendorf, *Noodklokken luiden bij Ten Boom: de historische feiten over de inval en ontsnapping bij Ten Boom, gedurende de Duitse overheersing* (Haarlem: Stichting Corrie ten Boomhuis, 1994).

40. See in this context, Cor van Stam, *Wacht binnen de dijken: Verzet in en om de Haarlemmermeer* (Haarlem: De Toorts, 1968), 68–94. Dan Michman, Jozeph Michman and Bert Jan Flim, *Encyclopedia of the Righteous: The Netherlands I* (Jerusalem: Yad Vashem, 2005), 128–29. Entry for Johannes Bogaard.

41. "Als je geen onderduiker had, was je geen goede boer," NIOD 251a LO-LKP LO/BO3 Hoogeveen.

42. M. Koster, *Ons leven in onderduikstijd* (Oosterbeek: Siegers, 1983), 14.

43. De Jong, *Het Koninkrijk*, 4:48–49; Moore, *Survivors*, 296–97. Indeed, some of the Jewish families in these initial call-ups were subsequently released and then asked for the return of their children.

44. Bert Jan Flim, *Omdat hun hart sprak: Geschiedenis van de georganiseerde hulp aan Joodse kinderen in Nederland, 1942–1945* (Kampen: Kok, 1996), 41.

45. Moore, *Survivors*, 299–300.

46. De Jong, *Het Koninkrijk*, 5:777 and 6:128; Gert van Klinken, *Strijdbaar en omstreden: Een biografie van de calvinistische verzetsvrouw Gezina van der Molen* (Amsterdam: Boom, 2006).

47. Moore, *Survivors*, 304–11.

48. Moore, *Victims and Survivors*, 233–39. Joël S. Fishman, "Jewish War Orphans in the Netherlands—the Guardianship Issue, 1945–1950," *Wiener Library Bulletin* 27, nos. 30–31 (1973–74): 31–36.

49. Moore, *Survivors*, 324–29.

50. NIOD 251a LO-LKP LO-BP3 Heerenveen; Yad Vashem M31/8339a Henricus Vullinghs: Michael Lachman to B. Visser, February 13, 1994. See also, Herman van Rens, *Vervolgd in Limburg: Joden en Sinti in Nederlands-Limburg tijdens de Tweede Wereldoorlog* (Hilversum: Verloren, 2013).

51. Johan M. Snoek, *De Nederlandse kerken en de joden* (Kampen: Kok, 1990), 146–47.
52. Michiel A. W. Gerding, *Drenthe 40–45* (Zwolle: Uitgeverij Waanders, 2014), 3, 62.
53. Gerding, *Drenthe*, 31.
54. Gerding, *Drenthe*, 6.
55. Gerding, *Drenthe*, 8.
56. Gerding, *Drenthe*, 9.
57. Gerding, *Drenthe*, 106.
58. P. Th. F. M. Boekholt, "De nieuwste tijd, 1850–1945," in *Geschiedenis van Drenthe*, ed. J. Heringa, et al. (Meppel/Amsterdam: Boom, 1986), 655.
59. This support was not sustained. While some farmers remained wedded to the NSB, others were known to have abandoned their former allegiances and in some cases sided with the resistance.
60. Boekholt, "De nieuwste tijd," 655.
61. Gerding, *Drenthe*, 106.
62. Gerding, *Drenthe*, 9.
63. Gerding, *Drenthe*, 46; G. C. Hovingh, *Johannes Post, Exponent van het Verzet: Een biografie* (Kampen: Uitgeverij Kok, 1995), 86. Also see Marnix Croes and Peter Tammes, *"Gif laten wij niet voortbestaan": Een onderzoek naar de overlevingskansen van joden in de Nederlandse gemeenten, 1940–1945* (Amsterdam: Aksant, 2004), 39; Lammert Huizing, "De ondergang van de joodse gemeente," in *Gedenkboek Hoogeveen 1940–1945*, ed. Lammert Huizing and J. Braker (Hoogeveen; Historische Kring Hoogeveen, 1999), 310, 314.
64. Boekholt, "De nieuwste tijd," 675; Gerding, *Drenthe*, 3.
65. See Pieter J. Bouman, *De April-Mei-Stakingen van 1943* ('s-Gravenhage: Nijhoff, 1950).
66. Boekholt, "De nieuwste tijd," 669–70, notes that the farmers affected were invariably compensated for their losses by the authorities.
67. Boekholt, "De nieuwste tijd," 670.
68. T. J. Rinsema, *Joden in Meppel, 1940–1945* (Zutphen: Walburg Pers, 2004), 216, 357; Gerding, *Drenthe*, 65; Lammert Huizing, "Steven, Albert en Gé Rozeman: onverzettelijk," in *Gedenkboek*, ed. Huizing and Braker, 160–61.
69. This "crime" was only made public in 1959, when the pastor wrote to the judicial authorities admitting what he had done. See Jack Kooistra and Albert Oosterhoek, *Recht op Wraak: Liquidaties in Nederland 1940–1945* (Leeuwarden: Penn, 2009); Frans Melein, *Verzet in Drenthe* (Rotterdam: VermeerBestseller, 2013).
70. Boekholt, "De nieuwste tijd," 673–74; Gerding, *Drenthe*, 3, 56.
71. The (Nederlandsche) Landwacht was established by the Germans in November 1943 as a paramilitary auxiliary police force composed primarily of NSB members. It should not be confused with the Landwacht Nederland created in March 1943 of Dutch volunteers to fight in the German army. This was renamed the Landstorm Nederland in October 1943.
72. Gerding, *Drenthe*, 56. See also Albert Metselaar, *Op de drempel van de hel: Hollandscheveld in de greep van de SS* (Hoogeveen: Metselaar, 1994) and ibid., *Fascisme en verzet: De NSB in de Gemeente Hoogeveen* (Hoogeveen: Metselaar, 1993).
73. Gerding, *Drenthe*, 3, 66.
74. Also known as Bloedploeg Norg. The leader of the group, Gerrit Sanner, went underground in 1945 but was captured and identified in 1946. Tried by the Dutch courts and condemned, he was executed in Groningen on May 1, 1947.
75. Gerding, *Drenthe*, 56, 65.

76. Less than 20 percent of the 2,498 Jews who lived here in October 1941 survived the Nazi occupation, and that figure could be as low as 10 percent. Croes and Tammes, *Gif*, 37, 39, have 20 percent. Gerding, who has the best overview of the topic, mentioned other figures, namely 1,600 Jews in Drenthe in 1940 but only 147 in 1947 (Gerding, *Drenthe*, 46). These last figures would imply a survival rate of less than 10 percent, but there were good reasons to suggest underreporting in the 1947 figures. For a more comprehensive overview of the statistics for the Netherlands as a whole see Marnix Croes, 'The Holocaust in the Netherlands and the Rate of Jewish Survival," *Holocaust and Genocide Studies* 20, no. 3 (2006): 474–99.

77. Gerding, *Drenthe*, 42.

78. Jozeph Michman and Bert Jan Flim, eds., *Rechtvaardigen onder de Volkeren: Nederlanders met een Yad Vashem-onderscheiding voor hulp aan joden* (Amsterdam/Antwerpen: Uitgeverij L. J. Veen/NIOD, 2005), 28, 33.

79. Rinsema, *Joden in Meppel*, 216.

80. Some of these camps were later used by the Dutch Nazi Labor Service, the NAD (Gerding, *Drenthe*, 54).

81. Rinsema, *Joden in Meppel*, 244.

82. Michman and Flim, *Rechtvaardigen*, 33, 41.

83. Hovingh, *Post*, 86.

84. Hans Leber, "Rompslomp door chaotische verdeling van Nieuwlande," in *Nieuwsblad van het Noorden*, March 23, 1985, 35.

85. Jan Engels, Jo Schonewille, and Jan van der Sleen, *Nieuwlande, dorp met vijf burgemeesters*, (Nieuwlande: private publication, 1988), 9.

86. Engels, Schonewille, and Van der Sleen, *Nieuwlande*, 24.

87. The first coal mine inside the Netherlands (Oranje Nassau I in Heerlen) began production in 1899.

88. A. C. van Oorschot, "De ruimtelijke ontwikkeling," in *Geschiedenis van Hoogeveen, 1815–1975*, ed. H. Gras and F. Nijstad (Amsterdam/Meppel: Boom, 1995), 35.

89. P. van der Eng, "De economische ontwikkeling" in Gras and Nijstad, *Geschiedenis*, 51.

90. Engels, Schonewille, and Van der Sleen, *Nieuwlande*, 40, 49–51, 58–59, 69–70, 97, 126.

91. Engels, Schonewille, and Van der Sleen, *Nieuwlande*, 71.

92. Engels, Schonewille, and Van der Sleen, *Nieuwlande*, 72.

93. The authors would like to thank Drs. Wim Berkelaar of the Free University of Amsterdam for the background information on the rise of Orthodox Calvinism in the Netherlands.

94. Hovingh, *Post*, 14, 16, 17, 22.

95. Hovingh, *Post*, 28.

96. Hovingh, *Post*, 64.

97. Hovingh, *Post*, 51.

98. Van der Eng, "De economische ontwikkeling," 52.

99. Hovingh, *Post*, 60, 65–66,

100. Hovingh, *Post*, 74–75.

101. Hovingh, *Post*, 87–90.

102. Gerding, *Drenthe*, 57; Hovingh, *Post*, 95.

103. Gerding, *Drenthe*, 57; Hovingh, *Post*, 93.

104. Hovingh, *Post*, 95, 395.

105. C. M. Schulten, "Johannes Post (1906–1944)," in Biografisch Woordenboek van Nederland, http://resources.huygens.knaw.nl/bwn1880-2000/lemmata/bwn5/post March 18, 2019; Hovingh, *Post*, 136–356.

106. Hovingh, *Post*, 357–59.
107. Hovingh, *Post*, 357.
108. Hovingh, *Post*, 360.
109. De Jong, *Het Koninkrijk*, 7:761.
110. Hovingh, *Post*, 371–75; Schulten, "Johannes Post (1906–1944)."
111. Pieter Lagrou, *The Legacy of Nazi Occupation: Patriotic Memory and National Recovery in Western Europe, 1945–1965* (Cambridge: Cambridge University Press, 2000), 26; Hovingh, *Post*, 11.
112. Hovingh, *Post*, 383.
113. Hovingh, *Post*, 11.
114. Hovingh, *Post*, 388–89.
115. Hovingh, *Post*, 11–12.
116. First conversation with the three daughters of Arnold Douwes, Jenny Dahan, Henny Assodi, and Irit Douwes, October 28, 2016. My notes on this conversation—signed by the daughters—are deposited in the archive of the Netherlands Institute for War, Holocaust, and Genocide Studies in Amsterdam.
117. First conversation with the three daughters of Arnold Douwes; Michman and Flim, *Rechtvaardigen*, 262.
118. First conversation with the three daughters of Arnold Douwes.
119. Second conversation with the three daughters of Arnold Douwes, December 2, 2016. My notes on this conversation—signed by the daughters—are deposited in the archive of the Netherlands Institute for War, Holocaust, and Genocide Studies in Amsterdam.
120. First conversation with the three daughters of Arnold Douwes.
121. The Dutch National Archives have no sources on the prewar years of this institution.
122. Michman and Flim, *Rechtvaardigen*, 262.
123. Second conversation with the three daughters of Arnold Douwes.
124. First and second conversations with the three daughters of Arnold Douwes. Also see Michman and Flim, *Rechtvaardigen*, 260.
125. Second conversation with the three daughters of Arnold Douwes.
126. First conversation with the three daughters of Arnold Douwes.
127. Telephone conversation with Max (Nico) Léons, November 24, 2016. My notes on this conversation—signed by Léons—are deposited in the archive of the Netherlands Institute for War, Holocaust, and Genocide Studies in Amsterdam. On Léons, see Diary, November 3, 1943: "We now do everything together."
128. First conversation with the three daughters of Arnold Douwes.
129. Michman and Flim, *Rechtvaardigen*, 260.
130. Michman and Flim, *Rechtvaardigen*, 260.
131. Second conversation with the three daughters of Arnold Douwes.
132. Diary of Arnold Douwes, Dutch Version, 1. NIOD 244/1065.
133. Second conversation with the three daughters of Arnold Douwes.
134. Diary, Dutch Version, 5.
135. Hovingh, *Post*, 82n25.
136. Hovingh, *Post*, 83, 93, 131–32. The act of arson was condemned locally by some as ill thought through, superfluous, vindictive, and irresponsible.
137. Michman and Flim, *Rechtvaardigen*, 261.
138. De Jong, *Het Koninkrijk*, 8:239–40.
139. Diary, Dutch Version, September 8, 1943, and September 24, 1943.

140. Hovingh, *Post*, 84. See Diary, Dutch Version, August 20, 1943; December 13, 1943.
141. Diary, Dutch Version, September 29, 1944.
142. Diary, Dutch Version, November 3, 1943; December 26, 1943; January 15, 1944.
143. Email from Mrs. Mirjam Bolle-Levie, Jerusalem, October 23, 2016. She remembered typing the English version in 1994.
144. See the prologue.
145. Diary, English Version, p. 1.

The Diary

May 10, 1940

I WAS WOKEN AT 5:00 a.m. by my landlord. [How can you sleep through all this noise!] I was at once fully awake and out of bed. Our work at the tree nursery began at 6:00 a.m. but no work was done this day. The skies were full of airplanes. The radio soon removed any uncertainties. War. The Krauts.¹ That which we could have seen coming but which we didn't want to believe had become a reality. We were at war. We couldn't understand it or comprehend it. At war with the Nazi-beasts, because we had known for some time that they were beasts.

In Boskoop people were out on the streets, standing in groups. We could see the antiaircraft gunfire from Woerden and other places attacking the Germans. In Boskoop itself, measures were taken to try and make life as difficult as possible for the expected German parachutists.² In this area with so many locks and canals, we removed all the road and footbridges so that any parachutists would land on islands surrounded by deep water. Steps were also taken to deal with [possible] fires and to create bomb shelters.

[As I was not in the army,] I decided to go to my sister and her family.³ They lived in Cuijck on the river Maas in Noord-Brabant. I left on the morning of May 11, 1940, and cycled via Den Bosch where my brother, who was a pastor in the Reformed Church, lived with his wife and eight children.⁴ I was stopped many times at checkpoints [but I had an easy way to prove that I was Dutch, simply rattling off a string of words with a *ch* in them, like *kachel* (fire) or *schuur* (shed) or Scheveningen. No Germans, or Englishmen for that matter, can pronounce these words properly, so I didn't have much difficulty in persuading my fellow countrymen that I was also a cheese head.] En route I also collected any number of letters from soldiers to be delivered to their mothers and sweethearts.

In Schoonhoven, I was not so fortunate and was arrested as a parachutist and not released for three hours. I saw a number of Germans, and there were rumors that many more had landed in the vicinity. Arriving in Gorkum [Gorinchem], there was a hive of activity. The town is a garrison and therefore prone to bombardment. In the main square, hundreds of civilians of all ages and of both sexes were digging shelters and building barricades. Suddenly there was a warning and everyone rushed for cover in nearby doorways or, as I did, with a stream of others, into the town hall. It was an air raid with machine guns. A hail of bullets sprayed over the town. We stood against the inner walls of the building. As soon as the "all clear" was sounded, we went back onto the street and the work recommenced. I myself saw at least one woman with a baby in a stroller [among them].

I needed a permit to leave the town, which I received from the mayor, although His Excellency advised me not to go any further because, as he said, "you will only meet the Krauts."[5]

Between Gorinchem and the Bergse Maas there was land that should have been underwater, but the planned inundation had not taken place.

On the way to the bridge over the Merwede there was an air raid, and another on the bridge itself. I stayed overnight in Raamsdonkveer and the following morning I saw my first Kraut [close up]. He was riding a motorcycle, one hand steering, the other by his side. As I watched, he turned into the road toward the bridge that I had crossed the previous evening. The bridge was still in Dutch hands and being defended. I didn't see any more Krauts until I got close to Den Bosch. The city itself stank of them, there were thousands and thousands.

[The bridges over the Zuid Willemsvaart, which I had to cross to get to my brother's, had been blown up, but an enterprising boy of some ten or twelve years of age took me across in his rowing boat for five cents. I gave him ten and he was happy.]

Jan, my brother, was very surprised to see me. He and his family were fine. I noticed that his neighbor's house had received a direct hit, a heap of rubble was all that was left, but his parsonage was untouched. [I asked about the people who lived next door, how many victims? Not one! The whole family had been "visiting" in my brother's bomb shelter!] Jan told me that there had been heavy fighting in and around Cuijck [although my sister and her family were okay], and that it would be stupid to venture into occupied territory and better to go back while it was still possible. [I told him that this was impossible because I had a stack of letters to deliver. I took the bag off my bicycle and showed it to him. Jan would not be my older brother if he did not have a perfect plan. "Clear the round table," he ordered. "Now pour letters onto the table and we will sort them out. All the letters for Den Bosch on one pile, other piles for Vught, Grave, and Oss. I'll get the teenagers from the youth club to do this. They'll love it. The letters will be delivered in no time at all."]

[I headed back toward Boskoop.] The Krauts were busy moving toward Geertruidenberg. They had huge amounts of weaponry and material with them. The villages in the Langstraat, through which all this stuff was passing, were closed to all civilian traffic. I was forced to turn right and make my way along the river hoping to find a bridge where I could cross before the Germans arrived. However, there was already a battle going on with much shooting and explosions that ended with the bridge being blown up. I went back about a kilometer and stayed overnight with a farmer near Waspik. On the following morning, I was taken across the river in a rowing boat, together with two escaping soldiers in civilian clothes, by the mayor of Sprang-Capelle in the Langstraat [who sported an orange bow on his jacket and a Dutch tricolor on his boat].[6] As had happened before, the mayor wanted to make sure I wasn't Kraut, so I said, "Scheveningse scheve schipperschuitjes" (small slanting fishing boats from Scheveningen)—anyone who can say that isn't a Kraut. After a few other questions and answers, he was satisfied. On the other side of the water I was met by two Marechaussees[7] and taken to the town hall, but later allowed to go on my way.

I thus continued my journey back to Boskoop, traveling more or less by the same route that I come. This time, I remember, I cycled into a very strong headwind. [On the way between Gorinchem and Schoonhoven I saw the devastation wrought by German air raids; of devastated farmhouses and burning hayricks.] I also saw enormous clouds of black smoke and was showered with half-burned pieces of invoices and other papers. Rotterdam was burning! [When I got to Schoonhoven I made a point of hearing the news. In a restaurant, I heard the news of the capitulation in German. Holland had capitulated because the Nazis had threatened to bomb all the other big cities too and General Winkelman, our supreme commander, thought it wise to give up the unequal struggle in order to protect our cities.][8]

The wind had shifted a little and between Schoonhoven and Gouda I rode into a cascade of Rotterdam ashes. In Gouda, I stopped for a cup of coffee and then on to Boskoop. Back in the village I volunteered my services and was appointed as a tower watchman or some such—a task I disliked intensely and I never did stand watch in the tower.

[The following day I cycled with some friends to Rotterdam to find out what had happened to friends in the city. I saw with my own eyes what the Krauts had done. It was unbelievable, but there it was in front of me. I could see it, smell it and hear it.] In half an hour the Herrenvolk had reduced Rotterdam to a ruin—a hell. There, where I saw for myself, only then and there did I realize and begin to hate them, and in ways that I didn't believe I could ever have hated.

My friends [in Rotterdam] had survived as they lived on the other side of the Maas and nothing had happened in their neighborhood. I cycled back to Boskoop with a great feeling of dejection hanging over me. Arriving back with my companions, we all had the feeling that we had been given an incredible beating.

Not long afterward I was stopped by a Kraut on a motorcycle who asked me for the quickest way to Leiden. I directed him to Utrecht.[9] He clicked his heels, saluted, thanked me, and headed off in the direction of Utrecht. [Lucky for me I never saw him again.]

[Before I went back to work and immediately after the capitulation,] my friends and I made a visit to our relations, including to my sister in Cuijck. She and her family had been evacuated for a few days to a farm outside the village, and when they returned home they'd found their house full of bullet holes. We also went to my hometown of Laag-Keppel, where I was born and spent my youth. The first stop we made there was at the home of the family doctor. He was Jewish and had been there only a few years [and had come fresh from the university. I happened to know him; he was bubbling over with energy. He was very well liked by the villagers, and I had met him because of his garden, which he had planned, laid out, and planted himself. I've always believed that one can rate a person by the looks of his garden. We rang the doorbell, but there was no response. It seems that he and his wife had committed suicide the day the Nazis arrived. If we had known of their plans, perhaps we might have persuaded them to think differently. The young couple had hatched the plan sometime before and had swallowed something as soon as they saw the German troops.][10]

There was one other Jewish family in the village who had been there for generations, Sam Jacobs the butcher, his wife, and two children. He was about my age and I well remember being invited to Shabbat meals at their house.[11] They invited us to stay, but we said we had beds waiting for us, which were in fact nearby haystacks.

[Within a week, we returned to our jobs in Boskoop as there was always plenty of work, even when the bottom had fallen out of the (horticultural) market. However, an unwelcome surprise awaited me on my return. During my absence, the nursery had been visited by two German Police men who had asked for an Arnold Douwes. My boss asked me, "What have you been up to? Have you killed one of the bastards?" I could truthfully say that I had killed no one and had no idea what it was about. "Well," he said, "what are you going to do about it?" Good question, but I had no idea what I was going to do yet. I racked my brains about why the Germans would want me but could think of nothing. I decided to do nothing and see what happened. My boss therefore formulated a plan. If the Germans came back, I would make myself invisible and officially I would cease to exist. But the Germans did not come back, at least not for several months.]

The general mood in Boskoop was depressed, not only because we were an occupied country, conquered by some of the meanest people on earth, but also because the world trade that supported the Dutch economy had all but ceased and even internal trade had dried to a trickle. On "our" nursery some interesting experiments were taking place to produce a new strain of azalea, but this did not bring in any money and such a "hobby" cost a small fortune.

In Boskoop itself we did not see many Germans, although the neighboring towns of Gouda and Alphen aan de Rijn were full of them. Nothing much happened, at least not in public. One day in July, or was it August, two Germans came again to arrest me. I had plenty of places to hide and my boss was a master of deception. He also tried to find out why they were hunting me, but without success. I decided then and there that I would leave Boskoop and did so the same day. I was drawn back to my birthplace, Laag-Keppel, where I felt I might be of some use. My boss gave me a month's salary, I said goodbye to everybody and was off.

I eventually found my way back to Laag-Keppel and found a job at a nursery, Huize Keppel.[12] In our village lived two policemen. The one, [Derk Willem] Berenschot, I knew from my childhood. He was a Marechaussee, a federal policeman. The other was the municipal policeman whose name was [Pieter] van Dalen. I struck up an acquaintance with the latter, and we became "friends." He, as a policeman, could keep his radio, and I sometimes went to listen to the forbidden broadcasts. His wife received me in a friendly fashion. We spoke about the Nazis, about the Jewish boys in the old mansion and how we should go about making sure they should never be caught. He promised his full cooperation in this matter. Then, one day, something happened, something terrible. The foul and damnable truth forced itself on me. This house, where the upholder of law and order lived, and with whom I had discussed the best ways to secure the safety of the young boys who were preparing themselves to go to Palestine, where I went to listen to the "voice of hope," this house was the nest of an agent provocateur. One who I had thought was a decent honest policeman was a Judas, dealing in treachery and deceit. How did I find out?

One evening when I came to listen to the BBC, there was a young man I'd never met. He spoke to me in a friendly tone, but I immediately felt an aversion toward him but did not let it show. He told me his name and that he had fled from the Germans in Enschede where he lived. There was something in the man's face that I did not like, and I smelled a rat. When I didn't respond, he said: "Do you want to know why I had to flee?" I said: "Perhaps it is better that I don't know." After a short silence, he volunteered the following information: "I killed a German and threw his corpse in a canal!" This crude and stupid attempt to ensnare me, the placing of the bait in the shape of that lowbrow numbskull cuckoo, suddenly opened my eyes very wide to this very unsavory truth. I played the game and had them fooled. After I left the house, I hastened to do a few very important things: firstly, I changed address within the village. Secondly, I told Berenschot that his colleague was not to be trusted. Thirdly I told the Jewish boys the same thing. Berenschot said: "If you had not told me this, I would have told you. I've been putting two and two together lately and have come to the same conclusion."

I think the discovery that the local policeman was a traitor gave me the rat-on-the-gallows idea. This was as follows: I took 12 large pieces of white cardboard. I drew and painted on each of side of the board a rat on the scaffold—24 rats in all. I wrote on each board: "Symbol of the NSB anno 194." One moonlit night I took my 12 rat boards with me on my bike and swung them over the German telephone wires. Swinging over the wires was simple because I fastened to each one a piece of string. On the other end of the string, I fastened a piece of stone, and the stone pieces swung themselves around and around the telephone wires. I let this happen halfway between two poles, not only within our own municipality but also in three others. My 24 rats became the talk of the town. It was not easy to get them off again. Ladders were useless for that job. All in all, I considered my little gimmick a success. After all, three or four villages were talking about nothing else for days on end and it proved very difficult to get my rats off the wires again.

[What I did not like very much was the insistent talk of the local community about who could have done this. "Who? You don't have to ask that, of course it was that 'Minister's Brat.'" Twenty years before I had always been the "Minister's Brat" and this epithet had stuck. My father had been minister in the local church and so I was, and remain, the "Minister's Brat."[13] Although I was proud of the title, I would very much have preferred that it not been so loudly and enthusiastically bandied about.]

During my time there, sometime in 1941, my friend, the Jewish butcher, Sam Jacobs, was arrested by a carload of Green Police.[14] I had been cycling toward the town of Doesburg when a young girl raced toward me, stopped me, and completely out of breath told me: "Go to Sam, warn him, they are coming." I had heard enough and was already on my way back. I've never before, or after, raced so fast. But it was too late! On the bridge over the river, 50 m away from the Jacobs residence, a Nazi assault van[15] overtook me at very high speed. I saw it all happen in front of me. Sam was dragged out of his house, thrown into the van and off they went. He was sent to Mauthausen, and nine days later we received news of his death: "the Jew Sam Jacobs is dead."[16] I didn't believe the report and said as much to his family; at this stage I had far too much trust in the Krauts. This trust was gradually eroded. It became clearer to all of us what we were faced with and that the bombing of Rotterdam had not been an exception, but that this was the mentality of the average Kraut.

Very slowly it came to me that we were not completely powerless against the might of the cruel occupier, and that we could do more than merely engage in passive resistance. Of course, you turned your head away when a Kraut passed by, didn't understand him if he asked you a question, left the ice rink if a Kraut came to skate. In all these ways we could show our contempt for this riffraff. But besides that, was there not something else one could do, something that could really make a difference, but what?

At this time the RAF was busy making nightly visits to Germany. They often flew over us and dropped pamphlets, small newssheets, and so on. I regularly visited the woods and the fields collecting these leaflets and then delivering them to houses in Keppel and Doetinchem. It gave me a certain satisfaction to drop them through the letterboxes.

In mid-August, person or persons unknown, who ostensibly had an unquenchable desire to carry out good deeds, took the opportunity to cut through a cable of the provincial electricity network between Hummelo and Keppel that powered various searchlights.

The Krauts found a certain level of opposition natural, but their vengeance was not.

After a week, news rolled across the community like an avalanche, "the cable has been cut again." Good!! There was all manner of speculation about what sort of reprisals might be carried out. Many crooks, I mean Kraut vehicles, could be seen driving through the community, Green Police, etc. All men in the village between the ages of 18 and 45 were ordered in squads of 17 men during the day, and 34 men at night, to stand guard over the cable. We were given official cards at the village hall and told where to go for three hours of guard duty. If the cable was cut within 300 m of a guard, the man would be shot on the spot. Summary justice! There were so many meters of cable and so few men that I had guard duty every other night. Later it became twice every three days.[17]

In the early evening of Saturday, August 30, Graaf van Rechteren had cycled at breakneck speed from Hummelo to warn everybody he could that the Krauts were planning to remove all the knives from every house in the community.[18] "They're coming closer," I heard the Graaf call, "they're already at Butcher B." Everyone began hiding or burying knives, scissors, axes, and so on before the Marechaussees, under German supervision, were forced to steal them. I can recall that in our house we only had a 1½-inch potato knife left to do all the household tasks.

In the meantime, we still had to stand watch over the cables twice in three days. It stretched across the country between Wehl, Angerlo, Steenderen, and Doetinchem. In Steenderen one could read on the cobbles the words "V for 'Victory,' Hummelo and Keppel are winning on all fronts."

Another incident that gave me great pleasure also comes to mind. A large British aircraft with a wingspan of around 36 m and damaged in a raid over Berlin was forced to crash-land between Hengelo and Zelhem somewhere between September 8 and 15.[19] The Tommies had brought their crate down immediately behind a house they had flown over, and two of them had escaped. When I put out feelers to find out what had happened I had an amusing conversation with the Kraut sentry.

I: "Can I get a bit closer?"

HE: (in low German) "No."

I: "It is a great plane, but the Tommies have ones that are even bigger."

HE: "Possibly."

I: "Have the crew been caught?"

HE: "Yes."

I: "Shame."

HE: "No need to ask whose side you are on."

I: "No, there's no need."

In reprisal for the repeated dousing of the searchlight cables, the age limit for sentries was increased to 55 years old and 30 men's bicycles were seized. My bicycle was not confiscated because it became invisible in the nick of time. The bicycles were then used by the 30 police detectives to track down those responsible and also to search for the missing British airmen. Finally, members of the civilian elite from Hummelo and Keppel were taken as hostages. . . .

On September 19, as I was about to post a letter to my sister,[20] I just had time to write on the back of the envelope, "Have just been taken away by the Marechaussee, nothing special, I'd been expecting it. Goodbye." I was thus arrested and after three days in custody in Doesburg,[21] I was taken to the SD[22] in Arnhem. With me was a gamekeeper and his two sons from Hummelo. We were placed in a cell next to another cell containing a young woman. She tried every way possible to make contact with us, but I didn't know her. Later it transpired that she was a Nazi spy.

I ended up in the prison in Arnhem among an elite company composed of seven people in one room. There was, among others, Mr. Smit, lecturer in English at the Seamen's School in Rotterdam, a man about 60 years old.[23] In addition, a hotelier from Zaltbommel, Eddy Kool, a first-class joker who, whenever the guards brought us food, treated them as waiters.[24]

"Oi, waiter, you can take this sausage away, we're vegetarians." And when it was time for exercise he said, "Gentlemen, make preparations for a stroll through our rose garden." He whispered in the ears of our guards while we were on way to the exercise yard, "I'm going by bicycle but don't tell anyone, understand?" This Eddy Kool told us why he'd been arrested. We had already experienced the liberation in Zaltbommel, he said. He had arranged a false broadcast through his radio. Someone sat in the cellar with a microphone connected to the loudspeaker from his radio. The voice came blaring out through the Zaltbommel air: "Hello, hello, this is Moscow calling. Broadcast for the Netherlands. We have wonderful news for you. Our brave paratroopers are at this very moment occupying Berlin. English landing troops have occupied the harbor at Bremen. Hitler has fled to Japan."

The result was that the good people of Zaltbommel were mad with delight, started to wear orange, danced in the streets, put out flags. . . . The Krauts objected to the joke and that was the reason why we could rejoice in Kool's company.

There was also a schoolboy from Wageningen who had written something in a school newspaper that had displeased the Kraut-lets. Mr. Smit died later in Germany, but the remainder survived the occupation.

After a few weeks, I was released. The only reason that they had arrested me turned out to be that I was thought to be anti-German. When I protested at the treatment I'd been given, I was told: "We are the masters. We won the war! End of." This took place toward the end of 1941 and I thought to myself, "For the moment," but I held my tongue.

In the spring of 1942, the SD from Arnhem came to collect me again. Reason: probably because I have been wearing a *Jodenster* [Jewish star] on my lapel.[25] On Wednesday, May 8, Berenschot managed to warn me five minutes before they turned up, so that I had the opportunity to leg it, or more precisely to wheel it, taking my identity card and papers with me. I was only 500 meters from my house and just made it into the comparative darkness of some woods when they arrived at my door. I could not only see them, but hear and understand what they were saying. They could not see me in the darkness of the trees or even if they did, they would not know it was me.

[I had no idea where to go, but decided to leave it to my bike and just follow its wheel. I thought about why they had come looking for me again, what did they know, and how could they know? Of course, there are those rats who for days on end had been hanging on to the German telephone lines. There were the Jewish boys in the old mansion. What would become of them? There was my Star of David. But how could the secret police in Arnhem know all about this? Unless Pietje van Dalen had betrayed me. How terrible that this man was a traitor! And also for his family and his young son and daughter to have a father who was *fout* at the time of the Nazi occupation.[26]

I was considering all of this while following the front wheel of my bike. I cycled via Zelhem and Ruurlo, but round these villages rather than through them. From there I went to Zutphen where I managed to buy a few things to eat without having a ration card. I traveled past Eerbeek and then hit the hay. After a bit of breakfast but no opportunity to wash, I turn my bicycle toward Arnhem with the intention of crossing the Rhine and traveling to my sister and her family in Cuijck, 18 km south of Nijmegen. This all went well, as there were no controls on the roads, no punctures, and no problems on the bridge at Arnhem. In Elst, halfway between Arnhem and Nijmegen, I stopped at some friends where I had a square meal and was given a bag full of sandwiches for the road.

I arrived in the early evening at my sister's place in Cuijck, where I found everybody healthy and happy. I turned in early and had a good sleep. Next morning, I was up early and inspected the very large garden—two and a half acres. I was at the end of the garden when my sister came running toward me: "The police are here, they want you." I asked "Germans?" "No, local police from Cuijck." "Oh," I said, reassured. We walked toward the back of the house. There was my brother-in-law standing in the company of Officer Jansen, a well-known member of the Cuijck police force. I heard him say: "Reverend, I'm truly sorry, if I'd known that he was actually here I would have first sent word, but what are we going to do now?" And he looked toward the neighbors' house where an NSBer lived.[27] I said: "You don't have to do anything, I'll do it," and I made a movement with my hand that meant "so long," grabbed my bike and was gone. And so I was on the run again, still following my front wheel—wherever it went I would go. I was totally without a plan.

Passing near Boxmeer I decided to visit Mr. Goudoever, the headmaster of the grammar school my sister's children attended.[28] My niece and nephews went back and forth every day by rail because in Cuijck there were no Calvinist schools. I had a breakfast there and decided to move on to the Van Vlotens' in Wageningen. The shortest way would have been back via Cuijck, but I did not want to do that, so I took the road to Grave where I crossed the river Maas and via a number of small villages I came to the river Rhine at Wageningen, which I crossed by ferry.

Arriving at the Van Vlotens' I got something of a shock. German Green Police had ransacked their house twice searching for me. "What on earth have you got on your slate?" Mr. Van Vloten asked me. I know it sounded stupid, but I didn't know myself why I was wanted. We talked for a few hours with everyone; I could hide behind the cluster of thujas.[29] Later on, I was whisked away to some friends nearby, where I spent the night. They were very nice people, also connected with the Rijks Landbouw Hoogeschool.[30] I noticed from books and other publications that the so-called Dutch elm disease was high on the agenda in the house. I say "so-called" because the virus came from the Far East and spread across all of Asia and Europe, including Holland, where it created havoc among the Dutch elm population. From there the virus migrated to North America, where it was erroneously named Dutch elm disease.

That evening we talked and speculated about what would happen next. One thing we all agreed on: Hitler would eventually lose, he would suffocate in his own foul plans, but that it would take a long time yet, too long. I went to bed. Early next morning I rose with the lark and was on my bike before sunrise. I found my cycle panniers full of neatly packed sandwiches and other goodies. I was again on the run but had no inkling of where I was going.

And so it came to pass that my bike and I found ourselves in Lunteren, in Apeldoorn, in Deventer, and in Raalte. Finally, I arrived in Dalfsen, where I was taken in by one of my brothers, although the Germans had been looking for me there too. How did they know this address? It was a mystery to all of us. That night I slept at his house. We took the chance that the Germans would not raid the same place three times. They didn't. Next morning, I went on to Dedemsvaart, to Frederik Stegeman's house, brother of Pastor Stegeman, my sister's husband in Cuijck.[31] I had never been there but had no difficulty in finding it. The only time I had to ask a passerby was when I was only a few hundred meters away from the house. It was a large villa called "De Flochte" with a large garden. Three people lived there: Frederik Stegeman; his sister Mrs. Homan-Stegeman, who was a widow; and her daughter, Dinie, who was eighteen years of age. I was warmly welcomed by all three. They knew what had happened in Cuijck as my sister had written to them. I lost no time in inspecting the garden. It was very large as gardens go, there was a pleasant arbor, with a rainproof roof over it, set back in the garden. There was also a greenhouse with grapes.

We had supper and after that we sat and talked. I told them of my narrow escape, thanks to the policeman Berenschot. Dinie's fiancé, Jannes Broenink, who lived across the road, also came, and we talked and talked into the wee hours. Next morning, I was up early. The day before I had noticed a large heap of rough wood that had to be sawn into small pieces for the stove. There was a sawhorse standing next to it, and Dinie had shown me where I could find a saw. I worked up a good appetite for breakfast. After eating I wanted to go on with the wood heap, but Stegeman had a visitor from nearby Zuidwolde, a farmer by the name of Hendrik Heerspink.[32] It turned out that Heerspink's father had known my father well, because Zuidwolde had been my father's second parish as pastor in the church. He had left there in 1902, four years before I was born. Heerspink invited me to come with him. He said I could stay on his farm for as long as I wanted. I told him I would like to come but not just yet as I had a little woodcutting job to finish first. Two days later, I left the Stegeman residence, with assurances from all three that I would be welcome back at any time.

The Heerspink farm was a pleasant place to be. It was a family of a man, his wife, and two teenage daughters. These youngsters and their visiting boy and girl friends treated us to song festivals in the evenings. I worked in the vegetable garden. Life was pleasant, but I was still restless and wanted to move on again but had no idea where. Then I heard that Pastor Volger, who had been in Nieuw-Amsterdam, had moved to Hollandscheveld, a village near Hoogeveen. I wanted to go to him and "talk things over." After a week or so with the family Heerspink, I left for Hollandscheveld.

Pastor Volger and his wife were surprised to see me.[33] They had heard that I was on the run from the Germans. Strange how information sometimes travels, using the grapevine and other means. The Volgers told me that Hollandscheveld harbored quite a large number of NSB-ers,[34] stupid people who thought they knew on which horse to bet. Stupid, yes, but potentially dangerous.

I had already noticed three things. Firstly, the garden attached to the Volger parsonage was located in the middle of the village. Secondly, the garden consisted mostly of a rundown lawn composed primarily of wild grass and weeds, and thirdly in a neighbor's garden I had seen about 1,000 seedlings all planted close together, of *Calendula officinalis* [marigolds], whose flowers are either orange or yellow. I ask the Volgers if the flowers in the neighbor's garden last year had been yellow or orange. A beautiful deep orange was the answer. "Splendid!" I said. "Just what I need to make my little plan a success." I revealed the little plan to my hosts, and they were enthusiastic.

I dug up the disintegrating lawn. It was interesting to note how quickly it was swarming with birds of all types, profiting from the free meal provided by the overturned soil. I had ordered 10 bags of old chicken manure, and it was properly delivered by a friend of the pastor. After I had finished turning over the area, I scattered the chicken manure over it, raked it in, leveled the ground, and planted my thousands of *Calendula* seedlings. The planting of the seedlings took an afternoon, and the whole operation took a week. I was lucky I did not have to water the plants, because minutes after I'd finished my last seedling, it started to rain, and it kept on raining all through that night. It could not have been better.

That evening, Pastor Volger had a visitor. He was Johannes Post.[35] Post invited me to come to his farm in Nieuwlande, a small village only 5 km from Hollandscheveld. The next morning, I set off to the farm. It was about a hundred yards off the road and connected by a private path. Alongside this path was a large Bouvier who had the run of an area next to the path, where he was fastened with a ring on a long cable, so he could freely run back and forth, or, if he so wished, sit still in his little house. A perfect four-legged watchman.[36] No one could enter, either by day or by night, without the farm inhabitants becoming aware of it thanks to this loud and boisterous canine friend.

The Post family consisted of Johannes; his wife, Dien; and their seven children. The oldest, Hilda, was seven years old; the youngest, Hermien, was in the cradle. Not to be forgotten, there was also Oma. She was Johannes's mother-in-law, and like all the others a very brave person. I shall never forget the spontaneous way in which I was accepted into the family circle.

Johannes Post was every inch a farmer. He had 40 hectares of land, which by Dutch standards was quite a large farm. One of his main crops was seed potatoes, which required careful cultivation. Johannes's fields looked wonderful. They gave an impression of being well tended, but I noticed that there was neither a flower garden nor a vegetable garden, so I suggested to Johannes that I should make a flower garden. Johannes thought this an excellent idea, as did his wife, but it was even more appealing to the children. To do this as cheaply as possible, I suggested that I make the whole thing out of seedlings I grew myself. Johannes ordered a list of seeds that I gave him from a well-known seed merchant. When they arrived, my nursery was situated in a sunny corner and protected against cold winds. I had dug up the ground, leveled it, raked it, divided it with narrow straight paths and made the beds. Everything was ready to receive the seeds.

One day Johannes came home with the news that he seen a picture of me in the latest issue of the *Nederlandsch Algemene Politieblad* [Dutch Police Gazette]. The story said that I was a terrorist and that the German security police in Arnhem wanted me and that I was riding a bike with an orange and blue banner on it—as if I would have left that on!

Johannes said: "It is high time for you to get a new identity card. Come with me, we're going to fetch one. Good thing you let the moustache grow." Johannes took me to the sextant of the church; his name was Willem Roffel.[37] After introductions, we talked about the Nazis—of course, what else! Then Johannes asked: "Willem, will you do me a favor?" "Of course, what is it?" "Will you lose your

Above, Portraits of the Post family with a superimposed earlier image of Johannes (his eighth child was born after his death). Collection Hovingh.

Right, Pastor Willem Volger of Hollandscheveld. Collection v.d.Sleen.

identity card?" "Lose my identity card? Yes, of course, but why?" Johannes explained that Willem Roffel would not really lose it, he would only tell the officials in the town hall that he had done so. He would then get a summons to come to the town hall in Hoogeveen at such and such a day to get a new one. I would be given that summons and would then go to Hoogeveen as Willem Roffel. Willem wrote down a few things that I had to learn by heart. Name of his wife, date and place of marriage, four children, [their] names, [birth] dates and places. "Of course," Johannes said to Willem "You keep your old, your real identity card and don't worry, although I cannot guarantee it, I don't believe there will be any trouble."

Everything went smoothly. On the day when I was ordered to attend the town hall, there were about a hundred others waiting for identity cards. Most of them were children who had turned 15.[38] My name was called, but I'd done my homework and answered all the clerk's questions. His last question was whether I could pay for the identity card. I said no, so I got it for free. From that day on I had a moustache on my identity card and a new identity! Fantastic!

Once, on a Sunday, as Johannes and I took a stroll over his land looking at one of his potato fields in bloom, he said: "You make nice gardens but is there really anything more beautiful than a field of potatoes in full flower?" Johannes loved his work and his farm, but his fight against the powers of darkness were his top priority.

In the meantime, I was still working away on my pet project: the garden. I worked long days. Before the sun rose I was already at it and when our "collective mother" sank below the Western horizon I was still there. With gardening however, it is like housework, it is never finished. Nevertheless, I wanted to test my new identity as Willem Roffel, and so when the garden was bringing forth a wealth of flowers, I said to the kids to take care of my "baby" and I left. Johannes and Dien said: "Whenever you want to come back, know that you are always welcome. Our house is your house."

I first went to the Stegeman family in Dedemsvaart, where I found everybody in good health. Through Stegeman, I met Sister Scholten, the district nurse in Dedemsvaart. Later on this brave little lady and I would work closely together, but I didn't know that yet. Two days later I went to Wageningen, to the Van Vloten family. Bernie, the oldest of the three sons, whom I met in the prison in Arnhem, was home again, released with a stern warning. I passed the time there delivering illegal newspapers, but I had a feeling that I should go back to Nieuwlande, where I had also had the honor of being their first *onderduiker*.[39]

It was only in the winter of 1942–43 that I asked Johannes Post what he wanted me to do. The farm was always a hive of activity. Johannes collected Jews from Amsterdam and distributed them in Nieuwlande and the surrounding area. He gave me the job of collecting identity cards, and I traveled the country stealing them: from family, from acquaintances, from strangers, i.e., I was given, stole, or

Resistance leader Hemke van der Zwaag and his wife, Frederika. Collection v.d.Sleen.

Jan Wildschut in his military uniform. Collection v.d.Sleen.

bought them. Every so often I returned to Post with my booty. He could use everything, greedily eyeing every identity card and turning over in his mind for what purpose it could best be used.

At Post's farm things became even busier. Thirty visitors in an evening was nothing unusual. The telephone was never silent. In spite of everything, Post always remained very calm.

On one occasion, he asked me if I felt able to visit some bureaucrats, with the idea of stealing identity papers and other blank official forms and destroying anything that could not be taken away. Naturally I was happy to do this, and so it transpired that on a pleasant afternoon on Wednesday, June 23, 1943, Jan Wildschut and I set off on our bicycles.[40] We went to Noord-Sleen, Zweeloo Oosterhesselen, and Nieuweroord. We took the identity papers and other things, for example, breeding licenses, cattle books, and rubber stamps. Everything went smoothly, although in Zweeloo a typist jumped through an open window and in Oosterhesselen I had to kick the door in to gain entry. In Nieuweroord we had to deal with an NSB civil servant, but he gave us no trouble.

After every raid, we gave the stuff to Hemke van der Zwaag or someone else who directed us to the next target and then met up again at a predetermined point. With a flat tire, we returned eventually to Post's farm. That evening there was a celebration in the kitchen. Together we sorted the whole lot out. Post sat in front of the fire feeding it with paper. Thick clouds of smoke billowed out of the chimney. Johannes Post danced with delight in seeing all these papers. He thought it wonderful that now the whole administration of four municipalities had been thrown into disarray. Everything was looked through carefully. The identity papers and blank forms were kept along with various other things, and the rest went into the fire, although it took a long time to burn so much paper. Thea provided the coffee.[41]

Around 2:00 a.m., Post said: "Now we have to take Hollandscheveld as well." No sooner said than done. He, Jan Wildschut, and I set out. Post led us through lonely neighborhoods. Everything went well, and the official was drummed out of his bed with the excuse that the Crisis Controledienst from Assen had arrived. "Look," said Jan Wildschut, "this is my authority," and he let him see his revolver. We came back around 3:00 a.m. with an impressive haul. Dien Post was still sitting there, feeding the fire. On the way back I had another puncture. Next day we heard that the news of the raids had spread like wildfire all over the province. It was also said that the two perpetrators came from Amsterdam. This was proof that our little gimmick of uttering a few words of Amsterdam slang had paid off.

Having a good bicycle and good tires was undoubtedly a priority if I wanted to continue my work effectively. This posed a problem because new bicycles could only be obtained with a permit from the Germans, but it was only NSBers and traitors who received them. It was Sister Scholten in Dedemsvaart who found the solution. She had the misfortune of living opposite a fanatical member of the NSB, but this now turned out to be a blessing in disguise as the man had just bought a new bicycle. And so, not long afterward, I "borrowed" this beautiful bike with first-rate tires and inner tubes from this Mr. Burgers. He was a nurseryman, and so I found an excuse to buy plants from him, but while his back was turned, I made off with the bicycle. I went straight to Jan Kats, the bicycle repairman, who rapidly made it unrecognizable with a few licks of paint and by changing the saddle and adding a bell and a strong luggage carrier.

Around this time, I began helping people go underground, Jews as well as others. I brought them to addresses that Post had found for them, not only in Nieuwlande, but also in other places such as Nieuw-Amsterdam, Dedemsvaart, and Zweelo. Gradually I also started looking for hiding places, which was not easy, especially in the beginning. Later, I built in more of a routine. Collecting identity cards became a secondary consideration. We certainly had need of them, but identity cards could be acquired by other means, either through forgery or by thefts from town halls.[42]

In that period, I didn't sleep at Post's farm because it was always very busy and I didn't want to add to their problems, so I sought refuge elsewhere. I often slept in a haystack nearby, and finding food was no problem because I was welcome at [the home of] just about every farmer and resident of Nieuwlande.

Given the nature of the work, I was often at Post's farm. There could be many people there, and all manner of things took place. On one evening, around midnight, we saw in the moonlight two uniformed individuals coming toward the farm. Post looked to see if his revolver was loaded, picked it up, and opened the door. It turned out to be two policemen who needed to go into hiding. Naturally they were given all sorts of things to eat and were allowed to stay the night.

If I arrived in the evening at the farm of the "Big Shot" as we called him, I would often see a bunch of onderduikers strolling in the flower garden, by the shed stood another group deep in conversation, here and there were children with black or bleached hair and dark eyes. If he was at home, and that was not always the case, the Big Shot himself sat in conference in his front room. Thea was always sociable and was usually at the center of a group. The living room looked like a clothing shop: stacks of socks, overalls, and other essential clothing were scattered everywhere, all intended for onderduikers.

I often visited Pastor Willem Volger in Hollandscheveld who sometimes received onderduikers that I was to take to various addresses, for example, a farmer's son [on his way to a] journeyman baker, or an office worker [being hidden at the home of] a bicycle repairman. In that period, I met one onderduiker who had hidden himself in a dog kennel. He claimed to have made the kennel cozy. If it rained, he had to lay curled up, but in better weather he could lay out flat. If he did that his head came out of the kennel. Ostensibly he had shared this hiding place with another onderduiker. Then they slept with neighbors, but now the latter had a haystack to himself.

I visited Dedemsvaart on a regular basis, with or without onderduikers. I could always find lodgings there with my friends the Stegeman family. I slept in a shed at the bottom of their garden [*vluchthut*].

I acquired a great many identity cards from Sister Scholten, the district nurse in Dedemsvaart. It was from behind a curtain in her house that I had spied on the NSBer whose bicycle I had stolen as he lived almost directly across the road from her. Sister Scholten asked me once if I knew of a place for young Jewish man, with a very typical appearance, who had to leave Amsterdam urgently. I said: "Let him come." The sister telephoned Amsterdam that the consignment of "surgical dressings" was expected as soon as possible.

An onderduiker hiding in Stegeman's house told me that there had been a *radja*[43] in the church last Sunday. Of course, he meant a raid.

I often visited Jan Kats, whom we called Vondel, in Hollandscheveld to listen to the English radio. From somewhere out of the wall came a voice: "Here is London." Masterfully hidden. There was a young Jewish girl at Pastor Volger's house who needed to leave there and whom I took with me to Dedemsvaart.

On a particular day, June 30 I think, a fire broke out in the bus station of the EDS[44] in Dedemsvaart. Seven buses that were to be examined the following day before being taken by the Krauts were totally destroyed. From a neighboring house, which was being showered by sparks, all the furniture was removed, a task with which I lent a hand and emerged from with two identity cards.

I was collecting money to help onderduikers, but that work was really not for me, anyone who had the enthusiasm might raise a hundred guilders against my Fl.10, but even I sometimes had donations of Fl.30 or Fl.50.

July 3, 1943, Saturday Evening

THIS MORNING I woke up early and by 5:00 a.m. I was working in the garden. There are persistent rumors that the Green Police will mount a raid in Dedemsvaart. All the physicians have gone underground and two pastors have also disappeared. One of the doctors in hiding has had constables stationed near his house. The wife of the other doctor has kept watch from the front of their house all night. However, up until now it has remained quiet.

My sleeping place in the garden has acquired a pair of lady's slippers, a nightie, a dress and some typical womanly odds and ends. This is to give plausibility to the story that the Germans would be told, namely, that Mrs. Homan-Stegeman sometimes sleeps there when she has headaches. The pastor of the Stegeman's church was tipped off by the Dutch Marechaussee[45] that he should go underground and he did so immediately. I am out of tobacco and prefer to smoke a mixture of cherry and bean leaves rather than ersatz tea leaves.

This afternoon I did more collecting and raised another 430 guilders. Everybody gave something, but it was still too little. One ruddy old man talked nineteen to the dozen and gave me the impression that he really would come across with something to write home about. "Yes of course he would give. Surely everyone ought to give and give plenty. Yes, he was old, otherwise he would also go out collecting." Then the old chap found a key somewhere and with it he opened a writing desk; inside the desk he opened the box; out of the box he took one guilder and gave it to me. I convinced him that a guilder was not enough, so he came up with two guilders and 50 cents. I explained this also was not enough. The old man gave this matter a lot of deep thought. I detected in him some nervousness while he was deliberating the matter with his daughter, and she decided that 10 guilders was appropriate. One young lady was going to give me two guilders and 50 cents but she could read my thoughts because she said at the same time, "Of course it's not enough, I'll talk it over with my husband when he comes home."

It is remarkable that so many cats are named Tommy these days, but appropriate considering that their task is also to rid us of gray parasites.

This afternoon I received a nice photo of the princely couple.[46] These days one can find a treasured "Oranje scrapbook"[47] in just about every home, with photos of Queen Wilhelmina, Juliana, and her family together with the lines from well-known songs, and of course a few Dutch lions.

This morning we received word that the whole administration of the regional secretariat[48] in Leeuwarden, capital of the province of Friesland, had been taken away in one master stroke. A telephone call had come from the German Ortskommandant:[49] a car would arrive to take everything and bring it to a safe place. A car with two Krauts and two Marechaussees arrived shortly afterward, and they took everything. However, the following day the real Ortskommandant called to say that men would come presently to take everything to safety.[50]

The six-year-old son of the of Pastor van der Sluys in Dedemsvaart has changed his mind about wanting to become a pastor, as he thought the risks of being picked up were too great.

July 4, 1943, Sunday Evening

THE PASTOR WHO had gone underground appeared unexpectedly in his pulpit this morning. He said: "It is all well and good to open your house for cousins, nieces, and other relations, but one must never forget, especially in these horrible times, there are many others that urgently need help." He also said this: "Don't be stingy but give for the good cause." He also spoke about present-day mores. "Morals," he said, "are going to pot." I thought this was an appropriate sermon for the times. [As soon as the church service was over the pastor disappeared again.]

I once heard Pastor Volger say in a sermon that David had had bad identity papers (he used the German word *Ausweise*), and he said that we must not forget to practice charity. On one occasion, the Volgers had a surprise visit from the WA[51] from Meppel who were looking for two onderduikers. The family had just sat down to lunch. There was Pastor Volger, his wife, the two children, two onderduikers, and two visitors: a man and his wife from Hoogeveen. When they saw the WA men coming, the onderduikers jumped like jackrabbits through the open window and ran through the garden into a rye field. At the same time, two chairs, two plates, two forks, two knives, cups and saucers were removed. The "gentlemen" were welcomed inside. "Where are the two onderduikers?" they asked. Nobody knew what they were talking about. "Don't try to fool us, you've got two strangers in the house." Pastor Volger pointed to the married couple from Hoogeveen: "These two people I have in the house and no one else." The parsonage was searched, nothing was found, and they left.

While I was in Dedemsvaart, there had been raids in Nieuwlande. The Green Police. They raced at high speed along the roads next to the many canals. They found no onderduikers, but took four men at random for work in Germany.

July 5, 1943, Monday Evening

THE POLICE COMMISSIONER in Enschede was shot dead on Friday. Hurrah.[52]

Sister Scholten gave me a beautiful revolver with ammunition, which I will give to Johannes Post.

Pastor Volger gave me two identity cards to be altered. He also had two onderduikers that had to go to a farmer in Slagharen and whom I delivered there.

July 6, 1943, Tuesday Evening

AT POST'S FARM, I handed over the money I'd collected and also the revolver that I'd received from Sister Scholten. He's very pleased with it and says it's the best. I also had a stack of identity cards and a few that had to be altered for customers of Pastor Volger. All my identity cards were from women this time, except one from a blind man. It was very busy in the identity card department. Never a dull moment! "Peter" was the identity card magician.[53] When Peter was finished with an identity card or any other document, it was better than a legal one.

There were not many people at Post's farm to see the Big Shot, and those who were there were disappointed. He was not at home to visitors. Post was sound asleep and his wife refused to wake him. I had a look in the garden, planted some petunias, and watered them.

In Nieuwlande they had been worried about me. The nearby rye field showed the evidence of the escaping onderduikers who had fled during the Green Police raid.

July 7, 1943, Wednesday Evening

TO DEDEMSVAART WITH two onderduikers. One was extremely slow in his movements. One had his own bicycle the other had one borrowed from Pastor Volger. On the way over we met Dr. Reijnierse on a byway, he had gone back home after being in hiding for a few days. [He joked with me about the fact that I was already in hiding permanently so I did not have that difficulty any more.] When we arrived in Dedemsvaart the three of us were perspiring like workhorses. It was very hot. One I took to a farmer who cannot work himself, and the other to a bicycle repairman. I was in a hurry because at 7:30 a.m. I had a rendezvous at a place just outside Dedemsvaart, to meet a Jew whom I was to bring to Nieuwlande. We were to carry red carnations and everything went without a hitch. I was there right on time. This rendezvous had been organized by Sister Scholten. My new companion was undoubtedly a Jew,[54] and for that reason it was probably best if he carried an identity card indicating that he was a half Jew. We cycled to Nieuwlande without his luggage, which we left at Stegeman's house.

My new friend had come from Amsterdam via an interesting route. Ostensibly volunteering to go to Westerbork with a yellow Star of David on his lapel, when he arrived in Hoogeveen he had removed the star from his coat and escaped on a bicycle. At the Stegeman household we had arranged for him to meet his girlfriend who did not look particularly Jewish, had good papers, and was in hiding herself in Dedemsvaart. They hadn't seen each other for a year and inevitably a lot of kissing took place. I took a walk through the garden. To prevent us arriving late in Nieuwlande, I had to bring an abrupt end to this idyll and insisted that we get on the road. Whenever we encountered anyone, my companion had a sudden attack of sneezing and used his large handkerchief, thus hiding his nose and much of his face. He and his girlfriend begged me to allow them to have contact occasionally, but I refused. Only letters would be allowed which I would censor, but with no names and no addresses. There was no question of any face-to-face meetings.

The escort who had brought our new friend had to return to Amsterdam. He was delighted with the list I gave him of addresses where Jews, especially children and babies, might be placed in Boskoop. A week before I had been canvassing there and had had a bit of success. I explained the list to him because it was in code and after that it became easy reading for him.

As far as possible, we used only byways to get to Nieuwlande. We had to hide only once, behind some shrubs, when we heard a car coming. It turned out to be a German police car. Arriving back at Post's farm, the place resembled a bicycle shed. The house was full of visitors. I exchanged a few words with Johannes and then left with my charge, following the canal. In a secluded place there was an old shed, inaccessible to vehicles. The shed had been fixed up to house onderduikers. It was already dark when we arrived. As we started singing "in the name of Oranje open the gate," the door opened and we saw 11 people. There was straw to lie on but the ventilation was none too good. The newcomer was enthusiastically received and was told to treat the place as his own and asked if he was hungry.

I went back in the pouring rain. I sat in Post's kitchen for a short time and then moved on to Hollandscheveld, where I had an appointment with Jan Wildschut and Jan Kats at the latter's house. The following day we were due to make a raid on a distribution transport. We were given tasty sandwiches with real cheese and afterward went to bed. [As I was undressing, Jan, who was an observant Roman

Catholic, started to pray so I stopped what I was doing and stood at attention. When he was finished, he said, "Hey, you're not in bed yet?" I said, "No, I waited for you to say your prayers." "You should not have done that." He said, "When I pray you just go on with whatever you're doing."]

July 8, 1943, Thursday

JAN WILDSCHUT AND I were on the road early, together with a guide, whom Kats had recommended as both good and reliable. Our route took us via Nieuwlande where we stopped at the house of Willem Roffel, the man whose name I was using as it was on my identity card, to borrow a raincoat. We held up the transport halfway between Coevorden and Steenwijksmeer. [Our guide had done his job well and had vanished immediately. Brandishing his gun, Wildschut shouted, "We are seizing these ration cards in the name of Her Majesty the Queen."] My task was to grab the consignment contained in one very large tin box, put it on the back of my bike and then ride to an agreed point where Kats was waiting with his Volkswagen. The box was so big that it took some time to get it in through the door of the car, but eventually we were successful. Kats took off, and so did Jan and I, cycling in different directions and meeting up again at Post's farm. Kats hid the booty under the floorboards of his house.

The same day, Pastor Volger had a visitor, a member of the church council. He begged the pastor not to come to church the following Sunday because he had heard rumors that the NSB had said that they would see to it that he would never preach again. Pastor Volger said that he would pay no attention to this. Later on, I took a male onderduiker, who had been in the parsonage, to Dedemsvaart. No difficulties on the way and Stegeman had a place for the new arrival. In Dedemsvaart I was told that that there had been a raid on a transport of ration cards. Surprise, surprise. I was tired and turned in.

July 9, 1943, Friday Evening

A DISMAL DAY with occasional sunshine. Jannes Broenink from across the road came over and asked me if I knew that Mussert got 13 guilders for every 10 guilder note. I looked nonplussed until he explained the play on words that each note carries the wording "De Nederlandse Bank betaalt aan toonder tien gulden," which could be rephrased as "De Nederlandse Bank betaalt aan Toon dertien gulden," where "Toon" was the shorter form of Antoon Mussert.

Some neighbors had noticed the rendezvous a few days previously, and there is now some talk in the village. "Hear, see, and be silent" seems to be a difficult thing for some people.[55]

The medical profession has won a "Victory" over the Nazis. They have agreed a few unimportant things, but there is no mention of the chamber of physicians (Artsenkamer).[56]

Stegeman received a pound of butter from one of yesterday's onderduikers.

Rumors have it that Italy has received an ultimatum, surrender or else, but there is no mention of it from London.

A "submariner"[57] whom I had placed on a farm had returned, claiming that he'd been put in the wrong place as he had to dig up potatoes. This he could not do as being so close to the Earth made his face swell up. What should one do in a case like this? I didn't say any of the things that I wanted to say. Stay calm? That is exactly what I did. I remained ice cool and tried to make the man understand that the purpose behind going underground was to save one's life, and that an onderduiker should thank his lucky stars if he was fortunate enough to have something to do, like him and his spuds. I told him that he was not only endangering himself by wandering around as if he was in some sort of paradise, having been made immune to all danger from the Nazis by the touch of some magic wand. I told him that I knew digging up spuds was hard work, but after a few weeks, he would get used to it. Besides, we do not run an employment office.

It so happened that I had another "submarine[r]" to place. He was younger, smaller, and thinner but, in his own words, not afraid of farmwork. I went with both of them back to that farm. I slept there overnight in the hayloft and took number one back with me. I was fortunate to be able to place him in a bicycle repair shop as he did not look particularly Jewish. He promised me that there would be no more running around and that he would forget the Stegeman address. Expunge it from his memory. He had good identity papers, so I counted on having no more trouble from him. His boss in the bicycle repair shop said he would try it for a month.

Rumors have it that Queen Wilhelmina has died. [I don't believe it.]

The NSBers in Hollandscheveld are afraid. They have asked for, and been given, additional police protection and there is one new policeman from Hoogeveen now living there, but it is rumored that he is *goed*.[58] This morning, I cycled via Hollandscheveld through Nieuwlande to Nieuw-Amsterdam. At Post's farm there was the usual hustle and bustle. Mrs. Volger and her maid, Aaltje, were also there. Mrs. Salomons, Mrs. Post's mother, was pacing up and down, nervously muttering, "This is getting ridiculous, this is far too bad, nothing is safe anymore, we are overextending ourselves, we will all end up against the wall." The situation is indeed very tense; raids, and talk about raids, shootings, that's how it is.

A Jewish woman who was in hiding with "Oal Jitse" van der Vinne [the local café owner] had to leave there at once because Van der Vinne himself had to go into hiding. She is typically Jewish and therefore cannot go out in public. She spent last night and the night before in the woods and then arrived at Post's front door, not exactly the best way to lessen the tension there. Onderduikers often have to be found new places to hide. To find them or not to find them, that is the question. Post remains calm at all times except on one occasion when someone called him a traitor and he threw the man out. At first I thought Johannes was going to kill him; I wouldn't have given two cents for the man's life at that moment.

Celina Kuyper (Thea).
Collection v.d.Sleen.

A truck driver from Dedemsvaart will take care of the luggage for various onderduikers, so that is one less problem.

Thea needs a change of atmosphere. I found a good place for her here in Nieuw-Amsterdam. The onderduiker whom I recently brought to the large shed has gone. No one knows where he went. The others told me that he couldn't stand the primitive life any longer. In Nieuwlande, two KK[59] and two WA men have been stationed in the village to keep an eye on things. With them around, life is no easier.

July 10, 1943, Saturday Evening

IT IS SAID that the radios burned in Zuidwolde the other day started playing the national anthem. It is dark, gloomy weather with lots of wind and rain. Many NSB farms are being burned down as well as local government offices, employment agencies, and warehouses where confiscated radios are kept. Van Ekelenburg, the assistant pastor in the church in Nieuw-Amsterdam asked me for identity cards.[60] We made an agreement. He looks for hiding places, and I give him identity cards. For every place he finds for a non-Jew, he gets two identity cards ready for use, and he gets three identity cards for a place for a Jew.

Everybody is talking about Sicily and everybody knows that whatever the Germans write about it in the newspapers is nonsense.

The doctors in Nieuw-Amsterdam are exceptional as they have not gone into hiding.

I received a non-Jew who had been sent to work in Germany but who had escaped from Essen. The city is bombarded nightly, and he said he spent a whole month in a bomb shelter. Essen was once a city, and now it is one vast ruin. I did not trust him really but had to help him and take a chance. He is now on a farm in the vicinity of Erica. He also said that the German people no longer believe what they hear on their own radios. Last night a lot of Tommies came over. This morning again, probably Yanks [this time].[61]

July 12, 1943, Monday Evening

I WENT TO see the pastor at Nieuw-Dordrecht, a small village on the way to Emmen, to talk about the placing of Jews.[62] Good prospects. He is a very careful man and is himself a quarter Jewish. In the pouring rain, I cycled back to Nieuw-Amsterdam using the country lanes. Lidia is a Jewish girl who I brought recently to Nieuw-Amsterdam for Johannes, and she is now at Van Ekelenburg's home. The assistant pastor just came home with some "black" milk.[63] Good news. He has a place for a Jewish housekeeper! Will bring him a Jewess and three identity cards.

Syracuse is occupied by the Allies.

July 13, 1943, Tuesday Evening

THIS MORNING I went to the pastor in Schoonebeek, who appeared rather afraid.[64] He took me to a farmer who was also scared. No success there. We went to other farmers, but nothing doing. One gave me, as a sort of tip, 25 guilders, another gave 10 guilders, but it was not primarily money I wanted. Places! Hiding places is what we wanted.

A guy from the Waffen-SS arrived at the offices of Zijlstra, the junior notary. He had with him a locksmith and wanted to break open the safe in a Jewish shop whose owner was in hiding. Zijlstra went with him and said he could not open the vault. It has remained shut up until now, and when the Germans find a way to open it, they will not have much longer to live. It is said here that the raid on the ration card transport was done with the aid of a German car.

[...]

We also have an onderduiker here from Friesland, a Jew who escaped from a raid in Drachten by spending a whole day up to his neck in water.

July 14, 1943, Wednesday

JOHANNES AND DIEN Post have gone underground. They are in the woods not far away from the Kerkhoflaan under a tarpaulin. "Peter," our identity card artist, has been evicted by his host, who became too fearful and panicked. He is also in the woods along with "Nico" and "Victor," two boys who are always together and who escaped from Hoogeveen after being betrayed.[65]

Thea has also had to move and has a new address, which I left with Mrs. Salomons, who is still on the farm with Miesje, the home help. I had expected her to be in a state, but no. Nervous, yes, but no more than that. Miesje is calmness personified.

[There was not much I could do for the "Babes in the Wood," so] I cycled to Pastor Volger, who was at his wits' end with what to do with two Jewish onderduikers. I took them to Dedemsvaart where I distributed them. [On the way we had to hide twice, once from the Landwachters[66] and once from the Germans, but everything went without a hitch.] The parsonage garden in Hollandscheveld is now a field of orange after my planting of spring marigolds.

The arch traitor De Kruyff from Assen is rumored to have spent a week posing as an onderduiker in and around Hollandscheveld according to reliable sources. The atmosphere is very tense and major raids are expected.

On a small pathway near Nieuwlande I came across Jan Dekker, the postman, who invited me for dinner.[67]

Jan Wildschut is no longer in Nieuwlande.

One of the onderduikers I brought with me to Dedemsvaart told me that one of his friends had been shot dead in Leeuwarden.

Pastor Volger told me the following joke: Hitler visited the school; he asked the children how they visualized his funeral. One saw this, the other that. Finally, little Moshe, disguised as little Wilhelm, raised his hand. "Yes, my Führer, I see all these things too, but I see more. I see the coffin slowly go down in the grave and slowly rise up again, then it goes down again and comes up again, it goes down, comes up, goes down, comes up, goes. . ." "Stop," the Führer shouts, "what is wrong with that bloody coffin?" "No, sir, nothing wrong with the coffin, it must come up again and again and again to receive the applause."

Good news from Sicily.

July 15, 1943, Thursday Evening

WE HEAR THE sound of artillery in the distance. [It comes from an easterly direction and may well be German antiaircraft gunfire.] Sister Scholten told me about the reaction of her neighbor, Mr. Burgers the NSBer from across the street, whose bike I had "borrowed." She and her sister had taken up ringside seats behind the curtains and they had had an enjoyable afternoon and heard the whole story. The mother was one of Sister Scholten's patients and from her they had a few more details. "Yes, and if they ever saw the man again they would recognize him at once." That seems unlikely because I had spectacles and a hat and was wearing a strange raincoat.

Seven bombers came over in two formations: one of four, one of three.

July 16, 1943, Friday Evening

I CYCLED TO Hollandscheveld. Everything was fine, both at Jan Kats's and at Volger's parsonage. I fetched the luggage of an onderduiker from a farm a few kilometers outside the village. He had to disappear suddenly because he had been betrayed. His suitcase had already been hidden in a haystack. Two Weerafdeeling [WA] spies had been seen sitting beside the canal fishing and the neighbors had recognized them as NSBers. The onderduiker had been careless. He had been walking around in his Sunday best city clothes complete with tie instead of wearing old working clothes or, of course, not being seen at all! Through his carelessness someone else will be killed because we now have one precious place less.

I went to Headmaster Wiegman's house to talk about Jews.[68] The door was opened by a stranger who said his name was Jansen. "Such a coincidence," I said, "that's my name too." Wiegman was not at home.

July 18, 1943, Sunday Morning

IN DORKWERD. I cycled first to Pesse, to Jannes [Broenink], the boyfriend of Dinie Homan. He is [now] hiding on a farm. With him, I went to a church minister[69] and to other VIPs, no success. They don't know me and don't trust me. Jannes has a good hiding place in case of trouble.

From Pesse I went to Groningen along the main road. Everything was quiet. I passed through two checkpoints and saw a German military train carrying anti-aircraft guns. Assen and Groningen, however, were filled with Krauts.

Julius, my brother in Dorkwerd,[70] has a little girl from Rotterdam as a guest. When they took the girl from the train in Groningen, the first words she said were: "I come from the rubble." The school she had attended had suffered a direct hit during classes. She was one of only 25 children from her class who had survived. Her home had also been destroyed.[71]

In Leeuwarden there had been a series of raids, many boys had been picked up, but many more escaped. They got away, for example, in bakery and bread trucks, and in milk tankers, standing up to their navels in the milk. [Who drank the milk afterward I don't know; let's hope it was the Nazis?]

In Groningen, I sought out Catrien Pronk, a nurse who was a colleague of my sister Guillette.[72] She had a message for me. There was a boy from Winterswijk who was in hiding in his grandparents' home in Groningen. He had a good hiding place but no ration cards. Well, this was easy to remedy through contact with a woman working in the local distribution center. His *stamkaart*[73] will be sent on from Winterswijk.

I also looked up brother Terpstra at the general hospital to talk about identity cards. He can get them for 40 guilders apiece from the patients, but this is too much money and I'm not interested. He should steal them and deliver them for free. This way there is too much danger involved. I also want to speak to "Doeks"[74] about Jewish children but she was not at home.

July 20, 1943, Tuesday Evening

IN NIEUW-AMSTERDAM HAVING just arrived from Groningen. A strong headwind all the way. In Dokkum, a member of the Marechaussee who had gone underground has been caught. He was found with five identity cards and a loaded revolver. I heard this in Groningen. Directly after his arrest there were serious raids in Dokkum, but the Marechaussee has once again escaped.

In Assen, Nico and Victor attempted the assassination of the traitor De Kruyff, but unfortunately he is not dead in spite of having been hit by five bullets.[75] Assen now has a 9:00 p.m. curfew. I tried to telephone Post in Nieuwlande, but there was no reply. Something is not quite right. There was an unsigned letter waiting for me in Nieuw-Amsterdam from Pastor Oppenheimer in Nieuw-Dordrecht, and I cycled there immediately.[76] He gave me the address of someone in Emmen who wanted a housekeeper. I went there, carrying a cornflower as a signal. The man was a widower with three sons in hiding. He had a red nose and smelled of alcohol but did not seem to me to be a bad sort. However, because of the three sons in hiding, I did not think this would be a safe address. Miss Pijl, of the housing inspection in Emmen, again acted as the intermediary between Oppenheimer and the widower. I have not yet made any definite agreements.

Van Ekelenburg, the assistant pastor, needs a place for a woman who is not typically Jewish. I have given him this address but told him about the three sons too.

Girls are not allowed to swim any more. Why? Because there are too many boys "underwater."

A surgeon in Emmen was arrested at his home by the SA.[77] First the house was surrounded, then a ladder was placed under the bedroom window (it was nighttime). In the prison van, there was another prisoner, also a medical doctor. On the floor there was a large pot filled with lard, obviously booty. They have been hunting for the surgeon's assistant, but could not find him, so they checked the identities of all the patients in the hospital.

[In Emmen] they have found a very good hiding place for the Jewish woman from Nieuwlande who had nowhere to go.

The assistant minister's brother also had to go into hiding, and I found him somewhere suitable in Friesland.[78]

July 22, 1943, Thursday

HERE IN NIEUW-AMSTERDAM I have an excellent Philips radio that I have hidden in such a way that it is totally invisible, easy to tune and to hear, but positioned in a way that it cannot be heard from the street. While I was doing this, two policemen arrived at the door. I went hell-for-leather via a small balcony to the back garden, through a pasture and into the wooded area of the parsonage garden. It turned out to be a false alarm as the police were "good."

We enjoy the summer weather.

July 23, 1943, Friday Evening

IN THE PARSONAGE at Hollandscheveld. This morning, in Nieuw-Amsterdam, the assistant pastor rushed over with a letter. It contained an alarming message: Johannes Post and Thea both arrested. It was possible that Thea had on her the address of a teacher in Nieuw-Amsterdam where a Jewess is in hiding. I went over there and brought the lady to my sister Mary. After that, I headed for Nieuwlande. The farm was deserted. Everything was gone. Luckily, no Krauts. It appears that Johannes and Thea had walked into a trap in Apeldoorn. No details. I went to Hollandscheveld where I heard that the farmhouse of an NSBer had been set on fire. The Volgers knew no more than that. I went on to Hoogeveen and heard that Johannes had escaped. I traveled to Pesse, thinking he might be there, but didn't find him.

Miss Kats in Hoogeveen told me that she has a brother who is a policeman in Giethoorn, and who is desperate for some action in his village. He had visited and asked if perhaps an NSB farm in his area could burn down or something. ["Well," I said, "What's stopping him."]

Fourteen onderduikers were caught near Meppel and transported to prison. There were two NSKK men in the front of the car when another car drove up alongside with two Marechaussee in it. Shots were fired and the two NSKK men were dead, dead as two doornails, and the onderduikers freed.

Near Coevorden I saw a lady on a bicycle with a boy of about 15. I caught a few pieces of conversation and deduced that she must be Miss Pijl and he was a Jewish boy.

July 24, 1943, Saturday

TO DEDEMSVAART. FARMER Melis had two identity cards that he wanted altered so that they were two years younger. Sister Scholten and I spoke about the possibilities of a mass rescue of Jewish children from Amsterdam [Mokum].[79]

Dinie Homan gave me a packet for Jannes, her boyfriend who is in hiding in Pesse. I went back to Hollandscheveld to meet Johannes at the parsonage but a message had come that he wouldn't be there, and we didn't know where he was. I telephoned Blanken, the baker in Hoogeveen, but he knew nothing.[80] I went to Pesse with the parcel, but he wasn't there either. I then cycled back to Nieuwlande as there were rumors that Mrs. Post had been seen there. I went to see Jan Dekker, the postman, and telephoned Hoogeveen. This time I was lucky and made an appointment for the next day. Finally back to Hollandscheveld.

July 25, 1943, Sunday (Early Hours Monday Morning)

I WENT VIA Hoogeveen to Pesse, where Johannes was rumored to be and where I met three of the six Post brothers, namely, Johannes, Henk (the pastor from Reinsburg), and Gerrit, at whose farm the other two were visiting.[81] There were also at least two children. As it was Sunday, Pastor Henk Post substituted for the pastor of Pesse who was in hiding.[82] Although Henk Post was also in hiding, he was prepared to take the risk but stood in the pulpit with a revolver in his pocket. Johannes also had two loaded revolvers and sat at the front of the church. The pastor took as his text Nehemiah 4:17, something like "in the one hand a trowel, in the other the sword."[83] After the service, we all had a long talk and agreed to attack the farmhouse of a well-known filthy NSBer called Meekof in Pesse.[84] To do this I went to fetch a flagon of petrol from Kats, and then we bedded down in the hay, fully dressed, and set the alarm for 2:00 a.m. Gerrit Post showed us the way, and at three o'clock we arrived at the farm. The back door stood open. I stuffed a rag drenched in petrol under the thatch of the house, threw the remaining petrol over the top, and then held a match to it. As I did, a dog started barking on the other side of the open door but then fell silent, I have no idea why. Johannes and Henk had their revolvers at the ready but did not have to use them. Cycling home, we stopped and turned to look. At first nothing but darkness, and our first thought was that something had gone wrong, but five minutes later the sky was on fire. Arriving home, we watched the fire through an attic window and then eventually went to bed. Sleep was difficult because the hay was new and infested with all sorts of small forms of insect life. But all things considered, a pleasant evening.

July 26, 1943, Monday Evening

THIS MORNING WE got up late, because we hadn't had much sleep on account of the insects in the hay. The children told enthusiastic stories about the fire that had destroyed Meekof's farm. They had no idea that we had been involved. Johannes Post, Henk Post, and I rode to Hollandscheveld. We went via the smoldering rubble of the farmhouse and asked the onlookers how this had happened. Pastor Post expressed his sympathy for the victims in the most beautiful language, very much like a sermon. We heard that Meekof had stood guard until 2:45 a.m. because he had feared an attack, but we had arrived at 3:00 a.m.

The three of us went on to Pastor Volger's, where we had lunch, and in the afternoon I went on to Nieuwlande, where I went looking for Van der Zwaag. Later in the day I met the Post brothers again at their brother-in-law Bouwe Zijlstra's house. We agreed that the following day I should go to another of their brothers, Marinus Post, in Kampen, to fetch a number of identity cards and bring them to Wolter Post, yet another brother, who had a farm in Staphorstermaten. Johannes and Henk will also be there and hopefully will have some news about Thea. She has probably been taken to prison in Arnhem. The plan is that I should go to Arnhem with 20,000 guilders to bribe someone to free her. This money is already available and more can be raised. It is lovely warm weather.

July 27, 1943, Tuesday

UP EARLY IN order to go to Kampen. I had to make several detours on account of raids and in Zuidwolde there were two police vans with Green Police.

[In Koekange I had to take refuge in the parsonage of Pastor Mooi because of a raid. After waiting 40 minutes I continued my journey but not on the route I'd intended. The pastor showed me a safer route along narrow by-ways where one could still cycle. Because this route was so isolated the Germans never went there. They like to be seen. NSBers also avoided being out in the sticks because they wanted to be near their protectors. While riding through these lonely stretches I reflected how lucky Holland was, being such a densely populated country but still retaining such desolate areas.]

As I approached Kampen, I saw a man working in an allotment and asked him the way to the Venedijk. He replied by asking if I was looking for Post. "How could you possibly know that?" I asked. "Well," he said, "There aren't many people living there but I wouldn't go there because the whole neighborhood is surrounded by Green Police and everyone is being arrested." Then he told me that there had been a raid on Post's house and shooting. Marinus Post had escaped, but his wife and one of his sons had been taken to the police station.

[I thanked the man for the information and went on, first toward and then past the police station to see what I could see but the answer was not much. Three police cars and many policemen. I reasoned that in a Calvinistic place like Kampen the police must be "good," but then I reflected, I am writing in 1943 and by now most of the good ones have probably been replaced by NSB or other scum.] He took me to friends in the city, but they couldn't shed any more light on the subject except that there had been a great deal of shooting, that there were some fatalities, and that some prisoners had been taken. I wanted to telephone Walter Post but there was no telephone so I left for Staphorstermaten as quickly as possible. [. . .]

When I arrived there was a policeman in front of the door.[85] As I was deciding what to do, Wolter Post came out of the house and called to me, "Arnold, it is OK, come in." The Staphorst police had been sent orders from Kampen to occupy Wolter Post's farm and arrest anyone who arrived, but this policeman was a good Dutchman. Johannes and Henk had fled into the reeds when they saw the police car coming, I went to fetch them and found them among the reeds ready for action with revolvers in hand. All three of us went back to the farm, and as they knew nothing, I told them what had happened in Kampen.

Marinus's twin sons and two other students in hiding had spent the previous night at their Uncle Wolter's place, and very early in the morning they had traveled to Giethoorn to do some sailing. Their plan was to cycle back to Kampen that evening. These boys had no idea what had happened and had to be warned. On the way back to Kampen, they had to pass the Black Water at Genemuiden, where there was a pond. I would go to the pond to meet the boys and tell them the whole story so that they would not walk into a trap.

It was a hot day, so I swam back and forth in the river. Every time I passed the pond, I scrutinized all the people passing. I carried on with this game until 11:30 p.m., but they never came, so I found a haystack and slept.

July 28, 1943, Wednesday Evening

IT WAS A beautiful morning and I left my haystack very early in the morning and set off for Giethoorn, asking all the boat hirers about four young men, but nobody knew anything about them. Finally, I cycled to Pesse. Near Gerrit's farm I came upon Johannes and Pastor Henk. I went with them to Hoogeveen. They were very worried, both about Thea and about Victor and Nico. The two boys had been to Diever, where they expected news from them, but they had heard nothing.

In Hoogeveen we were stopped by a policeman. Pastor Henk Post rode on, and the policeman asked us, "Do you know that man?" And then started shooting. We had, of course, never seen the man before. Johannes and I thought it best also to cycle away. I counted six shots from the policeman's revolver. We were reunited at Blanken the baker's. "Yes," said the pastor, "I had farmer's butter (a revolver) in my pocket so I thought it better to go on." Johannes's wife was also there. I was very happy to see her again, as well as Nico and Victor, who had also been missing. They brought word that everything is hunky-dory. Thea is currently being held in Westerbork and will be released. In Ruinerwold there was a raid on a distribution office. The weather is warm.

July 29, 1943, Thursday

ANOTHER BEAUTIFUL MORNING that started off with thick fog. I went to Nieuw-Amsterdam with ration cards.

The burgemeester, town clerk, and distribution clerk in old Schoonebeek have been killed.[86] Three boys have been picked up in Pesse and sent to KZ Vught[87] because they expressed their approval of the burning of the Meekof farm.

Back to Hollandscheveld and a meeting with Johannes and Pastor Henk in the woods near Nieuwlande to make plans for a raid to get ration cards from the distribution office in Oosterhesselen.

July 30, 1943, Friday Evening

THIS MORNING THERE were reports from everywhere about large-scale raids, including telephoned warnings from Hoogeveen. The whole town had been sealed, streets cordoned off, and Green Police everywhere with large vans. As usual, Aaltje, the quiet housemaid at the Volger's parsonage acted as a go-between and sought out the Post brothers hiding in the woods to warn them that two carloads of Green Police had left Hoogeveen heading for Hollandscheveld.

I myself was with two others in a fairly good hiding place in the Christian School run by headmaster Wiegman. Later on, the three of us went to a copse. After the all-clear came via the grapevine I called Nieuwlande. Yes, they had been in Nieuwlande too. Yes, they were Green Police. Yes, two vanloads of them. No, they caught no one. These Green Police had called on Jan Post (another of the six Post brothers), who had a farm in Nieuwlande.[88] Jan had to go with them to his brother Johannes's farm. In answer to their questions, Jan could truthfully

Albert Jan Rozeman, one of the founders of the Landelijke Organisatie in Drenthe with his father, Steven. Collection v.d.Sleen.

answer that he knew nothing about the whereabouts of his brother and that he knew nothing of his brother's comings and goings. Jan did actually know next to nothing about Johannes and did not want to know anything. He lived about 1.5 km east of Johannes's farm and went with the Green Police. They took all the foodstuffs they found there, like sausages, bacon, and so forth.

I have inspected the two churches in Nieuwlande for possible hiding places. Later I went into the woods and spoke to Johannes. He gave me a letter for his wife to be delivered to Ambt Vollenhove,[89] where she was in hiding. There were a few things she had to know at once. One of these was that she had to leave her present hiding place right away.

In Hollandscheveld a bunch of Hoogeveen WA men turned up and visited the ash heap of what had once been the NSB clubhouse.

On the way to Ambt Vollenhove, I met one of the boys near Kerkenveld. He warned me to be very, very careful and to take the byways. I did. In Koekange I went to Pastor Mooi, who told me that Meppel was not safe. However, all went off smoothly. In Ambt Vollenhove everything was peaceful, but in many other places there had been raids.

July 31, 1943, Saturday Evening

LAST NIGHT THE farmer in Ambt Vollenhove thought that there was likely to be a raid, and so his son and I took some blankets into the woods and had a good sleep. A raid did indeed take place.

Found a hiding place for a Jewish girl. An ideal location here among the reeds and water.

In Meppel, all hell had broken loose, so I gave the city a wide berth. As I've said before, never a dull moment.

Back in Koekange I called on Pastor Mooi again. His brother, who is assistant pastor in Zuidwolde, was also visiting, and he told us that he had had a visit from the "NSB police," as he called them. They wanted to know why he was not yet in Germany. Fortunately, his papers were in good order. They showed him an issue of *Trouw*[90] and asked him if he had ever seen the paper before. He answered, "Yes, but I always burn it."

I went to see Peter who is in hiding in Moscou[91] and told him all I knew about Thea. We talked a long time, and it was very late when I got back to Hollandscheveld.

I heard about the continuing raids in Hoogeveen, and things are also brewing in Oosterhesselen. Thirty Green Police arrived with motorbikes and assault vans.[92] In Hoogeveen the Green Police took possession of the technical college building.

August 1, 1943, Sunday Evening

I SLEPT LAST night in the haystack of the widow Zwiers,[93] who also gave me breakfast. At Jan Dekker's I called Hollandscheveld. Everything was calm there,

Marinus Post in disguise c.1943.
Collection Hovingh.

but not in the surrounding district. I met Pastor Post and Nico in the Kerkhoflaan. They had been to the farm to collect a sheet of canvas, as they are still together hiding in the woods.

A small bottle of phosphor dropped by the Tommies came down in Hollandscheveld. I buried it in the woods for future use.

The telephone at the Volger's must be red-hot. All of Hoogeveen is in turmoil and several people have been arrested. One of the VIPs, Rozeman,[94] managed to escape and came here this morning. All the policemen in Hoogeveen, including the three from Hollandscheveld, are ordered to report at two o'clock and even old Snorrebaard Seller, the amiable and jovial village constable, has to come as well. The telephone brought us the appalling news that Mulder, the notary; Baas, the teacher; and Jonkheer de Jong[e] had been shot by the Nazis.[95] A Hoogeveen policeman was ordered to bury all three.

A pastor from Hoogeveen and his wife arrived at the Volger's house. A telephone call from Hoogeveen warned that the Krauts were busy searching Blanken's house. He is currently on holiday, so I telephoned to warn him.

Willie, the Jewish girl hidden at the neighbors, slept in the church last night. Tonight, she wants to sleep out in the rye field.

This morning a short but heavy thunderstorm. Hot again now.

The Volgers are making plans to go underground. With Pim, the youngest son, on my back carrier, I was on my way to Nieuw-Amsterdam together with Joop and Harry, two fugitives.[96] Joop works with the *Trouw-groep*.[97] We got as far as Nieuw-Zwinderen when we were warned not to go any farther because there were raids everywhere and the district Oosterhesselen-Dalen-Coevorden was crawling with Green Police. Joop and Harry wanted to go on in spite of the warnings but I had the child on the back carrier and refused, so all four of us went back. Joop stayed behind in Nieuwlande, where he installed himself in the widow Zwiers's haystack.

I telephoned from Jan Dekker's to warn the Volgers that we were coming back. Pim remained seated on the bicycle fast asleep.

It was close to midnight when Nico dropped by. He was on his way to dig up a box of identity cards from the garden of a teacher named De Raad who had gone underground after being hunted by the Krauts. These identity cards were important for the Post brothers who had been photographed two days ago by Duiken, the photographer from Hoogeveen who had come to Hollandscheveld for the purpose. We wished Nico luck and went to the church for the night, taking turns on watch outside.

August 2, 1943, Monday Morning

WE DID NOT sleep much last night. Nico returned at one o'clock. All was well. He had gone into Hoogeveen crawling on his belly alongside a canal. Patrolling Germans were so near to him at times that he could have touched them.

We took turns guarding outside the church next to the Posts' bedroom window. He was beset by nightmares, to the annoyance of his wife and to our great entertainment.

August 3, 1943, Tuesday Morning

YESTERDAY MORNING JOOP and I visited the now deserted Post farm. We broke in to fix a motorbike that was hidden under some straw. We called in the help of a local mechanic to give us a hand. He came but was very nervous. He kept repeating: "This is no work for me, the Krauts will be here any minute, this will be the death of me," and so on. When a real German motorcycle and sidecar passed by, our friend just about died of fright and bolted. In the end, we got the thing in a state where we could push it to Van der Zwaag's farm, and we also took 20 pounds of sugar.

While we were doing this, a Marechaussee came to warn us that the Krauts were planning a raid in Nieuwlande and the surrounding area. After dealing with the motorbike we went around warning everyone. Eventually we arrived back in Hollandscheveld and prepared the rectory for a possible visit by the Germans for example by scattering a few Max Blokzijl[98] pamphlets in the study.

There had been a meeting in the woods planned for 10:30 p.m. to discuss a possible raid on the rationing office in Oosterhesselen, but this did not take place.

At 7:00 p.m., Kats telephoned the rectory: "The Krauts are coming, hide." We quickly warned a number of people, and then I and two others fled in the direction of the Christian School. I'd not forgotten this is a good hiding place, but Wiegman, the headmaster, had reservations because the place was already too well known.

We fled into the woods and no sooner were we in the shadow of the trees then we heard the Kraut vehicles driving along the Kerkhoflaan and could also make out the sound of motorcycles. It was good that we had telephoned Nieuwlande [to warn them]. We walked through the woods until we came to the Elim cycle path. Turning back toward the Kerkhoflaan we came across a solitary woman milking a cow and asked her what was happening. "The Krauts have gone," she said, "they are only still on the Coevorderstraatweg." We weren't at all confident about this but continued on until a group of girls shouted: "Go, go, they are here close by." We cycled back into the woods and soon saw motorcycle and sidecar come up the small path. We also heard the sound of other vehicles. We spent the night in the woods with two raincoats to cover the three of us and in the morning around 5:00 a.m. returned to Hollandscheveld without further incident.

We arrived at the rectory at about 6:00 a.m. where Mrs. Kurpershoek, Mrs. Volger's mother, was already up and around, but alone in the house. Pastor and Mrs. Volger had wisely disappeared. She told us that a luxury car had come and then gone again, and Mrs. Volger, who was then still at home, had gone out to her husband to tell him that the coast was clear, but he decided not to return home. She herself saw the entire rectory lit up as she was returning, and not trusting this also went into hiding. It transpired that 10 Krauts had been in the house and searched every nook and cranny. Told that the pastor was away on a trip, the Krauts refused to believe this because he'd been seen in the village earlier in the day. They took with them one of the pamphlets written by Max Blokzijl entitled "High Treason" and said that the pastor was very politically minded.

Jan Kats was arrested by the Krauts.

August 3, 1943, Tuesday Afternoon

[MRS. KATS BELIEVES that her husband will be released shortly. She is not unduly worried.] The Krauts have, as a rule, NSBers with them to act as guides. One of the skunks had said to the Krauts when they inspected the cellar and found preserving jars with meat, "You see, he is an enemy of Germany." I dug up the bottle of phosphorus out of Kats's garden just to be on the safe side. [I reburied it in Zijlstra's garden, the teacher at Wiegman's school. I had dinner with the Zijlstra's, or was it lunch, or both?]

August 4, 1943, Wednesday Evening

YESTERDAY I CYCLED to Dedemsvaart with Pastor Volger who had found his way to a farm in the middle of the night. He had tried to telephone Hollandscheveld but could not get through. At 5:30 a.m., he took the bus to Zwolle, planning to go on into Holland.

I am now at De Flochte, the Stegeman's [port of refuge]. I slept from seven until nine in the arbor at the back of the garden. Frits Stegeman from Doorn is also here as an onderduiker, along with Frederik Mooi, the assistant pastor from Zuidwolde.

The Broeninks across the street have a visitor from Enschede who told me that the police commissioner there, an NSBer, had suffered a nervous breakdown.

Everything in Hoogeveen is quiet at the moment. Stegeman gave me 25 guilders that he had received for the cause.

August 6, 1943, Friday Morning

YESTERDAY MORNING JACK came here.[99] He told me that he had slept in a bed at Slagharen, something that is a luxury for most of us. He also said that it was far from peaceful in Nieuwlande and that is why he had fled to Slagharen, but it was no better there.

The identity cards for the Posts are now in order and contact with Mr. de Raad has been reestablished. In Hollandscheveld, two Jews from Hoogeveen have been caught and, together with Kats, taken away. It is said that the two of them have been shot.

Yesterday evening, Broenink, Frits and I went to visit the widow [Zwiers] to listen to London on the radio. [To do this we had to crawl through a hole in the fence around the cemetery, walk across the burial ground and then crawl through another gap in the widow's back garden fence.] The news is good: Orel and Catania have fallen.

There is a new German decree: No person over the age of 16 residing elsewhere can now stay or visit in the provinces of Groningen, Friesland, Drenthe, Overijssel, or Gelderland on account, so it is said, of terroristic acts.

The Stegemans have taken in an 11-year-old boy from Rotterdam. An onderduiker staying in a nearby farm also sleeps with them every night for safety reasons.

This morning I distributed ration cards, [letters, and clothes].

Story of the week: Hitler placed an advertisement in the lonely hearts column, but not a single woman was interested. They all wanted someone with good prospects and a steady job.

August 7, 1943, Saturday

AFTER THE THUNDERSTORMS last Thursday, the weather has changed: rain and wind. Yesterday there was a telephone call from Hoogeveen: the Green Police have left Zuidwolde and Coevorden, but there is no certainty about Hoogeveen. Yesterday I saw Jack briefly. He is safely in hiding with a teacher, but he longs for some action.

I've had several requests for ration cards from people without valid papers. In the newspaper there is a list of people who have been shot. This time it contains 16 names. At Balkbrug and other places there has been bicycle requisitioning.

I walk around in old clothes, primarily to look as much as possible like a farm-worker, [and secondly because I have no others.]

August 8, 1943, Sunday Evening. Nieuw-Amsterdam

YESTERDAY MORNING I arrived here with four-day-old stubble and in general looking like a vagrant. I had cycled from Dedemsvaart, first to Hollandscheveld and to see Kats, who is now back home. He told me about his experiences, and how he thought at least once that his time had come. He told me about the two Jews who were picked up in Hollandscheveld and taken with him to Meppel in the same car. They had asked the Jews many questions, but they had steadfastly refused to give them any information whatsoever. They were later shot without having revealed anything. Kats also told me how he was slapped in the face by an NSBer, and he had answered in kind plus interest; how they had put him on the street in Meppel and had pretended they were going to shoot him too. How he then knew for sure that he would not talk. He told me how the tin box from the ration card raid had still been outside near his house, but a neighbor had taken care of it.

Mrs. Kats also told me a few details. She was in bed when the Krauts came. She heard how her husband was slapped in the face and she was scared stiff. Just before this unwelcome visit, she said, her husband had nailed down the carpet where the radio was hidden under the floor.

I went to the parsonage where Aaltje [Bisschop, the maid] was home alone. The whole family had gone underground. There was an obituary notice in the letterbox for Mulder, the notary. Aaltje told me that a girl in Hollandscheveld had been taken by the Krauts in order to find out the whereabouts of her boyfriend, in connection with the attack on the burgemeester of Oud Schoonebeek.

Johannes and Dien Post were back in their farm at Nieuwlande, N(ico) and V(ictor) were also there together with Pastor Post and his wife. I asked Post for an identity card for Jan Visser the journalist who is "underground" at Henk Visser's, his brother's house who is the pastor at Raalte.

At Berend's shop I got some butts for my pipe and also some tobacco on a ration stamp.

Cool and cloudy weather.

August 11, 1943 Wednesday Morning

MONDAY MORNING I left Nieuw-Amsterdam. The assistant pastor reminded me that I owed him an identity card. He also wanted a hiding place for "Tante" [Auntie] Aaltje.[100] This rather difficult lady gave me a package and a letter to give to her son.

Lidia had a letter for Peter, and she also gave me 10 guilders for the ration card. I left for new Nieuwlande loaded with these things.

Van der Zwaag had found a new hiding place for Henk, Tante Aaltje's son, on a farm deeper in the countryside. He was delighted with the package. Van der Zwaag asked me where Johannes Post was, but I didn't know. I visited de Maa,[101] the haberdashery shop owner in Nieuwlande, to visit Jack, but he had already moved on to Hoogeveen. I went to Peter with the letter from Lidia (his sister) and from there to the parsonage in Hollandscheveld.

Pastor and Mrs. Volger are back at home. In the evening, they were visited by Jack and Rozeman. I went to widow Zwiers's to sleep in the haystack. She gave me a cup of coffee and a sandwich.

On Tuesday morning I got up early after a pleasant sleep. After shaking off most of these tiny spiders, insects, and others that had left the haystack and taken up residence on my person, and after breakfast with the widow Zwiers, I left for Nieuwe Krim to Mr. Scholten[102] who is headmaster there in the grammar school, to find a place [for] an onderduiker. [He was always very friendly and asked me if I was hungry, which I was. Like I always was, hungry as hell. He took care of that.]

[This was very nice of course, but the hiding places, the very things I came for, did not materialize.] I talked and talked, [heaven and earth came into the picture, hell and damnation too. I reeled off all my usual arguments but, as usual, to no avail. I felt, as usual, out of frustration] at last they said (after Mrs. Scholten had joined us) perhaps, just perhaps, they knew another address. Perhaps I could come back some other time. [I said I was certain to do that, and left.]

I had an appointment to meet Johannes at de Maa's haberdashery shop. His house and shop are situated where the main—and only—street in Nieuwlande makes a turn. From that house one could scan the street for at least 1,000 meters. Johannes Post had chosen the house for our meeting so that we could see any trouble approaching.

Johannes had installed himself in an upstairs room and sat surrounded with various papers and lists. Mrs. Post was also on hand and the NV [Nico and Victor] were also there. A thick smoke hung in the room. In the distance we saw a single car coming; we decided to stay. It was a police car but it did not stop. Johannes and Dien were going to leave the neighborhood. [They had become too well known in the wrong places. Johannes was going to do other kinds of work, important work, Knokploeg work.[103] He would have a different name and a different face.] I felt sure his work would be very important. Johannes was going to place his unfinished business in my hands. To start with he gave me a basket full of ration cards that still had to be delivered.

[Peter was also there. He is a very important link in the chain because he is the artist who takes care of the identity cards and other important paperwork.] Johannes was writing down a list of addresses and names for me to learn by heart and then burn.

[We wished one another Godspeed, and I left. For the time being, I buried the list in a waterproof jar in the garden of Seine Otten, the schoolmaster.] I also traveled to Hollandscheveld and look in the parsonage garden where I buried a few things but found out that they were no longer there. Very unpleasant. Thank heavens the Volgers told me that Aaltje had dug them up because she needed a few identity cards. However, she was "on business" in Hoogeveen and the Volgers had no idea where she had put things. So I just had to wait for her. I have now buried it all in Mr. Zijlstra's garden.

After that I went back to a temporary headquarters. Johannes was still there, smoke much thicker than before. He told me that there was a shortage of ration cards. That was because of two things: firstly, in Meppel 1,500 cards had fallen into the hands of the Gestapo. Three boys had lost their lives in this calamity. Secondly the raid on Oosterhesselen had not materialized. It was perhaps possible that there were some cards left in Hoogeveen and the NV went to investigate.

Two boys walked into a trap in Zwolle and were killed. No particulars yet.

Later on, Van der Zwaag also arrived in Johannes's little "office." Johannes told us some fascinating stories about his experiences of late. For example, about his refusal to pay any taxes and about his escape from Apeldoorn. At around 10:30 p.m., the NV came back from Hoogeveen with 30 ration cards and 12 "smokers' cards," sufficient for the time being.

Van der Zwaag was the first to leave, but Jack and I left soon afterward. I again slept in the widow's haystack.

August 12, 1943, Thursday Afternoon

IN DEDEMSVAART. YESTERDAY morning I was up early out of the hay after a lovely night's rest. On to "headquarters" to finalize the scheme for the ration cards. I went round delivering ration cards and came back around noon. I had lunch with de Maa and then went back upstairs to Johannes's "office." He took his leave of us all and pleaded with us to be careful and never to take unnecessary risks.

The supplementary ration cards and smokers' cards we distributed as evenly as possible. I went on my travels and was welcomed everywhere, as the people had worried that with Post's departure and the current circumstances that there would be problems obtaining ration cards. En route I was beset by rainclouds.

[After leaving the office for the last time,] I went to eat with Seine Otten and his wife. Thereafter, I went to Nieuwlande and to Jannie Raak in Hollandscheveld. She works in the distribution office in Hoogeveen, and I gave her three coupons for three cards with three smokers' cards. She would leave them at the parsonage. I cycled to Dedemsvaart with ration cards, identity cards [and some copies of *Trouw*]. Included here were number of identity cards for Pastor Visser in Raalte,[104] including one for his brother Jan. The previous day there had been raids in the town to arrest doctors, but they had not found any. Pastor Volger's bicycle was here, and I'll take it to Hollandscheveld.

Yesterday I visited a farmer where the son of the family had hidden himself under the manure heap when the Green Police arrived. They had searched the

The Kerkstraat in Hoogeveen soon after the liberation showing Blanken's bakery. Collection Hovingh.

cattle barn with torches. In honor of Marinus Post[105] there has been a special edition of the Police Gazette [*Nederlandsch Buitengewoon Politieblad*, August 2, 1943] with his photograph and a warning that he is to be approached with caution as he is armed.

We were given three registration numbers that belong to Gestapo cars that operate from Assen, the provincial capital. The numbers are ZH 67400, ZH 7249, and ZH 46676. Of course they were passed on at once to everybody concerned. Jan Kats saw a suspicious motorcycle with a lady in the sidecar. They paid a visit to Kats's neighbor, the NSBer, Piet Schonewille. The number of the motor is 7903. An individual dressed as a gentleman has been going around Hollandscheveld supposedly collecting fountain pens for repair. We believe he is an agent-provocateur.

Broenink gave me a handful of identity cards to be changed, primarily the expiry dates. [Work for Peter!]

Jannes, Dinie's boyfriend, is back from Pesse and is now in hiding at De Flochte. Dinie conceals him perfectly when she hears someone coming. Every time someone comes or the bell rings, Dinie goes through the same ritual. Every time a cat meows or some leaves rustle in the garden, Jannes has to hide and stay put until Dinie gives the all-clear. Well, better too secure than not enough. But later on they took a walk into the village together.

August 14, 1943, Saturday

YESTERDAY I WENT to Nieuwe Krim. I took one ration card with me and searched for hiding places. No luck. From Nieuwe Krim to Nieuw-Amsterdam, partly along the railway tracks and partly via country lanes and trails. In Nieuw-Amsterdam I distributed ration cards and identity papers. In the evening, back to Nieuwlande, but first to Peter with a letter from Lidia and also to Mr. Pennings, the headmaster of the school in Moscou. I may bring them a Jewish lady. Sleepy and dead tired I rode to Nieuwlande and made myself invisible in my favorite haystack at the widow Zwiers.

August 15, 1943, Sunday Morning

A GOOD NIGHT's sleep. [I believe that haystacks beat beds any time.] Last night a heavy thunderstorm and hours of rain. [These two things make haystack all the more interesting as a bed.]

Rumors have it that some doctors and a notary public have been arrested.

Yesterday I was at Post's farm and found two policemen there (good ones). They said they had looked around to see if anything was stolen. They had with them a bag and they were situated under the plum trees.

Dekker, the mailman, had a card from Thea (from Westerbork).[106] She is in the hospital barracks.

August 16, 1943, Monday Morning

I SPENT ALL day yesterday at Jan Dekker's. There was cloudburst during the day. I smoked homegrown tobacco grown by Dekker. I did a lot of reading.

August 17, 1943, Tuesday Morning

YESTERDAY I WENT to Nieuw-Amsterdam. I had lunch at the Van Ekelenburgs. From there, I went to "Halve Ei" (half egg), the house where my sister Mary lives with three other people. There I took pleasure in helping devour pancakes baked in illegal oil. After that I fetched Tante Aaltje and a box of cakes for her son. I also brought Lidia back—30 km against the wind. [Good thing mother and son do not know from each other where they live. I censor the letters carefully to forestall that day for as long as possible. The day, I mean, that they do find out.] I brought her to the school headmaster Mr. Pennings in Moscou.

[It is a great, great pity that I have to use this new address for that woman. Tante Aaltje had an excellent spot with very pleasant people in a very good hiding place. She is very difficult and has already spoiled other addresses. I now hope against hope that things finally will click, that she finally realizes that we do not run a travel agency and that we are dealing with questions of life and death. I'm afraid that she's too eccentric to see this, but I bless the stars that she is exceptional rather than the rule.] I can see that Tante Aaltje was totally worn out and dead tired. I thanked the Pennings for their cooperation, but I cursed inside that I had lost this newfound place so totally unnecessarily.

Lidia, who doesn't 'look' at all Jewish has a good identity card and lives with the Van Ekelenburgs, came with me to visit Peter. She is his half sister. Peter was awaiting her in his office.

I had a flat tire and went to Jan Kats, [who gave me a piece of raw bacon for my landlady, the widow Zwiers. Kats put a new inner tube on my bike, still the old quality. I was very grateful for that.] I left for my haystack.

August 18, 1943, Wednesday Evening

YESTERDAY MORNING I had breakfast in the haystack. After that, I had a cup of coffee with widow Zwiers, and she had a message for me. It had come from Jan Dekker. He had a letter for me from someone in hiding[107] that also contained a ration card. He wrote that he had received two by mistake. [How that happened I have no idea, but I appreciated his honesty.] I went at once to Troost the baker's where I exchanged it for others [because it had almost expired].[108]

Last night the Green Police were in action in Oosterhesselen. Among others they were looking for the wife and children of the municipal secretary,[109] but luckily they failed to find them. They also paid a visit to the mayor's house where they turned the whole place upside down and inside out. They found nothing.[110]

I went to Henk (alias Ruby) to give him the box of cakes from his mother. I asked him if everything was OK, but he replied that the work in the rye fields was too hard for him. I believed that this was just an affectation and nonsense; [he is a heavily built, strong-looking young man, and besides by mid-August work in the rye fields is finished.]

I dropped in briefly at Van der Zwaag [who asked me to help with the destruction of the harvest in the East Polder because if we don't, it will disappear over our eastern border. I'm not so keen on this, partly because I have no time, and secondly that I have other work to do which, in my opinion, is more important in trying to save lives.]

I dug up a suitcase belonging to Tante Aaltje that was buried in the woods at Van der Vinne's The thing was full of mold, [and I delivered it with apologies to the Penning's house. So far so good there.]

I went to Peter and asked him what he thought about changing the numbers on blocked identity cards. This was in connection with the fact that the Hoogeveen municipal secretary had disappeared with 300 identity cards and 6,000 guilders.[111] Peter feels that this is possible [and confident that he can change such an identity card sufficiently for it to pass a normal control, and it would only fail in the case of careful scrutiny].

I had supper at Mr. Penning's, and we toured the school building looking for hiding places for people and for radios. Finally I went over to Jan Dekker and drank a cup of coffee before hitting the hay.

A pleasant day with an easterly wind.

August 19, 1943, Thursday Morning

BEAUTIFUL WEATHER, YESTERDAY even warmer. Last night there was a thick mist, but I crawled deep into the hay and stay dry. Johannes Post is in the vicinity, but he wants to remain incognito. I visited Van der Zwaag's farm to discuss the destruction of the East Polder.

August 19, 1943, Thursday Evening

HAVING BEEN TO the barber with a four-day-old beard, I went to "Willie" to make arrangements for a rendezvous between her, her mother, and her brother. Willie is of course, a Jewish girl, in hiding in Hollandscheveld. From there I went to Jan Kats's, where I ate pancakes. He told me that a friend had recognized Johannes Post, now sporting glasses, a beard, and a formidable moustache. [I met Jan Post this afternoon in Dedemsvaart. He told me about Marinus, who escaped during the shootout in Kampen but was badly wounded. He is OK and recovering but has to keep quiet for another three months. A courier brought a letter from him.]

I visited Tante Aaltje to deliver shoes and a coat. In Dedemsvaart a group of men working for the *Arbeidsdienst* (Labor Service) had arrived in the town to lift potatoes. Stegeman's neighbor had one of their leaders billeted on him.

August 20, 1943 Friday Morning

BEAUTIFUL WARM WEATHER. Last night Broenink and I went to the widow Hagen's house to listen to London. We went by bike and managed to get the machines through the holes in the cemetery fence so that we were able to use our secret passage via the graveyard, bikes and all. The widow has an excellent radio set and Broenink has hidden it very ingenuously.

Stegeman tells me that Pastor Visser in Raalte and his brother Jan, the journalist, are very happy with the identity papers and ration cards.

This morning I kept this diary more or less up to date. Not only with the aid of my memory but also with many puzzling, even to myself, notes, and scratches. When I go to bury them in the ground in the back of the garden I have another problem because the boy from Rotterdam must not see me, but the little chap follows me everywhere I go like a little doggy.

A true story from Hollandscheveld. Six hens have been taken from an NSB chicken coop. Next morning the rooster was found prancing through the coop with a ticket on his leg on which was written "Ausweis."

There has been an invasion locally of Labor Service men who go around shouting and acting like Germans with their spades over their shoulders.[112]

August 21, 1943, Saturday

I LEFT DEDEMSVAART and cycled to Hollandscheveld, stopping off at Moes, where I borrowed a bicycle for the mother-daughter-son rendezvous on Wednesday.[113]

The farmhouse of the NSB traitor Kist was burned down this morning.[114] They had just lit the kitchen stove, had gone to the pasture to milk the cows, and had just begun when they saw that the house was on fire. They couldn't understand it. A police tracker dog was brought in, but it was a "good" one. There is all sorts of speculation doing the rounds about exactly what happened.

I went to Mr. Zijlstra to fetch 44 ration cards that he received from Jannie Raak for me.[115] They had spoken about the fire, and Zijlstra thought he knew who and how it had been done because Joop had dug up a bottle of phosphor. However, it was not done with phosphorus, and it was Jan Kats who told me the real story.

I visited Kats because he still had a bicycle that belonged in Nieuw-Amsterdam. I took it with me to Nieuwlande and put it in Jan Dekker's garden. I also went to Van der Zwaag to talk about ration cards and the East Polder. [I explained why I was not interested, not only because I have no time for these things, but there is also something else. There are many people underground in the East Polder, both Jews and others. They would all become targets, much more so than they already are.]

On Post's farm, Miesje [the maid —translator] was busy with something and Aaltje was there too. She treated me to a plate of rice. I gave Miesje a ration card for an onderduiker she knew and then collected the bike from Dekker and traveled on to Nieuw-Amsterdam.

August 22, 1943, Sunday

IN NIEUW-AMSTERDAM. HERE too there are many Labor Service men, all lifting potatoes. The farmers have to pay 160 guilders per hectare and the boys get 25 cents a day. I have been collecting money for the underground, starting in my sister's house where she lives with three others; a trainee notary, an agricultural adviser and Annie de Boer, who is a schoolteacher and who gave me 10 guilders.

August 23, 1943, Monday Evening

TODAY I COLLECTED the whole day. [I hate this kind of work. It takes far too much time and what do you get? I think the Knokploegen should include robbing banks in their activities. That way we can save our precious time for searching out hiding places.] I went to large farms, but only those I knew not to be NSB. I also went to various schools, and to the parsonage where my sister had told me there was a meeting of pastors from the area. From there I went to Erica and via the pastor there visited various others.[116]

Today I found an address for a Jewess and also visited Tante Aaltje's former hiding place and was given another 25 guilders. I also took a letter from Lidia for Peter and collected a bag of stubs for my pipe from Berend's shop. Annie de Boer lets her class sing the national anthem every morning.[117]

August 24, 1943, Tuesday Morning

AT AROUND 11:00 p.m. last night the festivities began. Masses of Tommies flew overhead until 1:15 a.m. People came out into the street and sang "We're

Going to Berlin" a variation of a well-known Dutch song. Berlin was indeed the target as we heard the following morning at 7:45 a.m. My collecting activities brought in 556 guilders, not much, but it means I can stop this hateful work for a while.

August 26, 1943, Thursday Evening

ANOTHER BEAUTIFUL MORNING as I left Dedemsvaart early. I had slept in the arbor at the bottom the garden as usual. I'd been awoken in the middle of the night by strange noises at the back of the hut—like the shuffling of feet. An initial search brought nothing to light, but eventually I discovered a clandestine pig. Reassured, I went back to my dreams.

I received the latest editions of *Trouw, De Waarheid*, and *Vrij Nederland*. The leading article in VN was especially good and dealt with chatterboxes. Our evil deed was also mentioned: nice.

Our neighbor came to give us an extra warning about the NSBer whom she is stuck with in her house. He is a genuine fanatic, his room is hung with many portraits of the Führer [Hitler] and the leader [Mussert], and on his shelves there are books such as *Mein Kampf* and texts about racial theory and so forth.

Dinie Homan looks after me. She is always busy because I'm not the only one in hiding that she has "adopted." I spoke with Sister Scholten about finding places for children and the like.

On Wednesday I went with Mrs. Moes's bicycle to Tante Aaltje and took her to the rendezvous, namely, Van der Zwaag's farm. She told me that she had so many difficulties, as she could not get on with her hostess. I said that being in hiding wasn't a lark and that one had to compromise as far as possible as hiding places were thin on the ground, and we had to preserve them as best we could.

Mrs. Moes was very nervous and terrified that the Green Police would come back as she had a young Jewish boy in the house.

I dropped in on Peter, who asked me to get him something to smoke, and he gave me 30 guilders for the purpose. At the same address, there's also a married couple with two sons of 12 and 15. On Tuesday I'd also seen De Raad. He was the one that the Krauts were looking for in Hoogeveen, but he managed to escape and someone else was shot, ostensibly by accident.

At 11:00 a.m. I was at Van der Zwaag's and Joop was also there. After chatting for a while about the East Polder plan, we sorted out ration cards. Van der Zwaag has a corn warehouse near Vollenhove. The idea is to set it on fire in order to destroy the threshing machines there and then cross the waters by boat to Giethoorn, where a car will be waiting.

I went round distributing ration cards and was asked everywhere for milk and potato coupons. Many addresses where Jews are hidden I visited at night in order to prevent the neighbors finding out what is going on there. There are addresses where nobody knows that people are in hiding.

Yesterday evening I was at Dekker's in good time to make up my bed, in reality a new den in the hay. I slept well and had a cup of coffee with Dekker in the morning. From there to Pennings to collect the bicycle and return it to Mrs. Moes, who is looking after Hennie, Marinus Post's five-year-old daughter.

I dropped off 20 packets of papers with Peter, and then went to Kats to learn that the security police in Hoogeveen had been informed about Dr. Volger's family and that of Kats himself. From there to the widow Zwiers's to collect two boxes of cigarettes held there that were intended for Peter. To Mr. Scholten with a couple of ration cards (Nieuwe Krim) to find that he had a newly born son. The house was full of visitors, and I took the opportunity to collect a hundred guilders.

An old Jewish lady (hiding) in Nieuwe Krim is threatening to become mentally ill. She says she can no longer stand being underground. Her host would like to be shot of her, but I left her there for as long as possible.

I cycled through Dalen on my way to Nieuw-Amsterdam. Jan Deik, the assistant pastor was sitting on the floor of his study repairing a radio that he just been given. Marinus Post is in England, at least that's what we think, and was fetched by seaplane. Spread the word, because that is the intention.

Annie de Boer had a message from Delfzijl—"Winchester and Zwaantje have been caught"—and asked me to pass it on to those in charge. The names meant nothing to me.[118]

August 27, 1943, Friday Morning

PETER GAVE ME a box with all sorts of nice things for Thea, who is still held in Westerbork. I gave it to Lidia, who packed it with other things and will send it off. A transport of Jews has left Westerbork for Poland.[119]

August 28, 1943, Saturday Evening

YESTERDAY I DID a bit of collecting; incredibly tedious.

I was given an address in Friesland for Jewish children from Mr. de Vries.

I had a plate of tomato soup at Dirk's, and he gave me a couple of addresses that I then visited. Later he came home with the news that Thea had been on the transport to Poland from Westerbork the previous Tuesday. I telephoned Nieuwlande, but they already knew.

This morning I traveled to Nieuwlande early on after a telephone call. At Dekker's I heard that there had been a postcard from Thea thrown from the train and postmarked Groningen. She was excited and sent everyone her greetings.[120]

I went with Seine Otten and Joop to see Kats (known to us as Vondel). Kats had tobacco from me and a pair of repaired shoes. Then to Pennings to collect newspapers and on to Peter.

Yesterday six luxury cars with NSB leaders, including Mussert, arrived in Hollandscheveld. Meekof from Pesse was also there.

Kats has made preparations to disappear at short notice.

I received two registration cards with inserts from Jan Post, and I ate there.

I went to Mrs. van der Zwaag[121] with a coat for an onderduiker. Hemke van der Zwaag also knows nothing about Winchester or Zwaantje.

August 30, 1943, Monday Evening

THIS EVENING I took the young Jewish girl to the Adema family. There's supposed to be a hundred guilders for the month, but we'll see. Yesterday I came back from Delfzijl with 30 guilders. In Delfzijl there are regular collections for the wives of sailors who are serving with the Allies.[122]

August 31, 1943, Tuesday Evening

THIS MORNING I left Nieuw-Amsterdam for Nieuwlande. Visited Van der Zwaag, Joop, Dekker, Boertien, Kats, the rectory, and Peter, giving the latter 500 guilders, which had come from Lidia. Bouwe Zijlstra's son[123] has been arrested in Apeldoorn, as has Post's brother-in-law [Jan Mulder] in Diever. I traveled to Dedemsvaart.

September 1, 1943, Wednesday Evening

YESTERDAY EVENING I just crawled into my bower and was nearly asleep when I was rudely awakened by a bomb explosion. I put on a few clothes and went into the garden, everything was ghostly illuminated. There was a hellish spectacle in the sky, with shooting and bombs.

Sister Scholten gave me 2,000 flyers with a call to the Dutch people to resist the Krauts, and to help those on the run. This missive was drafted by a reserve officer in hiding. She also had a new tire for me. A teacher was hit by a firebomb and died soon afterward. The Russians have broken through near Smolensk.

September 2, 1943, Thursday

I WAS WOKEN early by Jannes, who had my pipe between his lips. I have written a letter to Willem Stegeman in Utrecht asking for a mimeograph machine.

September 3, 1943, Friday

SLEPT WELL IN the haystack and then had a cup of coffee with the widow (Zwiers). Johannes Post and his wife were caught by a policeman on their way through Zweelo at an identity card control.

"Identity card?"

"Here you are."

"Is this not a forgery?"

"No, what makes you think that?"

"Now, stop playing games. You are Post from Nieuwlande, so stay away from the roads here because it is too dangerous."

To Nieuw-Amsterdam and first to Jan Dirk to offload all the illegal materials my pockets. He gave me some leggings because it was raining and then I went on my travels to Groningen and Friesland. I also had an old umbrella that I put across the handlebars, but in spite of that, I got horribly wet and had the wind against me.

There was an intensive identity card control on the Heereweg in Groningen, perhaps because of the raid on the distribution office by Ten Boer, where two lads dressed in German Wehrmacht uniforms had broken in during the night, handcuffed the NSB watchman, and then stolen anything of any value. I was also stopped, but everything was in order.

In Groningen I went directly to Doeks's house, rang the bell, and got a number of looks from two German policemen in black uniforms. I asked the maid if Doeks was at home. (Post called her "the woman with the horn," because she was very deaf and had a listening device.) "I wish she was," she said. "I was informed that she had been arrested by the Krauts some ten days ago and was still in Groningen prison." She had not heard anything more.

I went on to [my brother] Julius and Mimi but saw Mr. Koning on the way who was at the end of his tether because of the tobacco shortage. Julius spoke of a Dutch officer who had gone into hiding with a neighbor. As a result of a betrayal there had been a Green Police raid, and he had lain on the roof flat on his stomach for two hours; a lucky escape as the police had shone their torches on the roof, and had searched the entire house. Julius had also had an officer in his house and the man had an identity card that he had previously seen in my hands.

September 4, 1943, Saturday Evening

I AM NOW in Nieuw-Amsterdam. This morning in the early light I set off from Dorkwerd into Friesland. The address I had been given was occupied by two young Jewish women. The man of the house promised to use every effort to find new places. On the way back I went to Dorkwerd again. Julius and Mimi promised me that they would make a collection among their acquaintances.

On the Friesche Straatweg, just outside Groningen, a huge cement barrier has been installed. I went back to Nieuw-Amsterdam but had serious saddle sores and tiredness on the way. It proved to be an endless journey, and I counted the telephone poles and trees, jumping on and off the bicycle in desperation. But even this journey eventually came to an end.

In Friesland I heard that the Allies had landed on the Italian mainland. In overall terms this trip wasn't a much of a success primarily because Doeks was in jail.

September 5, 1943, Sunday Morning

SLEPT BEAUTIFULLY AND awoke refreshed. Have now heard with my own ears about the invasion of Italy. Guillette is very upset about Doeks.

September 6, 1943, Monday Morning

THE LOCAL MARECHAUSSEE told me that my identity papers in the name of Willem Roffel have not been canceled. The Labor Service [NAD] was in action early; and some bloke screamed something about them not being one of Stalin's Bolshevik gangs, but honorary Germans, and that they should conduct themselves accordingly.

I went to Nieuwlande.

September 7, 1943, Tuesday Evening

YESTERDAY I WENT initially to Van der Zwaag. There was a checkpoint on the main road, but I was warned by an old lady who told me, "The Germans are on the road and stopping everyone," so I took a small diversion.

There is an additional bunch of ration card addresses that have come via Post, exclusively Jewish onderduikers, so I took them round. At Dekker's I saw Aaltje, who told me about a car with Krauts that had driven through Hollandscheveld, stopping occasionally but without doing any damage.

Ds. Volger has spent a few days at the rectory but has now moved on after several warnings that it wasn't safe. Jan Post has also gone underground. He was supposed to report to the security police in Arnhem but refused that honor.

Van der Zwaag is very keen that we get a mimeograph machine and also a typewriter.

Toward evening I arrived at Dekker's, where I encountered a middle-aged man: an onderduiker. I had a huge argument with him over the well-known hackneyed theme that the Jews were dangerous and ungrateful. He quoted his own experiences, and I gave him mine in return. I told him that speaking as he did was playing into the hands of the enemy. After this argument, I sought out the hay. A nice night. Fresh.

This morning I went to find Jan Post, who is himself underground. I washed and had an egg for breakfast. A [female] courier arrived on time from Johannes Post and I gave her a letter to take to the big boss about the ration cards for the Jews as we did not know all their addresses. I had been round with most of them but there were still about 15 left over. In Johannes Post's garden, in the middle of the wilderness, I found a beautiful orange rocket.

In the afternoon, I ate with Seine Otten: beans with bacon. I was given books for Jewish children, study books, which I distributed to three onderduikers who were 10, 12, and 15 years old.

I visited Peter and then went on to Dedemsvaart. On the way, there was lightning and I went into the woods, just in time. Four Kraut motorcycles with sidecars came past. In Dedemsvaart, the Christian Center has been taken over. I slept in the *vluchthut*.

September 8, 1943, Wednesday Morning

I SPENT A whole morning writing in my diary, working from a host of short notes. A hellish task, but worthwhile I think.

September 9, 1943, Thursday Morning

YESTERDAY SOME GREAT news, Italy has surrendered. Broenink, Frits, and I went to the widow Hagen's at about 8:15 a.m. to listen to the radio. I went across the cemetery and through the fence without being seen.

Mrs. De Jong, who lives nearby, asked me to find a place for two onderduikers, one of whom gets his ration cards from Meppel, and I fear that his *stamkaart* card may be suspect as in Meppel many of the cards have been confiscated.

Pastor Stegeman and his wife from Aalten are visiting.[124] They told me about a really good warning system against raids.

This morning early I went to Heerspink, the farmer near Zuidwolde. I brought three ration cards and two identity cards. They have again one more onderduiker, the boyfriend of one of the daughters. I have again insisted on a foolproof hiding place. Miss Scholten, the sister of the district nurse, brought me a new tire and inner tube for my bicycle.

September 9, 1943, Thursday Evening

A MESSAGE FROM Amsterdam via Sister Scholten. A place wanted for a mother with a two-week old baby. I told her to let the mother and child come as I had a place for them. [This wasn't true. I was introducing a new tactic: never say no. First get the victims, then find the places. Of course, Sister Scholten doesn't know this.] She'll phone Kats when she hears something further.

I stopped by at Peter's and he had a message from Tante Aaltje. [How did she know Peter's address?] She couldn't stand it at the Penningses' any more. She had already left the house three times and was therefore a great danger not only to herself but also to the Penningses and to all of us. I went over there and witnessed a shouting match between Mrs. Pennings and Aaltje while Mr. Pennings stood silently looking on. Aaltje was impudent and downright insulting. [I have no solution to this problem. I'm not going to waste another one of my all-too-scarce hiding places for which I have to search for days on end to find. I'm not going to waste any more of the secret places on this woman, who thinks that she alone is of any importance, that her comfort, her cup of tea at 3:05, her you-name-it was all that mattered in September 1943, with a swarm of brutal killers all over our land. What is she up to? What am I up to? What is my next step?][125]

I went to Jan Kats's to eat, where we heard a feast to celebrate the Italian capitulation. Kats asked me about an identity card for Karelse, the policeman who had gone underground. I thought this had been taken care of ages ago, but I'll look into it.

Later I went to the teacher, Zijlstra, who told me interesting story. Mr. Leenhouts, the registrar at the town hall in Dedemsvaart had offered to "organize" a new identity card for me. It will be so good that would almost be better than a real one. I had just left Kats's when he ran after me, he had an identity card that had to be made three years younger. Zijlstra will look after the mother and baby, and a schoolteacher from Hoogeveen who was visiting told me he would look for hiding places.

Jannie Raak came to tell me that there had been a successful raid on the distribution office in Staphorst.[126] I cycled to Jan Dekker's where the same onderduiker whom I had the row with was still there. We acted as if nothing had happened. He told me about his experiences with the Krauts. His whole family is now in hiding, including his son-in-law. All his furniture and other possessions have been confiscated. I gave him an address in Terwerd [Ter Aard] as a possible hiding place.

September 10, 1943, Friday Evening

WHEN I LEFT this morning the Dekkers were still asleep and I cycled to Seine Otten's where I washed and had breakfast. From there to Van der Zwaag to discuss the identity papers for the policeman. Next stop was at de Maa's to telephone Dedemsvaart about the mother and baby, then to Nieuw-Amsterdam with Otten's five-year-old son on my back carrier. At Van Ekelenberg's I picked up a few identity cards that needed to be altered and some new editions of illegal newspapers. I found a place for a Jewish girl young woman, but no more news from Friesland.

My young friend behind me on the bicycle was having fun, telling me jokes about the Krauts, but then immediately correcting himself and calling them Germans.

Before I crawled into my haystack, I drank coffee with Jan Dekker and his wife and exchanged jokes about Hitler.

September 11, 1943, Saturday

I HAD A good wash at the Dekker's and had a breakfast of baked potatoes. [I went to look at the red-hot poker in Johannes Post's garden. It is still there.] From there to Van der Zwaag and then on to Hoogeveen with 10 identity cards. The raid on Staphorst was a great success. I took two cards to Peter and then a message to Kats. The two cards will be ready next Monday but the identity card [for Karelse] is not yet done but will be ready soon.

Cycled to Nieuw-Amsterdam.

September 12, 1943, Sunday Evening

A CALM DAY and beautiful weather. Likewise the news from London. I took a walk with Guillette and two others. Lidia has asked me for three identity cards for relatives in Westerbork who want to escape. She is in clandestine contact with them and has been trying to weaken their simple belief and trust.

The NSBers in Nieuw-Amsterdam are beginning to lose heart.

September 13, 1943, Monday Evening

I SPENT THE night at Nieuw-Amsterdam and in the morning cycled to Nieuwlande. I met Van der Zwaag at Buikema's the cycle repairman, and returned with him to his farm, where we cut coupons from ration card sheets. Back on the road I encountered Tante Aaltje who had vacated a hiding place yet again. She is a real danger to all of us.

I went to Peter's to collect the two identity cards. He does fantastic work and these were beautifully altered. Peter also gave me a letter for Johannes Post and one for Lidia. I delivered the coupons we had cut out to Jannie Raak and then went to Jan Kats with the identity cards and gave Mrs. Post the letter for her husband.

There was a thunderstorm in the afternoon.

September 14, 1943, Tuesday Afternoon

THE WEATHER IS still warm. I saw Hilda, the eldest daughter of Johannes Post, who is 11 years old. She needs a better and a safer hiding place. "They are working on it," she said. "What a situation to be in."

I visited my namesake who promised to take an onderduiker.

I also ran into Trijn Post from Pesse and went with her for lunch with Jan Post. Hilda was there and her mother was also due, but she was late. While we were at the table, the "boys" also turned up—a whole bunch together. Trijn told us that her aunt in Diever (Johannes's sister) was very worried about her husband who had been picked up by the Krauts.

September 14, 1943, Tuesday Evening

THIS EVENING I was at the Katses' when a young man arrived who said his name was Tien Zomer. He showed us his identity card in that name and said that the boss of his group whom he called "Hans" had sent him to ask if Kats would lend him his car for a raid on a ration office. We didn't know either of these men and so of course Kats didn't bite.

I looked up Willie and gave her a letter from her brother. She told me about a Green (policeman) who had been sniffing round in Hollandscheveld in the company of an NSBer. He had been particularly interested in the parsonage.

At Bouwe Zijlstra's, Johannes Post's brother-in-law, where I ran into grandma again—Mrs. Salomons, the mother of Dien Post-Salomons. She reminded me that the last time we had met, she had made me a stack of bacon sandwiches and that I had left them behind, completely forgotten them. This was certainly something to shed tears over.

I spoke to Jannie Raak. She gave me a message for Victor: "She would like to receive the challenge cup." Also spoke to Van der Zwaag in Nieuwlande. He had also never heard of this chap Tien Zomer.

September 15, 1943, Wednesday

IN DEDEMSVAART. THIS morning I went round warning a number of young men not to take their identity papers to the distribution office, because they would be confiscated. Next I went to Mrs. De Jong to assure her that she would receive ration cards for her two onderduikers.

In Hoogeveen, I picked up a packet with 25 ration cards for Pastor Volger. Visited farmer Heerspink who has now created an excellent hiding place for his onderduikers and gave him three ration cards. Also saw Sister Scholten and told her that I had found six places for Jews.

September 16, 1943, Thursday

SISTER SCHOLTEN WAS here to talk about the Jews. The mother and baby I will fetch from the station at Hoogeveen, the others will come to Dedemsvaart. The weather has become much cooler.

September 17, 1943, Friday Morning

BELOW IS A scheme that shows how within Nazi theory, Aryan children can be born to Jewish parents and vice versa. According to the Nazis a Jew is anyone with at least three Jewish grandparents. [They have decreed that a full Jew must have a J on his or her identity card[127] and that a part-Jew must have a B stamped on his card. The B stands for bastard.[128] Frits Stegeman, who is in hiding at De Flochte, came up with an interesting diagram to show what situations could be created by this decree.]

Yesterday Mr. Leenhouts was here, but had no idea why he had been summoned. I showed him the note from Zijlstra and then he understood everything. We made an appointment to meet at the town hall at 12:45 p.m. and that he would then expedite matters. He told me that he'd recently received a letter from The Hague congratulating him that his registers were in such good order.

Mr. de Jong from Avondlicht[129] asked me for five copies of *Trouw* and he also needs six or seven ration cards.

Yesterday evening I went, via the cemetery, to the widow Hagen to listen to the radio.

Miss Scholten (the sister of the district nurse) came by for six ration cards which she will get. She also wanted a revolver for an army officer who had gone underground, but I couldn't help. I gave her a letter to be typed which is for the owner of the house in Hoogeveen whose current tenant, a good patriot, has gone underground. The owner wants to rent out the property to someone else but the letter exhorts him to abandon this plan or face the consequences.

September 17, 1943, Friday Evening

THIS AFTERNOON I cycled from Dedemsvaart toward Hoogeveen. Razzias (raids) have taken place in Noordscheschut again, but only on a small scale. I cycled on through the drizzle to Hoogeveen. Rozeman was not at home, but I did find Victor there, who was making himself useful by doing the washing up. I left a note with my requests, like the quantities of *Trouw* editions, ration cards, inlay sheets, and so on. I left Peter's message that he would like to work for *Trouw* or another illegal newspaper and also the typed letter for the recalcitrant house owner.

Went back to Hollandscheveld and to Jannie Raak to collect ration cards. She was a little piqued that more than 400 cards had not yet been collected, and she didn't want to keep them in the house that long, especially now because of the raids. I took 160 from her. I also spoke to Victor in Hoogeveen about the possibilities of getting people out of Westerbork, but he was not optimistic. I have a request letter from someone with family members who have been caught and who are now in Westerbork.

September 18, 1943, Saturday Evening

YESTERDAY EVENING I was again with Dekker before crawling into my haystack. Hilda Post is temporarily staying with the widow Zwiers. To Van der Zwaag, where Seine Otten was also to be found. We talked about this and that before I went back on the ration card route.

Tante Aaltje is now in another place. She made so much of a fuss at the Pennings, so she is now in a small worker's house in an isolated part of the country. I have 200 guilders for Willie, the girl at the bakery in Hollandscheveld.

We have written a piece that I will take to Dedemsvaart for printing and mass circulation. It's a call to resistance.

Seller, the Marechaussee at Nieuwlande, has been ordered to Groningen, where his NSB masters told him that they'd received reports of onderduikers hiding with this or that family, and that he, Seller, had known about this.

September 19, 1943, Sunday Evening

IN NIEUW-AMSTERDAM. CHIEF of Police de Vries had a warning for Johannes Post to be extremely careful because he was being actively sought (by the Krauts). Headmaster Venhuis arrived with 65 guilders that he had collected from his colleagues.

September 21, 1943, Tuesday Evening

YESTERDAY EVENING I was at the Ottens' and last night I slept there too. Today I spent the whole day distributing ration cards. I also visited Peter. He wants to go into the woods, he's had enough of sitting still, and he wants to find a hole somewhere and work for a newspaper or something.

I rode past the Zijlstra's as fast as I could because the mother and baby had not yet arrived and I am scared stiff that Mrs. Zijlstra will change her mind.[130]

I went via Kats to Bouwe Zijlstra, where I delivered 10 *stamkaarten* with inlays and ration cards for Jews. We listened to Professor Gerbrandy broadcasting from London.[131] [Bouwe is married to one of Johannes Post's sisters and his farm is one of the very scarce places where we can always count on understanding, aid, and advice.] He has constructed a wonderful hiding place in the hay, complete with electric light, radio, grain mill, and sleeping places for three. To get into this hiding place one has to first crawl through a narrow tunnel. This hiding place is also well known to Johannes Post and his wife.

We have a new list of names on the ration card list. [These are all in code, a code that can be read only by me.]

In Hollandscheveld, there's a guy who has fought on [the] Eastern Front and was wounded, unfortunately not fatally, and has been given a month's sick leave at home. He spent his time shooting at children and dogs.

My shoes have gone completely to pot. Jan Dekker has given me a pair that fit fairly well except for my toes. On my travels today I was rained on twice and blown dry by the wind twice.

Mrs. Roffel stopped me as she has three new places for Jews. Her husband will try to get me a coupon for a pair of shoes.

September 22, 1943, Wednesday Evening

IN NIEUW-AMSTERDAM. IT was cold last night so I covered my blanket with lots of hay and that did the trick.

This morning I visited the Gereformeerde (Calvinist) pastor in Pesse. He promised me that he would make the rounds with me this coming Monday to try to find hiding places for Jewish kids. I passed the charred remains of Meekof's farm. There is now a temporary building made out of requisitioned chicken houses. It has been furnished with furniture stolen from Jews.

Traveled round distributing ration cards.

September 23, 1943, Thursday Evening

IN DEDEMSVAART. YESTERDAY morning I left Nieuw-Amsterdam and came [via the railway track] from Coevorden and De Krim to Dedemsvaart. There was only one checkpoint, near De Krim, and that was easy to skirt. In Nieuw-Amsterdam farmer Wiggerink gave me some of his homegrown [tobacco-substitute], which is good to smoke. A. P. Zijlstra, the trainee notary, gave me an identity card for a girl.

I went to Sister Scholten with the piece to be printed. She said it would be OK and promised 2,000 copies.

I have a wound on my leg.

September 24, 1943, Friday Evening

LAST NIGHT I slept in the *vluchthut* and this morning continued this diary with the aid of my extremely limited notes. Sister Scholten gave me six torch batteries. This is great as they are not to be had anywhere. These are stamped "state property."

September 25, 1943, Saturday Evening

BROENINK HAS PRINTED 500 pamphlets for me. Wonderful. Yesterday I went via the cemetery to the widow Hagen's and listened to London. I found a better place for her to hide the radio. [My leg wound is getting worse.]

September 26, 1943, Sunday Evening

THIS AFTERNOON, I left Dedemsvaart with the 500 pamphlets. I am now at the Ottens' but don't feel too good, so I decided to stay here tonight.

An onderduiker [H. Lips] was shot dead by NSKK men in Oosterhesselen.[132] The local population was infuriated. The culprits fled to a tram, but the driver refused to start it. Two hundred Hitler youth have been installed in a camp at Langerak, and a bunch of SS men have arrived in Coevorden.

September 27, 1943, Monday Evening

FEELING ILL. NO desire to smoke or eat and also aware of my leg getting worse. Retired to bed, where Mrs. Otten gave me a glass of wine. I had intended to go to Pesse today, but Seine Otten went in my place. He also visited Bouwe Zijlstra with a message from me to the Posts. Geert Schonewille from Nieuw-Zwinderen, who has been in jail for some time, has returned home from the Oranje Hotel.[133] The news is good: the Russians have crossed their own frontier.

September 28, 1943, Tuesday Morning

MY LEG IS much worse, and the district nurse advised consulting the doctor.

October 1, 1943, Friday Afternoon

A RAID ON the distribution office at Nieuw-Zwinderen has failed. Four men were involved, all carrying revolvers; there was shooting and two of the four were injured, but all got away. Seller, the local Marechaussee from Nieuwlande, was on duty there and was grazed by a bullet. He is now held in high esteem by the Germans, who described the raid as "Bolshevistic *Schweinerei.*"

On Wednesday, there was a telephone call from Kats saying that I should be at the station to meet the 10:20 a.m. train from Amsterdam on Thursday morning. I went there in spite of the doctor's advice, but nobody came. I waited for the next train. Nothing. I went to Rozeman to talk about ration cards and identity papers. At Bouwe Zijlstra's I met Mrs. Post. At Kats's, I had a rabbit for dinner, but it may possibly have been "roof hare."[134]

The KK have been in a bad mood recently. In Hollandscheveld a young man slipped through their fingers by intimating that he would fetch his papers from his home. Mrs. Post raised objections to allowing more Jews to come here, as she felt that there were no more places for them. Yesterday I was over at Van der Zwaag, who also thought that there should be no more Jews from Amsterdam[135] because there were no more hiding places and no more money. I refuse to pay attention to all this rot.

The doctor was livid with me because I had been walking and cycling. My leg was red and swollen. This evening I sat with my leg raised.

We have put 350 pamphlets in envelopes and address them to people in Nieuwlande and elsewhere.

Today we sent a courier to Dedemsvaart to ask Sister Scholten what went wrong with the rendezvous at Hoogeveen station. I then received a telephone call from Kats saying that the mother and baby would be on the same train tomorrow.

All NSBers are to be armed with hunting rifles and carbines.

I have been sitting reading *Trouw*.

October 2, 1943, Saturday Evening

AT THE APPOINTED time I met the train from Amsterdam in Hoogeveen, wearing an Aster in my lapel. It was a woman from Amsterdam who called herself Nel. She had nobody with her. I took her to Blanken the baker's where we were given lunch. We talked about this and that and she soon got around to talking about the Jews. I told [her] to bring as many as she could. That meant that we would have to find places for them, but if the onderduikers come, the places will also come. She told me that the mother and baby already had a hiding place. She left with the three o'clock train and I gave her two rye bread loaves. I then cycled back to the Ottens' and gave my leg some further rest.

October 3, 1943, Sunday Evening

I KEPT STILL all day today and feel much better as a result. This evening there were lots of Tommies in the sky. A letter from de Maa: I should be in Hoogeveen to meet the 10.20 a.m. train. An unknown person had called, he said.

October 4, 1943, Monday Evening

THIS MORNING I went to Hoogeveen. On the way, I called in at Kats's to ask about the telephone message. He knew nothing about it. I called de Maa. Yes, it had been a male voice. We didn't understand it. I had only given Kats's number to Amsterdam Nel. Who can have called? We immediately thought about the possibilities of betrayal.

Kats dressed me as a motor rider, and thus I went to the station. But everything was in order, Nel was there with the Jewess and her baby. We took the tram to Bouwe Zijlstra, ate there, and then were collected by Kats in his car and taken to Mr. Zijlstra. Zijlstra had almost forgotten that I was bringing these two. The baby is one month old! The mother, a German Jewess, told me long stories about the shocking things she had seen Amsterdam, how she fled from address to address with her newborn baby and how all-around her people were being dragged away by the Krauts.

Nel had not been able to reach Kats by telephone on Sunday, but had remembered the number of the baker Blanken, and it was he who had phoned de Maa.

Bouwe Zijlstra has been to Amersfoort, where his son is being held, to see what he could do to free him. No success.

Peter will be able to hide underneath the church in Nieuwlande. A place is being prepared for him with electric light, keys, straw, etc., and he will also be able to work there.

October 5, 1943, Tuesday Evening

TODAY I WENT to Pesse, and went around with the Calvinist pastor. In the evening we met two other farmers at the church, and in two groups went trying to find hiding places for Jews. The results were poor, with very few commitments. It was one o'clock in the morning before I returned to the Ottens'.

October 6, 1943, Wednesday

THIS MORNING I took Mrs. Otten and her son, Arie, to Hoogeveen on a tandem. She is going to Apeldoorn to try to find some hiding places. She will also stop off in Zwolle to visit the Roman Catholic hospital there, where she had once been a patient, to try to get them to take a Jewess as a nurse.

I went to Van der Zwaag to cut coupons and brought them to Jannie Raak for new ration cards. Joop arrived unexpectedly; he is going back to Groningen to the Maritime College.

October 7, 1943, Thursday Evening

LAST NIGHT THERE was a telephone call that today at 10:55 a.m. "something" would come to Dedemsvaart by bus. (The town is not on the railway line). "Something would come." Good! I set off early and the bus was only a half hour late, but it did not bring me the "something." The next bus was at 4:00 p.m., and it brought Nel and another lady. Nel told me that the children that should have come had been found another place. "But," she said, "there are many more that need places." I said, "You know what I told you." Nel will come back this Saturday with a consignment. The lady she brought today was a young girl—who looked like a student to me.

I went to Broenink and asked him if he could fix me 500 pamphlets. "Consider it done," he said. I also gave him coupons for new "inlay sheets." I fetched 20 liters of gasoline from a secret depot for Jan Kats.[136]

[There is a break in the diary here. Probably the result of Douwes's original notes not being recovered or being illegible]

I met the boys (NV). They thanked me for what they described as a "beautiful" automatic pistol. I had given them the address of a farm where I knew there was a revolver hidden in the hay. They had acquired it by peaceful means.

I saw Peter to collect three sets of identity papers and to deliver a few others for alteration. Peter cannot stand doing nothing, as he calls it, any more. I told him that his bed is being prepared in a safe place complete with work table, light, etc. etc. I did not tell him where—that is a surprise.

Tomorrow evening, I have to meet the last train in Hoogeveen. Nel is coming with surprises, but I also received a phone call that I need to be in Dedemsvaart at the same time. As I cannot be in two places at once, we decided that Broenink and de Jong will help out by providing lodgings for the night. I will be there Saturday morning. Never a dull moment. The weather is fine.

October 18, 1943, Monday Afternoon

FROM APELDOORN CAME the news that Doppenburg, the foul creature, has been shot.[137]

Johannes Post was in Nieuwlande. His red hair is now pitch black, his moustache is also black. He has now gone again.

In Hoogeveen there are seven Gestapo agents in civilian clothes walking the streets.

Friday evening I was at the station at the agreed time but no Nel. What I did see were many Germans on the platform. I was at my "hotel" under two blankets and a thick load of hay at 11:15 p.m. In Hoogeveen, Faber, the baker (called Pencil in the diary), has been arrested, and the same happened to a police constable in Nieuwe Krim and to the burgemeester of Hardenberg.[138] Where are all these people? Nobody knows.

The clergyman to whom I delivered the little red-haired boy came bellyaching and moaning that his wife was scared—after all these raids and shootings. She had lost her nerve and become a nervous wreck. He asked me nicely but urgently to find another place for the boy. I told him that at the moment, I did not have the time, but that sometime I would come over and that in the meantime I would look for another place. The last thing is, of course, perfectly true, but when I do find a place it will be for someone else from Amsterdam.

Seine Otten and I agreed that whenever the man asked for me, I would not be at home and Seine would not know where I was. The clergyman knows only one of my addresses—Seine Otten.

Nel came Saturday morning with the first train from Zwolle, where she had spent the night. I went to have a look at the station, just in case. And there she was. She had with her an eighteen-year-old youth. I brought him temporarily to Mr. and Mrs. Otten. First we went to Bouwe Zijlstra, where Nel spent the night. On Sunday I brought her to the train on a bike [borrowed —translator] from Bouwe.

In the meantime, four boys arrived here in Dedemsvaart (where I am now). The four have to be brought to Nieuwlande and tonight another four will come. These second four can sleep in the same beds as the first four. I ordered a car for tomorrow night to take them further. The father of one of the boys was taken to Mauthausen two years ago.[139] His mother was subsequently sent to Poland. Every few minutes, the boy had a weeping fit. The other three are brothers who have two sisters in Westerbork. Soon Frits and I will take them to Nieuwlande. One of the boys keeps asking for Hennie, who brought them here.

It has been a very cold few days, today it is much warmer again, more sun. Yesterday I borrowed a suit from Seine Otten. The change was phenomenal; I looked like a gentleman—downright creepy.

In the newspapers (which I never read because they are censored by the Germans) there are threats against the "criminals" who have hidden radio receivers.

October 19, 1943, Tuesday

YESTERDAY EVENING TWO women, one of whom was called Hennie, and each with two children, should have come. However, at the appointed time of 8:15 p.m. no one had arrived. There was a telephone call to say that they would arrive at 10:30 p.m. Sister Scholten, Frits, and I waited in vain. Then a message came through that the bus had broken down. Frits went home at 11:00 p.m. and I sent Sister Scholten to bed at midnight. The bus arrived at 2:15 a.m. being pulled by a breakdown lorry. Hennie stepped down from the bus with two boys. They had had a pleasant time on the broken-down bus. There were only "good" patriots on board, and they had tried to outdo one another with jokes about Hitler as well as Mussert and his aunt.[140]

The bad news was that the other lady, whoever she was, boarded the same train in Amsterdam accompanied by a boy, but got off the train in Zwolle. I knocked Broenink out of bed and handed the two boys over to him. We had agreed that the two ladies were to spend the night at Mrs. De Jong's, but she had long since gone to bed, and Hennie did not want her to be awakened. I therefore took her to the *vluchthut* and took a walk myself. Arriving at the Stegemans' house, I tried all the windows and eventually found my way inside. I then called Hennie from the *vluchthut* and offered her a divan to sleep on while I went back to the shelter. Her sleep did not amount to much as she had to catch the 6:45 a.m. tram.

At seven in the evening we took the boys in a car owned by Mars, the garage-owner, to Nieuwlande where I "dumped" them on the Ottens who now have a house full. Mars had given his car and his time for free. By 9:00 p.m. I was back.

Van Geelkerken[141] has written in the newspapers that NSBers will be armed and will defend themselves.

November 3, 1943, Wednesday Morning

MUCH HAS HAPPENED in the last two weeks, for which I have no notes and have probably forgotten more than half. The general impression that has stuck in my mind of the last two weeks is of flying from place to place on my bike; of sprinting to Hoogeveen station to fetch people; of being at a loss about where to go with them all, and a desperate search for hiding places for boys, girls, babies, and adults, both men and women. Everyday new ones arrived.

Also an avalanche of telephone calls, telegrams, arguments over ration cards, identity cards, luggage, etc. The persistent whining of people where I had placed onderduikers "temporarily" and who found my definition of "temporary" too elastic. [Of that infuriating intrigue, the scheming and plotting of those who got scared and who changed their mind and who wanted desperately to palm off their charges, who tried to bamboozle me somehow or other. More nightmares from Tante Aaltje, who found a perverse pleasure in spoiling and poisoning precious hiding places.][142]

And just for a change, the story of the Tommy, who had to be found a hiding place. He had been shot down near Pesse and was a real Brit. I sat pleasantly talking to him and informed him about the situation here. He was very naive in his thinking about the Krauts as he thought them nice and decent people with whom he was accidentally at war. I tried hard to rid him of these mistaken ideas and told him the current thinking on Hitler. He is temporarily settled with an excellent farmer in a small upstairs room. He was also very concerned about the fate of the other member of his crew. His friend had jumped first but had to be pushed through the hatch because he got caught on something. He jumped immediately afterward. At first, he had no idea where he was as the plane's instruments had been damaged. After landing safely he went to explore and found an old clog; he knew then that he was in Holland or perhaps Belgium. Soon he also found part of a Dutch newspaper. For now, he is in a fairly safe place, and plans are being made to take him elsewhere.

Searching for hiding places for the diverse Jewish onderduikers always takes some doing. First always "temporary" placements. People find it hard to refuse if you tell them that the "client" would have to sleep out in the open if they didn't take them in. Naturally, the result is often an argument, but it usually turns out all right in the end. In any case, I have told Amsterdam that they can send more.

There is one boy who is full of sores. [I took him to a doctor in Zwolle with a letter from Sister Scholten.] Another was very ill when he arrived here. A Jewess gave me a pair of boots that fit perfectly and will be of great use. I also received two blankets, which will come in very handy in the haystack, which can become extremely cold at night.

At Amsterdamscheveld [a hamlet near Nieuw-Amsterdam][143] I visited a Roman Catholic orphanage and spent some time talking to the Mother Superior trying to persuade her to take in Jewish children, but she refused. I worked on her feelings, and on her Christian duty, but nothing would move her. I also went to the deacon, who had a large parsonage that could have accommodated a dozen onderduikers, but he claimed not to have any room.

Last Sunday there was a control at the front door of the Calvinist church in Nieuwlande. A warning was passed to those inside via a young girl who made her way into the church through the consistory door. The pastor in the pulpit asked all his parishioners to remain calm until the service was over, and those who did not have identity papers, or only bad ones, to remain behind. And so it came to pass. Those who remained were spirited away via a trapdoor under the pulpit.

I warned the other church in the village, which emptied in no time. Among others, I saw an eighty-year-old man who lost no time in disappearing.

Hiding places, or rather holes, have been constructed in the woods around Nieuwlande. They are well camouflaged and, in most cases, provide somewhere for onderduikers to sleep. The weather has remained remarkably warm throughout the autumn.

Nel van den Akker (*far left*), the four Bolwijn sisters, and Hans Lelie (*far right*) with Max Léons in the centre. Collection v.d.Sleen.

Postwar view of the Orthodox Calvinist church and parsonage in Nieuwlande. Collection v.d.Sleen.

In Seine Otten's garden (*from left to right*) an unknown Jewish hidden child, Ies Davids (Peter), Lou Gans (Herman), Arnold Douwes, Seine Otten, c. 1943. Collection v.d.Sleen.

The other day, I really vented my spleen at a farmer and his wife. I had, after a lot of discussion, persuaded them to take on a child and had brought them a nine-year-old girl. Two days later I arrived with her luggage and discovered that they had evicted her. Headmaster Wiegman had taken her in, although his house was already full. I took her to another address, to a place I had reserved for a newcomer from Amsterdam.

You experience everything in this work.

There is not much cooperation from the Dutch people as a whole. Those who bother about the enemy are the exception. The majority are too self-centered and too cowardly. Typically, those involved in the most active resistance and who do the most come primarily from the ultra-right and the ultra-left, thus from the Anti-Revolutionaries[144] and from the Communists. The people in these parts who take in the persecuted and help in other ways are nearly all Orthodox Calvinists.

"Herman" is one of our onderduikers who is being sheltered by Dekker and has dug a hiding place from himself in the woods.[145] He has a guitar with him, which he plays very well, and is also a first-class sketch artist and caricaturist.

He drew a caricature of Hitler for me. I had a row with Herman because he had written a dangerous letter to Amsterdam, and he promised to improve his behavior. The plan is to dig more hiding places for up to 30 people and Herman wants to help.

The other day I was given a revolver and a blackjack [by Berenschot, the policeman] that I passed on to the Knokploeg.

One evening I received a mother with a 16-year-old daughter and a 15-year-old boy from the last train. I took the boy to Pesse and the mother and daughter to Nieuwlande, having first taken them to Blanken the baker's where we were treated, as always, to coffee and cake.

The latest edition of *Trouw* was splendid.[146]

Nico is helping me these days. Not Nico of the NV but another one.[147] He was underground with the Van Dijk family in Nieuwlande,[148] and I did not trust him at first, and neither did Van der Zwaag.[149] His movements were very carefully investigated and letters addressed to him were opened. He asked me several times if he could help me, but I refused. Now we do everything together.

November 21, 1943, Sunday Afternoon

NICO IS NOW a great help and we are very busy. It is difficult, without any notes, to remember what has happened over the last three weeks. During that time, we took a young boy to Deesker, the baker in Nieuw-Amsterdam. I had promised him a little girl, but it turned out to be a boy. He didn't mind.

I have had more problems with Tante Aaltje. For the umpteenth time she has run away from her hiding place, gone to Van der Zwaag, who had no idea that I had earmarked Deesker's as a hiding place for the young boy, and demanded that he provide her with a taxi to take her back to Deesker's, where she had been previously. He was good enough to take her back. Van der Zwaag also told me later that "Sweet Aaltjelein" had moaned to him and to Deesker with all sorts of negative things about me. The people that she left now won't take anyone else, so another hiding place has been lost. The plan is that the boy, whose name is Henkie, will go to school.

We also went to the Calvinist pastor. Mr. Gorter, who has a Jewess under his roof and who gave us his address, said to us that "I do hope you succeed with our pastor so that I may respect him again." Up to that point, he had refused to be involved in anything illegal. It went like this: when we met him, his reverence was sitting in his chair shivering. I do not know if this was because of fear or something else, but the fact was that he thought the whole idea of him giving shelter to an onderduiker, and a Jew at that, was absurd and that his wife would never tolerate it.

Our ration card route is expanding every day. Last week I had been to Amsterdam to do various things. Collected clothes for a number of onderduikers and also visited an address given to me where a non-Jewish woman lived who needed to go underground. The residents there knew nothing about it, and I suspect they did not trust me. During the time I was there, Amsterdam was quiet: no air raid warnings, no raids, and no identity checks at the station. During the outward journey, there was a baggage inspection but as soon as the officials had gone, three sacks of apples appeared from the WC.

All sorts of rumors are circulating in Nieuwlande and the surrounding area, all to make the people fearful. We get a good deal of opposition from various quarters. In the first place, this comes from the general public who refuse to give shelter to those being sought. We get all sorts of excuses—which usually do not make sense: lack of space, no hiding place, talkative children or domestic servants, the fears of the housewife, too close to the street, too far from the road, no children in the house, too many children in the house. All of these well-known excuses mean the same thing: namely, I will not help, I am too selfish, I don't want to risk my goods and chattels or my freedom to help someone else.

Even within our own camp we get complaints. "People" say that we shouldn't bring more Jews to the neighborhood (Nieuwlande). There are already too many, "people" say. We need to have a purge and send some away. There are also objections because Nico himself is Jewish. We are also accused of being reckless because we bring in onderduikers without having guaranteed hiding places for them. In practice, the system works extremely well, even though we are sometimes tearing our hair out, but it works.

We got word of the fact that the SD was on our trail. We had to go underground ourselves for a month. We were warned by reports from a number of sources. I told Nico directly that I didn't believe any of it and wasn't prepared to give them any credence.

For the sake of our fellow illegal workers and for the wider community, we did have a purge and took various Jewish onderduikers away from Nieuwlande,[150] but we continued to receive newcomers from Amsterdam, something we tried to keep as secret as possible.

We put together a code to indicate what sort of onderduiker we were dealing with. The numbers 1, 2, and 3 were used to describe, respectively, Jews who were typical, somewhat typical, or not typical at all. Letter were then used to indicate gender and age, thus Type A—old woman either 1, 2, or 3.

A.1 Old Woman—very typically Jewish
A.2 Old Woman—somewhat Jewish-looking
A.3 Old Woman—not typical at all

Other letters described different categories as follows: Type B—young woman; Type C—young girl; Type D—female child; Type E—male child; Type F—female baby; Type G—male baby; Type H—old man; Type I—young man.

We went to Pesse a few times, where we did poorly and only managed to place one E.1 type Jewish boy. We were able to offload many more "Aryan" onderduikers there, and we didn't have to provide them with ration coupons as the village did that for them.

From Amsterdam we received a number of A.1s and B.1s who were safely hidden at a "summer farm."[151] It is quite a chore to get each onderduiker to his or her appointed place, with all their luggage, and it takes a great deal of time.

One evening, Nico brought an A.1 old Jewish lady to her hiding place on the back of a tandem, traveling along a narrow path. The woman was frightened to death from beginning to end, having not been on a bicycle for years, let alone a tandem.

We also received a cute little E.2 chap. This kid had already been caught by the Nazis in Amsterdam but escaped on his own initiative, jumped on a tram in spite of having no money and found his way to an address he had been given by chance. When he got there, he said, "Bring me to so and so in Utrecht and I will be fine." Now we have him. His parents have been picked up, and we hatch a plan to get them out if they are still being held at Westerbork. It is said that several contagious diseases, including polio and diphtheria, are rampant there.

Johan is type E.1 and asthmatic and has a very good place to stay—at Sister Scholten's. I had taken him to a doctor in Zwolle, but it was Sister Scholten who had collected him from there and taken him in.

We have ordered 1,000 liters of gasoline at Fl.1,50 per liter. It is horribly expensive, but there is nothing to be done about it.

Herman is the boy we took to Jantje Dekker [and] is now with Kikkert, who owns a small farm a bit out of the way. He had been with Dekker for a month and then moved here. In a month's time he can go back to Dekker for another month. Dekker is prepared to shelter him on a one month on, one month off basis, which he thinks is safer. It was a perfect moonlit evening when we took him to Kikkert. He played tunes on his guitar and sang; for example, "Thoughts Are Free."[152] It was a great evening.

It was very late when Nico and I walked back, I to my haystack and Nico to the Misses Nieuwboer, "the Ladies" we call them for short. One is a teacher at the same Calvinist school where Seine Otten teaches, and her sister looks after the house. They have a Jewish girl called Bep hiding at their house whom no one in Nieuwlande knows about. I am often told: go to Miss Nieuwboer, she has room, she can take someone. Such things are, as a rule, said by people who themselves do not want to help or are too scared. Those who use this excuse then say: Go to so-and-so, he has a large house, he can obviously take someone.

Nico needs a new identity card, and they are working on it in Hoogeveen. We went to the Rozemans for it, from whom we also get large quantities of ration cards. They are a father and son. The father is a tailor and the son works in the local poor-relief office. Nico gets one of the blank identity cards stolen in Hoogeveen, which is ready save for the number that still has to be altered. It is a shame that it is not ready as we have to make a trip to The Hague.

Tjitske and Hendrika Nieuwboer. Collection v.d.Sleen.

Recently, the Krauts have been all over the place where Nico had created his hiding place, hunting [for rabbits].

We have had a lot of planes fly over recently, probably going to Berlin. They fly extremely high up and leave condensation trails behind. German fighter planes are often shot down and once one fell very close to us on a return trip from Hoogeveen, setting off the air-raid alarm in the town.

For various reasons we sometimes exchange onderduikers [a girl for a boy, an old lady for a younger one; this has happened quite a lot recently], for example with Dedemsvaart.

It is said that a joker has daubed the words Psalm 7:8 on Doppenberg's grave in Apeldoorn.[153]

[The Lord shall judge the people: Judge me O Lord, according to my righteousness, and according to mine integrity that is in me. —translator]

In Diever there has been a successful raid on the ration card office.

November 22, 1943, Monday

I SLEPT IN Dedemsvaart last night. To Nieuwlande in cold, rainy weather. I found Nico at the Misses Nieuwboer's and heard that telephone messages had been pouring in warning Arnold and Nico that they were being shadowed, that they should stay out of sight for a while. This time, it was the real thing. I told Nico straight away that I thought I knew where the warnings had come from and that we should not take it too seriously. The Misses Nieuwboer were not entirely convinced and advised Nico to stay inside for the time being.

We talked about our plans for the trip to The Hague, where Nico can acquire a bicycle, together with clothes and money. There is also a plan to visit De Steeg where Bep knows a Baron so-and-so who can perhaps help with hiding places or other things. With one eye on our visit to the baron, Nico has christened me Lord Wanhoop [Despair] and I him Lord Haw-Haw.[154]

November 23, 1943, Tuesday

NICO WILL STAY with the Misses Nieuwboer for another day. I went to Van der Zwaag, who asked me where Nico was, but I said I knew nothing.

More telephone warnings came in about our being shadowed. I continued not to believe them and decided to do some research of my own, via the police. My feelings were entirely correct. There were no grounds whatsoever for the shadowing rumors. Some "good" Dutchmen, who wanted us out of the way, were trying to intimidate us.

I made a visit to the constable in Hollandscheveld—an old, pompous man full of his own importance who had a whopper of a nose. He was a character who could have come straight out of the pages of a Dickens novel. He admitted that all these rumors and telephone calls had come out of thin air and were designed to scare us and make us quit. Because "we brought far too many Jews into the district," and "ultimately you could never trust the Jews" and "if one Jew were to be caught then we would all be lost," etc., etc.

I listened to all these canards quietly. He also told me precisely where all the rumor and warnings had originated—exactly as I suspected—and he then offered his own advice. "Stop now," he said. "You need to call a halt. Everyone knows who you are and what you are doing, and it is also becoming difficult for us as policemen."

When he had finished, I promised that we would be very careful and try not to repeat previous mistakes but that it was impossible to quit now because those who were already here had to be looked after. "Moreover," I said, "It is a myth that there are so many Jews here, and I'd wager that you couldn't name more than twenty in Hollandscheveld." He began to list the ones he knew of, and I soon realized that there were many he didn't know.

I went immediately to Nieuwlande and told the Ladies the results of my enquiries. Nico and I went into the village to try to put the gossip to bed, as the locals were uneasy as a result of their being circulated. Some began to talk about it and wanting to be rid of the onderduikers.

Nel came with two sisters, aged eight and five. The elder one has been placed with Dr. Reijnierse in Hollandscheveld and the younger with widow Zwiers. I used peroxide [dye] on her hair to the great interest of the whole family that consisted of a mother and four young girls—all of whom were redheads.[155]

We have a whole series of plans for Sinterklaas.[156] All the children in hiding will get something. We have ordered *taai-taai* dolls[157] from Klaas Blanken, the baker, and *speculaas* from his fellow baker Bolwijn—who received sugar and butter coupons from us. We have asked Peter and Herman to help with the verse writing and so forth. Peter is now in hiding under the church. The weather is wet and cold.

November 24, 1943, Wednesday

I WENT TO Hoogeveen and collected Nico's new identity papers. There I ran into Van der Zwaag who again asked about Nico, but I stayed silent and indicated I had no idea where he was.

Jan Kats had telephoned. He was nervous and said that we had to do our disappearing act again as an onderduiker in hospital had said something to the Gestapo at his bedside and betrayed some hiding places. Two hours later came another call: We had to go urgently to Headmaster Wiegman in Hollandscheveld as great danger threatened. Nico and I went there at once. On the way over, we stopped at widow Zwiers's, where I emptied my pockets of anything incriminating and asked her to hide them. It turned out to be quite a lot, and I urged her to be careful and promised that I would be back as quickly as I could—either that evening or the following morning.

At both Wiegman's and Zijlstra's, who live next door to each other, there was great consternation as there had been a mysterious telephone call asking who had phoned from Amsterdam the previous Thursday morning between 10:00 a.m. and 11:00 a.m. This was seen as an omen and the houses had to be "cleaned" straight away. We therefore needed places immediately for a mother with a two-month-old baby, two elderly ladies, one one-year-old boy, one girl of 18, and one Jewish boy of 21.

The young mother, for reasons that I did not understand, needed her breasts binding and the district nurse was there. We found places for them all in the neighborhood, but on the strict understanding that this was only temporary. It was gone midnight when we finished. Earlier in the day, we had been to Jan Dekker, the postman, and had been told that Herman could not stay with the Kikkerts because they had also received a warning that someone had been talking and mentioned Kikkert's name and address in the wrong places. Jan Dekker refused to take Herman back because, he said, that had not been the agreement. He was right about that, and so Herman was accommodated in the hay loft above widow Zwiers's cow byre. We decided that I would go to Mokum [Amsterdam] in the morning to warn Nel and Hennie and to fetch clothes and money.

That night, I went to the Ottens' to sleep.

November 25, 1943, Thursday

LAST NIGHT I didn't get much sleep. I went to the Ottens' because they had told me that they were also going to Amsterdam as Mrs. Otten, who has health problems, had been recommended to see a specialist in Amsterdam by Dr. Reijnierse. The doctor has said that she needed a good night's sleep before her journey. I was still up when the doorbell rang. It was well past midnight. Obviously, I didn't go to the door but crawled on my hands and knees to the upstairs hiding place in the house, where I also found Henk Sweepe, another onderduiker.[158] We were all safely hidden before Mrs. Otten opened the door.

It was Herman. He emerged from behind the nearby well. Mrs. Otten gave the all-clear sign and we came rushing down. Yes, it was Herman, but hardly recognizable. He was plastered from head to foot in mud, and the mud was mixed with blood on his face and hands. He was a mess. He told us that there was a raid in progress. The Germans had arrived at the widow Zwiers's. He had heard them from his hiding place in the hayloft above the cow byre. Herman had let himself down [from the loft] by hanging from his hands until he was only two feet above the barn floor and then letting himself drop. He made only a dull thud as he landed. He then crawled on his hands and knees through the dark to the haystack where he thought I was sleeping. I was not there so he crawled to the edge of the woods. There he was able to stand up without running the risk of being seen. He crossed the woods, crawled across the Kerkhoflaan, crawled over farmland to a ditch by the roadside, and via the ditch came to the bridge in the middle of Nieuwlande.

Via various gardens, he made his way to the Ottens', rang the bell and then hid himself, so that he could run away if required. This proved unnecessary as Mrs. Otten opened the door rather than a Kraut.

He said he had seen lights in various farms and heard the sound of Krauts talking. He also said that he had heard the sound of a door being forced at the widow Zwiers's. After all this, we were naturally alarmed, and I was scared stiff because of the little Jewish girl I had hidden there, and also because of the stack of ration cards and other contraband that I had given to widow Zwiers for safekeeping. I had no doubts that my hiding place in the haystack had also been betrayed and that the widow would be in serious trouble.

The fire was lit to start drying Herman out, and Henk Sweepe set to work to burn various bits of incriminating paperwork. Seine Otten and I went outside to see what was happening. We went out the back garden and across those of one or two neighbors before coming to the back of de Maa's house. There was nothing unusual to see or to hear. We went over the bridge and each took one side of the road, keeping behind the trees. At one or two farms, we saw a light. At Roffel's we called in, but what we had seen was only a nightlight. Roffel knew nothing about Germans or a raid and went back to sleep.

Eventually, we got to the widow Zwiers's but there was nothing unusual there. The door had not been forced and elsewhere there were no signs of Krauts. We walked round the house and looked at the haystack. At a sign from me, the dog stayed quiet, otherwise he would have barked. We retraced our steps and said to each other "Herman must have dreamed it." Just as we said this, a policeman appeared behind us, demanding to know why were on the road at that hour. He was a new Marechaussee who had only been in the locality for a week. He told us that there had been a group of German SS together with some Dutch KK. They had been at the widow Zwiers's only to ask the way. They had arrested an onderduiker at Elema's house and had visited a number of other addresses.

Widow Zwiers had been upset but had had the presence of mind to hide all my contraband in the oven attached to the stove. At around 3:15 a.m., we drank coffee back at the Ottens', and Herman and I spent the rest of the night reading *Volk and Vaderland* and other trash.[159]

The KK men must have been very nervous because at one point they apparently aimed their revolvers at each other, thinking their own comrades were the onderduikers they were seeking. Only one onderduiker was caught, at Elema's.

November 26, 1943, Friday

YESTERDAY THE OTTENS and I went to Hoogeveen railway station in Buikema's car. Standing on the platform we met Van der Zwaag. Between Zwolle and Harderwijk, we saw a dogfight above the Zuiderzee and one plane was shot down. In Amsterdam, the trams were packed.

First I went to Hennie in the Zuider Amstellaan [to tell her what had happened]. While there I telephoned Mrs. De Bruin. We agreed to meet near the Concertgebouw and she would be carrying a copy of the *Haagsche Post*.[160] She gave me Fl.500 for various onderduikers as well as wristwatches, pens, pencils, and other trinkets.

Hiddo Buikema and his car, with Arnold Douwes, Seine Otten, and two unknown children, c. 1943. Collection v.d.Sleen.

Then to Nel, to let her know about the events of the last few days. Then I went to Hilversum to visit a perfume shop where I collected money for "Tante Louise," one of our charges. There was an [identity card] checkpoint at the Central Station in Amsterdam, but I slipped by. In the evening, the [return] train was held up near the army camp at Oldenbroek.

I spent the night at Albert Nijwening's in Hoogeveen. Most of the other houses I could have lodged with were full of onderduikers. Albert also had his share of them but managed to squeeze me in too, and the luxury of having a bed meant that I overslept the following day. From there I went to the photographer to collect photos for the identity card of a Jewish onderduiker, and luckily they were ready for me. I went back using the little steam tram, but it jumped the rails near Noordscheschut, so I walked the rest of the way to Hollandscheveld. Many aircraft in the sky and a myriad of condensation trails.

Klaas, the [non-Jewish] onderduiker arrested at Elema's, is free again. He says he talked his way out of it. I think it is unbelievable.

December 2, 1943, Thursday

ON SUNDAY I went back to Amsterdam to fetch the two girls, having slept on the Ottens' divan and then cycled to Hoogeveen. Van der Helm called me in to eat a couple of *oliebollen*, and I left my bicycle at Blanken the baker's.[161]

In the train between Amersfoort and Amsterdam I encountered J. P. Strijbos, the ornithologist[162] and an old seaman who had been with Shackleton to the South Pole. We had an interesting conversation and they competed to see who could curse the Nazis the most. In the same train there were twenty Allied prisoners of war, all airmen.

I met Mrs. de Bruin at the Concertgebouw again and asked her about the girls. "Tomorrow you may take two of them." Went to Nel and said that we had more hiding places. Slept at the house of the Winkel family on two stools, because the house was full of onderduikers—so full indeed that Hennie slept elsewhere. On Monday morning I went to Carl Denig's clothes shop to fetch a skirt for Tante Louise. This skirt, she had told me, was paid for and ready for collection. At Denig's they knew nothing about it, even when I showed them a letter from Tante Louise herself.[163]

My agreement with Mrs. de Bruin was that I would meet a certain Annie at the Central Station who would hand the two girls over to me. It all went well. Two lovely children: sisters. We went first class to Amersfoort and then second class to Hoogeveen, mainly because of the congestion in third class, [but also because first class compartments had no connecting doors and could only be accessed when the train arrived at a station].

The younger of the two girls got all the people in the compartment laughing when the train stopped in the middle of nowhere. As people speculated on the reasons for the delay, she piped up and said, "I think the wheels have fallen off."

As we arrived in Hoogeveen it was clear that the station was surrounded by Green Police. I got off on the wrong side of the train and then lifted the girls, their luggage and then myself over a fence. I left them with their luggage by a lamppost and told them not to move. Nico was nowhere to be seen. We had agreed that he would meet me by the station, but he had seen the whole area full of rogues but had no means of warning me. Eventually I found him [and we were able to get the children safely to Blanken the baker's where there was coffee and sandwiches. From there we took them to a temporary address from where they would ultimately be taken to Sister Scholten in Dedemsvaart].

The gasoline we ordered has not yet arrived. I did a whole series of small errands: Taking a pair of clogs to a little boy. Fetching girls' clothes from one address and taking them to another. Collecting taai-taai from Blanken for Sinterklaas and taking it to the Ladies for safekeeping. [Blanken] became known to us as the "taai-taai man."

On Tuesday night there was a rendezvous between a Jewish man and his wife at Blanken's. A plane crashed near the station at Hoogeveen. Nico and I went to Nieuw-Amsterdam for the night and on Wednesday morning we cycled to Stadskanaal in Groningen Province. It rained again, and we collected a suitcase of clothes for Bertha, a 20- to 22-year-old Jewess. From there we went to Groningen by train, but had a race with time to catch the train at Zuidbroek station.

December 6, 1943, Monday

IN GRONINGEN, WE first went to Doeks (Mrs. de Clercq-Zubli). She had connections with the university hospital and promised to investigate the case of the talkative onderduiker and let us know what she discovered.[164] She also gave us 50 ration cards, which made a welcome addition.

Later in the evening we went to my brother Julius and his wife, Mimi, in Dorkwerd;[165] Mimi was at first frightened when we appeared, as there had been two house-to-house searches in the village looking for missing Allied airmen, and their house had also been thoroughly searched. Eventually we went to bed convinced that the parsonage would not be raided again, which turned out to be right, although three other houses in the vicinity were searched that night.

We agreed that Guillette would bring a two-month-old baby on Monday.

The following day, we cycled to Nieuw-Amsterdam, keeping Groningen on our left as there was a raid going on in the city. We had a nasty journey into the rain and the wind, and it seemed that it would never come to an end.

That night, from Thursday to Friday we slept at my sister Mary's house. [She shares with three others; Peter, a notary public; another woman who is a teacher; and Job, who is an agricultural expert.] Job made a fuss because he objected to Nico sleeping in the house on security grounds [but was outvoted].

We urgently needed a temporary place for an elderly Jewish man in Nieuw-Amsterdam as his existing refuge had been hit during a dogfight and completely destroyed. We tried to find somewhere for him, but we were not quick enough (the telephone lines to Nieuwlande were down). The man committed suicide.

From Friday into Saturday we did not go to sleep but spent the night wrapping Sinterklaas presents at the Ladies' house. It was a great occasion and we had 50 presents.[166] During the night we heard many planes flying overhead and saw one shot down in flames. On Saturday, we delivered the presents. Nico went to Nieuw-Amsterdam; I went to Dedemsvaart. Eventually I became so sleepy that I couldn't cycle any more.

Masses of *Vliegende Hollanders* have been distributed by the Tommies.[167]

It is early Monday morning, December 6, and I am about to depart for Hoogeveen.

December 13, 1943, Monday Afternoon

IN DEDEMSVAART.

Last Monday I cycled from here to Hoogeveen via Zuidwolde. First to Blanken the baker's where the baby would be taken, to be picked up by Guillette to be transported to Julius and Mimi in Dorkwerd. Mrs. Blanken was cross with me because I had not told her that the baby's mother would also come the night before. That was without my knowledge and against the agreement I had with her. Not pleasant, of course, but in this work one gets used to being scolded. The baby had been looked after by Bouwe Zijlstra's daughter for a week.

I cycled to Hollandscheveld with a borrowed pram in tow, had lunch with Bouwe Zijlstra and then on to Nieuwlande.

Herman is now hiding under the church with Peter. [Besides all their other work] they are now also producing a small weekly newsletter, *De Duikelaar*.[168]

Nico and I went to Mrs. Jonker's baker's shop in the center of the village and extracted from her a promise to take in a Jewish girl. "No, not a Jewish boy, far too dangerous with all this circumcision going on."[169] [When we left the baker's we said to each other, if we have a Jewish boy, we'll just have to dress him in girls' clothing, and it will take a while for Mrs. Jonker to find out, and by the time she does, she'll have grown attached to him.]

In the afternoon we cycled to Hoogeveen and took the 6:00 p.m. train to The Hague. We arrived very late and headed for an address in the Van Alkemadelaan. Because we were late and with an eye on the curfew, we decided to take a shortcut across the Malieveld, but the field had been ploughed and we ran into barbed wire and a tank of water, so in the end we had to walk round anyway.

The address in the Van Alkemadelaan appeared to have been evacuated, but by this stage it was 11:00 p.m., and we needed to be off the streets. We asked at various unevacuated properties, but no one was willing to take us in. We were advised to go to the police station, but we were none too keen. Finally, we went to a Roman Catholic parsonage but met with the same excuses. Then we approached a night watchman, whom we thought was a policeman, and who had been following us for a while. We told him what our problem was, and we then walked with him on his route [while he tried to find somewhere for us to stay]. Our vision of a comfortable bed for the night had gone up in smoke.

When we had walked a short way, he tried at a couple of addresses for us. At one house where he rang we heard a woman's voice.

"Who's there?"

"Night Security Service (*Nachtveiligheidsdienst*) Madam"

"What? Filth? (*Vuiligheid*)"

"No, not filth—security."

Oh, no, she had no place for us and advised us to go to the police. She was thanked for her advice, and we moved on.

He tried again for us at a shop where the light was still on. Here a man and two girls were packing up the entire contents of the shop because they had to leave the following day. We were allowed to sleep there. In the window, there were some curtains and tablecloths and we had a good night's sleep. Before we left (around 6:00 a.m.), one of the girls brought us breakfast.

We went from there to an address in the Tasmanstraat where Nico had been hidden [previously]. There were other onderduikers there. They were all still asleep when we arrived. Nico phoned a well-to-do acquaintance who was also looking after his parent's affairs and asked him for financial assistance, which he promised to provide. After that, we went to visit his parents. [They are in a house in the center of The Hague with 11 other Jews.] They were in a place where it was easy to escape in case of danger or betrayal. Nico's father was far from good to his son, calling him a daredevil and a stupid idiot and so on. But it was undeniable that deep down he also took great pleasure from the fact that his son was trying to thwart the Germans.

In the evening, we went to Voorburg, to a bicycle manufacturer where Nico used to work. The man looked up when he saw Nico on his doorstep. He promised a new bike, which had to come to Rotterdam. That night, Nico spent the night with his parents, while I stayed at the address in the Tasmanstraat.

On Wednesday, we went to De Steeg, to Baron Heekeren, who lived in the famous Middachten Castle.[170] There also were a group of noble women, who were all scared as weasels.[171] They were exceptionally friendly toward us, but they had no space for onderduikers. They had only 30 rooms in the castle, perhaps a few more.

From there we went to another address in De Steeg, the Van Ginhovens.[172] [Given to us by Bep—the Jewish girl underground with the Ladies, who had stayed there for a while.] One of their brothers had been shot by the Germans and another was in jail. We negotiated a hiding place for a B.3 [not Jewish-looking] "housekeeper" with one of their neighbors, but she could not go there before January 15 because there were family visitors. After a good deal of negotiation, we were allowed to bring her a week earlier.

We went looking for other places but found nothing, although we did get promises of financial assistance. We also heard that the baron did not enjoy the complete trust of the locals. In De Steeg, we stayed overnight at the Van Ginhovens.

Thursday by steam tram to Doetinchem, where we arrived late at the "Aunts'."[173] The tram went through Laag-Keppel, [where I had escaped from the Gestapo and where the local policeman Pietje van Dalen had done everything to find me]. I sat in a dark corner of the tram wearing glasses and a hat. I saw a number of people I knew, but no one recognized me. The Aunts worried about us but plied us with all sorts of gifts.

The next morning we took the first train from Doetinchem to 's-Hertogenbosch to see my oldest brother, Jan, who is a Calvinist pastor there and to ask for a place for a Jewish onderduiker. At my brother's we were greeted at the door by a young black-haired and black-eyed girl. In the kitchen, there was a son of the Chosen People washing plates. In the living room there was the daughter of the same people darning stockings. My brother was delighted to see me and asked the reason for our visit. We told him it was no longer important. Upstairs he also had an elderly Jewish couple. My brother's children (he had nine) called the house "Duikerslust."[174] The children say nothing about this to friend or foe alike.

We moved on to Geldermalsen, to acquaintances of Nico to place another onderduiker, but this didn't happen as the man [of the house] was already in hiding and his wife expected to have to do the same shortly.

On the platform at Geldermalsen we saw the "Giant of Rotterdam," the Netherlands' tallest man.[175] On various occasions, I had said to Nico that all the tension of being on the run would do something to me and I would start seeing things. As we were on the platform, I suddenly saw a giant in front of me—a man taller than any I had ever seen, with hands like soup-plates and shoes like canoes. If he stood on his toes he could see over the top of the train. I nudged Nico, who seemed completely unmoved, and asked him:

"Nico, do you see anything unusual about that man?"

"Which man?"

"Him, in front of us."

"Anything unusual? No, I see nothing."

"There you have it then," I said, grabbing Nico by the arm. "I have gone mad. I see things others do not, I can see a giant very clearly in front of me and would swear to it."

Nico started laughing out loud, and I thought he would never stop. "That is the giant of Rotterdam," he said.

[When we had calmed down, Nico explained that he knew right away who the giant was. The tallest man in Europe. In the Netherlands, everyone knew about him, but I had lived for ten years in the United States and subsequently had three years of study in Boskoop at Horticultural College, so had had no time for anything else.]

In Utrecht we took the train for Hoogeveen and got into a compartment with two young women. It soon became apparent that they were in the same line of work as us. This was not a compliment to their caution. Nico began singing, "Everybody's doing it, doing it, doing it." They also got off at Hoogeveen and made their way to Faber the baker's.

We had left our bicycles at Van der Kerk's,[176] collected them there and then cycled to Nieuwlande. We slept at the Ladies', me in a bathtub.

On Saturday, we did all manner of small chores and eventually found our way to Faber the baker's, where we met the two young women again and took them to their train. We went to Blanken the baker's to pay the bill for Sinterklaas and to collect baby clothes. In the evening, we went to Zijlstra's, where we collected more clothing for the baby in Groningen. Later to Kats who was annoyed with me in connection with the case of a 14-year-old Jewish boy. I had in fact nothing to do with it. Kats thought he was one of our customers and demanded that we take him with us. The details of this case I do not know, but he is not one of ours. Someone, unknown to Kats, had arrived with the boy, begging to give him shelter for 24 hours, and then had not returned. Where have I heard stories like that before?

We have found a place for two girls with a single family. Someone gave us a name. We went to a small farmhouse by mistake. We had been given an address but had lost it, but thought we were in the right place. Nico stayed with the bicycles while I crossed the small bridge to the farmhouse, where I met a man, his wife, and their daughter.

"Good evening," I said, "Are you Mr. Duinkerken?"

"And what if I am?" He was obviously raving mad about something.

I said, "Sorry, I've made a mistake, you will pardon me for the intrusion. Good night."

"Oh, no!" he shouted. "That's not the way we do things here! Tell me first, what do you want with my wife? Tell me what you want with her?"

The man tried to block my way, but I skipped out and made my way back across the bridge. He followed me, shouting, "What do you want with my wife?" He repeated this over and over again while jumping on the small bridge, and I was lucky not to end up in the water. I got safely to the other side, but he followed. When he saw Nico, he said, "And who are you, you want my wife too?" And to me again, "I am Van Duinkerken, and who are you?" I got disgusted with the whole thing and said, "I am Van Puffelen from Assen and this is my assistant, Lord Despair, and if you don't go back where you came from, you'll go headfirst down the well." This seemed to do the trick and we escaped. Later we heard that he had betrayed two Jewish onderduikers to the Green Police and that his wife had many Kraut visitors.

That evening we were still on the road at 11:30 p.m. and slept in the hiding place at Bouwe Zijlstra's—in the middle of a large haystack—having listened to the BBC on the radio. We had breakfast at Zijlstra's after a good night's rest, save for one incident when I had an attack of claustrophobia. I awoke and forgot where I was. I wanted to stretch my legs and stand up, but that was impossible. I was truly afraid as I had never experienced this before. The hay all around me made me afraid, but after a short while, it passed, and I went back to sleep.

We cycled to Nieuwlande and passed by Jan Dekker's. He knocked on the window and passed on a message from Van der Zwaag. Things were not normal in the neighborhood and there were some cars with Germans in the vicinity. We warned everyone: phoning those with telephones and visiting the others in person. We ate at Jan Post's, and Seine Otten also appeared with information on what was happening.

We cycled to Nieuw-Amsterdam via Nieuwe Krim where "Tante Loes" is in hiding with the Hoogeveen family. This refuge had first been used by an elderly Jewish lady who had a nervous breakdown as a result of being in hiding and was transferred to a bookshop in Nieuw-Amsterdam. Tante Loes is content there and her daughter will be able to join her. [Hooray. One more place freed up for someone else.]

In Nieuw-Amsterdam we met Guillette, who told us that Mimi's parents had become so nervous about having the Jewish baby in their house in Dorkwerd that it had been moved to a nearby farmstead.

We went to Van Ekelenburg, the assistant pastor, who had a letter for us from Doeks about the loquacious onderduiker in the hospital. It went as follows: "I met your friend in hospital. As far as I can tell, his condition is stable. He is now quiet and says only a little. But in my opinion this is no cause for alarm. From my bookshop, I hear that you have got your books from someone else. Should this not be the case, let me know and I will try to take care of it." The "books" were, of course, ration cards.

Guillette is going to Groningen with a suitcase of baby clothes and is ready to undertake other tasks. Yesterday evening, I cycled to Dedemsvaart (De Flochte, which we now call the Vinery Hotel), where I slept well in the arbor at the rear of the garden. This morning I took this diary out of the ground and made additions.

Van Ekeleburg called to say that it was canceled. This concerned a woman whom we were taking to De Steeg. I need to tell Nico this. Later we met a young Jewish man, who told us that he had hidden in a closet during a raid in Amsterdam but that the closet door had swung open. He had handed a gold watch to the Green Police man with the words "zu haben,"[177] and the Kraut had taken it and he remained free.

[The text then includes a verbatim account of an Italian army report dated November 10, 1943.

Also recorded is the fact that Douwes and Nico gave the Misses Nieuwboer a book containing a poem as a Sinterklaas present.]

December 14, 1943, Tuesday Morning

STILL IN DEDEMSVARRT. Yesterday a huge number of planes flew over on their way back from Germany. I went to see Mikie Ruys (from the nursery) to get the address of Mien Ruys (the garden designer) with a view to finding new hiding places.[178] It is much less cold now but I am afraid that snow is coming.

I received a card from Ds. Visser in Raalte with the following message: "Friend, I assume that the photos have got lost. I have not seen or heard anything from the photographer. It's a shame now that film is so scarce. Best wishes, H. Visser." Again, this is a message about lost ration cards.

A letter from Jo (Sister) Scholten where she asks for a domestic servant who must look good, thus Type B.3 for a family with three children who own a bakery and grocery store.

A "wants" list from Amsterdam:

> Non-Jewish boy,[179] 23 years old, prepared to do any work, having escaped from forced labor service.
> Jewish boy, 26 years old, prepared to adjust to anything.
> Non-Jewish woman, 30 years old, urgently needs a new address, will also work.

Another letter from Hennie with, among other things, the following: "I'm bringing Mia to the Vinery Hotel on Wednesday. I will go to Dorkwerd for Marie and when I fetch Mia I will also bring [undecipherable]. The second one goes to Favorite and for the baker Gijs, I have one of the things that I have kept back, from Leon Vlesman. No other news, Greetings, Hennie."[180]

December 26, 1943, Sunday Morning, Second Day of Christmas

I RECEIVED THE following letter:

> This morning someone was here, sent by Mien from Amsterdam. The larger and the smaller plant will come on Saturday via the same route. The person

who is bringing them is keen to meet you because she does the same type of work. She also has other large and small plants that she would like to send to you, mainly smaller ones. She also has a very old m., a j of 20 and one of 24, who looks very good, and a m. of 14.¹⁸¹ Bert.

From J in 's-Hertogenbosch I received the following epistle:

Seven little froggies, sitting in the farmer's ditch. You know the song, but that is old hat. I now have a new version, Ten little froggies, sitting way down in the farmer's ditch. How do I get them through the winter?

A few days earlier, I had also received from him, among other things, the following, . . . "I find again and again that morals are deteriorating fast. All sorts of dirty tricks are taken for granted. Hoarding food, black marketeering, extortion; and where forgery is seen as a well-loved sport. Where is it all going to end for our people, when there are no curbs on their behavior?" Someone also told me how people obtain identity cards these day. One approaches [bribes?] the civil servant and he looks in the population registers for children who died young, who are then issued with an identity card as though they were still alive. A photograph is handed over and a card made up for the dead person. The paperwork is then sent to The Hague so that the individuals are included in the Burgerlijke Stand [population registers] and the rest is simple.

I told him [J from 's-Hertogenbosch] that such an attitude [his worries about morals] is fatal and undermines people's confidence, leaving aside the severe punishments when something comes out.

[My brother asked me about this system, not knowing that it was how I had come by my latest identity: Hendricus Marinus van der Vegt. He had been a farmhand, born the same year as me, who had died when he was 20 from a kick by a horse. His name was expunged from the death registry and given to me. He "moved" about four or five times before becoming a farmhand in Nieuwlande, working for Frans de Graaf, someone I knew well. I went to see him and told him that I worked for him—on the grounds that it was better that he knew of the deception. My brother continued in his letter:

I forgot an important point. You asked about stamp collectors who would like to trade stamps with you. I spoke with someone who is interested and who has a nice Dutch collection that he will trade for equally valuable examples. You had better write to him about what you have. In this way, he gave me information about identity cards and the stamps were, of course, onderduikers.

The last time I wrote any notes was twelve days ago, so that there will be many things forgotten.

From Mr. Emmens in Nieuw-Amsterdam we received 50 half ration cards that we distributed quickly.¹⁸² Last week I went to Amsterdam, Haarlem, Hilversum, Utrecht, 's-Hertogenbosch, and The Hague. In 's-Hertogenbosch I met one of Jan's acquaintances with whom I discussed the exchange of onderduikers. The NSB burgemeester of 's-Hertogenbosch had invited all his fellow NSB burgemeesters from Noord-Brabant to a dinner.[183] Somebody [my brother] phoned them all to say that the dinner had been canceled because the host was prevented from attending. The guy waited in vain for hours, but nobody came and he was suitably cross.

My brother's children have created a "revue" that they perform in the attic. The building itself plays a role because it is filled with onderduikers, one of whom is named Baron Ata because he helps with the washing up.

In Haarlem I collected clothing for a 16-year-old boy. In Hilversum, money and women's clothes, in The Hague, money, and a revolver (for the Knokploegen) and distributed ration cards. Lenie and Piet are a student couple who trade in Jews (*in Joden doen*). They brought us a mother with a son of seven, also a girl of 18. The mother is a B.2. I dyed her exotic-looking black hair red. Her son is at Nieuwe Krim.

I received a letter from Doeks as follows:

> Dear Arnold. Just a few words about my cousin, who is doing fine. I spoke with the doctor about him who said that there has never been any cause for concern. He has no idea how this rumor got out, but you know that there are always people who like to scatter sensational tales around. About the Christmas cards, it is difficult to get good ones at a low price, but I will do my best.[184]

In Nieuw-Amsterdam I took "Riek" to a new address in the pouring rain. Riek is the Jewess who had been with the Ottens. Her husband is in hiding on a farm in Nieuwlande.

A telegram came asking me to go to the station at Assen, but it arrived too late. It was probably about a raid on Westerbork—where plans are at a preliminary stage. Doeks and a man known as Ata are also involved in it.[185]

Piet (of Lenie and Piet) brought a gem of a revolver the other day. I'll give it to Johannes Post. We also got another one from Van Thalens, a farmer in Nieuwlande, but this was a much older one.

One night recently, a gang of eight guys from the Dutch Security Police (Hollandse Sicherheitspolizei) were in Nieuwlande looking for a man of about 50 who was underground at various addresses. They didn't find him, but at Jan Dekker's they went straight to the peat stack where they unearthed a radio. Obviously, there is a traitor in our midst. Dekker told me that they had been a stupid and disorderly band of numbskulls. They had searched his house but had not found his brother-in-law, who was upstairs in hiding. The same group reappeared a couple of nights later and raided a couple of farmhouses, but with no result.

It was said, and then contradicted, that the Green Police had been in Dalen. The Krauts have occupied the Ijssellinie[186] and placed the defenses in a state of readiness.

Nico and I have been busy for the last few days with the normal routine of delivering ration cards and the like.

January 5, 1944, Wednesday

ON TUESDAY, DECEMBER 28, I went to Groningen to see Doeks. The whole story about the chattering patient was entirely false. It is becoming clearer and clearer to me that this is just one more case of sabotage, one more attempt to make life difficult for us, one more attempt to get us off the streets.

This "sabotage" emanates from people who call themselves "good" Dutchmen, the same ones who are responsible for the rumors that we were being shadowed. I know who they are. It comes of unbelievable naivety, jealousy, or whatever. Maybe it is fear.

We know how to react, [but] the great danger is that we won't be able to able differentiate real warnings from the false ones.

Good news. Kikkert and his wife, where Herman was but who had to leave because of these rumors, want to take in another onderduiker.

I went to visit Elly in Groningen, but she was not there. On Wednesday I went to Amsterdam, collecting and delivering letters and collecting money for some people. I also spoke to Lenie and Piet [Veenstra], and handed over a batch of copies of *Wervelwind*.[187]

I also visited Hennie's married sister [Kitty] in the Michelangelostraat and found several onderduikers there, including Nico's sister [Chelly]. He has no idea that she is there. There was an identity card control at the Central Station, so for safety's sake, I entered the building through a side door.

I was also in The Hague, where I visited Nico's parents and then went to Voorburg to find out about Nico's bicycle. It is ready at an address in Rotterdam, and I can collect it from there. In a fortnight we can send a married couple to the address where Nico's parents are hiding. My plan was to have stayed overnight at the house in the Tasmanstraat, but I heard from Nico's parents that all the people there had been arrested. Thus, I slept in Voorburg and had a long conversation with the man in a mixed marriage trying to persuade him that he should go underground rather than give himself up to be sterilized. He had no idea what to do.[188]

On New Year's Eve I went from Voorburg to Groningen in a packed train, went to Elly's house, where Ata was also present, and discussed plans to free 40 people from Westerbork. On the same day, an NSB police inspector had been shot dead. In reprisal, 60 hostages had been picked up, of whom three had been shot. There was no checkpoint at the station when I left, but somebody pulled the emergency brake on the train just as it was picking up speed.

In Hoogeveen I found Nico at Blanken the baker's. He was just having some *oliebollen* and the whole family were at the table, including the servants. With Nico and me, we numbered 23 in all. Nico stayed there to sleep. I went on to Nieuwlande to "pitch my tent" with the Ottens. Joop was also there. He is in Groningen most of the time now and busy with illegal work, I believe.

The girl, whose name was Suzy, whom I had brought from Groningen to the Ottens, had been moved on to Nieuw-Amsterdam by Nico in my absence. While I was away, I had left Nico a note: "Dear Nico, I have brought you a present from Groningen in the form of a 20-year-old girl. She is at present with Otten (Beaver). She is very nice, but do not attempt to flirt with her as she is not interested. At 'Snorretje's'[189] there is an identity card in the name of Ote—born in Hungary, or something like that. Ask 'Snorretje' for this and the ration card that goes with it and send it all to the address in R."

We had a place free for a housekeeper in Nieuw-Amsterdam, and another in De Steeg, as well as places for three children and perhaps a married couple. I received a letter from Nel [van den Akker] asking urgently for places for two children—well, we have these ready. Also a place for a boy of 15 to 20 who is prepared to sleep in a hole. I also had a suitcase of clothing for Liesje, who was lodged with the widow Zwiers. A few days ago, I peroxided her hair again, and did the same with a little boy lodged at De Krim.

A letter from Lenie and Piet. "Dear Arnold and Nico, Here is compensation for the vacuum cleaner that you repaired for us. We are keen to know if your little rabbit has given birth and if things are OK. If this is the case, we want to know as soon as possible. With regards, Lenie and Piet."

From Mr. Schouten in Utrecht we received the following:

A list of wishes:
Harry, one year old, money there
Jan, 10 months old, money there
Edith, five years old, special case, small family
Ladies, 62 and 70 years old, [need] good milieu—pastor, schoolmaster or similar

We are still being hindered by people who want to be seen as "good" Dutch citizens, through spreading of false alarms, insinuations, or withholding help. As long as these things are aimed at us personally, we could not care less, but they border on treason.[190]

The day before yesterday, Nico was forced to sleep under the church floor, with Peter, Herman and Dirk. Peter and Herman were working on their newssheet *De Duikelaar* while Dirk is someone who was forced into joining the Dutch SS and was sent to the Russian front. When he had a few days leave, he escaped and went underground.[191]

I had been worried stiff about Nico as I had no idea where he was and thought he might have been arrested. Only the day after, when I saw him again, did I discover that he had been locked inside the church as the sexton had forgotten about him.

We went to see Geert Schonewille in Nieuw-Amsterdam to talk about the Westerbork raid. We decided that he would go to Groningen to fix a time and place for a meeting in Hoogeveen. I would then call him today. He is only lukewarm about the project, and I think he regards it as too risky. He's afraid that Ata and Elly are too reckless. I hope we will agree a good plan.

Nico met an onderduiker in Nieuw-Amsterdam who can get a police uniform for us. He also got two dozen fuel ration cards, which will come in handy sooner or later.

Yesterday I went to Pesse to visit Petertje (not to be confused with Peter under the Church). First I went to Daling, where I had often eaten, to talk about this and that, and about the relationships between illegals and how they sometimes go wrong, but thank heavens not very often. Daling had been warned against me by Snorretje's (Van der Zwaag's) father. I was not to be trusted.

Daling wanted revolvers. I cannot help him with this. I asked him for ration cards. Perhaps he can help us in the future. We haven't received much from Hoogeveen recently.

The organization in Pesse will provide 15 guilders per week to support Petertje. I gave him my overcoat, which made him very happy, but he needs so many other things; he has almost no clothing.

Many people have been arrested in The Hague in the last few weeks, and there are rumors of major raids all over the country, but these have not materialized so far.

We received the following (wish) list from Mrs. de Bruin in Amsterdam.

1. Housekeeper, 35 years old, dubious appearance[192] and should only go to the door in an emergency. Easygoing and nice person. Very good cook.
2. Nurse, 45 years old. Has recently finished a nursing stint entirely on her own in Nijmegen. Appearance also not very good and should not go out during the day. Very cultured.
3. Nurse, 35 years old, plus husband. She has a good appearance, but he does not. He is a composer and reclusive. They pay Fl.120.—at the moment. Want to stay together if at all possible.
4. Girls, 18 and 22 years old. They are sisters and both look safe. The younger one has mild asthma and should not be placed in or near woodland, and has difficulty being alone. The elder is very good with housework and makes a good impression. Nice kids, both of them.
5. Girl, 15 years old, said she looks more like 20. Will see her soon. Fairly safe face. With a bit of guidance will be good for household help. Has a sweet tooth [and] comes from a simple milieu.
6. Young woman, 25 years old. Fairly safe and can come to the door, but cannot run errands. Slight German accent. Piano teacher but has had three years of housekeeping education. On account of her shyness is a little overfriendly, but that will disappear as time goes on.
7. Girl of 21. Has to stay indoors, from a good milieu. Can pay Fl.100.— per month. Willing and able to help with housekeeping. [Formerly] a pupil at the art academy, daughter of a professor. Slight German accent.

8. Tailor's apprentice, 17 years old. Not fully qualified and cannot work at an atelier. Spent two years at a tailoring school and one year at a good tailor's. Can, with guidance, make a suit. A very nice boy. For him, we are looking exclusively for a tailor.
9. Carpenter, 24 years old. For him, the same applies as for No. 8. Can, I think, be turned loose in Limburg.[193] German accent. A fine, stocky fellow who will try anything.
10. Male domestic servant, 24 years old. I only know of him through recommendation. It is said he could run around free.
11. Dutch Reformed domestic servant, 21 years old. Wants to stay in Amsterdam or nearby. Was a ship's carpenter, from a simple background, good impression, willing.
12. Married couple, about 60 years old. Ostensibly able to move around freely. I do not know them personally but they are said to be very nice and cultured. Can pay Fl.400.—per month.
13. Very well-known psychiatrist, 70 years old. Healthy, busy writing a book. I believe can move around freely. Can pay well.
14. Married woman, around 35 years old. Can move around freely. Good for housework.
15. Girl, 15 years old. Household help, lowest class in the gymnasium. Looks well.

We can thus provisionally go ahead [with finding places for them]. Finding addresses is getting increasingly difficult. The people who you can rely on through thick and thin are already overloaded. It gets harder to find people prepared to offer hospitality. [At the same time] good addresses are also lost through betrayal, carelessness or the requisitioning of houses.

January 15, 1944, Saturday

I AM IN Dedemsvaart again and will try to forget as little as possible. I have no notes, and have to rely entirely on Nico's memory and my own. The last time I was here, I was looking for hiding places, but apart from some promises, concrete successes were limited.

I also went to Zanting the farmer who, my sister had told me, had a Dutch airman in hiding at his house. He wants to get to England, and I have taken his name and unit and will see if Post knows how this can be done, or whether he can use him himself. He is good with weapons. I had a good meal with Zanting, bacon and so forth.

I cycled from there to Hoogeveen, where we had a six o'clock meeting with the people from Groningen (Ata and Elly) and Geert Schonewille to discuss the plans for Westerbork. No one came, not even Nico. I waited for the train from Groningen, which was very late.

In the station, I met a man who was a caravan-dweller[194] but that the Germans had confiscated his caravan and left him to find a roof for his wife and six children. He loudly cursed the Germans over and over again, to the point where I warned him to be careful. The Germans have confiscated all the serviceable caravans. That night I went to Nieuwlande and lodged with the Ladies.

The following day Geert Schonewille told me over the phone from Coevorden that the meeting would take place next Friday, same time, same place.

A letter from Schouten in Utrecht with a request to swap the redheaded boy currently placed in Emmen with a black-haired one. He has acquired legal illegal papers for the boy proving conclusively that he is half-Jewish, and the family in Utrecht [who sheltered him previously] would like him back, because he has safe papers. This is a difficult case because the foster parents of the redhead in Emmen do not wish to lose him.

We have no shortage of such difficult cases; they are an everyday occurrence.

Nico has acquired 15 ration cards in Nieuw-Amsterdam.

The woman whom we originally placed with the Hoogeveen family in Nieuwe Krim but who subsequently had a nervous breakdown and was moved to Nieuw-Amsterdam is now seriously ill and needs to be in an institution. I have written about this to Doeks, who has many connections. The woman is suffering from paranoia and the delusion that she is being made to suffer for her sins [*zondewaan*]. The situation is worsened by the fact that the lady of the house also has weak nerves. We don't dare go there anymore because we don't have a solution.

We tried Van der Zwaag, who promised to help. He ordered a car and had the woman taken to Licht en Kracht, an institution in Assen,[195] but they would not take her there—because she was Jewish—so the driver brought her straight back. As a result, Dr. Hovink was cross with us because we had acted without asking him; Van der Zwaag was cross with us because we had not consulted sufficiently; and Van Wieren, the host of the lady in question, was cross with Van der Zwaag because he had been careless on the telephone. Everyone was cross with everyone else, and we got it in the neck everywhere we went.

On Friday, Nico went to Dedemsvaart and I went to Nieuw-Amsterdam, carefully avoiding the house sheltering the mentally ill woman. I had letters for Riek, Suze, Hennie, Tante Aaltje, and Lidia, as well as money for various people. Riek was ill in bed. I had Fl.200.—for her. Her own money has been stolen by the director of a butter factory, four Fl.1000 notes and two of Fl.500. I also had ration cards with me and, on my return, had a whole lot of other letters to deliver.

Suze had to leave her last address because her host fell in love with her.

I had to be in Hoogeveen at the appointed place by 6:00 p.m. It rained and there was a very strong headwind, so I was late. Ata and Elly were there with Nico and Geert. On the table was spread out a map of Camp Westerbork. We discussed everything at length, but the time and place [of the raid] could not be determined because there needed to be further contact with those inside the camp.

Nico had brought a pamphlet to Dedemsvaart to be printed. It contained instructions to the population on what to do in the case of an invasion. One

Nieuwlande in winter. Collection v.d.Sleen.

thousand copies will be produced. He also had a list of all the NSB members in Hoogeveen. The list had come from the NSB itself as its members had been exempted from a tax related to the burning of a government office or some such, as a result a list had been prepared which the local officials had lost no time in copying and circulating. Ata gave us a list of Gestapo agents operating across the whole country, [nearly all Dutch] with photographs.[196] It is far from complete, but we will have 500 copies made. [The list is nearly all men but also some women.]

That night we stayed at Bouwe Zijlstra's haystack, first listening to London and some American music on the radio. Bouwe's son, who had been arrested and held at Amersfoort, had been put on a transport but managed to escape.

On Saturday we went to Pesse and heard that the previous night Gerrit Post's haystack had been set on fire. Arson. I brought Petertje a pair of shoes that were too small for me. He was delighted with them. He is in a very good hiding place, and we do not have to support him as Pesse provides. I gave him Fl.25.—pocket money.

Sunday the weather was filthy. We asked Dr. Brouwer to take us to Dedemsvaart and Nieuw-Amsterdam in his car, but he was too busy with patients. So we went to Kats's (Vondel), ate there, and eventually persuaded him to put his car at our disposal. Nico went to Nieuwlande while I went with Kats to Dr. Brouwer, where we still had 20 liters of gasoline stored. The purpose of the journey was to fetch little "Vs" from textile cards that Mr. Emmens had saved for us. They were necessary in order to get "legal" smokers' ration cards. I didn't get "home" to the Ottens' until 11:30 p.m. [That night] I slept in a bed.

Monday afternoon, January 10, I went to Amsterdam on the 3:00 p.m. train from Hoogeveen. The weather was awful; snow, wind, and rain. Nico went with me to the station and I rode [directly] onto the platform and just jumped on the moving train. Henk Sweepe, the hidden and then not hidden, both fake and real assistant pastor from Nieuwlande was also at the station. I had to stand until Meppel, when a seat became free and I decided that I would not give it up for anything less than a grandmother. No one like that was on the train, so I was in luck, not least because this was a through train to Amsterdam. En route, there was a baggage inspection, but luckily I wasn't carrying anything.

In Amsterdam, I went to Elim, the Salvation Army building in the Singel. Ata has a room there that he can use without registering, which means he doesn't get troubled by the police.[197] There was a man with Ata who had put up Fl.30,000 for the raid on Westerbork. This man, who will play no part in the raid, was very critical. He wanted to know everything, including every detail, but was not very confident about it. I stayed the night in the room with Ata. He told me that he had also run a clandestine meat market from the building but had stopped because it had been too risky and not important enough.

When I had arrived at Amsterdam, there had been a checkpoint at the station exit. I had no desire to be "controlled" and headed for the Wehrmacht exit. I thought I might be stopped there too, but I shouted "Wehrmacht!" on my way through, and it worked.

The following morning I visited Nel and Hennie. Hennie returned with me to Elim as she has some cases she wants out of Westerbork. Ata can help with this. By the time we got there, Geert Schonewille had also arrived. Piet (from Lenie and Piet) has been picked up. Hennie thinks it is contagious. Many planes flew over the city and the air raid warning sounded three times.

In the evening I went to and from Rotterdam to sort out Nico's bicycle. It will be sent to the Stegemans in Dedemsvaart. The trains were packed. In Leiden I pulled six people onto the train through the window; a mother with two kids, two young girls, and a woman of about 65.

I slept at Elim. Next day, I left for De Steeg with a Jewish woman who has three grown-up sons in hiding. There, I met Nico, as we had planned. Ata can place the woman with the nervous breakdown at the Veldwijk Foundation in Ermelo.[198]

According to our list of Gestapo agents, one of them is at Laan 22 in The Hague, where Nico's parents are lodged. I wanted to go there, but Hennie had already been to warn them.

When I arrived in De Steeg, everything was upside down. At the Van Ginhovens there was a tense atmosphere. The people who were going to take the woman I had brought did not want her anymore, because it was far too dangerous (although it did finally happen). An illegal organization has been rounded up in Velp. Betrayal. A series of arrests resulted.

In De Steeg, a six-year-old girl was hauled from her hiding place across the road from the Van Ginhovens. The Van Ginhovens' nephews, the sons of an accountant who had been shot, were also staying with their uncle.[199] We slept the night there. The next day we left, taking two young girls [sisters] with us. They had been hiding in a hole in the woods and in haystacks for some time, but had been betrayed. [That day, there was a gathering of "traitors and other filth" in De Steeg.] In order not to arouse suspicion, we left most of the baggage behind and walked via the back routes to Dieren, where we caught the train for Hoogeveen. In the compartment of the evening train, we shared out sandwiches thick with butter and jam. After Zutphen we had the compartment to ourselves.

In Hoogeveen we went first to Blanken (the taai-taai man), where we were given coffee and biscuits, and then onward by bicycle, with each of us having a girl riding pillion. We were stopped by a policeman at Noordscheschut, but luckily he was only interested in the fact that we were contravening the law about having two people on one bicycle. We got off and walked a few meters and then got on again. We arrived in Nieuwlande long after curfew, I via the Kerkhoflaan and Nico via the main road. One of the girls remained at the Ladies'[200] while I took the other to the Ottens'. Seine and Jan had already gone to bed but, as usual, this was no problem. I think Jo—that is her name—can probably stay with the Ottens. I slept on the couch.

Yesterday I went to visit Albert Neutel and his family in Moscou to tell them that I had found a good place for the 11-year-old girl he had staying there. It was no longer safe for her there because of the talk about her being there and the large numbers of NSBers in the area. I told them that I would arrive unexpectedly to take her away and that she should be kept ready. I ate lovely *kruipertjes*[201] and then traveled on to Dedemsvaart, where the mood was somber. There had been raids, but luckily these had been signaled in advance by the police so that all the onderduikers had been able to disappear. However, there and in other nearby places a number of doctors have been arrested.

The news about the war is good. The Russians are performing miracles.

Near Nieuwlande, four American airmen were shot down. They have all been brought to safe places. In Emmen, there is another airman who has been completely overlooked by the Krauts.

I have received 100 copies of the list of NSB members in Hoogeveen. We have also been given some NSB pins and membership books from a couple of executed traitors.

January 19, 1944, Wednesday

I RECEIVED A letter from Groningen: "Dear John, The snowdrops are lovely, what an early spring? But what about the money? You know that something has to be done with it. Here everything is good. Just send a postal order or transfer. Greetings A."

A letter from Hennie:

I wanted to come, but Jan and Kees have been caught, among others and I cannot leave here. Don't send anything else to my house. Please give me answers to the following questions:

1. Is the aunt, who you call Johanna [indecipherable]? Perhaps she's doing it to be with her husband. Talk with her. If it is simply a case of her being man-mad then as far as I am concerned you can get rid of her. After all, if Jan and Kees are probably dead, there is no reason why such a creature should remain alive.
2. Have you got inlay paper no. 66506. I'd like it back.
3. Herewith the identity card for Mia. Occupation still has to be filled in. 'Evacuated' can be written under her address. Her mother can get a card that fits with this one if need be.
4. Herewith five blank identity cards from [the village of] Avereest. Don't use these for yourself. You can get a good identity card if you send a good photo of a 'black' Dutchman from Avereest. You need to know the precise numbering and issues dates, so be sure to discuss this with the responsible civil servant. Then a number of Avereest identity cards will be printed with a clear example of the signature of the clerk who issues the cards. The best way is to send the stolen photograph of the collaborator with the dates and numbers.
5. An identity for Frits. When he has an Ausweis you have to fill in the number on it. On the left-hand page under the photo his identity card number, signature, and so forth. Profession: Assistant inspector
6. Identity card for Dekker.
7. Letter for Bep [Ursula Zimak].
8. From whom is this idiotic letter full of Yiddish expressions? I don't want to be arrested for it, and I have no idea who to give it to.
9. Letter for Mrs. Hovink.
10. A whole lot of money.
11. Parcels for Hans, Mia, Bobby, Hanny, and Auntie.

All the best.

. . .

Cuijk January 11, 1944

Dear Arnold, Do you have a place for a young Jewish woman? She is the mother of the baby I was going to bring (who is now well looked-after). She is 30 years old, a qualified nurse and very handy and is happy to help with the housework. How long is the damnable war going to go on? Although it has been going well for a long time, we do not seem to get any further. Bep

Dear Arnold,

I got your letter. Sorry to say that Edith cannot come to visit you as she was unexpectedly admitted to a sanatorium. She is well taken care of and there is absolutely no danger, but the visit naturally cannot take place. Here everything is as good as can be expected. J.

Dear A.
We have completed a lot of work recently and with some good results. I know you are very busy, but can you give some thought to the one case for which I have not found a solution, namely, the two elderly acquaintances of my mother whom I spoke to you about recently. You will remember that these two old ladies were thrown out of The Hague and are now quietly boarding in a milieu not that different from the one they came from. They lived with us for a while, but the house was commandeered (more than 180 houses in three days) so they are now homeless again. The elder one is slowly getting to the stage where immediate help will be a necessity (fatigue, constantly crying, insomnia). The other one is also in a bad way, but she is younger and can stand more. Can I bring this case to your attention again, and it would be greatly appreciated if there is anything you can do, as I am at my wit's end.
Best wishes, Schouten

. . .

These notes and letters are a sample of what we have received recently.[202]

Last Saturday I went in the pitch-black to Nieuwlande and spent the night at the Ottens'. On Sunday morning, Nico came to visit and in the afternoon, having already eaten, the two of us went to see Geert Schonewille. We inspected the spot on the heath where the traitor De Kruyff stood [with his binoculars trying to spot onderduikers], while right in front of him was a young Jew in hiding under a pile of heather. He was not found.

From Geert we got clothes and food for onderduikers. Back in the pitch-dark via the by-ways and spent the night at the Ottens'.

Monday via Nieuwe Krim to Nieuw-Amsterdam. We spoke to Tante Louise, Henk, Riek, Tante Aaltje, Suze, Lidia, Annie, and Bobbie.

From Emmens we got 15 ration cards and from an onderduiker, a pair of Marechaussee trousers and a pair of boots that fit Nico.

We went to Nieuw-Amsterdam via Coevorden, where we heard from Geert Schonewille that Ata and Elly had been arrested at Elim on the Friday that we had had plans to go there.[203]

There was a lady at Geert's place who had come from Groningen. She warned us to be very careful.

In Nieuw-Amsterdam we had discussions at the Emmens' about the new German measures, for example the new ration distribution cards and stamps. It is clear that these have been well thought out. I slept at Gorter's[204] and Nico at Suze's.

The following morning we set out in filthy wet weather. We had two non-Jewish[205] onderduikers with us whom we were taking to their destinations. We traveled as a foursome, dropping one of the men at Aasman, the farmer in Nieuw Zwinderen, and the other at a teacher's in Nieuweroord.

I cycled on alone to Pesse. On the way, I visited Annie, who is nine years old and hiding with a teacher. I brought her from [the village of] Elim, where she had also previously been lodged with a teacher, but there had been rumors that she was Jewish and for her own safety she needed to be moved. Now she goes to school, just as she had in Elim.

I visited Heerspink in Zuidwolde, where I delivered ration cards and an identity card. He gave me an address where a revolver could be found. I will pass this on to the boys (Nico and Victor). Also dropped off an identity card in Pesse. Identity cards and ration cards for a farmer in Dedemsvaart and ration cards for Sister Scholten.

Now it is Wednesday morning and I am going to Nieuwlande.

January 28, 1944, Friday

IN DEDEMSVAART AGAIN. In the meantime, I had been to Cuijck and back to see the Jewess who needed a place to hide. She was at a small farm in Vianen, not far from Cuijck but she really could not stay there, on account of the fact that (1) there was no room for her and (2) the danger.

I was in Grave and had been given the address of a single lady [who might accommodate the Jewish woman], but she was not in. Arriving at the address, I saw the Jewish woman and another, unknown to me, coming from the other direction. We reached the front door at exactly the same time completely by accident. The other woman was the wife of a headmaster in Wageningen: Mrs. Plomp. Henceforward I named her Mrs. Nuphar after the botanical name for the plant the Dutch call *plomp*.[206]

She turned out to be looking after the woman's baby, at home in Wageningen. None of us met the woman at whose address we gathered in Grave, but we spent some time talking in the garden. The ladies did not agree with my ideas about security, for example, not allowing contact between brothers in different places, or between mothers and daughters. They thought it cruel.

Large squadrons of German planes flew westward while I was cycling back to Grave, all two-engined bombers.

The following day I went to Zutphen. First to an address given to me by Mrs. Otten, one of her aunts. There I was given all manner of nice things, as well as the loan of a bicycle. Then I went to an address where Mirjam (Marie) had previously been in hiding, a widow with two children. She told me that Marie had escaped in the nick of time because the following morning a troop of Green Police and WA men arrived and turned over everything and searched the whole house. "Where is the Jewess?" they had demanded. One of the WA had sworn: "Damn. Ten liters of fuel wasted and caught nothing." Some of Mirjam's things were still there, and these would be made ready to be collected by friends.

I then cycled to Hengelo to another address given to me by Mrs. Otten. The house was full of people evacuated from The Hague.[207] I spoke to the daughter of the house who worked at a distribution office about the possibility of a raid there. I went to a rest home to find places for onderduikers, but had no luck. The director was far too afraid. Storms and rain on the way back to Zutphen. Collected Mirjam's clothes and returned to Mrs. Otten's aunt, where I spent the night. A dear elderly lady, she has great difficulty coming to terms with present-day life.

To De Steeg early on Sunday morning for an arranged meeting with Nico. The widow of the executed Van Ginhoven was also there.[208] She told us how he had been betrayed and arrested, how he had spent five months in jail after being sentenced to death, how her nine-year-old son went every day to the prison but never got to see his father. On the mantelpiece there was a picture of her husband, taken clandestinely in prison. Next to it were two bullets.

In De Steeg, the locals think Nico and I are Gestapo agents.

In the evening, we traveled through to Wageningen. From Ede station we had to walk. Stayed with the family Van Vloten overnight, where we were, as always, warmly received. We can place five girls—type B.3 in a villa neighborhood known as the Sahara.[209] In Wageningen there was a raid on a football field, and 82 boys were picked up. Why do these [stupid] donkeys go there in the first place? There are also many hundreds of Krauts billeted there, so-called destruction troops. We also heard stories emanating from high-ranking Krauts about the total destruction of Amsterdam, The Hague, and other cities if there was an invasion.

Mrs. van den Bergh, Mrs. van Vloten's mother, has a house full of Jews. One is leaving, so that frees up a place. The Van Vloten's also have someone hiding with them.

Monday, we went to Cuijk. In the evening I made an unsuccessful attempt to find our protégé. Next morning we had more success and agreed to meet at the railway station. We went with her to Wageningen and for her it was a pleasant surprise because her baby is there. We delivered her to Mrs. Leenderts and promised to take care of an identity card.[210]

One of the onderduikers at Mrs. van den Bergh's received a message that his parents had been betrayed and arrested. He is very down.

Wednesday, we went back to Nieuwlande. I bought two cakes on account of my birthday.[211] At the Ottens we had a lovely time. Herman came with his guitar and played many nice songs, including "KK man wat doe je weer raar," one of his own compositions.[212] From Jo I received a bag full of cigarette butts and from Mr. Otten a smoker's [ration] card.

We heard that a Jewish lady had been caught in Hoogeveen. She had been in hiding with the Pennings, the headmaster at Hollandscheveld. She had gone on her own accord to Hoogeveen and been betrayed. Otten thought she had been one of our customers, but that was not so.

[Herman had been under the church with Peter, but both had ended up at the Ottens' after an accident. Only five people knew they were in the crypt, Nico and I, the sexton, the pastor, and Bolwijn the baker's daughter, who brought them food every day.[213] If Herman or Peter wanted anything, they listened for the sexton in the church and then tapped out *V* in Morse. However, one day the sexton was ill and his daughter was doing some superficial cleaning in the church to help out. The onderduikers, thinking it was the sexton, started knocking and the daughter became hysterical and rushed out of the church shouting, "Spooks in the church!" The boys had to get out immediately and went to the Ottens', where they dug themselves a place as deep as they could—limited by the height of the groundwater.]

We stayed overnight in the hiding place at the Ottens'. There were rumors that Green Police were being drafted in to Hoogeveen, but it turned out to be KK men in civilian clothes. They had arrested six young [non-Jewish] men on the market. Some onderduikers never learn.

Nico went to Nieuw-Amsterdam yesterday with a sack full of letters and came back with just as many. He has also found two hiding places. I also have two, for a type A.1 or B.1. In this way, we have four places that are urgently needed. I suspect that Nico is becoming infatuated with Suze in Nieuw-Amsterdam.

Was with "Big" and Mr. Zijlstra.[214] Everything there is under control, but I had to bring news that the identity card for Zijstra's brother-in-law has gone missing. Back in Dedemsvaart, I found a very nice pair of gloves that an acquaintance had knitted for my birthday. I received Fl.10.—for the good cause from my sister Mary and a further Fl.80—that she collected from one of Frits's friends.

The 1,000 copies of the pamphlet showing how to sabotage the new distribution system[215] are ready. Nico's bicycle has now arrived with new tires sent separately. There is also a whole load of ration cards and a stack of letters [to be censored—it is essential we read all the letters as lives may depend on it.] A telephone call from Nieuwlande: Nel is planning to come tomorrow.

A letter from Jan in 's-Hertogenbosch: "Dear Arnold, This afternoon Mrs. Marlijn was here to ask if you could come over to them for a weekend. She has a big job on hand and wants your co-operation."

Here, a nice little ditty:

> Go back, go back, these are our tactics
> Because the Russians follow in wild panic
> We entice leader Stalin to leave his land
> And come to Berlin as he had planned
> But you are fooled, Berlin is no more
> And so we defeat the Russian Bear

We received an address in Almelo where a revolver can be collected. Will pass the information on to the NV.

February 7, 1944, Monday

ARRIVED HERE IN Dedemsvaart yesterday evening with Hannie, a young girl eight years old, whom I took to Sister Scholten.

On Saturday, January 29, we went to Wageningen with Mirjam on the 6:00 p.m. train from Hoogeveen. It was an uneventful journey, and we were able to sit. In Ede there was no bus to Wageningen, but we were able to find a taxi.[216] We sat in the back of taxi but were stopped by two Green Police accompanied by a young boy in a Hitler Youth uniform.[217] The driver put on the interior light. I tried to position my arm so that it obscured Mirjam's face [while Nico did his usual trick with the handkerchief]. Naturally we were extremely stressed, but it transpired that these men were only interested in going to Wageningen.

The question then was how they would all be fitted in until Mirjam said, "The youngster can sit on my lap." And so it transpired that we rode with two Green Police men and a Hitler Youth all the way to Wageningen.

We took Mirjam to Mrs. van den Bergh's, where I also slept, while Nico went to the Van Vlotens. Mrs. Leendert came over to talk about her "domestic servant." Relations are very good, and she has never had such great help.

On Sunday I went to Amsterdam and tried to get hold of Lenie, but I failed. I went to her parents in Oegstgeest, but she was not there either. I was sent to another address and from there to another address on the other side of Leiden, which turned out to be nonexistent. I was furious and went back to Amsterdam. Various addresses are now ready. In the evening, Nico arrived with the identity cards that we needed in Amsterdam.

The following day to Utrecht to visit a friend of Frits who works at the chamber of commerce and has collected money for us. From Utrecht to Hilversum to try and place children in an orphanage. This address I was given in De Steeg. No luck. In Hilversum, I collected letters and money at the Favorite Perfumery. To Naarden, where someone was at his wit's end with a "bakery assistant." Back to Amsterdam, arriving at the Winkel family's very late at night.

The same day, Nico went with Hennie to The Hague. The previous evening we had a lovely reunion between Nico and his sister, who is in hiding with one of Hennie's sisters in the Michelangelostraat. We had not told either Nico or her, so it came as a complete surprise.

The story about the Gestapo agent at Laan 22 in The Hague is untrue. The people arrested in the Tasmanstraat are all back, except for the Jewish onderduikers. At Laan 22, there are 15 Jewish onderduikers. Nico and Hennie stayed there overnight. Nico slept on the floor, but it was too cold to sleep and thus he paced up and down the room, smoking his pipe.

In the afternoon, Nico, Hennie, and I left for Arnhem. She needed to be in Arnhem and we in Elst. In the train we sang all sorts of songs from songbooks that I had brought for Herman from Amsterdam.

In Elst there is a plan in the offing to raid the distribution office, but I didn't think much of it; it seems like a reckless adventure to me. [This was not our sort of work. We did not work with firearms.]²¹⁸

We went back to Arnhem, took the tram to Velp, and then walked to De Steeg. Nico's shoes were too small and mine had too many nails sticking out. It was rainy and stormy, and we grumbled a lot.

The following morning to Wageningen with a suitcase of clothes for Mirjam. She complained to us that she could not stand living at the Van den Bergh's and recounted all sorts of things about the everyday routine in the house. I begged her in the nicest possible way to exercise some patience.

In the evening I went to Amsterdam as planned. I had a meeting with Mrs. de Bruin and agreed to meet at the Central Station at 6:00 p.m., when she would bring a boy of 15 and a girl of 17.

In Amsterdam, I had a nice [and unexpected] meeting. I was walking down the Zuider Amstellaan when there was a hand on my shoulder. It was Johannes Post. He was doing well, and we agreed to meet in an hour's time. I told Nico who I had seen. Post came at the agreed time and the three of us sat and talked. Post gave me Fl.2,000 and promised some gasoline coupons as well. He asked us about all manner of things and told us that he had executed a guy from the SD or some such.

At a certain address where a Jewish girl was hidden, two "gentlemen" came to fetch her. "Someone you know," said Post, asking one of the two, "You are Mr. So and So, and you have come to fetch the little girl, is that correct?" "Yes" was the answer and at the same moment he was shot and killed. The other one got away because the revolver misfired.²¹⁹

Johannes seemed to be busy with surprise raids and so on. We promised him a first-class revolver and the NSB membership lists, and Nico gave him an NSB pin. Post also told us, "There are people who do not appreciate the work that you two are doing, but don't take any notice. This happens to me too."

At the Winkel home, there is a Jew with his wife and daughter. This man has escaped in the nick of time on a number of occasions, once through bribery.

To Hoogeveen on the evening train with my two protégés. I was famished and a lady sitting opposite me gave me a cheese sandwich. Wonderful. We traveled in second class with second-class tickets. After Zwolle we had a compartment to ourselves with the cheese lady. We sat reading things out of the *Wervelwind*. At Hoogeveen, the Green Police were on the station, so we got out of the train on the wrong side and walked next to the track for the 200 meters to the level crossing. The signalman saw us but said nothing.

At the taai-taai man's and greeted as always with coffee and huge slices of cake. We pumped up our bicycle tires and each with a pillion passenger we went on the road. Nico went with the boy to Headmaster Wiegman (Big), and I brought the girl to Seine Otten. The family was already in bed, but I rousted them out. We got bread and coffee from Jo and then went to sleep. The following day I took the child, who is slightly crippled and also homesick, to the Padding family.

Nico had taken the boy to Kikkert temporarily (and not to Wiegman), but we collected him from there yesterday and took him to [Roelof] Bisschop, the father of Miesje, Johannes Post's domestic servant. Bisschop lives on a small farm in a tiny house on the cycle path to Elim so it is inaccessible by car. There is also plenty of woodland to get lost in, so it is an ideal hiding place.

I went to Neutel and collected the eight-year-old girl and took her to Dedemsvaart. I had arrived late and the girl was already sleeping. Later she slept on the back of my bike.

Otten told me that a farmer in Nieuw Zwinderen had warned him about me, saying that I had been reported in *Trouw* as a Gestapo agent. At present I am in Dedemsvaart, writing, while Nico is on the couch resting.

We have been given a map of the airfield at Teuge by Broenink that marks the spot where 1,000 aircraft engines are stored. We will try to find someone who can get this information to the Allies.[220]

February 21, 1944, Monday

IT IS ALREADY two weeks since I last wrote. Who knows where the time goes?

On Monday 7th, Nico and I went to Hollandscheveld. On the way over we had problems. The bracket that held my bicycle light broke and the light caught in the spokes and got jammed in the forks. Catastrophe: a wrecked front wheel and front forks. I stopped dead and Nico, not expecting anything, collided with me and broke his bracket as well. We made our way through the pouring rain to Zijlstra, who promised to get my bike fixed. Wiegman loaned me a bicycle to get to Hoogeveen, where we left them with the taai-taai man and took the train to Wageningen.

We were also in Arnhem, Elst, and De Steeg. Why we had to be there, I forget. Oh yes, in De Steeg we collected Jo's luggage, a huge suitcase. We were also going to move a small girl from there, but this was no longer necessary. Later I went to Amsterdam. Oh, yes, and Nico had acquired a beautiful revolver with a load of ammunition in Arnhem, which we reserved for Johannes Post.

From Wageningen, I took a Jewess to Kitty, Hennie's sister, but that was a mistake as she [the Jewess] was too well-known in Amsterdam. We slept at the Winkels', I on two chairs and Willy (as we called her) on the floor. I was assured in Wageningen that she was a first-class housekeeper. Hennie doesn't sleep at her house anymore because there are so many onderduikers there is no room for her.

I am puzzled because I have lost a bundle of letters from onderduikers and the map of Teuge airfield. I assume someone must have robbed me on the train.

On the train, I met Baanders, who was a fellow student at the horticultural school. I hadn't seen him for years. We agreed to meet in Nijmegen the following Saturday to have, according to him, a fruitful exchange of views.

Next day I left Amsterdam with Willy (now christened "De Bijenkorf"[221]— as she had been employed there). I also had two little boys of nine and seven, brothers, in tow. One of the boys had to walk with a leg brace as a result of polio. De Bijenkorf acted very stupidly in the train—she sat fiddling with a torch and shined it into the face of a policeman sitting opposite us in the carriage. Arriving at Hoogeveen station I had to carry the lame boy on my back and the suitcases in my hands. De Bijenkorf offered no assistance whatsoever, save to ask if we were nearly there.

"Yes," I said, "only another 12 kilometers to cycle."

"If I had known that, I wouldn't have come."

"Thank you," I said.

We arrived at Blanken the baker's and met Nico there. He had telephoned Amsterdam and had been told by Mrs. Winkel that I was on my way with a single packet. For that reason he had thought that I would not need his help at the station. We received, as always, coffee and cake, borrowed a bicycle from the taai-taai man and set off on our way. Nico went with one of the lads on the back and I was to follow with the other one and De Bijenkorf. It was already late. De Bijenkorf could not ride a bike. She tried several times but always fell off. I took the bicycle back and handed the young lad over to the taai-taai man, where he could spend the night.

I tried to get the girl onto the back of my bicycle, but she could not climb on top of her suitcase that I had so carefully tied onto the carrier so I took it off again and left it with the taai-taai man. After many fruitless attempts, I finally got her onto the carrier and cycled to Kikkert, where luckily she can stay for the time being. On the way, I heard Nico's well-known whistle. He had brought the boy to Anne, on the Krakeelse Wijk, and his brother will be welcome there too. I spent the night in the hay at Kikkert's, Nico stayed with Big. I don't know much more about the following days except that we were busy with all sorts of small tasks.

There have been many raids on distribution offices all over the country.

A couple of days later we took De Bijenkorf to Zweeloo. First we walked her to the Ottens' (Beaver) and then with a car from Coevorden, took her the rest of the way. There, Mr. De Jong [a headmaster] had asked for a good housekeeper. From Kikkert and his wife I had learned that this woman could really do nothing, absolutely nothing. She couldn't wash a single cup, could not shine a shoe nor wash a window. With a heavy heart I set off, accompanied by Seine Otten.

I was very short of time because I had to be back at the railway station at Hoogeveen by 9:00 a.m. because Hennie was arriving with a "transport." For that reason, I wrote down everything I wanted to say about this "housekeeper." For example, that she would find it difficult to begin with in a strange environment, that the housewife would need to have some patience with her, that the girl was undoubtedly willing and that I would drop by in a couple of weeks to see how things were going and with a bit of give and take . . . and so on and so on. Short and sweet.

However, when we got there, we had the wind taken out of our sails. The housewife said that it was a mistake and she no longer needed a housekeeper as her mother-in-law had come to stay and could help out. She therefore had no room for anyone else.

I said, "Listen to me Mrs. de Jong, we will talk about all these things later, but right now I have no time as I have to meet the 9:00 a.m. train at Hoogeveen. I have written down everything I wanted to say about this lady because I have no time to talk now." Mrs. de Jong protested. I said, "Look here, one thing is certain, I am not taking this lady back with me, and that is final."

Finally, she was allowed to stay on the understanding that I would return soon. Of course I would do that.

Seine Otten sighed as we made the return journey in the rear seats of the car. "That was one hell of a stunt, and when do you intend to return?" "That's something I don't want to think about right now," I replied.

In Hoogeveen there was a message that Hennie would actually arrive the following day, at the same time and place. The next day she was there, with Lia and Tineke's mother. Hennie went back with the next train, accompanied by a girl who was abnormal and whom we had not been able to do anything with. She was adamant that she wanted to go to Amsterdam.

If we had hung on to this child, we would have had to shoot her or find some other way of ending her life. She was a danger to herself and to others. Hysterical, incapable of reason, subject to visions and generally making a fool of herself—a pathetic and, for us, a troublesome case. Hennie intended to place her in an institution for the mentally ill, or in the last resort, give her an injection. The girl went willingly, blissfully happy that she was going to Amsterdam, where, she thought, she would find heaven on earth.

We took the mother of the two girls to Pencil (Faber the baker) and in the evening to the Ladies'. She was completely unaware how close she was to her children there. We also received a non-Jewish man from Amsterdam who had been tortured by the Krauts but had been freed from the hospital where he was under guard.

I received a smart black suit from Geert Schonewille (for myself).

Have heard nothing from Ata or Elly since their arrest in Amsterdam. In Groningen, nothing is known about what has happened to them. Our Westerbork plans are a shambles.

The provision of ration cards is very unreliable, and it is a real problem securing enough of them each month.

February 22, 1943, Tuesday

HERE BELOW ARE a few recent letters:

> Dear Arnold,
> A black Hollander is an identity card issued in 1943, which has the word Nederlander printed in black. The numbers begin at a certain point at a

certain date and then reach a certain number as of now. I will need the numbers and dates to give for a specific municipality. At the moment, this will take time.

If I have to get an identity card for "Tante Loes," I need all her real details and I'll just change de Raay to de Raaf.

You need to tell "Tante Ammi" that she must not write such stupid Yiddish letters. I don't want to take the risks for them.

The reason why little "Peter's" letters have not arrived is probably because his guardian angel has gone underground.

Keep smiling,[222]
H

Wageningen, February 21, '44[223]
Dear Mr. Roffel,
We are waiting for you expectantly. May it be soon, please? Mrs. C also desperately hopes it won't be long.
Best wishes,
Mrs. M. J.

Dear Janus,
Here in Jubbega there is someone with a canary, the normal sort that many people round here have in cages. He has no seed for it. Do you know a suitable supplier?[224]

Do come over if you have time; it's ages since I heard anything from you.
G.

This is the text of the leaflets printed for us in Dedemsvaart.

Pass On   Pass On

Tricks with *Stamkaarten*

You are already aware that the Krauts intend to issue new *Stamkaarten* soon. This is not just to replace the old *Stamkaarten* but to

1. Make it more difficult to go underground
2. Create a new administration that will be used to extend the system of forced labor[225]

Soon every citizen will receive a green application card (*oproepingskaart*) in order to obtain a second *Stamkaart*. You need to fill in this form and it is of vital importance that you do so as carelessly and badly as possible. Here below are a few guidelines:

1. Make sure the card gets dirty
   a. Let it fall in a puddle
   b. Make grease spots on it
   c. Use a pen with a hair in it
   d. Blot what is written
2. Fold the card

3. Make mistakes in everything
4. Do not write in block capitals
5. Do not go along at the appointed time
6. Forget to take your old Stamkaart along; lose it or allow it to be stolen
7. Sign the card at home and make the signature different from the one on your identity card.

This way everything will go haywire and the treacherous purpose of the Krauts will fail.

KNOW YOUR DUTY   WE COUNT ON YOU

Another letter:

Dear Arnold,
You were going to send me a reproduction of that Femma-Cactus, but this is no longer necessary because we got it from someone else.
Best wishes,
M. L.

Yesterday, I could not find my hidden tin in the garden. I was worried that it had been discovered but a hiding place had been dug nearby and everything was OK. Yesterday, large swarms of flying fortresses protected by fighters, leaving condensation trials in the sky. Krauts were regularly shot down, and we saw four tumbling out of the sky.

On Sunday, the KK surrounded all the churches in Dedemsvaart and carried out searches. A number of onderduikers were caught but most were able to escape. They searched inside the organs and the towers, behind pillars and window recesses, and in the altar of the Roman Catholic church. There was also a raid in the village. One onderduiker was caught in his house, but was able to escape over the roof. Frits and Jannes were not in the church.

Yesterday, it is rumored, there was a lot of shooting and bombing at Coevorden. A potato flour and cardboard factory was involved. There were eight dead.[226]

On Saturday, Nico and I went to Nijmegen and Venlo. As arranged, we met Wim Nolet, Bram Slikker, and Baanders [all three alumni of the Boskoop Agricultural College].[227] The previous night, these gentlemen had set fire to the population registry in Venlo and, according to Slikker, only the X IJ and Z remained intact, but the fire brigade had done such a good job that these were also rendered illegible.

The following morning we left early, long before sunrise, via a back door, through the garden and over a fence as the owners said that the house was being watched.

I broke my journey in Cuijk, where my brother-in-law is a pastor while Nico broke his journey in Arnhem. I was just in time to listen to the church service—held in the parlor of the parsonage because of the lack of coal.

My sister [Al]ber[ta] told me wonderful stories about the local NSB mayor, who walks around the town in his monkey suit trying to sell copies of *Volk en Vaderland* and generally makes a nuisance of himself.[228] The civil servants in the town hall dislike him intensely and are continually on the warpath; one by one they are resigning.

A young boy who works as a cleaner but is reputed to be not all there often arrived late for work and was reprimanded by the mayor. "Well man," he replied, "Stay calm, I'll come when I'm ready but not before."

"Don't be rude," blustered his excellency, "You are speaking to the mayor."

"So what?" said the boy, "If I join the party, I'll be mayor within 14 days."

On another occasion the mayor said that the boy was crazy. "That is perfectly possible," said the boy. "But you are crazier still because before too long you are going to be hanged."

Yesterday I got a package of clothes and toys for the eight-year-old girl we had taken to Dedemsvaart.

In Hoogeveen, a house where Nico sometimes sleeps was raided by the Green Police. He had been there the night before.

In Dedemsvaart, a pile of letters was waiting for me. One of them was from that Mrs. D from Wageningen. She wants a revolver to kill her husband. She is becoming a nuisance and dangerous.

Baker Blanken had received some documents from a woman unknown to him that related to a Jewish boy who, according to the documents, is actually half-Jewish and therefore "legal." We don't trust this 100 percent.

Sunday night we ate with the Pencil (baker Faber) and had delicious "three in a pan."[229]

In Hoogeveen, all the men in the Bentincklaan, Van Echtenstraat, and Alteveerstraat were told that they had to undertake 14 days of work on the airfield at Havelte. Of the 250 called up, six went. Then the mayor was taken hostage and they all went.

When Hennie was in Hoogeveen the other day, she slept one night in the hospital. In the morning, she was weighed, declared in good health, and discharged.

Nico asked me what the difference was between a pig's tail and the death of a Kraut. Answer: nothing, as they were both the end of a swine.

I need to get my teeth seen to. They are going to the dogs.

Collected a list of onderduikers who need ration cards from Sister Scholten (no addresses). I'll also ask for a similar list from Mr. de Jong of "Avondlicht" ["evening light," an old people's home but where some Jews were also hiding].[230] This is to avoid anyone getting two cards.

February 22, 1944, Tuesday Evening

THIS AFTERNOON I went round with some parcels. At Loekie's, Nico was also there. While I was there, she said to me: "Uncle Arnold, I shed a few tears today, as it was my mother's birthday." I also visited Piet in Pesse, Bisschop on the Elim Path, and Kikkert as well. In the evening, I returned to Bisschop with a young boy.

Some bombs fell on the Zwindersche Canal. Nico was in the vicinity but took cover in a ditch until it was all over.

February 23, 1944, Wednesday Evening

TODAY I VISITED the Ladies (the Nieuwboer sisters) with packets sent from Amsterdam for Lia and Tineke. I wanted to show them to their mother first, who is hiding with the Ladies, although she has no idea that her children are nearby, at Headmaster Griffioen's house.

Went to De Krim to pay board money to the Hoogeveens. At Scholten's I tried once again to get someone placed. Cycled on to Stieltjeskanaal, where I found a place for Mia and her mother. I got this address from Hilly Bolwijn,[231] the daughter of Bolwijn the baker in Nieuwlande.

On to Nieuw-Amsterdam with letters and then back via Coevorden where I received word that there would be a "delivery" at Hoogeveen station that same evening, but not fit enough to travel by bicycle. We therefore had to find a car. Finally, we got hold of a doctor's car and our bicycles were left in Coevorden.

On the way, we visited our petrol dump, but we had little left, and it was mixed with water so the driver was unwilling to use it. He hoped to be able to get to Hoogeveen on wood alcohol, but he ran out close to Hoogeveen and had to switch to petrol. For the return journey he borrowed some petrol from a local garage.

Hennie alighted from the train with just one young man, whom we could have fetched much more easily with the bicycles. I was in a bad mood. Lots of trouble and expense—and all for nothing. The young man was a German Jew who had escaped from Westerbork. Nico remained in Hoogeveen and I went with the newcomer to Coevorden by car. I negotiated a bed for the night at Geert Schonewille, and our client was accommodated in Coevorden.

February 24, 1944, Thursday

WENT WITH GEERT Schonewille in his car to Coevorden, where we looked first at the bomb damage. Two factories gone—direct hits—both chimneys still standing, but damaged.

I left Coevorden with our German Jew riding Nico's bicycle and went to Kikkert where he can stay for a week. Not longer, as they would prefer a younger person whom Mrs. Kikkert would be better able to control. I promised the Kikkerts a child's bedstead as they already had a small Jewish boy in the house, whom we call "Hoedag" as that is the way he greets us.

Herman, who is now almost permanently at Seine and Jans Otten's (Beavers), gave me a hand fetching a child's bed from a farmhouse at 't Kanaaltje to the Kikkerts.

The Beaver has made a hiding place at the bottom of the garden using straw bales and earth.

A decree has been issued by "six and a quarter" (Reichskommissar Seyss-Inquart)[232] that anyone caught falsifying identity cards will be executed.

February 25, 1944, Friday

MR. GRIFFIOEN PESTERS me every day as he wants to be rid of the two girls because they are too much work for his wife who is, according to him, sick. Lia was visiting the Ottens. I spent a few minutes at the Ladies and in the afternoon, I went to Zweeloo and to Mr. Jonker, where I had left de Bijenkorf [the woman who could not wash dishes or do any other housework]. I went with a heavy heart. First, there was hell to pay, but later things calmed down and she could stay. Thank goodness!

I visited a smith in Zweeloo, looking for a place for a smith to hide.[233] He said he would let me know, which almost invariably means nothing doing.

I went back by bicycle and managed to get a tram from Oosterhesselen to Hoogeveen for a prearranged meeting with Nico.

Hennie got off the train with six people.[234] I went with Kats, whom I had asked to come to the station with his car, with a couple to Nieuwlande. Nico took the others to Blanken the baker's and other addresses in Hoogeveen. The couple are the parents of Hans, who is currently lodged with Bisschop. Nice people with a sense of humor. They have no luggage, the result of a couple of hasty escapes. "Makes things so much easier," said the wife. "Now we don't have anything to carry."

I went from house to house trying to find a place for them. First to Jantje Dekker: They could not accommodate anyone as their radio had been discovered and they had farmed out all their bedding, as the punishment for having an illicit radio is the confiscation of all furniture.

Then to a couple of others who were still up, but no one wanted to take them, even for one night.

Mr. Eppinga, the evangelist, tried to palm me off with all sorts of difficulties and excuses.[235] He also reproached me because a boy I had placed with him and agreed to collect after a few days had now been with him for a month. Finally, after a long argument with him I left saying that I was deeply disappointed in him and was going to get help from Mr. Otten, where anything could be done.

They were not yet in bed and Mrs. Otten asked me why I had not come directly to them, "You know of course, that it is always OK and that you can count on us."

Jo made something for the newcomers to eat, and we sat talking before going to bed. Mattresses and blankets were juggled until everyone had a place to sleep. I slept well on the kitchen floor with two tablecloths as blankets. Peter and Herman are also now staying at the Ottens'.

February 26, 1944, Saturday

UP EARLY AND cycled to Hoogeveen on Otten's bike. My first task was to find Nico. He was not at the Pencil's nor with the taai-taai man. Nico and Hennie had spent the night at the Bentincklaan, where they had watched an entire film. "Tante Koos" had insisted that they all slept in one bed, but Hennie eventually slept at the neighbors across the road.

At the taai-taai man's we discussed both children and adults with Hennie before she left on the 9:03 a.m. train. Then we had to deal with the four onderduikers who still needed permanent addresses. Two had spent the night at the taai-taai man's. We telephoned Koekange and found a place for one of the men. He was from Zeeland and made his way there during the day.

There were 19 of us for breakfast at the taai-taai man's table, plus five children sat in the corner with plates on their laps. Johannes Post had also intended to come to Hoogeveen but did not show up. The taai-taai man was worried about him; we all were.

We promoted one of our onderduikers to baker, as at some time in his life he had learned to bake sweet rolls, and took him to Bolwijn. Nico took the other two to a couple of farmhouses in Elim. He left Hoogeveen long before me, but when he had not returned by 6:00 p.m., I got worried and telephoned everywhere. He had vanished without trace, leaving me wondering if he had been picked up.

At 8:00 p.m., thank goodness, he resurfaced. Trouble with the bike and later in finding addresses. He had to use all his abilities and talents to offload the two onderduikers properly. The German Jew we had left with Kikkert we have now collected and taken to Padding, a good address.[236]

Later in the evening we took the couple from the Ottens' whom we had christened "Tante Marie" and the "Lifeguard" to the Nienhuis family, who had a farm well off the beaten track. Seine Otten and I had been there before to try and soften them up. "No, they couldn't take anyone," they said. "Far too much work for the womenfolk and far too dangerous." We had drawn attention to the motto above their door: "Believe in God and always build well." That evening we got nowhere, but on another occasion Nico and I got a half promise to take one person. But now we were bringing a couple, and Nico and I had agreed beforehand that we would not take no for an answer.

When we arrived, we told the Lifeguard and Tante Marie to wait outside on the pretext of making sure that everything was safe. Nico and I went in where we found the whole family in the kitchen gathered around the stove. We were greeted very heartily until we told them that there was a couple outside waiting to be invited in, at which point the expressions changed on their faces as if by magic. Every possible difficulty was raised. The same song, but sung in a different way. Eventually it boiled down to us having to take the couple back with us, but where to?

They could not go back to the Ottens' because they were full. "The Ottens are full to the rafters." (We could say this because it was a well-known secret that the Beavers had Jews in their house.) Moreover, it is now so late that we can't go back there as everyone will be asleep.

Eventually, eventually they were allowed to stay . . . but only for one night. This we contrived to make 14 days. The family would receive Fl.100 for board and lodging from the couple. The couple, who had by that stage been invited in, heard the debate, and the woman did nothing but cry.[237]

[Back at the Ottens'] Nico slept with Herman and Peter in the hiding place under the floorboards, and I slept in the hiding place in the attic.

February 27, 1944, Sunday

UP EARLY AND did the household chores together: vacuum cleaning, fetching water, washing plates, laying the fire and the kitchen stove and so forth. Nico, Herman, and Peter had not slept well in the hiding place as it was cold there. At 2:30 a.m. sleepy-headed Nico had given a performance. Mrs. Nienhuis came with a bottle of milk (she was on her way to church). I saw that as a good sign. Luckily, she saw the table set for lots of people [so giving weight] to my occasional references to the Ottens' being full to the rafters with onderduikers.

For the remainder of the day we rested, played games and went to church.

*[Inauguration of a new pastor in Nieuwlande.[238] A rumor went through the village that Johannes Post was in the church. We were behind him and Mr. Otten. Nico and I met him at Bouwe Zijlstra's. Johannes prayed at the table that we would have the strength to continue our work and that we would be spared from death. We spent a long time talking and listened to the news together.

Sister Zijlstra has gone to Wageningen to fetch a patient with heart trouble.]

[Entries marked * appeared later in the original Dutch diary as recollections but have been restored to their chronological position. —translator]

February 28, 1944, Monday

WE WENT TOGETHER to Nienhuis and spent five hours talking and finally arranged for the couple to stay for good. We would pay Fl.100 per month per person and the couple would have their own room. Now we have to try to find some clothes for them.

*[In the evening, we were again at Bouwe Zijlstra's where we saw Post again. He gave us Fl.2,000 and rations stamps.

We traveled on to Hoogeveen to collect a woman and her daughter. Hennie was there with the luggage for another onderduiker.

Spent the night at the taai-taai man's. Nico and I drew lots as it was a single bed. I won. Nico slept on the floor in the front room. Early in the morning, little Roelie came downstairs, saw Nico on the floor and shouted, "Mama, Uncle Nicolo!"]

February 29, 1944, Tuesday

*[WE WENT TO see the heart patient in the hospital, he was very nervous.][239]

Then to visit Vondel and discussed the onderduiker who had to leave because he had molested the daughter of the house. It was agreed that he would meet us at a certain place and go with us to Dedemsvaart.

I had been to Zweeloo with baggage for de Bijenkorf, and then to Jopie in Emmen with paperwork that would legalize him. He is now a half-Jew. On to Nieuw-Amsterdam and did the rounds there. Slept at Van Ekelenburg's and away again early in the morning.

March 2, 1944, Thursday

I BROUGHT TANTE Loes's daughter Mia to Wageningen. She couldn't stand where she was any more. She was at Bolwijn the baker's. From Ede we had to walk to Wageningen, no more buses, no more taxis. Very bad weather and we carried a very heavy suitcase. I left it with an acquaintance at Bennekom (which is about half way). First I dropped off Mia and then went to the Van Vlotens'.

Next morning, I went to a family in the vicinity to talk about an onderduiker, and after that to Mia. I found her in tears and suffering from homesickness. I tried to comfort her a little.

Then to Marie/Mirjam. Same story, different tone. She was also at the end of her tether. I asked her to hold on as there were no other places available.

I also went to Femme, where everything was fine.

At the Plomp family (Nuphar) I heard about a man, his wife and their daughter who needed to go underground urgently. I told them to send these people to us.

From Wageningen, I went to Cuijk via Nijmegen. Nijmegen has suffered a great deal of damage, around the station there were two hotels full of Krauts that suffered direct hits and were completely destroyed. Many German officers[240] killed. A waiting room at the station flattened. A diesel train was hit by falling overhead cables and all those inside were killed.[241]

My brother-in-law was in Nijmegen during the bombardment and barely escaped. If he had not been delayed by a colleague, he would have been on that train. A horse was killed by shrapnel near him and houses collapsed. He was injured in the hand by a grenade fragment. I spent the night in Cuijk.

March 4, 1944, Saturday

MY SISTER BER told me a dreadful story about a boy of eight who had said, "Mof" (to a German). His father was called to account and given the choice of being sent to Vught Concentration Camp himself or having the boy whipped. He chose the latter and brought in the boy, where he saw his son beaten to death before his eyes.

From Cuijk I traveled back to Hoogeveen. The trains were incredibly full. A policeman from Nijmegen on the train spoke of how many dead Krauts he had pulled from the rubble. There was a troop of Landwachters on the train.

In Hoogeveen, I found Nel on the platform with a large suitcase. We went to the taai-taai man where we had coffee and cake and we borrowed a bike for Nel. Nico was also there. We went to Nieuwlande where Nel stayed with the Ladies. The suitcase had things for Lientje and Liesje and for two brothers.

All the way along the line there were yellow and blue flags indicating a danger of air attacks. In Nijmegen, the sirens were sounding, which means it was safe there as the sirens only ever sounded after the danger had passed.

At the Beavers' there was an urgent message for us about six people who were hiding in the heath near Zuidwolde and needed help immediately.

March 5, 1944, Sunday Evening

THIS MORNING WE had a talk with Haspers, a farmer who went with us to one of his laborer's houses in a very lonely spot. We agreed that the six people out in the open on the heath can stay there for Fl.20 per day. It will be very primitive as there are no beds, only straw and two blankets. The family consists of a man, his wife, and a baby. The place looks filthy, but the people seem to be very friendly, especially the baby.

In the afternoon, we fetched Nel, who was still at the Ladies', and we had a nice afternoon at the Beavers'. Herman played the guitar and sang songs. Peter and Herman performed an opera that they had created while they were under the church. It related, of course, to present-day circumstances. It got great acclaim.

An onderduiker came looking for Snorretje (Van der Zwaag). We took him there and then took Nel to Hoogeveen to Bouwe Zijlstra's. Here we discussed the people on the heath. One (type B.3) already had a place to go so that left five. It was agreed that they would be fetched in Kats's car and taken to Griffioen's school.

Of course, we took them to the Ottens' first, where they could warm up. Kats had to make two journeys because of all their luggage. They consisted of the Cohens, a married couple from Hoogeveen—he was typically Jewish and could not be seen out during the day; a brother and sister of around 55; and a man of around 50 whose wife was in New York. After an hour at the Ottens' we were on the move. The very poor worker's house looked far nicer than it had in the morning, and we finished everything about 12:30 a.m.

Nico still had to find a place to sleep for himself that night. I said that he had to come with me to the Ottens' but he refused, knowing that it was already overfull there.

March 6, 1944, Monday Evening

WE GOT TO work early this morning, looking for places for our five newcomers in the straw. They cannot stay there, far too cold and too primitive. In Nieuwe Krim we were in luck. The Hoogeveen family, where Tante Loes is staying, can accommodate the brother and sister, and their neighbor Hartemink can find room for the single man. The Cohens can stay where they are for the time being.

While at Nieuwe Krim, we talked to the headmaster, Mr. Scholten, about Bobby, the six-year-old son of "Tante Anny," who is with his mother next door at the Hoogeveens. We want him to go to school and decided in advance that if Mr. Scholten refused, we would tell him exactly what we thought of him. He agreed.

Scholten told us that his doorbell had rung in the middle of the night, and he, in a panic, had burned in the stove whatever might have been considered contraband, including an issue of *De Duikelaar*. I told him that I thought it scandalous and that he had no right to destroy such a thing! When he finally opened the door after some insistent ringing it turned out to be two men on the doorstep wanting to phone the doctor to attend the birth of a child.

When we were in Nieuwe Krim, we saw masses of American planes fly over in formation. A dogfight started with heavy shooting. Everyone took cover. Suddenly we saw a German fighter coming down.[242] An enormous fountain of mud sprang up as it hit the ground, around 400 meters from us. Just as we were about to head in that direction, we saw a pair of legs appear out of the clouds. Above the legs was a man, and above the man a parachute. We asked several people the quickest way to where he had landed. Nobody wanted to tell us but eventually we found the parachute and a little farther on the pilot—an American. He was already surrounded by a group of people but none of them spoke English. I greeted him and suggested that we needed to leave immediately.

"Yes, I want to get out of here," he replied.

I assured him that it would be fine. Firstly, I asked the bystanders to disperse, which they promptly did. Then we took Roberts—that was his name—to a shed where we disposed of his uniform and hid his helmet, goggles, boots, and gloves under a pile of potato leaves. We acquired a pair of clogs and a pair of overalls (that Nico got from Van der Vinne the farmer) and left the area as quickly as possible as he had sprained his ankle on landing. With Roberts on Nico's bike and he on the pannier of mine, we rode to Otten's. There we borrowed a third bicycle and rode into the woods, where we had a hiding place (*hol*) for emergencies. Unfortunately, there were too many people in the area, so we went to Bouwe Zijstra. On the way, we passed a Kraut motorcycle and sidecar out looking for parachutists.

At Zijlstra's we put our friend into the hay hole—a brilliant hiding place—and sprinkled pepper in and around the farm to put off bloodhounds. It was Bouwe's birthday, so there were all sorts of good things in the house, *oliebollen*, cake, etc.

Roberts told us that they had been to Berlin and were shot down on the way home. His plane was a Liberator with a crew of eleven who had all bailed out. I also went looking for his comrades but didn't find them. Two of them, I soon found out, had been taken in by Dr. Brouwer but had later been arrested by the Krauts.

I went to see Kats, who asked me how it had gone with the American. I was flabbergasted that he knew about it. In fact, the man who had shown us the way when we carried out the raid on the ration card distribution office had seen the whole operation. Kats promised his complete cooperation with his car if we ever needed it.

In the evening at the Ottens' I was told to "sit down and tell us all about it." They already knew everything and all sorts of stories were doing the rounds.

March 7, 1944, Tuesday Evening

NICO STOOD GUARD over Roberts last night. Peter and Herman had been busy until five in the morning to make a drawing for him. He had given me a photograph, and Herman had used this to make the drawing. Mrs. Otten made a poem to go with it, which I then translated. Peter then wrote the poem and the translation on the back of the drawing bordered by a Dutch and an American flag. We searched all through Nieuwlande to find a copy of an American flag because we could not remember if the top stripe was red or white.

I received a message from Griffioen: when was I finally going to collect the children from him? His wife was sick and was lying in bed groaning. I sent a reply that everything was fine and that the girls would be taken away before next Tuesday.

I went back to Bouwe Zijlstra's, where Nico was sleeping, having been up all night, and I spent several hours chatting to Roberts and eating pancakes. We had asked Dr. Reijnierse to come and see to Roberts's foot as it was badly swollen. He came and enjoyed the situation. "Call me Texas Slim," Roberts told us.[243] I handed over the drawing and the other things, which he was delighted with, but could not really take with him, so he asked us to keep them for him and send them to him at the end of the war at 1008 Jefferson Street, Fort Worth, Texas USA.

We had a very pleasant time until one evening he was dressed in a nurse's uniform and with two genuine nurses from the Bethesda Hospital, cycled to Hoogeveen. One of his guides was Sister Tinie, one of Bouwe Zijlstra's daughters. He was going to present flowers to Her Majesty the Queen in London from the Underground Movement in Drenthe and also took with him a blank *stamkaart* that could be copied and reproduced in England.[244] Roberts gave me a fountain pen and a book as a souvenir.

A Landwacht division is to be stationed in Hoogeveen. It is the talk of the town and people are worried.

Nico sleeps in Hilbrand and Wietske [Veenstra]s bed because they are not at home.

March 8, 1944, Wednesday

MANY PLANES CAME over. Nico and I cycled all over the place looking for other Texas Slims, but no one fell to ground. Everywhere we went, we heard discussions about an escaped American pilot, the strangest stories were told. On one occasion, we stood guard behind Post's farm. I went into the garden, but it is now a sorry mess. We visited various onderduikers and listened to their problems and complaints.

In the evening, we delivered the three people from their temporary hiding place and took them to Nieuwe Krim. We followed one of the most isolated paths in Drenthe, and it seemed to be an endless journey. We had a whole lot of baggage with us, even though we had left some of it behind for the time being. We saw a light following us and for safety reasons hid in the heath. It turned out to be the Beaver on his bike, who brought word that we should meet the evening train in Hoogeveen, but who or what was coming we had no idea. On the basis that we could only be in one place at a time, we could not do both and the people in Hoogeveen would have to do without us for once.

In Nieuwe Krim, we dropped off all three; the brother and sister at the Hoogeveen's and "Oom Cor" at Hartemink's. We once again stressed the rules very clearly; no contact of any kind with the outside world other than by letter—and through us—which we reserve the right to censor. Never divulge addresses or names, no matter to whom. Don't go out and preserve the peace in the house with tact and goodwill. This seemed particularly important because the woman in the group wanted to start writing letters straightaway and mentioned two addresses where she had lived previously. Although I told her I was not interested, she kept throwing out other pieces of information. I am sorry to say that she does not come over as particularly sympathetic and the man we took to Hartemink is much nicer.

In the evening, we returned to the Beaver, and Jo gave us coffee and cake. Nico slept in the bed with Peter, Herman on two chairs, I on the divan, and Jo in the hiding place.

There is a cute little boy of three who looks like Napoleon at the Ottens'. His parents have been sent to Poland, and he was lodged with Albert Nijwening but had to leave there on security grounds.[245]

March 9, 1944, Thursday

UP EARLY AND to Hoogeveen. Hennie was there with two Zeelanders.[246] We sent her on to Groningen, to Julius and to Joop to fetch two revolvers. We stopped at Bouwe Zijlstra's to give Texas Slim a copy of *De Duikelaar* for Queen Wilhelmina. We put the two Zeelanders on the steam tram to Noordsche Schut while we went by bicycle and then took them to Elim. To Seine Otten, to the bicycle repairman (Kats), to the Ladies. We also went to Post's deserted farm to observe some fighting overhead, but nothing came down. We always carry the overalls with us.[247]

A batch of oranges has arrived. We passed them on to the kids. In the evening, I collected a load of blankets and luggage belonging to the five [from the heath] from a farmhouse near Zuidwolde. It was very late when I came back. Ten bombs had fallen near the farm and the people had already gone to bed twice before I got them up for a third time.

March 10, 1944, Friday

THIS MORNING I met the 9:03 a.m. train at Hoogeveen. Hennie was on board going from Groningen to Wageningen. I gave her a whole written list of commissions as there was no time to talk.

De Bijenkorf was also on the platform. She said she was going to Amsterdam. If I said nothing, then we would be shot of her. She thought that it was now safe in the capital. She asked why I had not come to Zweeloo. There had been a phone call yesterday for me at Jitse van der Vinne's shop. Van der Vinne had brought the message over to me—would I go directly to Zweeloo? When I got the message, it was too late to do anything about it.

I asked de Bijenkorf what was going on. "I want to go to Amsterdam" she replied. "And for this I was supposed to make the long cycle ride to Zweeloo? Are you mad?" I replied. I also tried to make it clear to her that we were not a travel agency and we took no further responsibility for people who traveled to Amsterdam without letting us know.

The taai-taai man will see to it that I get a pair of glasses with window glass in them.[248] He gave me a nice strong flour bag to have a bike bag made out of.

In the afternoon, I visited Nienhuis and found everything in order there. There had been the beginnings of a fire in the scullery, but the Lifeguard had seen it and put it out. This event can only improve matters there, where we pay Fl.200 a month. The couple had all sorts of requests; writing paper, identity cards, clothes, shoes, soap, letters to give to their son Hans. They don't know where he is in hiding [as the crow flies about 500 meters!]. Hans and little "Peter" turn out to be cousins.

In the evening to Cohen and his wife, who are still sleeping in the straw. I brought them the blankets that belong to that very difficult old woman (whom we have Christened "Ouwe Taaie")[249] who is at the Hoogeveens. These blankets were still in Zuidwolde, and she does not need them as she has more than enough bedding, whereas the Cohens have to lie on the bare straw with a few old sacks.

March 11, 1944, Saturday

WHEREVER WE GO, we hear the most ridiculous stories about 'Texas Slim'.

Up early this morning to go and look at an "air-mine" that has been lying at the side of the road to De Krim for weeks. It's a huge thing with a small red flag next to it.

We have been looking for one night's lodging for the Cohens because their hosts are expecting visitors. We first asked Elema. He was at least honest, that he was too frightened. "No, my boy, I can't do it because I will be so scared I will shit my pants."

We finally alighted on an address where success was assured, at Thalen's house. He is a church warden in Elim and furthermore a [business] rival of Cohen, competitor and enemy. They are both cattle dealers and cannot stand each other. Thalen had no time for us until he heard for whom he was required to be the Good Samaritan, and moreover it was only for one night. This was therefore a very cheap [gesture] and virtually without risk.

Snorretje came to see me at Otten's and talked to me about cooperation on the understanding that I would have to let go of Nico. It didn't go well, as Vondel would say.

In the evening, Nico and I went to the Nieuwe Krim again, laden with blankets, suitcases, and knapsacks. On the way along the canal, we met some curious people who wanted to know if we were busy moving house. Nico gestured to the canal, and they went on their way.

I had a row with "Ouwe Taai," the difficult woman, when I told her that I had given her blankets to the Cohens. "Blood is still thicker than water," she said. She was furious. I told her it didn't concern me at all.

Later in the evening, we went to where I had buried Texas Slim's boots, cap, and spectacles. We took them over to Otten to show him and then hid them securely. On the wall there is the drawing of Texas Slim. When Dr. Reijnierse came to visit Mrs. Otten, he asked, "Who is that?" "A friend of Arnold's," she replied. "Yes, I know him well," replied the doctor, "I treated his foot yesterday."

March 12, 1944, Sunday

THIS MORNING WE were all busy with household chores. Later in the day we played games. A really pleasant day.

Reports from Russia are very good. In Italy, the weather is still poor. According to reports, Italy has the least favorable climate in the world.

Kats has lost his clandestine car through betrayal. The KK who came to take it away will probably keep it themselves, but at least Kats will have no further trouble.

A radio has also been seized in the neighborhood.

There was a raid expected in Elim. We were warned immediately, but in the end, it wasn't that serious. It concerned three SS men who had gone on the run to avoid being sent to the Eastern Front. There was a huge manhunt for them across the fields and ditches.

March 13, 1944, Monday

CENSORED A WHOLE pile of letters. Tedious work.

In the evening, we fetched the two young girls, Lia and Tineke. Initially we took them to their mother, who is lodged with the Ladies, and they spent a happy time together.

Overtaken by a snowstorm on the way, so much so that the children were numb with cold sitting on the bicycle baggage racks. Halfway to Dedemsvaart we stopped at a farmhouse to warm the children up. We dropped them off late at night with Sister Scholten.

March 14, 1944, Tuesday

SPENT THE WHOLE morning writing my diary. I'm fully aware that I'm forgetting many things.

[Here follow supplementary diary entries for February, 27, 28, and 29.]

It is now Tuesday evening. I left Dedemsvaart in the afternoon. I went to the farmer near Zuidwolde where Ouwe Taaie used to be. I had been warned about her. She will, for example, try to send letters secretly through the post, and she is prodigal in naming names and addresses.

At the Beavers', there was a letter waiting for us from Cohen and his wife that we took notice of. It read as follows:

> Dear Mr. O,
> Will you be kind enough to ask Arnold and Nico if they can arrange for our departure from here? We leave it to them which evening it will be but it needs to be before the following Sunday since that day we will not be able to be here. With thanks in advance.
> With friendly greetings
> P and M

At 9:00 p.m. we were at Hoogeveen where Hennie arrived with a woman. We went with her to the taai-taai man and talked together over coffee and cake. Nico went with the woman to Big. Hennie had brought a wish list with her. She slept at the widow Baas's, whose husband had been shot the previous summer. I cycled swiftly to the Ottens'.

March 15, 1944, Wednesday Evening

UP BEFORE DAWN and off to Hoogeveen, where I found Nico and Hennie at the widow Baas's. For Hennie we had a whole range of tasks, for example messages for Wageningen, Hilversum, Naarden, De Steeg, Amsterdam, Zwolle, and Groningen. She left on the 9:03 a.m. train.

After that, I bought things for Peter, for example, materials he needed to falsify identity cards, *Ausweisen*, and so forth, high-quality paper, drawing ink, and pens. Hennie had two counterfeit identity cards with her that cost Fl.50 each, but we took them.

In Hoogeveen I had a good look at the Landwacht, who were busy marching through the streets. They had left their double-barreled shotguns at home.

We received some ration cards from Amsterdam, and I got some homegrown tobacco from Bouwe Zijlstra.

Masses of Americans flew over and we had our overalls to hand, but nothing happened. Late in the evening, we got a message from Nienhuis that his house had to be "cleaned" immediately as his three sons were being sought (probably for black marketeering). We agreed that Nico would come and collect the Lifeguard and his wife and take them to Kikkert.

I had to go with Herman to the photographer in Hoogeveen to get an identity card photo. We didn't get very far, as I had several errands to run on the way. Thus we went to Dr. Reijnierse in Hollandscheveld, who insisting on hearing the whole story about Texas Slim, and I also had to deliver clothes to two onderduikers. By that stage, it was too late for the photograph, and we went back. In the direction of Dedemsvaart, we saw something glowing falling from the sky.

March 16, 1944, Thursday Night

WE WENT TOGETHER to visit the new pastor and ask for his help with the onderduikers. He promised to do all he could.

We paid a visit to the hole in the ground that Nico had habitually used to sleep in last summer. It was full of water. After dark, we took the Lifeguard and his wife from Kikkert's to Van der Helm, but not before we had given them the opportunity to see their son and nephew, who are staying together at Bisschop's house. The nephew is little "Peter," who had been at Pesse but who had to be evacuated suddenly. He had been taken to Tante Koos "for three days" but where he stayed two weeks. [Tante Koos lives in Hoogeveen and helps with this and that.]250 After that, he was taken to Bisschop's, where he was pleasantly surprised to see his cousin. The two boys have a nice and safe hole in which they sleep.

The meeting between them took place on the Elim cycle path. The Kikkerts now have one of their relations underground with them, so that means one less place for us.

A telephone call from Nieuw-Amsterdam. "Tante Ammi" has to disappear this minute—immediately. Nico returned the call and said that she wasn't a biscuit that can be swallowed and then is gone. . . .

March 17, 1944, Friday Evening

THIS MORNING WE went to Van der Helm, where everything was fine.251 Then on to Wietske's, where we left the bikes and walked through to the Ladies. Wietske and Hilbrand [Veenstra] live under the same roof as the Ladies and the two dwellings are connected by an internal door [that looks like a cupboard]. To the outside world, it looks as though we are visiting Wietske when in fact we are with the Ladies Nieuwboer. Nobody knows that the Ladies have two permanent onderduikers under their roof and that Nico sometimes sleeps there, as do I.

Two of Bouwe Zijlstra's sons, who saw our bikes, asked Wietske where we were. Wietske told them that we were out the back in the woods. I would have liked to have seen the boys, but it is better this way.

We went to see Padding, who would like to palm off his onderduiker. He is not open to reason. He wants rid of him, "because," he says, "the man is a German, also a Jew, but mainly a German, and I don't like Krauts."

The whole day we spent looking for new hiding places (addresses). We do this together as experience has shown us that we have a better chance than if we operate separately. We complement each other's words. Unfortunately, on this occasion we had no luck at all. The best hiding places have gone, the cream has been skimmed off. The people are afraid and the majority are terrified as soon as we come in. They are happy to give us something to eat, but then we mustn't bother them with onderduikers.

Hilbrand en Wietske Veenstra. Collection v.d.Sleen.

On the way, I let off a bit of steam. I cursed and swore and Nico laughed, and the more I cursed the more he laughed. Afterward we looked in our little tin box [*trommeltje*] which contained identity cards and *stamkaarten*. One identity card where Peter had removed a stamp, I have treated with mud and urine to make the colors match, much to the amusement of Jo and Herman.

Broertje, the three-year-old at the Ottens' has developed a new expletive sentence. "You mustn't say that, you naughty boy." He's a nice little chap who looks like Napoleon.

It is always busy and pleasant at the Ottens'. Peter is busy with forging and printing while Herman draws.

In the evening, Nico and I went to Wietske and Hilbrand, ate there, and then sang songs. Tante Ammi, Bep, Nico, and I also went for a walk and went past Hilbrand Veenstra's father's house on the corner of the Nieuwlandse Straatweg and the Coevorder Straatweg. "Uncle Dirk" is in hiding there but does not want to stay as he thinks it is far too dangerous.

We read in the newspaper a wonderful headline: that the Central Cemetery in Rome has been bombed and that there are many dead!

March 20, 1944, Monday Evening

WE DID NOT do much on Saturday and Sunday. Yesterday we went to church, where the pastor reminded the congregation of their responsibilities to shelter the persecuted.

Today we again went looking for hiding places. "The pastor and his elder making house calls" is [apparently] often said when people see us coming.

At one farm, someone spoke ill of Johannes Post and the result was a huge fight.

At Jan Dekker's, a place for one girl, or at least the promise of it. Elsewhere, absolutely nothing, no luck at all.

In the evening, Snorretje came by to tell us that Albert Rozeman and his father had been arrested in Hoogeveen around 6:30 p.m. There had been a car with Green Police and the two had been taken to Assen. Snorretje had found it suspicious when he had telephoned them and a strange voice had answered. He had asked if the men of the NV (Nico and Victor) were there. "What do you mean?" came the reply. "Oh, nothing, I'll come right over." Snorretje then raced over to Hoogeveen just in time to see the two Rozemans loaded into a car.

We were worried stiff about Seine, who had been in Hoogeveen and due to collect a bundle of ration cards from them. Luckily, at around 10:30 p.m. he came home and told us his story.[252] Before he had come back, we had rounded up all manner of illegal items—newspapers, identity cards, etc.—and got them out of the house. Peter and Herman disappeared into the parsonage while we took little Broertje to the Ladies'. We got there around 9:30 p.m. with the kid wrapped in blankets. As long as the Krauts haven't found any ration cards at the Rozeman's...

The Russians are streaming into Bessarabia.

March 21, 1944, Tuesday Evening

ALL DAY LONG we have been searching for places, but the results are meagre. We visited Schuiling. Beaver had offered us Fl.10 if we could place anyone there. Well, we were [sort of] successful—we can bring an Aryan onderduiker to hide there.

This evening there was a panic in the village. Jonker, the baker, came rushing in through the door, "The Landwacht are coming!"[253] The poor man was near a nervous breakdown. We went to have a look what was going on and it turned out to be a group of soldiers out on exercises.

March 22, 1944, Wednesday Evening

I SPOKE WITH Hennie on the telephone from Dedemsvaart and agreed that she should bring her next delivery (*vrachtje*) to Dedemsvaart rather than Hoogeveen because the Landwacht were always at the station there.

Yesterday I spoke to her mother on the telephone [and was told] that we should expect a music ensemble, including a violinist and singer, and a troupe of acrobats from Zeeland. I went to all the neighbors, Broenink, de Jong, etc., to arrange for temporary shelter, but they did not arrive. Probably stayed in Zwolle.

The Cohens, who were living in the straw in that lonely place, can now go back to their old address as a new, and very good, hiding place has now been built for them.

March 23, 1944, Thursday Morning

THIS MORNING AT seven, Nico was here. Yesterday there was all sorts of activity overhead. We saw a Kraut fighter fall from the sky in flames. Didn't see any parachutes but we stood ready with our overalls.

March 24, 1944, Friday Afternoon

HENNIE DIDN'T ARRIVE yesterday. We waited for one bus and two steam trams. We telephoned Amsterdam. Her mother was very surprised and worried because Hennie had left Amsterdam at 6:04 p.m. on Wednesday evening. Then we went to the Neutels in Nieuwlande to see if they would take a married couple. The woman was not at home, and the son could not say yes without his mother's consent.

In Nieuwlande, everything had gone to pot. Mrs. Otten lay on the divan. The rest of the house was empty. The Beaver had joined the ranks of the onderduikers. He had been "dismissed" from the school.

The Green Police have been in Oosterhesselen. Van der Zee, the municipal clerk, has been arrested.[254] They raided Van der Zwaag's, but luckily he was not at home. They kicked the door in and drove the horses in the stable out onto the road. They found nothing. They also visited Janny Raak.[255] She was not at home, but took her brother, who had only been released from prison 14 days ago.

At the Ottens', we "cleansed" the whole house. Mrs. Otten was very brave. She had had great difficulty in persuading her husband to go into hiding and take their five-year-old son, Arie, with him. At the school, the children were told that their teacher was ill.

In cleaning the house, we found a German army uniform, a rubber truncheon, an old revolver, and a whole load of other forbidden things. It is all gone now.

Jo [Otten] is at the Norders' for the time being, where we have also buried things in the garden. Other stuff has disappeared under the church where Peter has reconstructed his bivouac. Herman has gone to Kikkert, where he is going to dig a shelter. We'd had plans to make a solid shelter at the Ottens'. The American pilot's clothing has also been moved to a safe place.

There was a stream of people who came to the Ottens' house looking for ration cards, identity cards, *stamkaarten*, and the like, some making a great fuss, but they were all shown the door.

A small group of Landwachters came through the village just as Nico and I were taking the German uniform to a safe place. They didn't notice us. Most of these villains are not very bright. The mood in the village remains in turmoil. Henk Sweepe, the assistant pastor, has had to go deeper underground.

Jo was in a very bad mood, but Herman remained his usual self. He joked with her. Jopie Vetex, he calls her, and drew a caricature of her. Eventually he did one of me too.

We cycled over to the Ladies' and were called over by Mrs. van de Vinne when we passed her shop. There was a telephone call from Amsterdam about Hennie, who was coming to Dedemsvaart that evening. She had been delayed. There was also a telegram from Nijmegen that Hennie should go there too. They could take children because they had found places for them.

We visited Wietske and found the young Jewish girl there whom we had placed at Wietske's parents in Hollandscheveld. She had wanted to go for a bike ride and wanted to go out, she said. We gave her a good piece of our minds. People didn't go underground as a joke and this wasn't a holiday camp. We gave her a long lecture. We ate at the Ladies': wonderful baked potatoes and bloodwurst.

We removed some savings bank books belonging to Jews from behind the wallpaper at the Ottens' and moved them to a safer place. After that, we took the Cohens back to their old hiding place. This was not easy as they could not really ride bicycles or see clearly in the dark. It took us about two and a half hours before we arrived, along muddy paths and in thick darkness.

It was far too late to go to Dedemsvaart, so we slept in the hay, but not before we had had a long talk with the farmer and his family. At a quarter to twelve we heard the good news: The Russians are making rapid progress.

In the morning, we left for Dedemsvaart with two extra bicycles. Hennie had arrived the previous evening with a musician and a lady. She had already left on the six o'clock bus but had left behind all sorts of things for us; ration cards, money, letters, parcels, etc. It was a shame that she had gone as we had so many things to talk over.

The musician is going to stay here with Stegeman and the lady at the neighbors. Because of the disruption in Hoogeveen we don't yet have a place for the musician, but that'll be OK.

March 24, 1944, Friday Evening

I VISITED SISTER Scholten looking for help. The musician can stay there temporarily, and we'll see what happens later. In the meantime, we had asked Broenink to take him in, but this wasn't possible. Then we went to the Calvinist pastor and he promised to do his best for us.[256]

Nico has taken the lady, who looks as though she is from the South and has a very youthful appearance although she has been married for ten years, to Nieuwlande. I will follow tomorrow. From the bottom of my heart, I begged Nico to be careful [as things are getting more dangerous by the day]. The Sister came over later in her car to tell me that she had found a place for the musician. Great. I'll take the man to her at 8:00 p.m. He told us dire stories about the persecution in Amsterdam. He had previously contracted a mixed marriage and was therefore put to work at Schiphol (airfield) [under German control], where he was not allowed to shelter from the rain or sit at meal times etc., etc.

I have managed to scrounge some homegrown tobacco, and I'm now busy drying it on the stove. A radio has been stolen from the wreck of a large Liberator that crashed near here, right under the noses of the German guards. They are furious.

March 25, 1944, Saturday Evening

DELIVERED THE MUSICIAN yesterday evening and set off for Nieuwlande. I had a suitcase of clothes for the lady that Nico had taken to Neutel (in Moskou), again temporarily. I stopped at Mr. Zijlstra. "Tante Eef," who is hiding there, is very depressed. I tried to cheer her up but not with much success. I had a letter for her from her brother's children, who are safe underground. She was obviously pleased with this, and I was also able to give her money and clothes. I also went to see Big, where I delivered a letter and money for the two sisters, and from there, I went to Elim with letters and packages. Last night a Lancaster bomber crashed half way between Nieuwlande and Hollandscheveld. Five bodies have been found.[257]

I went to see Mrs. Otten, who told me about the arrest of Van der Zee in Oosterhesselen, betrayed by the NSB headmaster of the primary school who lives across the road from him.

Today there was a run of people looking for ration cards. I buried a few more things in the garden.

Nico and I have been to see the pastor to talk about an onderduiker. Back to Mrs. Otten's, where we tried to persuade her that it was no longer safe to stay here. We ordered a car from Kop that took her to relations in Hoogeveen. Tomorrow she'll travel on to Apeldoorn. I'll go with her because she is unwell and cannot travel alone.

After she had gone, the rumor went around in Nieuwlande that she had been arrested by the Krauts. At the Ladies', where I spent the night, they also asked me who had been arrested.

March 26, 1944, Sunday Evening

THIS MORNING EARLY to Hoogeveen, and on the way saw the crashed aircraft with the Krauts standing guard. In Hoogeveen, I ordered a carriage to take Mrs. Otten to the train. In Zwolle there was a Landwacht checkpoint on the platform, and we had to wait there four hours for the connection to Apeldoorn. We spent the time with some of Mrs. Otten's acquaintances there.

One of the sons of the house was there having had a couple of free days. He was a nurse at a hospital in Amsterdam where four political prisoners had escaped. He had been "worked over" with chloroform a bit, [but it was only for show]. I think one of the four is Uncle Dirk, who is now in our care.

In Zwolle, two German soldiers who had been posted to the Eastern Front tried to drown themselves in the canal, but they were hauled out, put in a hospital, and when they were recovered, taken out and shot.

The city center in Zwolle is full of barbed wire. It has become a veritable fortress.

When we arrived in Apeldoorn,[258] there was no one at home. They had gone for a walk because of the good weather. We waited with their neighbors. When

Mr. Otten and Arie arrived, they could not believe their eyes. The Beaver was, of course, desperate to know about everything that had happened in Nieuwlande.

Churchill spoke [on the radio] at 9:00 p.m., but it was not worth the trouble or the risk to listen.

March 27, 1944, Monday Evening

THIS MORNING EARLY I had a walk with Otten and Arie. Krauts everywhere. Arie's comments were amusing. "Do you see the **** over there, Dad," and so forth.

The Palace[259] has been turned into a military hospital. We heard all sorts of stories about the Landwachters who steal even more than the Krauts.

In the afternoon, I went back to Hoogeveen. At the station, there was a bike for "Johan" a Jewish onderduiker hiding in Dedemsvaart, so I sent it on there. The ration card supply system is in chaos. I slept at the Ladies'; Nico this time in the bath tub.

March 28, 1944, Tuesday Evening

WE WENT TO de Groot[260] for ration cards, which were buried there. I heard that Van der Zee had said nothing to the Germans, or so it was claimed.

Nico and I had lunch in Ottens' empty house, and Henk Sweepe, the assistant pastor, dropped by. Joop from Groningen came to ask if we could find a place for a 52-year-old Jew. We will try to exchange him for the musician, who would like to be somewhere where there is a piano.

We have been busy with the ration cards; we have 230 and a list from Seine Otten that we have not yet sorted out. Nico went to Hoogeveen with a portion of them and I took a different route. Everywhere I go, people are whining about *stamkaarten*, identity cards, stamps, *Ausweise* and so on, it's enough to drive you crazy. Everyone is worried that it will all collapse because of the arrests and so many people having to go underground in a hurry.

The news from the Eastern Front is really good. We are longing for it to end.

March 29, 1944, Wednesday Evening

I SLEPT IN the Ottens' empty house last night. Around 2:00 a.m., I thought the Germans had arrived, but it turned out to be mice behind the wallpaper.

Griffioen, the school headmaster who lives next door, came with a surprised expression on his face. He asked when Otten was coming back as he was grievously missed at the school. "He'll be back after the war, not before," I said. That he found very worrying and uncalled for.

Rumor went around that Otten had been seen. Yes, so-and-so had seen him.

We were busy distributing ration cards, yesterday evening until 11:00 p.m. and then on our way early again [in the morning].

I tried to place the pianist with Mr. Pennings. "An artist whom you could have here perfectly well." I said. (Mrs. Pennings is very musical and plays the piano a lot). It was a "no," and "no" it remained. It was a great disappointment as I had counted on them to take him in.

Otten came to see me at Pennings' as he saw my bike there. He had come via the early train from Apeldoorn and was staying with his brother for the time being who lived about 100 meters from the Pennings'. I told Seine what Griffioen had said. "He can get the pip,"[261] he replied.

Mrs. Otten is back at home.

March 30, 1944, Thursday Evening

SPENT LAST NIGHT on the Ottens' couch. Mrs. Otten does not think there is any immediate danger and neither do I. As long as Rozeman and Van der Zee don't say anything, nothing will happen.

I went to Kikkert to see how Hoedag was doing as he had been very ill, but the crisis has now passed.

Went to see Peter and Hans, the two cousins. Peter has adapted better to the circumstances than Hans, who sometimes has complaints. I brought them some old clothes, rubbish, but they were very happy with them.

Their foster mother took me to one side and opened her complaints book for me. According to her, the boys were not very good: dirty shoes, torn clothes, a lot of extra work. It amounted to this: that I would have to find other places for them. It then dawned on me that I had not yet paid her for the previous month so I mentioned in passing that I still owed her the money; 2 x Fl.65 = Fl.130 and would pay in advance for the next month, thus Fl.260 in total. I counted the money out on the table, and then there was a miracle. She turned like a leaf on a tree, and suddenly saw everything through rose-tinted glasses, and it was all perfectly fine. "It was not that bad" and "boys will be boys," and she was prepared to make a little extra effort for them.

I patted her on the shoulder and thanked her for her goodness and said to her that it was such a great pleasure [to work with those] who carried out their Christian duty so unselfishly. She was very flattered and in the best of moods when I left her.

"Lekkere Liebe Lutschie" want to leave Padding's. It is apparently not chic enough for him there. LLL is the German Jew, better described as the Jewish German whom we placed with Kikkert for one night and then with Padding. We called him that because he begins all his overlong letters that he writes to his girlfriend (a married woman in Amsterdam) with those three words. We have told him that he has to limit his writing as we have to censor all the letters. A short letter once a week is "plenty." He holds all manner of grievances against his host and hostess. He is an annoying, unpleasant person. Nico and I have said to each other, "no more Krauts," but there are of course good German Jews, for example the Herz family, who are at the Norders.[262] Fine people.

We have recently been shuffling our "clients" around. This woman needs to go there, this one to there, the Ouwe Taaie to Almelo, this one in her place. We have to make best use of the limited number of places that are available. This is the first priority. The second is to take account of the wishes of the various onderduikers, as well as those of the hosts and hostesses.

I visited Douwe Doornbos (where Jo had spent a couple of nights). I brought a ration card and a bicycle. Ate delicious pancakes with scraps. Through to Nieuw-Amsterdam, where I found everything in order. There were inevitably some small complaints and frictions at certain addresses, but that is to be expected. It's exceptional where everything is 100 percent harmonious. Went to Van Ekelenburg and was given a hard time because I had not taken Tante Ammi away in time. I slept there.

March 31, 1944, Friday Evening

THE LANDWACHT IS more of a presence. They are a bunch of idiots, but dangerous, and one has to look out for them. Many underestimate the danger they represent. We hear some priceless stories about them. For example, the case of a judge in Groningen who was stopped by the Landwacht and asked to show his identity card. He refused. They asked again. He refused again, and then a third time. So they took him to the police station. There he produced his identity card. When asked why he wouldn't obey the Landwacht, he replied, "Because I have sentenced the man in question three times."

Yesterday, I was given a large box full of torch batteries for the "good cause" by a bicycle repairman. These things are normally no longer available.

This morning woken up early by the sun shining into my room. Downstairs in the kitchen, Van Ekelenburg was busy writing the name *Frits* onto a cake with cream or something similar. Frits is Lidia's fiancé, and it's his birthday today. Frits was in Westerbork and has been sent on. He [Van Ekelenburg] had also made an enlargement of a photo of Frits that he had stolen from Lidia.

I also encountered a young Jewish girl of about 12 who also appeared to be staying in the house.

I went to see Gorter (the man with the electric light) and where I had taken Tante Ammi. She can stay there for a while. Not permanently, and I understand that as his house is often full of fugitives from German camps, prisoners of war who come over the border at Schoonebeek. [Tante Ammi had originally been taken to the Blok family], but she could not stay there as the whole village was talking about it—at least according to the Blok family. I promised Gorter to do my best to fetch her as soon as possible. I told him that between me, him, and the lamppost I would try to place her with her son at Nieuwe Krim.

I telephoned Hennie.

At the Berendses' to collect cigarette stubs as they always save them for me and they are becoming increasingly scarce. Some of them come from surrogate cigars.

I went to Nieuwe Krim. Tante Ammi can go there, and Mia can also join her mother, but Ouwe Taaie, who is also still there, has to go first. She may go to an address in Almelo where her daughter is lodged. The sooner she goes, the better it is for all of us. Behind our backs, she's been sending letters containing both names and addresses. I scolded her in the most terrible way possible.

At Hartemink, everything was fine. Our man can stay there for the time being.

I went to ask [Headmaster] Scholten if Mia could work there during the day.[263] This was fine.

Bobby is ill. Miesje, the girl who used to work at Johannes Post's farm and now works for the Scholtens, came to ask what I thought about her coming to help us in our work. I answered that I thought it was a wonderful idea. She will now give up her job and join us.[264]

In Hoogeveen, I bought five pairs of clogs for onderduikers.

I found Nico at the Ottens'. There was a telephone message that Joop would be in Hoogeveen with a Jew. It was far too late to go there now, so he would have to find shelter for the night there, but it was agreed that he would come with a car from Groningen to Nieuwlande.

There was a raid at Bunschoten-Spakenburg involving 500 Krauts.[265] They had come from Amsterdam, fully equipped, including field kitchens and so forth. The many onderduikers hid themselves in every possible place, including in roof gutters or by dressing in women's clothing. Four were caught. They also took the pastor of the church because he was caught with some copies of *Trouw*.[266]

April 1, 1944, Saturday Evening

IN HONOR OF it being April 1, I allowed Nico to go and see Mr. Eppinga, the evangelist with whom I had had the stand-up row.[267] On that account, I had told Nico, he would only speak with Nico and not with me about the placement of a young boy.

Van der Helm is starting to be more proactive in finding hiding places for onderduikers.

Joop came early on a bike from Hoogeveen, angry that we had not come last night. It had been extremely difficult for him to find somewhere for the man to stay the night, and he had been reduced to walking the streets knocking on doors. If only he had gone to the taai-taai man, everything would have been fine. I agreed to collect the man this evening.

A warning arrived that the Landwacht in Hoogeveen were going to raid Hollandscheveld.

This afternoon, I went to Hoogeveen, where Hennie had been and gone. I had a suit of clothes for the musician, a few photos of [known] Gestapo agents and a packet of letters for various clients. This evening I'll take the Jewish man back to Nieuwlande with the extra bike I had brought with me for the purpose.

I sat in the window with Albert Nijwening to watch the Landwacht marching in formation to their eating place. They eat altogether between 6:00 p.m. and 7:00 p.m. in a restaurant in the Schutstraat. The good people of Hoogeveen use the time to fetch [illicit] milk. On this occasion, they didn't come. I phoned Hollandscheveld and was told that they had inspections across the whole district. I decided to wait until morning to transport the man.

I learned from Mrs. Nijwening that Lekkere Liebe Lutschie had sent a letter the other day behind our backs and had received a reply from Amsterdam.

Broertje [the little boy who looks like Napoleon] is [back] with the Nijwenings and doing fine.

April 2, 1944, Sunday Evening

THIS MORNING I waited for the Landwacht to have breakfast and then set off with my "cargo."[268] Lovely weather, if a little cold.

Arrived at the Ottens' and learned that there had been some disquiet about us. For example, Nico had kept saying, "He's been caught and arrested." In Nieuwlande they had known all about the Landwacht inspections on the roads.

We drank delicious coffee substitute there, and then I went to the pastor, where the newcomer whom we have named "Oom Gerrit," can stay temporarily. He is very entertaining and knows lots of jokes.[269]

Seine and Jans are back at home like they have never been away. Seine is back at the school and Peter, Herman, Jo, and I are also there [back at the house].

The day before yesterday, Norder, the carpenter, had made a hatch in "our" house, which gave access to a hiding place behind the stairs and from there to the space under the floorboards. It is completely invisible and can be locked from the inside. As Mrs. Otten put it, "We have added two rooms to our house." There is not much room under there and we have to crawl in using our elbows.

The place at Padding's formerly occupied by Lekkere LL has been taken by an Orthodox Calvinist student. Nico brought him there—which was a mistake, as we should have reserved the place for a Jew. A Calvinist student is not so easy to move on.

I tried to palm off a couple of onderduikers on the new tenants in Johannes Post's farm but without success. "They had no space."

The newcomer (Oom Gerrit) lodged with the pastor is a wise man. He doesn't want to see his three hidden daughters until the liberation.[270]

April 3, 1944, Monday Evening

VISITED MR. BOS [the headmaster of the nonconfessional school] to persuade him to take another onderduiker.[271] He already has a Jew under his roof, a journalist whom we know only as "the journalist." He wants to think it over, but I think it will be OK. Then to the widow Muller, with the same result, and to

Visser, the postmaster, who for some time has had a young Jewish widow in his house.

To Bouwe Zijlstra to ask if his daughters will escort Ouwe Taaie to Almelo. It will be done the day after tomorrow.

April 4, 1944, Tuesday Evening

ON THE LOOKOUT for hiding places today and had success with Dijk, the painter. Spoke with Wieten, the grocer, about food supplies in times of ever greater need.

There was a report that all airmen who made emergency landings should not be returned to England but be interned in Belgium.[272]

Last week, five English pilots were buried at Hollandscheveld. Pastor Volger spoke in English. The following day, another was also buried.

April 5, 1944, Wednesday Evening

UP EARLY. BOUWE Zijlstra's daughter came at 6:30 a.m. as arranged. We set off for Nieuwe Krim, but the roads were bad. We took Ouwe Taaie on the back of a bike to the station at Dalen. [Good riddance.]

I went alone to Nieuw-Amsterdam with the extra bicycle to fetch Tante Ammi. She scolded me for not coming earlier. She hadn't ridden a bike in two years, and it was therefore very difficult cycling against the wind and the rain, and the only way we made progress was if I pushed her. [This was not easy because the heavy trunk on the carrier of my bike drove the rear wheel into the mud.] The meeting between mother and son was [nonetheless] a sight to behold.

I went back to Dalen station with the extra bike and arrived at the same time as the train. Zijlstra's daughter and Ouwe Taaie had had an uneventful journey with no inspections. The weather was getting worse so we decided to avoid the muddy byways and made our way to Nieuwlande on the main roads via Coevorden and De Krim, arriving sodden, cold, and tired.

Nico left a message for me that he had gone to meet Hennie at Hoogeveen. I'll follow him tomorrow morning. A message from Mrs. Dijk that she won't take one, but two, people as long as a double bed comes with them. Herman has written to his former neighbors in Amsterdam, asking them to send on the double bedstead that belonged to his parents. I'll give the letter to Hennie tomorrow morning.

Oom Gerrit was here and played chess with Seine Otten. He is the director of the Magneet Bicycle factory in Weesp.[273]

April 6, 1944, Thursday Evening

I WAS UP early and went to Hoogeveen. Nico was still in bed at De Groot's house and Hennie did not arrive. I had some errands to run and tried to buy a postcard that has been banned by the Krauts. It shows two fishwives from Scheveningen staring out with their hands above their eyes saying to each other, "There they come." [I want that particular card so that I can make copies.] I bought a series of maps of the various fronts.

Rozeman's house looks all forlorn, sealed up by the Krauts.

Nico and I cycled back to Nieuwlande. Near Hollandscheveld, the Landwacht were shooting birds. Nico took a diversion, but I went on because they had already seen me and I wasn't stopped. We met each other again in the Kerkhoflaan. Old Jitse [v.d. Vinne] the shopkeeper had a message for us from Hennie. She was in Dedemsvaart and hoped to be in Hoogeveen tomorrow.

April 7, 1944, Friday Evening

IT WAS WIETSKE'S birthday today, but because there were so many visitors I did not go to congratulate him.

Job van der Vinne has come back from Germany.[274] He looks like a living corpse. He has been away seven months, and his family bought out the remainder of his sentence for Fl.500.

Herman and I took a walk through the woods looking at various hiding places and followed the flight path the burning plane must have taken. Nature is doing its best. Buds on the beech and chestnut trees are swelling.

This morning I went to Hoogeveen early. Nico didn't come with me. Hennie had stayed the night at Tante Koos's. She spoke of the Landwacht being everywhere. She also told me that Mrs. van den Bergh in Wageningen had had a stroke, and because of this, her house had to be cleared.

Versteeg has been looking for a place for Marie in Zetten.[275] "Tante Thea," who is in hiding with Hennie's parents, is very ill and will probably soon die. I'd made another list of things that Hennie could do for us, and I took her to catch the 9:03 a.m. train.

Leaving the station, I was stopped by the Landwacht. I made as though I could not find my identity card. I looked in all my pockets but found nothing. I moved across to where there were no passengers passing, forcing two of the Landwachters to come with me, which meant they couldn't inspect anyone else. I stood for a while and grumbled. I said (in the vernacular) something like, "I always have it with me and I am never stopped." Finally, I acted surprised to find it. In the photograph I had a moustache that I had subsequently shaved off. The men apparently did not find that suspicious.

I collected Oom Gerrit's overcoat, typewriter, photos, and letters as they were still at Albert Nijwening's house.

April 8, 1944, Saturday

FROM 8:00 A.M. to 9:00 p.m., the Beaver, Herman, and I have been digging under the house. The beginning was the most difficult as we had no room to move and had to dig lying on our bellies. We pushed the soil we dug out under Ham's house, the neighbor who own the other half of the semidetached dwelling. It was one hell of a job, but the result is worthwhile as we have dug out a passage that leads to a great space that can sleep six people, and if needs be, eight. Whenever we heard people above our heads, we had to stop working and be dead quiet. Arie, the five-year-old, knew exactly what was going on. He became very mysterious and said very little. On one occasion he said, "Mama, they must be very large mice . . . because they are making so much noise." The radio was also moved below and stood on a shelf.

Seine Otten and I then went out, unwashed and filthy, to collect Easter eggs and to collect a pack of tobacco that had been promised to me a long time ago.

Peter recently made a mistake when he was hiding under the church, when he heard someone walking through the church itself. Thinking it was the cleaner, the sexton's sister, who was aware of his presence, he knocked on the floor. However, it was not the girl who usually worked in the church, but a replacement who knew nothing about it. She let out some dreadful screams when she heard the knocking and heard a voice from below calling "Liesje" and fainted from fright. Luckily, she is also someone who can keep a secret.

While I was under the house, I heard Nico come in four times, but he didn't come down once.

April 9, 1944, Sunday Evening

LAST NIGHT, THE three of us slept in our new hiding place. A deep layer of straw with mattresses on top where we could stretch out. Excellent. From this night on, we'll not be sleeping on beds or divans.

A beautiful morning, the first day of Easter!

Masses of airplanes and dogfights, but no parachutes. I did see a gas tank come down. I found it in a rye field. I gave the thing to a couple of boys in the village, who can make a canoe out of it after the liberation. For the time being, they have hidden it underwater [in one of the canals].

April 10, 1944, Monday Evening

SECOND DAY OF Easter.

I had a long walk with Jo in the woods. Twice we bumped into one of our onderduikers with a girl. The weather is perfect and everything is in bud.

April 12, 1944, Wednesday Evening

YESTERDAY EVENING, OTTEN and I went to Hoogeveen to collect ration cards and stamps for identity cards. We paid Fl.51.50 for the cards, the same price that the Trouw-groep had paid for them.[276] I also received a packet of homegrown tobacco from Bouwe Zijlstra's son.

This morning, Otten and I cycled to Dedemsvaart. We went to the distribution clerk with 40 inlay sheets. Such good service. I can collect 40 ration cards this evening. I took some of them to Sister Scholten and Mrs. de Jong.

Went to the widow's house via the cemetery as usual to listen to the radio reports. The news is excellent. They (the Krauts) are getting it in the neck on all sides.

April 13, 1944, Thursday Morning

I AM LEAVING here (Dedemsvaart) in about an hour. It was the same story as always here: letters, money, packages.

A doctor in Hardenberg was stopped by the Landwacht, who asked to see his papers. "Which papers?" he asked. They didn't know. "So, come to my surgery hours to see me when you know which papers you want to see."

April 14, 1944, Friday Evening

NICO HAS GONE, without a trace. I have tried everything but can't find him. I've called everyone with a telephone I know, but nothing. I fear the worst.

April 15, 1944, Saturday Evening

YESTERDAY EVENING OLD Jitse got a call saying that Nico could not write letters at present. He had no idea where the call came from, but later in the evening we got a message to from the hospital to bring clothes for Nico as he had been admitted there. I went to Wietske, and she packed a few things, including a letter from Bep for him.

I found him in the hospital, lying on a bed, covered from head to foot in ointment, and under the care of a nurse. He had contracted scabies.

Nel came yesterday and left today. I took her to the train.

Ate at the Pencil's, delicious bacon.

April 16, 1944, Sunday Evening

ZWART HAS COME to Nieuwlande, bringing me greetings from my brother Jan and a request for ration cards.

This evening at the Ottens' there was a meeting between the Lifeguard and his wife, and their son Hans and nephew Peter.

I went with Herman to Kikkert to ask if Peter could stay with him. He said he'd have to think about it.

In the evening at Ottens', we played Academie.[277] Oom Gerrit wandered in, told a few dozen jokes, offered us some advice on how to play the game, and then disappeared again.

I was supposed to go to Hoogeveen with shaving things for Nico, but I had no desire to cycle 25 kilometers just for that.

April 17, 1944, Monday Evening

EVERYWHERE YOU GO people are talking about an invasion.

This morning I gave Zwart 15 ration cards to give to Jan, together with milk and potato coupons. Collected ration cards from Van Aalderen in Hoogeveen as well as milk and potato coupons for a lady to take to The Hague.[278] Last night the Landwacht had been busy daubing slogans all over Hoogeveen. "Mussert Wins" is everywhere and also "Mussert or Moscow" and other slogans. To their great annoyance, many people had washed or scratched off the slogans on their houses and six were arrested. They were threatened with punishments if they did not replace the slogans, but not all of them did.

I had been to the photographer to arrange an appointment for several onderduikers to have their pictures taken at Otten's for identity cards.

In Hoogeveen I ran into Zwart, who has had to flee from 's-Hertogenbosch and who told me a long story all about it. I went to the hospital, but Nico had already left. For Mrs. Otten, I bought seed-beans and flower seeds.

In the evening, I took ration cards round and stopped at Jan Dekker's to drop off Herman's "sister" (neighbor's girl). Here I was scolded; city people this and city people that, Herman was lazy and wouldn't help peeling potatoes, etc., etc.

Otten, Peter, and I have been digging in the shed at Johannes Post's abandoned farm looking for a tin box containing *Ausweisen* and so forth. We didn't find it.

April 18, 1944, Tuesday Evening

UP EARLY THIS morning to visit Bouwe Zijlstra, who told me that the Landwacht are constantly patrolling near his house. They, the Zijlstras, are trying to catch them doing something [illegal] but no luck yet. Yesterday evening, Bouwe and two of his sons had gone out about 9:30 p.m., well-armed and looking for the Landwachters, but found nothing and came home around midnight. This morning they found out from the neighbors that there had been three Landwachters posted near their house from 10:00 p.m. and had stayed until around 11:00 p.m.

Visited Big and ate there. Collected letters, delivered ration cards. Menno is now growing into a big chap.[279] He runs away whenever he gets the chance and likes nothing better than to be fetched back.

Went to Loekie. Something is wrong as a strange man and woman, not from these parts, were there. [They did not introduce themselves.] The atmosphere was tense and Loekie, who usually rushes to greet me, barely said hello to me. I concluded that there were communications taking place behind our backs. I pretended I saw nothing unusual but I was very cross.

I visited some of our Zeelanders, who wanted all sorts of things, including clogs, overalls, letters, and so on.

Saw the son of the bookshop owner in Nieuw-Amsterdam, Van Wieren. His hostess did not have a good word to say for him, describing him as stuck-up and demanding.

In Elim, I secured a place for a young Jewish boy who is prepared to do the simplest farm work. At Padding's, I was only there for five minutes before he threw me out of the house. He was obviously overwrought, and I won't blame him for it.

Arrived at Otten's, where there was a letter waiting for me from Piet Muller, who wanted me to find a place for a father and a son.[280] He is the third person to ask me this for the same father and son.[281]

Nico was in bed and did not feel well after his attack of scabies.

Herman went to Jan Dekker in high dudgeon. He had come back late and spoke of a war of words where at one point he was thrown out of the house but drawn back in by the argument. He also reiterated another set of slanders that had come to him from a completely different quarter.[282]

Oom Gerrit was again there in the evening, full of jokes and stories. He also told us about the persecution of the Jews in Amsterdam: how the South and East [of the city] had been cordoned off, how one Jew had been able to rescue his wife in the nick of time because a German guard who knew him had looked the other way. Another Jew had escaped by breaking the seal on a nearby property and attaching it to his own so that the raiders passed him by.[283] Some children also managed to escape.

For the last few days, the news from London has not been worth listening to.

There was a telephone call from Hennie to say that she would be arriving the following Thursday with Tantes Lies and Marie.

I got a letter from Mr. Jonker in Zweeloo about de Bijenkorf. They want rid of her. This is urgent because a grandmother is arriving and there is a baby [and all that rubbish]. With the letter was one they had received from de Bijenkorf, who had gone to Amsterdam, but found it far too dangerous there. In any event, she intends to come back.

A letter from Van Ekelenburg:

> Dear Arnold,
>   For little Kenki at D, at least four months [board and lodging] due; For R at V at least 2½ months. In total therefore, 6½ x 50 = FL.325.—No other news. Send some milk and potato coupons. See you at our independence day celebrations. V.C.

April 19, 1944, Wednesday Afternoon

THIS MORNING MASSES of airplanes on their way to Berlin. The cat had kittens while the Yanks flew over. Something fell out of the sky that turned out to be a gas tank. It was almost undamaged as it had fallen into a ploughed field. There were a few liters of gas still in it, which I of course removed. The tank I hid under the water until after the war. It will make a nice canoe. It is reported that a German fighter has crashed nearby. Let's hope so.

April 20, 1944, Thursday

BOUWE ZIJLSTRA CAME to tell us that the much-discussed father and son would be arriving. He and I went to Bos in Alteveer to see if he would take them.[284] There was no one there. Had they gone underground?

We went from there to Bouwe Zijlstra's house, where we were due to meet Nico. We waited until 11:00 p.m., but no one came. I arrived at the Ottens' at 11:30 p.m., where there were some late visitors—two farmers from Nieuwlande who reported a telephone message that they had received from Coevorden about potatoes for eating. This was code for raids being imminent.

Today I made lists of Gestapo agents, some with photos.

We have no money.

April 22, 1944, Saturday Evening

OTTEN, PETER, HERMAN, and I spent the whole day digging under the house. We have made the hiding place a whole lot bigger. It was a major task as every shovelful of earth had to be moved three or four times lying on one's back or stomach before it was safely under the neighbor's house. [But] the results are really good. Once I was in there, I was not available to anyone and spent most of my time under the neighbor's house [moving soil] but was very careful as they mustn't hear anything.

Bouwe Zijlstra came and told us that the father and son had arrived soon after we left. I went on working in the "catacombs" while he and Nico took the father and son to the Bos family.

Mr. Otten had to go to Hoogeveen and dropped out, as did Herman soon afterward with a hand injury. That left Peter and me and we had everything finished by around 10:00 p.m.

Herman is nearly always smiling and has the happy knack of seeing the funny side of almost everything [even when Peter had sliced into his hand and he was bleeding like a cow in the slaughterhouse].

Oom Gerrit came as usual.

April 23, 1944, Sunday Afternoon

FOUR OF US slept in the catacombs last night safe and sound. We scrabbled around like pigs in straw. Nel and Riek (Herman's "sister," who is lodged at Van Veen's, the farmer)[285] sneaked over, and we went into the woods, Jo, Herman, Nel, Riek, and I. Herman had his guitar, and we sang all sorts of songs.

This afternoon, we did the washing up, snatching the plates from each other while we dried them. [Not one of them broke.]

Last night there were many planes in the sky. We thought that an invasion was imminent.

Nel left to go back to Amsterdam.

The Germans who were posted from Hoogeveen to Noord Holland were attacked [from the air] on the Afsluitdijk.[286] Result: panic and 50 percent casualties.

April 24, 1944, Monday Evening

THIS MORNING HENNIE was in Hoogeveen with a woman destined for Dedemsvaart. I took them to the taai-taai man's, where there were 24 of us round the table. I sorted out everything with Hennie quickly and then went out with this woman. All the other things I was supposed to do in Hoogeveen fell by the wayside. The woman couldn't cycle, so I took her to the edge of town and then showed her the byways to Nieuwlande while I cycled with the luggage, letters, and packets that Hennie had given me. There had been a Landwacht inspection at the station, but everything had gone well. I took the woman to the *dominee* [pastor] to stay for the night.

The riddle of Lia and Tineke's missing Christmas parcel was solved; we had given it to another girl (Lientje) by mistake.

April 25, 1944, Tuesday Morning

THIS MORNING I took the newcomer to Dedemsvaart in Beukema's car. She is very nervous and simpering and enormously grateful for everything [done for her].

Late yesterday evening Peter, Herman, and I took all the remaining things out from under the church. It included Texas Slim's clothing and the German army uniform. We couldn't take it all at once so left some of it under some rubbish at Hilbrand and Wietske's house. We were back at around 11:45 p.m. and fetched the rest early this morning.

Nico is in bed as his trousers have to be mended.

I went back with the same car that brought our new lady to Dedemsvaart. I left her with Stegeman and gave Frits a letter for Sister Scholten.

Every night as we go to bed we do the same pig-like performance [to arrange the straw]

Bep is going to make biscuits and a tart for Arie Otten's birthday and I need to see if I can find eggs for her.

April 27, 1944, Thursday Evening

IN DEDEMSVAART; IN Dinie's room writing in my diary. Yesterday I was up early gathering information from various people for the new *stamkaarten* that Hennie can get for us.

The Landwacht is becoming more and more active.

I've been given 23 eggs.

Yesterday evening Mr. Jonker came from Zweeloo, and unfortunately I was at home as I saw him too late. He gave me an ultimatum: "Either you take Willie [de Bijenkorf] away, or I'll bring her here to Nieuwlande and just let her loose." A real hassle. I said, "Please sit down, I'll be back in a minute. I'll just fetch my partner."

Nico came back with me (he was with the Ladies).

We talked and talked, but Jonker was immoveable. Finally, we said that she would have to go back to Wageningen. Jonker went away and will telephone us if she is prepared to go or not.

This morning I was at the Stegemans' and saw the woman I had delivered the day before yesterday sitting in the [living] room. She was not what they had expected as they were looking for a young girl, not an old[er] woman. I found a place for her today.

This evening an unusually large number of planes flew over. The noise was apparently terrific, but I heard nothing. Recently Hennie had given me a packet of letters that had ostensibly come from Dedemsvaart but were undeliverable. I didn't know any of them, and neither did Sister Scholten.

April 28, 1944, Friday Morning

IT IS VERY early in the morning. Jannes has already gone to the bakery, where he now works. Frits is still in the chicken coup, where they both usually sleep. It sits at the rear of the garden on land belonging to a neighbor.

The lady we call "Tante Johanna" has a good hiding place—starting next Monday, so for the time being she is staying at De Flochte. She gave me two letters for Amsterdam.

From Sister Scholten I received two identity cards belonging to people who have died.

Two onderduikers had jumped on a vehicle between Dedemsvaart and the Balkbrug, but realizing that it was a German car used in raids, they lost no time in jumping off again.

I went picking flowers for Arie's birthday tomorrow.

April 29, 1944, Saturday Evening

IT IS ARIE's birthday today.

I arrived back in Nieuwlande yesterday laden with flowers. In the evening, Jo, Peter, Herman, and I picked more tulips and narcissi in a nearby nursery. I went to Nieuw Zwinderen to rustle up a couple of rabbits for Arie, but with no success. I bought a beautiful box of building blocks from Dinie Homan.

This morning early, Peter, Herman, and I decorated the room. Herman had made a whole series of delightful drawings portraying a young birthday boy and hung them on the wall. Peter had created a very artistic clock.

I went with Buikema's car to Zweeloo to fetch de Bijenkorf, for whom I had found a place in Dedemsvaart for Fl.150 per month. On the way, I lectured her about the letters she had sent secretly in the mail and alluded to the "onderduikers syringe." [She laughed and that made me really angry. I told her it was nothing to laugh about and that six people had already gone to their deaths through her Goddamn antics.]

We took Arie for a little ride to one of his friend's. Seine Otten came with us to Dedemsvaart.

I went to the distribution clerk in Dedemsvaart with 80 inlay sheets. Joop came with a colleague from Groningen. There is strife [*hommeles*] in the North with many arrests. Joop brought a large quantity of cigarettes for us.

April 30, 1944, Sunday Evening

IT IS PRINCESS Juliana's birthday. We heard her voice on the radio and the little princesses also said a few words.

Enormous amounts of bombing taking place in Germany.

May 1, 1944, Monday Evening

ALL THE TELEPHONES in the Netherlands have been cut off, except those for the doctors, police, and some other institutions. Naturally the NSB are allowed to keep all their phones.

This morning I went looking for hiding places but found nothing. Returned home exasperated and despondent.

Yesterday evening Herman sat on top of the shelter at the bottom of the garden singing songs and playing his guitar. He collected a large group of children. Later on we headed for the streets and someone asked him to play some more. So we sat by the waterside. [By this time] it was dark, but he carried on playing, while I illuminated him with a flashlight.

May 2, 1944, Tuesday Evening

I TOOK CLOTHES round for onderduikers. I also visited various "mussels" as we called the Zeelanders in hiding.[287] I had overalls for two of them and three pairs of clogs. They were much appreciated.

Ouwe Veenstra, Hilbrand's father stopped us on the street and asked us how the search was going for a new place for "Dick." He had had him for long enough, he said. He was really angry. He doesn't know it, but we'll never be coming to collect Dick as he's in a safe place and there is no reason to change things. I did my best to keep him in line.

Mrs. Post came past. Everything was fine.

May 3, 1944, Wednesday Night

GREAT UPHEAVAL. YESTERDAY evening a special courier arrived from Groningen with a message from Van der Zee, now out of the prison in Groningen where he had been taken from Assen. In his interrogations by the Nazi executioners, they had mentioned Otten and Pol, the leader of the distribution system, as well as Luten, a manufacturer in Gees. His advice: go underground immediately.

Otten promptly vanished and is now completely hidden at Doornbos's house in Nieuw Zwinderen. Mrs. Otten wanted to stay at home with Arie, but in the evening a message arrived from a young woman in Hoogeveen who was originally from Nieuwlande and married to a committed NSBer. The message was that there had been a meeting of NSB leaders at her house where it was said: "We'll get that Mr. Otten from Nieuwlande." We persuaded Mrs. Otten that it was also time for her to leave, and she went with Arie to stay with Norder, the carpenter. We "cleansed" the house.

Peter, Herman, and I spent the night in the woods. We took a tin of provisions with us and later returned to fetch some blankets. I left early in the morning.

Mrs. Otten has returned home today and intends to stay. I think it's stupid.

Jo is with Nijwening and has cut back enormously [on activities].

May 4, 1944, Thursday Evening

RECEIVED A TELEGRAM from Hennie yesterday that she was coming with Mia and Annie. Two hours later, [another] telegram to say it wasn't going to happen.

This morning I left the woods, where we had spent a second night. Peter and Herman, who had stayed in the woods, had moved the camp farther into the interior, so when Nico and I arrived back in the afternoon, we could not find the new site. We whistled our secret tune, the first bars of "Yankee-Doodle" and got an immediate reply. When we heard the reply, we discovered Herman, who was alone. He looked like an aborigine king on his throne. Peter wasn't there. Frans de Graaf and Lidia had come to see him, and he had gone with them to the civilized world.

Nico and I had hauled a tarpaulin about eight meters square from Post's farm so that we could use it in the woods. In the evening, we took it to the campsite. It is great to lie on and to sit under when it rains.

This morning I visited Otten in Nieuw Zwinderen to tell him the latest news and the plans of the NSB in Hoogeveen. In the afternoon, he went to his house and then on to Hoogeveen in order to make an early start for Groningen in the morning.

May 5, 1944, Friday Evening

PETER DREW A text for me. Isaiah 16:3: "Hide the fugitives. Do not betray the refugees."

No more news from the fronts, but plenty of guessing about the "invasion." The waiting is awful.

This evening, Peter, Herman, and I went into the woods about 11:30 p.m. We looked for our camp, where we'd left food, blankets, and a tarpaulin, and discovered that everything was gone except two spades that were hidden under the moss. Herman had left everything under the tarpaulin, but not camouflaged. All gone, including a briefcase with writing materials and flashlights in it.

We stood there dismayed.

I asked Herman, who always saw the funny side of things, whether he could see anything funny in this situation. "No, not yet," was his reply. "But it will come." And he started laughing. He found it so funny that we were standing there, soaking wet in the rain. But however comic it might have been, we had murder in our hearts.

It started to rain harder and became colder. We held a council of war and decided that our stuff must still be in the woods. It is surrounded on three sides by water. There was therefore a chance that it might be by the side of the water, or that there would be evidence of a tree trunk having been used to cross the surrounding waterway, and that it could be found near one of the small cottages nearby. Perhaps at this very moment there were people examining the booty they had found?

Armed with a knife and the two spades, we set off. Everything was soaking wet, not least ourselves. It poured from the sky, and in the middle of an impermeable wood, we stood telling jokes and trying to light cigarettes and a pipe, but it was all far too wet.

Then we saw a light burning in the window of a small farm (it was around 2:00 a.m. by this stage), and we thought, "Ha, this is where they are dividing up the loot." To get to the light, we had to walk a long way round to circumvent the water. When we got there, we found the family asleep and just a night-light burning.

After some further wandering we arrived in Nieuwlande about 4:00 a.m. and went to Van Veen's farm. We knocked and got them out of bed, giving them a terrible fright as they thought it had to be the Krauts or something like that. Instead they found three drowned cats[288] on their doorstep.

There we were greeted by a glowing-hot stove that we huddled round and were given real tea to drink. We took most of our clothes off and hung them above the stove to dry. We sat there until 7:30 a.m., by which time we were completely dry.

We thought we were alone in the room and said all sorts of things that were not meant for other ears. Then suddenly from all sides doors opened to reveal wall beds and the heads of three girls sticking out, two of Van Veen's daughters, and Riek [the Jewish girl] who was staying there.

We got three pairs of shoes from Van Veen. Peter's shoes had uppers and soles that were completely separated, Herman's were not much better, and mine were also full of holes.

We went to Nijhof, the local policeman, to report the theft. There the drama unfolded in a funny and unexpected way. Nijhof himself had taken our stuff out of the woods, thinking that it belonged to us. There had been some boys searching for eggs in the woods, and they had told Nijhof about their find. Herman found the whole affair very funny and is going to make a drawing. In the evening, we fetched all the stuff back.

May 6, 1944, Saturday Evening

WENT TO NIEUWE Krim to be scolded. Teased "Tante Louise" a bit. Bobby is going to school now, and he came to sit on my lap. I gave "Tante Annie" a peroxide treatment. [She is now a charming redhead.] I promised to send Norder, the carpenter, to make the entrance for a bomb shelter.

Yesterday evening Otten returned from Groningen. He had spoken with Johannes Post and came back with all sorts of stories about the Groningen underworld.

That night we slept, as in the old days, in the catacombs. Peter and Herman had a snooze there during the afternoon. I didn't want to go to bed but had to give in eventually and spent some time sleeping on the divan. First I had done some shopping and came past Van Veen's, where the three girls stood outside, laughing.

Joop came from Groningen this afternoon with two onderduikers for whom we have places. He also had smokers' coupons, so now we have four each. It means I don't have to smoke butts or cherry leaves any more.

Joop told us that controls in Groningen were very intense. The four of them had arrived in Hoogeveen yesterday evening and got through the controls there on their false papers. In Hoogeveen they'd had a real problem finding lodgings for the night. The taai-taai man was full to overflowing, and they had to try several other addresses before they got lucky.

It was again very busy in the Otten household. Seine is also going to try staying there again. "We have being so good with the underground shelter that there is not much to fear." He said.

Later I cycled to Dedemsvaart with eggs for Dinie, smokers' coupons, issues of *Trouw* and *Vrij Nederland* and other things.

May 7, 1944, Sunday Evening

MANY PLANES CAME over today, on their way to Berlin.

It was very busy in the Stegeman household with two birthdays and many visitors. Guillette [Arnold's sister] was also there with Van Aken, a retired missionary from Africa. We decorated the living room with all sorts.

"Tante Jo" came in the evening to stay for a few days because there was a family reunion at her host family's. I stole a couple of identity cards from the visitors and spent last night sleeping in the chicken coup.

May 8, 1944, Monday Evening

A COUPLE OF letters we received:

> Dear Arnold and Nico,
> Here are the summer clothes from the kids. Pass them on quickly, because they have only winter clothes. Mali
> B.A.

> Give me the exact monthly financial shortfall and perhaps I can make it up. I'd intended to come this evening with a very presentable eight-year-old girl, but I waited in vain at the station. What a misery with the telephones.[289] Herewith two identity cards. I can get the stamps from most municipalities in Overijssel on demand. Keep smiling, Hennie

> Dear A and N,
> This is to tell you about a change. Apart from Mia, Simon is also coming with me. He is the oldest of the family at 23 years old. We are going, I hope, Tuesday night or Wednesday morning to Pension Druivenkas.[290] Greetings, Hennie

> Dear A,
> Try to get a room for P. and G., perhaps at the taai-taai man's. You must not tell people who have rooms to let that the renters are NSB. I know from experience that they don't let rooms to NSBers and besides it is dangerous (assassinations and so forth). Just say that he is from the CDK, like Herman or Mrs. Hovink.
> I hope you have no objection to them coming. It is much better and nicer like this, and they play bridge very skillfully.[291] Greetings, Hennie

Last night I slept in the chicken coup and this morning listened to the news from London. Nothing. Hopeless.

A father and son visited Stegeman's office. They showed their match boxes.[292] They were Wietske's father and his son, who had been arrested but escaped and were therefore now underground. I took them to a farm.

Masses of planes and dog fights, but no parachutes.

May 9, 1944, Tuesday Evening

A RUMOR IS going round that Herman has gone to Amsterdam. He had said goodbye to a number of people beforehand. I cycled past the Dekkers' and was called over by Mrs. Dekker, who wanted to know exactly what the matter was with Herman. Of course I left with the impression that he had indeed gone to Amsterdam. I dropped in to see Jo at the Nijwenings', and when I told them that Herman had gone to Amsterdam, she winked. So she knows.

Peter and Herman are to stay in the hiding place at the Ottens'. I'll provide them with food if Mrs. Otten has to go away. Otten doesn't sleep at home any more.

May 10, 1944, Wednesday Evening

FOUR YEARS AGO today, the Krauts invaded our country. Four years of the greatest oppression in the history of our people.

The reports [on the radio] are not worth listening to. Spirits are low and nerves are on edge, but the weather is beautiful. The little rabbits dart through the woods, the cuckoos sing their familiar refrain. Lucky animals.

Peter has created the first issue of a new paper, *De Nieuwsflits*. It is neat piece of work and Oom Gerrit, who saw it, offered Peter a job after the war.

This afternoon we listened to London and heard the queen speak of the heroic attitude of the Dutch people, etc., etc. We were irritated when we heard this particular, and uncalled for, praise. It was much criticized. The queen, we agreed, was the victim of completely erroneous information. It would have been better if London had told the Dutch people about the situation in a far more forceful way. Then perhaps a small minority might wake up.

Herman went round with coupons and ration cards today, pretending that he had come back from Amsterdam.

Mrs. Otten has finally decided to leave her house for good (at least temporarily). She didn't want to, but we all urged her to do this and she left this evening on her bicycle with Arie and went to Douwe Doornbos in Nieuw Zwinderen. She took a very roundabout route along the byways, to lead those watching up the garden path. Otten and I took a different route and met her at a prearranged place. We pushed her the rest of the way between us as cycling was a bit too much for her.

Otten and I went back via Lunenberg to visit a smallholder on 't Kanaaltje where a Jewess is hiding. Otten and I wanted to place another onderduiker there as well, but the Jewess had contracted scabies and was being treated with ointment [by the doctor], so it was better that no one else was placed there. We were sad about this [but what could we do?].

I also went to see Snippe[293] and dropped off two ration cards and then went "home." Otten went back to Bouwe Doornbos. Beautiful weather.

At Otten's house Peter and Herman sat in the kitchen drinking milk. There was a whole load of milk that needed drinking else it would go sour. We chatted about this and that and then took everything that might look suspicious into the underground hiding place and then also ourselves. I went up again as I realized that the front door key was still on the inside of the lock. We had arranged it so that the entrance hatch would be covered by a broom and a dustpan when it was closed. We listened to the news from London and then went to sleep.

May 11, 1944, Thursday Evening

TODAY WAS A day that we'll find hard to forget.

We were lazing in the straw when Peter awoke me with his hand over my mouth, whispering, "Pssst. Danger." We heard the hum of voices and a car engine. The doorbell rang, and then rang again. Someone shouted, "Shoot through the door, that'll wake them up." "Kick the door in." "You do it, I don't have my boots on."

Crack! There went the door.

I slowly raised my body and looked through a ventilation grid. I stared at two things in particular, the rays of the rising sun and the face of a tall guy in a Sicherheitspolizei (Sipo) uniform. Very carefully I lowered myself down again. Peter looked at his watch; it was a quarter to six. Above our heads was a thunder of boots. Everything was searched.

We thanked heaven that Mrs. Otten and Arie had gone just in time. We had a difficult time down below because we were likely to cough and sneeze but had to find the strength to suppress any such coughing. We also had to do what one always does in the morning. Herman peed into a cushion to dampen the noise. I let it out very gradually into the straw. We also heard shots. First one, then another.

Later I saw Dr. Reijnierse on the street through the grating that I was sitting behind. I tried to draw his attention with straws, but it didn't work.

[We had also acquired a carrier pigeon from a farmer's son who had seen it fall in a cage attached to a parachute. We had already attached a message to its leg, telling of a large cache of V2 spares on the airfield at Teuge, near Apeldoorn.] The pigeon in its cage was with us in the underground bunker while all this took place. For the whole three hours, the bird kept quiet. We could not hang anything over the cage as that would have required movement and made the straw crackle.]

After those three hours, by Peter's watch, we heard one car leave, and then another. We had some idea what was happening by bits of broken conversation outside. When we saw schoolchildren heading home, we knew that something had happened at the school or at Griffioen's, the headmaster. Then people gathered in front of the house, and one said, "I'll go in and put the light out that they've left on." When we heard this person come in through the doorway, we knew that they [the Germans —translator] had gone.

Herman and I were completely out and Peter halfway out when we heard a car. Peter dived down like lightening, and we followed him. Luckily the car went past so we came out again, shut the hatch, placed the broom and other things on top, and went outside. People on the street were astonished to see us come out of the house that had been the subject of an SD search for three hours.

[It turned out that] Agatha Griffioen, the headmaster's 17-year-old daughter, had been shot through the leg when she opened the door to the [Nazi] thieves. They wanted to take him away, but he chewed them out and that seemed to help. His daughter was lying in the passageway with a bullet in her leg. Griffioen demanded that they make one of their cars available to take her to the hospital. This they refused to do.

They then telephoned Dr. Brouwer [in Elim]. His wife answered and, when she realized she was talking to the SD, told them that her husband was not at home but attending a birth. So they called Dr. Reijnierse [in Hollandscheveld]. He was also very distrustful, but came anyway. He left his motorbike at home but came on a bicycle along the byways to Nieuwlande where he found out what was happening and then hastened to the scene.

Mr. Slik from Elim has also been taken away by the scum [*boeven*].[294]

The three of us went to Mrs. Dijk's via the back gardens of Otten, Griffioen, and Dijk. The fellows [*kerels*] have also taken our bicycles. Mrs. Dijk gave us pancakes and coffee. She was an angel.

The Krauts (Dutch traitors, most of them) knew more or less what had been going on at the Otten household. For example, they knew that Broertje [little Napoleon] had been there.

Herman went to see Kikkert to find out if we could stay there. Yes, that was OK.

From Kremer's, the only telephone left in Nieuwlande apart from the post office, I called the Bethesda Hospital in Hoogeveen to ask about Agatha Griffioen. She was apparently fine [as the bullet had not hit the bone].

I went to visit the Ottens in Nieuw Zwinderen. They were terribly worried because they had known since 7:30 a.m. that the SD had raided their house.

There were many rumors circulating (as was normal) that all the school staff were to be arrested.

Nico and Bep had gone into the woods. We took our little box with identity cards, *stamkaarten* and so forth to a safe place. Oom Dirk was, as always, very afraid. Nico, who had come back for the day, took him to the dominee.

In the evening, we mobilized a group of youngsters, some of whom did service as lookouts. One stood in the middle of the bridge in Nieuwlande from where he could see the whole road as far as the Coevordenstraat. A second boy stood on the next corner, about 100 meters from the first, and the third stood by the Ottens' house. In the other direction, toward De Krim, there were also two sentries, a little way apart from each other.

We completely emptied Ottens' house: all the bedlinen, blankets, sheets, silver, cutlery, photo albums, in short anything we could take out, and took it to neighbors

Simon and Ida Dijk. Collection v.d.Sleen.

and acquaintances: to Dijk, Griffioen, Norder, and a number of others. One of Seine Otten's brothers, Arend, came to help, also Oom Gerrit, who is staying at Dijk's but for safety reasons had fled into the fields, came back to help. In total there was Peter, Herman, Oom Gerrit, Arend, Otten, six other young boys, and me.

At 2:00 a.m. we had finished the removals. Mrs. Dijk gave us coffee and bread, and at 2:30 a.m. we went into the woods, loaded with blankets and fell asleep to the sound of the nightingales.

When I went to the Ottens in Nieuw Zwinderen the following morning, little Arie asked me, "Uncle Arnold, did the Krauts also get my elephant?" I reassured him and told him that I'd bring over his beloved elephant (which he had got for his birthday).

[Early that morning we had let the carrier pigeon go with its message. For a moment, it sat on the roof and then was gone—and in the right direction. That evening we listened to the radio and heard the message "Carpe Diem and all is well." This was our signal that the pigeon had arrived safely, and the following day, the airfield was successfully bombed.]

May 12, 1944, Friday Evening

HAD A GOOD sleep and was up early. We took the blankets to Kikkert and had breakfast there. I then went to Nieuwlande and Herman followed later. Collected tobacco from Wietske.[295] For us she had supplies; for those who came after—none.

Herman and I wanted to collect the radios we had hidden under straw at Jan Post's farm. One had disappeared; some ass had found it and handed it in to the police. The police had sent it on to [the Germans at] Assen.[296]

Clutching a radio, an elephant, and some other things we cycled to the Ottens [in Nieuw Zwinderen]. I was really worried about Nico, who was insisting on going to Hoogeveen. Around 200 Landwachters have arrived in the town to patrol the streets. This is in connection with the escape of Ds. Frits Slomp [Frits de Zwerver] from the prison at Arnhem.[297]

We arrived with the radio at Douwe Doornbos just in time to hear the broadcast from London. A new Allied offensive has begun in Italy.

We discussed plans for the night. We are going to do roughly what we did last night.

Ham, the owner of Otten's house, wants to change the locks and give the key to the police, but that's not going to happen. Ham is a malevolent and frightened dog [*kerel*].

I went back to see Otten and warned him to stay off the roads. Too many controls. NSBers had reported him in Hoogeveen a couple of days ago. Peter wrote in his clandestine newspaper *De Onderduiker*, "The Landwacht is waiting for you, don't wait for the Landwacht."

Near Elim I saw some boys fishing. "Shouldn't you be at school?" I asked. "No," came the reply. "Our teacher was dragged out of the classroom by the shits this morning."[298]

May 13, 1944, Saturday Evening

YESTERDAY EVENING WE cleared more from Otten's house, for example a folding bed that we took to Dijk's as a couple of guys now sleep there when necessary. Very late last night we had a pancake banquet at Dijk's and then went to Kikkert to collect the blankets and then into the woods to sleep.

I went to Van der Helm's to place the boys (Peter and Herman) there.[299] He asked me to take "Minister de Geer" away because he couldn't get through the hatch into the hiding place. We had a long talk with them all. Minister de Geer is an elderly Jew who claims to have various diseases. He is very difficult and looks like the former prime minister [hence his name].[300]

In defense of Van der Helm, I would point out that if every Dutch citizen had done as much as he did, then not a single victim would have fallen into German hands.

Yesterday was the second anniversary of my "going underwater." Last night I again slept well with the nightingales.

The pressing need now is a place for Peter and Herman where they can work. Van der Helm won't have them. Kikkert would but doesn't have the space. Nienhuis, no. With Dijk perhaps?

Beukema has found me a new bicycle. "We'll talk about the price later," he said. It's a top-quality bicycle from before the war and with excellent tires.

I ate at Dijk's and took a chamber pot (*pispot*) from there to Jo. Went via Ham to talk about the garden. I had the chamber pot on the handlebars of my bike, and people stared at me as though they had never seen one before.

Little Arie sees himself as a real onderduiker. He told me that he had been playing with the Doornbos children until the baker's boy from Nieuwlande arrived, who wasn't supposed to know he was there. "I couldn't get away quickly enough," [he said]. "But I lay flat on the floor between the [other] children, and he didn't see me." Otten has also become a real onderduiker, dressed in an overall and carrying a dung fork. They have planted a small field of tobacco. Arie is over the moon with his elephant. "That is one thing they didn't get. Right, Uncle Arnold?"

May 14, 1944, Sunday Evening

YESTERDAY EVENING WHEN we were at Kikkert's, Pastor Hoogkamp from Elim was there and he has to go underground.[301] He's a good guy and had received a warning. He told us a few things about the raids in Bunschoten-Spakenburg where his father had been arrested.

He told one story of a man who had hidden in a manger with a radio. The radio was discovered but not the man. Another hid in a wardrobe; he was all but touched but not discovered.

One young man whose father is an NSBer had stolen a membership list. On the list was one name whom no one knew was a member and who was assumed to be a patriot [*goed Nederlander*]. He had [deliberately] paid his membership fees in another town.

The runways at Havelte [airfield] will be ready in about twenty years if the current tempo of work is maintained.[302]

Two onderduikers had hidden themselves in a hayloft and two Krauts had lain on top of them to take a nap.

The raids in Bunschoten-Spakenburg had been carried out by 1,000 men between 2:00 a.m. and 5:00 p.m. Result: five onderduikers caught [three men and two boys].

Yesterday evening, Jansje Boer, who we strongly suspect of being the traitor in our midst, was given a severe beating by the police for being on the street after 11:00 p.m.

Snorretje stayed the night with Beukema and arrived around 11:15 p.m. Half an hour later a car pulled up outside. They were, of course, frightened, but it turned out to be a false alarm. It was Johannes Post, who left a few minutes later on a motorbike. Snorretje handed Fl.2,000 to Nico.

We took a few more things from the Otten house and now everything has gone. Herman and I have been sorting the things out [temporarily hidden] at Norder's, Visser's, and Dijk's to take to Seine and Jans. Beukema gave me 15 pictures of Thea to give to Peter.

Herman and I ate at Visser's. Peter is coming [to stay] at Dijk's house.

May 15, 1944, Monday Evening

THIS MORNING HERMAN went round with ration cards. Nico has dropped out on the orders of Johannes Post and must no longer be seen on the street, not least because of the much greater risks he runs because of his "typical" Jewish nose. He has gone underground at the Ladies' and no one will know if he has left Nieuwlande or not. He will now go completely underground, in the way that he has advised and helped so many others to do.

Last night I slept late in the "Singing Nightingale Hotel,"[303] [and although it rained we had a tarpaulin over us.] I had breakfast at Kikkert's. Pastor Hoogkamp was also there but left before we ate. The Kikkerts are very religious and very good people.

May 16, 1944, Tuesday Evening

WE WERE COLD last night. Frost. The flowers, tobacco, potato, and bean plants were all damaged.

Rumors about the invasion—we yearn for it.

A decree from six and a quarter [Reichskommissar Seyss-Inquart] about conditions in the event of an invasion. Herman is also going to stay with Dijk. We have taken Otten's folding bed there.

I went to Bouwe Zijlstra, where there was a message for me about a place for a man and his wife. I was given 100 [ration] cards.

Telegram from Henny: She is coming to Dedemsvaart with Mia. I went to meet her. There were controls on the roads, so I took the tracks and byways and everything was OK.

May 17, 1944, Wednesday Evening

ARRIVED IN DEDEMSVAART yesterday evening. Henny is here with Mia. She (Henny) has all sorts of problems. Traveling is becoming very difficult with all manner of controls. She wants to place two people with the employment exchanges, distribution offices, and town halls in Drenthe. I don't think much of this plan.

Mia spent the night at Sister Scholten's and Henny at a photographer's.

May 18, 1944, Thursday Evening

ASCENSION DAY. A beautiful morning.

I took Mia on the back of my bike to Nieuwlande via the backroads without any trouble from controls.[304] I dropped her off at Visser the postmaster's and then went to fetch Herman and Hillie for a meeting. Herman and Mia embraced.

We went on the Nieuwe Krim, where the meeting between mother and daughter was wonderful. I stayed with Sister Scholten after much squabbling and chatter.

May 19, 1944, Friday Evening

THERE ARE RUMORS that there is a Gestapo agent in the area passing himself off as an onderduiker. He had been at various addresses but had not been liked and nobody trusted him. I was given an address where he was now. I went there and he had spent the night, but had gone into the heathland. I found him in the middle of the heath and had a conversation with him, but I still don't know what to think. I'm inclined to think that he's OK [*goed*]. [But I am not sure so I'm warning everyone not to say anything.]

There have been problems about Mia [not of her doing, poor girl]. It had been agreed that she would spend the day working at Sister Scholten's and then sleep at Hoogeveen's, but Hoogeveen has now objected. He says: "Scholten is running no risks but gets the advantage of Mia's work, so let the coward also take someone in." How this is going to pan out, I have no idea. Scholten says that she cannot possibly spend the night there because of the children talking. Of course, that's just an excuse.

I talked to the Hoogeveens about a hiding place and after much debate we agreed on a place. I'll give Norder the carpenter a prompt to go there. At the minute, they have a potato cellar but it is far from safe.

Back to Nieuwlande and to Dijk—our new headquarters.

I went to see the Beaver and told him about Henny's idea for these two from Amsterdam (it is a man and wife) to work in the town halls, etc. He was also unenthusiastic, and we decided not to go ahead with the plan.

Wietske did not know that her brother had left Dedemsvaart. She was surprised. He had had disagreements with the farmer's wife.

This morning I spent clipping out the coupons that need to be taken to various distribution offices.

Van der Helm stopped me and spoke about Minister de Geer. He wants me to find another place for him as he [Van der Helm] is getting nervous. I told him I had no time and that everyone was getting more nervous and that it was a very normal and nothing unusual in these times.

Arend Schonewille[305] stopped me to say that he had heard indirectly from NSB sources that they were again looking for me and that I should be careful. Drukker also stopped me with the same message.

I went to Bouwe Zijlstra with coupons and then to Dr. Reijnierse, who wanted to know all about the raid on the Ottens'. He laughed out loud when told about Ms. Visser, at the post office, who had treated the "gentlemen" who had come to use the telephone correctly, but as [if they were] dirt.

I took some ration cards round. Pietje Schonewille, the NSBer who lives across the road from Kats, was walking around with his gun over his shoulder and wearing an armband.

In Groningen 133,000 ration cards were stolen in broad daylight straight from the printers.[306]

Dijk and his wife cycled from Hoogeveen, having been to Groningen by train. Mrs. Dijk was stopped on the train and asked her name. She had replied: "Little man, my name is on my identity card" but then spent ages trying to find it. The Landwacht were not amused.[307]

The Landwacht from Coevorden have been patrolling the countryside. Otten is very careful and has a brilliant hiding place in which to disappear. I took him the chamber pot.

Eight onderduikers were arrested at Op 't Landschap. They were having a film evening, the asses. Geert Schonewille on his motorcycle was shot at [by the Landwacht] guys with their shotguns. The pellets bounced off his leather coat, and he only got four in his leg.

Herman and I were packed and went into the woods.

May 20, 1944, Saturday Afternoon

HERMAN AND I had a good night's rest in the woods. We built a sort of bunker to store the blankets. Well camouflaged, but it took a lot of work. We heard voices and stopped work. It turned out to be four Landwachters heading eastward. Herman is sitting editing a letter from Minister de Geer that consists of 18 sheets of very small writing. "Hopeless work," he says.

May 21, 1944, Sunday Evening

YESTERDAY AFTERNOON AROUND 3:00 p.m. had wonderful pancakes from Mrs. Dijk. Yesterday evening, two Landwachters went round Nieuwlande handing out summonses to go and work on the airfield at Havelte; no one went.

All men's bicycles are to be confiscated. At Zweeloo, a raid on an *Ausweis* shipment[308] failed [but no one was caught].

Bouwe Zijlstra persuaded me to try to find his new hiding place, but I couldn't. It's perfect. Bolwijn has offered to take Herman in, but it is not necessary. Herman likes to sleep in the woods and for the rest he relies on Mrs. Dijk.

May 22, 1944, Monday Evening

THERE WAS A message from the widow Swiers asking me to come at once. She was very nervous and told me that Liesje, the five-year-old, had been seen by an NSBer and that sometime after an unknown man had come and warned her that she had to get rid of the girl right away. I took Liesje with me to Dijk's, and then to Padding's, where she can stay for the time being.

I took ration cards to Hendrik Bleeker, the wagonmaker, who was busy pressing oil seed to make oil illegally, and to Teun de Vries. From there I went to Bouwe Zijlstra with 17 inlay sheets for Albert Nijwening.[309]

I got a telegram from Nel:[310] "Arnold go immediately to your sister." It meant nothing to me.

A letter from Henny. She will be in Dedemsvaart tomorrow morning.

I have a place for "Oom Dirk," a perfect spot, nice people. Bombs have fallen near their house twice.

Tinie Zijlstra was also there, looking for a place for a couple.[311] I can help with this.

I went to Jan Post. The radio from Otten's is still at the local police station. Bleeker had a letter for Otten about ration coupons.

There is nervousness in the area about possible reprisals related to Havelte, as no one is going there [to work].

Minister de Geer has left Van der Helm after he [Van der Helm] found an alternative place. I made no objection. As far as I was concerned it was a good place.

I had a terrible problem with butter. A mass of onderduikers had been given two halves of a ration card rather than one whole one. On the second half was a coupon for butter that had expired but I was able to trade them in with Wieten and still obtain the butter. Now I have to go all over the place selling butter, but it's an uphill struggle as everyone thinks they are not getting enough. It's a complete shambles.

I went to see Jo, who is very down.

May 23, 1944, Tuesday Evening

I LOOKED UP Nico. He does not like his forced unemployment.

I gave Peter a bundle of identity cards and other things to be "doctored."

Eventually I arrived in Dedemsvaart via the back routes. There were checkpoints everywhere. I have a list of things I need which I'll try to get one by one.

Agreed with Sister Scholten that she'll go with "Freddy" this week to Groningen to take measurements for a *beugel*.[312]

Again, there are many death sentences listed in the newspaper. Yesterday evening there were masses of planes and flares in the sky. We thought it was the invasion.

Delivered identity cards to Dr. Brouwer and went to Mr. Slik, who is now free again. He warned me: "Get out before it's too late."

Controls in the trains are now targeting women.

Letter from Henny:

> Dear Arnold,
> Mrs. van Houweningen's daughter is longing to see her mother. Now the mother can stay at the same place as the daughter. The next time I come, can you make sure I can take her on the 6:30 a.m. tram to Zwolle. You'll be rid of the old bat and have an additional place free.
>   I want to bring a 17-year-old girl, Type 2 [B.3] I had intended her for the Sahara, but she has baulked at sitting in the kitchen all day and of course, she is right. The Sahara is simply a place of Jewish exploitation by those stuck-up women [*KK-dames*].
>   Bye, Henny

May 24, 1944, Wednesday Morning

ILLEGIBLE ON ACCOUNT of its time in the ground.

May 31, 1944, Wednesday

THE ENTRIES FOR the intervening days are unreadable.

It is Herman's birthday today. We wanted to have a party and had everything arranged, but Herman did not want any recognition of his birthday.

There was a raid in Hollandscheveld.

A gas tank fell nearby. I heard and saw the thing fall and found it in a rye field. Dr. Reijnierse, who was in the village at that particular moment, got the leftover gasoline.

Went to see Mr. Zijlstra and Big. Everything was fine.

"Auntie Eef" has homesickness.

It's no longer safe in Hollandscheveld.

The rest illegible.

June 1, 1944, Thursday Evening

A LETTER FROM the couple hiding at Dekker's—Wietske's parents. They want a different hiding place as they don't think it's safe anymore. Naturally I'll leave them there. It is no less safe than anywhere else.

The rest is illegible.

The last photograph of Johannes Post, June 1944. Collection Hovingh.

June 2, 1944, Friday

DE RAAD AND Johannes Post reportedly arrested.
ILLEGIBLE.

June 3, 1944, Saturday

JOHANNES POST HAS not been arrested but De Raad has. Took ration coupons round. Got a bottle of acetone from Zijlstra to give to Peter. Also got a bottle of 30 percent peroxide from Dr. Reijnierse to make victims blond.

Jo can go to Baker Bolwijn.

Large sections unreadable.

June 5, 1944, Monday Evening

I PAID A visit to the Haitjema family. Mrs. van Houweningen is a crushing bore, and they would love to be rid of her. Their wish will now be granted because Henny can take her to her daughter in Almelo. I bought things for Peter and Herman, various sorts of ink, paint, pens, pencils, and paper. It's a real problem getting all these things as stocks are nearly exhausted.

Received letters from Lia and Tineke to go to their parents. Lia's letter was full of heaven and hell.

It is rumored that Mussert will be in Dedemsvaart tomorrow.

June 6, 1944, Tuesday

THIS MORNING I was about to set off for Nieuwlande when a message arrived that the invasion had begun. We didn't set much store by this as there had been so many [false] rumors in the past, but to be certain, we went to listen to the radio at Avondlicht. There was Mr. de Jong already with the radio out from under the floor, and it was true. They had landed between Le Havre and Cherbourg. Everyone went wild. Frits jumped a meter in the air and came down on Dinie's toes, who was not best pleased.

Klaas Reine the fat NSBer's house was bedecked with flags. Not because of the invasion but because he was expecting a visit from Mussert.

Dijk received an anonymous warning letter through the post:

> Dear Mr. Dijk,
> We want to stress to you that if the free movement of people to and from your house continues as it is, you will get into serious difficulties. We are asking you to draw the necessary conclusions from this letter and we assure you that we are doing this in your own interests. You will not be warned again.

Peter and I were busy sorting out identity cards, as many of our clients still need one.

This evening we listened to the radio at Griffioen's. Everything is going well.

The rest, illegible.

June 7, 1944, Wednesday

THERE ARE UNCONFIRMED rumors that Albert Rozeman, Jan van der Zee, Henk Raak, and many others have been shot.[313]

This morning I collected a confiscated radio.

Paulien Zijlstra, the daughter of Bouwe Zijlstra, came in the afternoon with the remaining ration cards. She confirmed the rumors about Rozema, Van der Zee, and Raak. She told me that she had coupons for inner tubes for my bike.

June 8, 1944, Thursday Evening

WE HAVE HIDDEN the radio in the chimney and listen on a regular basis. Coevorden is empty; there are rumors going round that the town will be heavily bombed. Shops are shut and the schoolchildren have a free day.

The rest illegible.

June 9, 1944, Friday

A RATION CARDS and *Trouw* day.

June 10, 1944, Saturday

PETER GOT A package of identity cards ready, which I then brought to our customers. All the buses in the Netherlands have been confiscated [by the German army].

June 11, 1944, Sunday Evening

RECEIVED A MALE onderduiker from Sister Scholten. I took him to a farmer halfway between De Krim and Nieuwlande, a nice, lonely spot.

Sister Scholten gave me Fl.1,000.

I sought out Johan, and all is well there. People think he is an evacuee from Rotterdam. The musician is also doing well.

Large raid in Balkbrug.

June 12, 1944, Monday Evening

THIS AFTERNOON I took an onderduiker with a heart complaint by car from Dedemsvaart [to Nieuwlande].

The Landwacht have raided the Douwe Doornbos farm, but they didn't find Mrs. Otten.

Jansje Boer, whom we think is the traitor in our midst, stopped me and asked me for ration cards. Of course, I had no idea what he meant. Teun de Vries came to me with a plan to eliminate him [*uit de weg te ruimen*].

Bleeker also came to see me, but I pretended not to be at home.

Fat Jo ["Jopie Felix," as Herman calls her] is at baker Bolwijn's and it is going well.

Bouwe Zijlstra and his entire family have gone underground. The army of onderduikers grows and grows.

June 13, 1944, Tuesday Evening

THE INVASION IS one week old. A week of storms and rain. We have subscribed to various newspapers, including the NSB *Nationale Dagblad*.

Mrs. Otten and Arie have gone to her brother-in-law's in Moskou.

Today there are NSBers going round all the farmers and checking their acreages of rapeseed to see how much each farmer will have to hand over.

Peter and I went to the writers of the threatening letter. First, we told them that we had received it, and we asked them what they thought of such a thing. They agreed that this was dirty sabotage. Then we told them that we knew where the letter had come from.

Sister Zijlstra visited me accompanied by another nurse in the pouring rain to talk about "Tante Johanna," the young woman placed in Norg [a small village between Assen and Groningen]. At first everything was fine. She helped with the housework and for the rest minded her own business, but later she started to go out with Krauts, so she has to go.

This is a difficult and dangerous case.

We asked Mrs. Dijk to take her, but she, who is always willing to help, will have nothing to do with it. "No," she said, "that's not going to work, especially with Oom Gerrit around. He's crazy enough as it is." Tomorrow we'll try Visser. We have moved the radio to under the floor; it is much safer there than in the chimney.

Van der Helm visited me with an urgent request to find somewhere else for Minister de Geer. He says he has had more than enough of him.

There are rumors going around that KZ Vught is to be evacuated and all the inmates taken to Germany.

Peter is busy sending out rye bread loaves.

June 14, 1944, Wednesday Evening

A SURPRISE RAID on a prison in Rotterdam has freed 16 condemned men. One of them was Pastor van Ginhoven, a brother of the Van Ginhoven at De Steeg. In Arnhem 40 prisoners have also been freed.[314]

Mrs. Otten came here on her bicycle and told me about the tense moments she had experienced during the raid at Douwe Doornbos's.

Peter and I went to see Visser to see if he would take "R. de H" but no luck. "R. de H." is short for "Rachab the Whore,"[315] which is what we have christened Tante Johanna since we found heard stories that she was going out with Krauts.

It is said that the Landwacht is being called up for service in France and that many of this noble guild are now going underground. Mussert has put on a German uniform and has volunteered to serve with the German army in the event of an Allied attack on our country. I am sure this will give the Allies pause for thought about their plans.

Herman is still ill. Fat Jo has scabies, and we considered taking her to the Bethesda Hospital in Hoogeveen. Joop was here with a friend of Oom Gerrit. The atmosphere is very tense, and it feels as if we are living on the edge of a volcano.

I remembered something from the illegible period. Little Liesje had to leave the widow Swiers in a hurry as a result of a betrayal. I took her to Padding's, where she stayed a week before being moved on to Dedemsvaart.

June 15, 1944, Thursday Evening

I WENT WITH a package of ration cards to "Geer." On my way back I picked some wild flowers for Mrs. Dijk.

The Hitler Youth was out practicing and being drilled by German officers. Such an uplifting sight, all these noble Germans.[316]

Herman is now better. He and I went into the woods to find a suitable place for an underground bunker and found one. We also fetched a roll of tar paper from Norder. Henk Sweepe asked about identity cards and *stamkaarten*. We will have to see what is in our tin box.

June 16, 1944, Sunday Evening

YESTERDAY EVENING I got a message via the Nieuwlande Post Office from Dedemsvaart that a present had arrived. The present was a new identity card for me, which I could collect the following morning.

[The identity card was in the name of Hendrikus Marinus van der Vegt who had been born in 1906—the same year as Douwes—but had been killed in an accident in 1923. The officials at the population registry removed him from the death registry and provided a narrative that had Van der Vegt moving from one municipality to another over the following twenty years. His new identity card showed that he was working for farmer Frans de Graaf in Nieuwlande, and Douwes lost no time in telling de Graaf about the subterfuge.]

Went to Sister Scholten and brought her some clothes for the children.

Everything is fine with the onderduikers. The musician is longing for a piano, but he'll have to make do with singing as his hiding place is otherwise perfect.

Everything is also fine with Johan, who works with great satisfaction to himself and his boss at a vegetable nursery.

Things with de Bijenkorf exceed all expectations, although a lot of money is being paid to keep her.

It was Frits Stegeman's birthday, and he had lots of visitors.[317] The conversations lasted the whole evening: about Krauts, the war, onderduikers, bombs, and the invasion.

June 17, 1944, Saturday Afternoon

ONCE AGAIN THERE is a list of death sentences in the newspaper. This morning I went to see Leenhouts at the town hall. He is the clerk in charge of the population registry and who provided the priceless identity card for me. I have now been "placed round," as the experts term it. I was born in Wije, my name is Hendricus Marinus van der Vegt. I have lived in Dalfsen and Ommen and now reside in Dedemsvaart but will be moving to Oosterhesselen next week—all entirely legal.

I can also get all my rations legally and naturally, also have a new *stamkaart*.

I have found a good place for Mrs. Otten and Arie with the Krabbe sisters, who own a small shop. The weather is extremely bad.

June 18, 1944, Sunday Night

CYCLED TO NIEUWLANDE this afternoon. No checkpoints on the way out, but there on the way back. I went to Seine Otten's brother in Moskou to tell them about the place I had found for Jans Otten and Arie, but she was not there as she was visiting her husband in his hiding place.

Little Arie looks well. He came up to me and said, "Uncle Arnold, I have to talk to you, go with me to the bench in front of the house." I went with him and then he asked me in a whisper, when he was sure that there was no one listening, whether I had found a good place for him and his mother. "I don't want to know where it is, just that it is a good place. Mamma has found a place at Schuinesloot, but it is not very good." While we were talking, a little girl came to stand by us. "No Marie," said Arie. "You have to go away as we have to talk."

The Landwacht kommandant in Assen has got what was coming to him. He has been shot dead.[318]

I went briefly to Visser to return the envelope in question. "Broertje" was at home and recognized me immediately.

I looked up Herman. This young man is completely recovered. Tomorrow or the day after we hope to start work on digging our bunker [hol]. Now that we have acquired the asphalt/tar paper that is one major obstacle overcome.

Jo is getting much better. We didn't take her to the hospital as the doctor is looking after her at home.

I took some maps of the fronts to the Ladies. Nico is very happy with his new identity card. No one knows that he is hiding there.

I went via De Krim to Dedemsvaart and was stopped by six Landwachters, who examined my new identity card closely. Eventually I was given it back with a "Yes, it is good." I agreed with them, that it was indeed good and went on my way, warning everyone I met of their presence.

June 19, 1944, Monday Morning

WENT TO THE population office [in Oosterhesselen] about my "move." Everything was in order.

I managed to lay my hands of a quantity of brown wrapping paper for Peter's rye bread and also a hank of old [good quality] string. I ordered Z-maps,[319] blank identity cards, and *Ausweise*.

I have found a place for R. de H. from July 1 onward at Fl.150 per month.

The Russians have broken through the Mannerheim line.[320]

June 20, 1944, Tuesday Evening

WENT TO NIEUWLANDE yesterday evening along the paths and backroads, but there were still checkpoints at specific places, so it took me an hour longer than usual [I had to avoid the checkpoints as I was carrying a large quantity of an underground newspaper, *Ons Volk*.][321]

Today I was busy distributing the newspaper, which had a very good headline article.

I also conjured up two axes, put handles on, and sharpened them, as well as getting together everything we needed to create our bunker. The idea is that we start tomorrow.

I have been to Henk Sweepe with one of our [precious] tins and he has taken out some identity cards and *stamkaarten*.

The story being told by our mysterious onderduiker that he came from Nunspeet and had helped Allied pilots is not true. No one in Nunspeet knows who he is. [If he really had helped British and American airmen he would not have spoken about it. Something must be done to stop him for good.]

I went to Hans and Little Peter with clothes and letters. The latter is sick, so I asked Dr. Brouwer to look in on him. The two boys have a safe hiding place where they sleep. They are always pleased to see me. Soon we hope to organize a reunion between them and Hans's parents.

Heading back, I crossed the bridge in the center of Nieuwlande and saw loads of people around, but before I had time to get over my surprise, I saw a young man cycling furiously past me. He was waving a revolver and shouted, "Long live the Queen!" The background to this story is as follows: During the afternoon, the distribution office at Coevorden had been raided.[322] Two collaborator [*verkeerd*] policemen, a civil servant, and a driver were in a car [looking for the perpetrators].

The civil servant saw two of the perpetrators on the Straatweg in Nieuwlande and there was a veritable shootout, but the two boys escaped, and it was one of them whom I saw.

The other crawled through the canals and was eventually taken in by Elema, soaking wet, and then taken to a hiding place at Jan de Boer the shoemaker's.[323] I put his wet clothes in a bundle and dumped them underwater with an eye to the possible use of bloodhounds, who duly arrived later. I had also sprinkled pepper.

I spent a few minutes with Nico. He gave me two packets of cigarettes and pills to keep fit for the boy in the hiding place. He lost his revolver, and it is probably somewhere in the field. I'll attempt to track it down.

Herman is busy drawing cards that will be sold in aid of the onderduikers.

June 21, 1944, Wednesday

UP EARLY.

Our friend is well and I spoke to him. He told me where, according to him, I could find the revolver. This turned out to be wrong, but I found the thing and returned it to him. Van Goor had found it on his land and had accidentally discharged it twice.[324]

I went to Van der Helm's, where Hans's mother gave me a package for her son.[325]

Went to Herman and arranged for him to be at Dijk's at 3:00 p.m. to have his photograph taken. He had slept the previous night at our old place with the man from Bolwijn's.

The papers for my move came in the post from Dedemsvaart. I took them to the town hall. The only thing I do not have is an old *stamkaart*, but that can be arranged.

Lidia was here. She told us that a list of "invasion hostages" had been discovered in Nieuw-Amsterdam. Gorter was top of the list.

Tinie Zijlstra came with a message: "R.de H. must have a new place." She also wanted to know if we needed ration cards. Herman and I are going to sleep in the woods tonight with plenty of provisions. Tomorrow we will begin our bunker.

June 22, 1944, Thursday Evening

SPENT THE WHOLE day digging in the woods. First, we removed the moss covering and then the black earth. We put these on separate heaps and then began to dig out the hole. All the shrubs that got in our way were tied back with string so that no branches were broken. From now on, at least one of us will be in the woods until the whole job is finished so that we will know for sure if we have been discovered or not.

Herman dropped out for a while so that he could be photographed by Peter. He came back with a message that Bouwe Zijlstra and his son were waiting for me there, so I went over to them. Bouwe Zijlstra talked about a ration card distribution. I hope that it will all come right.

In my absence, Herman has done a lot.

June 23, 1944, Friday Evening

HERMAN AND I spent the whole day in the woods, working. The hole is not very deep because of the groundwater. We have laid branches on the floor to a depth of 15 cm and then straw on top. The roof is good and watertight. About 45 cm of black earth sits on top [of the tar paper]. Herman left in the afternoon to eat. I went in the evening. I got a card from the municipality saying that my new *stamkaart* was ready for collection.

June 24, 1944, Saturday Evening

LAST NIGHT WE slept in our new bunker. Lovely. I went to the distribution office to collect my new *stamkaart*.

I went to see Frans de Graaf, who told me about a load of confiscated bicycle tire inner tubes at the home of an NSBer in Nieuw Zwinderen. He asked if I'd go with Dirk to remove all this stuff. I'd be happy to do it, but not with Dirk, because as a former SS man who had gone underground, I will never trust him completely.

There should still be a hidden radio in the peat stack at Van der Zwaag's farm. De Graaf and I looked for it but could not find it.

Two hundred SS men have arrived in Hoogeveen.

This afternoon went back into the woods to continue camouflaging the hideout. It looks good. In the evening, back to Dijk.

Peter had a list of things for me he wanted. But more important was the fact that R. de H. had arrived unexpectedly. Peter came into the garden to tell me that she was in the house. We always came across the meadow from the woods to Dijk's and in via the back garden so that we could be seen from the kitchen.

Tinie Zijlstra had brought her by car, the "creature" having also been dumped on her doorstep without notice. I greeted her (R. de H.) coolly. Mrs. Dijk didn't want her in the house (because unfortunately we had let slip the story of her behavior).

Peter had written a letter to the dominee and got Frouke to take it to him "that we once more wanted to make use of his kind help . . . , etc., etc." Frouke returned with his reply—he would not help.

I tried various places and did a lot of talking, but all in vain. Eventually, I went to see Dominee Bos personally and, after a lot of talking, got her a place for one night, which was not a great deal of help.

At Slijkhuis's[326] I had better luck, and they will have her for a week, but no longer, and not starting before Monday. Eventually Mrs. Dijk agreed to keep her for that long and so we didn't take her to the parsonage at all.

Oom Gerrit, who was far from stupid, knew that there was something not quite right about R. de H. and wandered through the house. Finally, he couldn't keep quiet anymore and asked me outright to let him in on the secret and tell him what was up with the woman. I didn't make him any the wiser.

Mrs. Otten arrived with an identity card that we had requested for her husband, but it was no longer necessary as he already had one. A whole load of people have been round with requests and questions about identity cards.

I also went to see Van der Helm about R. de H. but came back with a flea in my ear.

The atmosphere in the Dijk household is tense. Oom Gerrit's behavior was amusing. He knew that there was "something" amiss with R. de H. and was dying to know what it was.

I finally got back to the woods at 12:45 a.m. Herman was lying awake as he had already been asleep for a while. He had been philosophizing about the miracle we call life and all its implications. It is cozy living underground, under the trees. I didn't tell Herman what had happened that evening, but kept it for the following morning.

June 25, 1944, Sunday Afternoon

HERMAN AND I slept really well. I told him about R. de H. He is in favor of getting rid of her [op te ruimen] but won't do it himself. I won't do it either. I think she deserves one more chance. Peter has read her the riot act more than once and Oom Gerrit now knows everything because he was eavesdropping.

I took her to Slijkhuis's,[327] where she can stay for a week but in general, they want nothing to do with Jews [Jeuden].

June 26, 1944, Monday Evening

ONCE AGAIN, SLEPT really well in our bunker. Herman left to make drawings while I stayed the whole day improving the camouflage. A layer of one and a half to two feet of earth is on top of the bunker, which I have planted full of all sorts of shrubs that I gathered from various parts of the wood with root balls attached. I only leave the intact branches and throw the rest away. Naturally there shouldn't be any dying leaves, but this is not easy in the middle of summer. The shrubs were mostly rowan, birch, buckthorn, and a few oaks. Once they were all planted I brought moss and clumps of grasses, dry leaves, and dead branches. Even the entrance was covered by dry branches.

In the evening, I heard shooting nearby, probably the Landwacht. There was also a thunderstorm. I went to sleep early. Herman did not come back.

June 27, 1944, Tuesday Evening

HERMAN CAME BACK very late and spent half an hour looking for the entrance. This speaks well of the camouflage. He did call out but I was too deeply asleep. He was soaking wet by the time he came in.

There had been a raid on the Van der Kerk house in Hoogeveen, but he had not been "at home" and had a lucky escape.

Nel arrived from Amsterdam without warning with clothes for all the children. She wants to visit some of them, but I am against it. She is completely trustworthy, but she doesn't need to know their addresses [or does she?]

Nel was carrying a letter from Henny. Jan and Kees have been picked up. At her own place there is also "scarlet fever," as it is called, and she has also gone underground, so she is no longer Loekie but Wil.

I ran into Geert Schonewille, and he gave me an account of the shooting the other night as it happened outside his house.

Peter and I discovered that we had ordered 100 fewer ration cards than we needed. I immediately wrote a note to Tinie Zijlstra to try to rectify the situation. I visited Pol, the distribution leader, about a shoe coupon. He said it would be all right.

Nel slept in our bunker last night. We have no mosquitoes in it—unlike outside. The other day we sent Mrs. Dijk to Hoogeveen to buy citronella to combat the mosquitoes. She couldn't get that but came back with something else "that was even better." We smeared our arms with it and the result was that all the mosquitoes in the wood came to taste it, whereupon they died. As we did not want to serve as a mosquito cemetery, we didn't use it again.

June 29, 1944, Thursday Evening

THE LANDWACHT HAVE left Hoogeveen. It is rumored they have been sent to the coast.

I went in search of a bundle of copies of *Trouw* that I hadn't received. No sign of them.

June 30, 1944, Friday

NOBODY WANTED TO have R. de H. in their house, but finally I had some luck with Koekoek in 't Langezak.[328] A wonderful address with nine adult women in the house. I'll take her there tomorrow. The Koekoek house is full of onderduikers. Broertje is there at the moment, as well as Dinie Post, Johannes's second-youngest child.

I also found another address, a worker's cottage in an out-of-the-way place where they'll not have someone permanently but certainly for a few days.

I spoke to our radio repairman, who told me that the Krauts had arrested my brother [Jan, minister in Den Bosch]. Jan's sister-in-law was visiting and saw the opportunity to grab a Jewish girl and some illegal newspapers and escape through a window in the roof and disappear via the neighbors.

All police leave has been canceled.

July 1, 1944, Saturday Evening

THIS MORNING I overslept in the bunker again. Had a quick wash and then went to fetch R. de H. and delivered her [at the Koekoeks's]. Once again, I spoke to her forcefully, and she made me angry by reeling off the names of people whose houses she had stayed in.

On my way back I stopped to pick flowers in Posts' garden and took them to Wieten. I got a prewar cigar and a glass of prewar orangeade [*ranja*].

July 2, 1944, Sunday Afternoon

OUR BUNKER HAS stayed dry in spite of the heavy rain over the last few days. This has helped all my planting, and there's barely a dead leaf to be seen.

I got a card for R. de H. written by her husband that he had written on a bus on the way to Arnhem. He had been in custody for 18 months and not sent on until now. When R. de H. read the card, she cried. [It means she is human. Sometimes I doubted that.]

July 3, 1944, Monday Evening

HERMAN IS BUSY drawing cards. We sell them all over the place, and it is going very well.

Oom Gerrit is complaining about his stomach and buys "black market" eggs whenever he gets the chance, to the great consternation of Mrs. Dijk, who thinks it is all humbug.

Frans de Graaf came over. According to my false papers, he is my employer.

I went to Nieuwe Krim to fetch Mia so that she can put her fingerprints on her new identity card. I got into a great argument with the Hoogeveen's neighbors about Oom Cor. They want rid of him—preferably immediately. I said that I'd come and fetch him in a few days.

There were still some of Ouwe Taaie's clothes there that should have been sent on [to Almelo, where she had been sent to live with her daughter]. I thought this had been done long ago. I took a few things out to give to other onderduikers, for example a gown for Ammi, a dress for Louise and a few other small things. She still has plenty left.

"Oom Cor" told me that his host and hostess wanted him out because he had refused to be baptized. In addition, they were scared. This is probably the main reason, I think. "Yes, there have been raids in Coevorden again . . . , etc."

Mr. Scholten [presumably the father of Sister Scholten] will no longer allow his daughter to borrow books from the library in Coevorden for "Tante Loes" because he thinks it is too dangerous.

Mia and I were caught in a thunderstorm, but got home just before the heavy rain started.

Peter has to put up with the constant nagging and harping of baker Jonker about the loaves of rye bread. They are not ready on time, not properly baked, it is too dangerous, etc. We still have three weeks' worth of rye from Jonker, after that Peter wants to switch to baker Bolwijn.

Bobby needs clothes. I will give him a few things meant for others, who will not miss them. We simply have to compromise with these things.

Our people in Nieuwe Krim would dearly love to have maps of the fronts, and I hope I'll be able to oblige.

Albert Nijwening asked me if I could find out any details about the NSB farm where all those stolen goods are being hidden, for example the security of where the goods are stored. He knows a couple of well-armed lads who would like to go there and "tidy up" [opknappen].

July 4, 1944, Tuesday Evening

I WENT TO Zwinderen to find out about the NSB farmer, but it appears that everything has been taken away. Four full truckloads.

Oom Gerrit left the house at 3:00 a.m. to go fishing. I went to find him to warn him that a squad of NSBers were expected who were coming to check the rapeseed grown by the farmers. He was scared stiff and would not go home but fled into the fields.

Hendrik Bleeker came. I had completely forgotten that I was supposed to go with him to Gramsbergen last evening.

Bouwe Zijstra and his inseparable son were also there. They told me that there would be a lag in the supply of ration stamps on account of a [new] overprint [achterdruk], but that it would get better and that the printers were working at full speed.

In Groningen, 100,000 ration cards had been seized so the Krauts or their lackeys had insisted on all cards being printed on the reverse as well, thus rendering the 100,000 [stolen] cards worthless. It won't do them any good, but it does mean more work for the printers and all the others involved.

There are all sorts of ugly rumors circulating about arrests in Dedemsvaart and that many members of the organization have been picked up.[329]

Nurse Smid was here with a message from Leenhouts [the clerk who supplied my most recent identity papers]. He is in Hollandscheveld—deep underground—and wants to speak to me. I think I'll have to find a hiding place for him.

Oom Cor can come to the Dijks. "But," said Mrs. Dijk, "what will Oom Gerrit say about it. I'm sure he won't like it." Naturally, I really couldn't care less.

I went to farmer Van Dijken, where Henk—Riek's husband—is living. Geert Schonewille took him there to stay for a week and he has now been there for 18 months. I asked for rye and was given 2 hectoliters [70 kilograms].

I also went to Schuiling find a place for another onderduiker. (We already have one there.) But even after a lot of talking it didn't come good. He did give me a packet of tobacco and bought a set of Herman's cards. It rained continuously and I got soaking wet.

Bleeker is running his oil press at full speed, but it is likely to come unstuck at least once. Bleeker acts as if there is no danger. He has already been betrayed once but managed to use the oil as a bribe.

A letter arrived for R. de H. from her husband in Westerbork. A cheerful letter.

July 5, 1944, Wednesday

I WENT TO see R. de H., who was delighted with the letter from her husband. All seems to be going well with her.

There was a telegram from Annie in Amsterdam. She is coming to fetch two children who, according to their parents, are being fed too much Christianity. This isn't going to happen. The children are in a safe place, and I'm going to leave them there for as long as it is secure. I immediately wrote a letter to Sister Scholten to say that I am nowhere to be found and that she knows nothing about the children.

Peter is once again up to his ears in rye bread.

Received some information about the events in Dedemsvaart. The bicycle maker Bonsius, the baker Kwaat, and three others have been picked up, as well as a number of onderduikers. An American plane came down near Ommen. Some of the crew escaped, but the people who helped them initially have been arrested.

I went to Gramsbergen with Bleeker, stopping at his parents on the way to listen to the radio, which was hidden in the mattress on which his sick father lay.

Success at the town hall in Gramsbergen. We were given identity card stamps and promises of more help. In cases of urgent need, we may be able to get identity cards like the one I have, where someone is turned around [*rond gezet*—brought back to life].

I received all manner of things for nothing from a shopkeeper in De Krim. For example, 1,000 [blank] postcards for Herman, pencils, rubber, paint, ink, blotting paper, wrapping paper, string, and lastly a huge cooking pot for Mrs. Hoogeveen to use to cater for all her onderduikers.

Broertje is now back with postmaster Visser. I took a number of orders for Herman's drawings. Lanting gave me Fl.25 for four of them.[330]

We received a request [to help] a carpenter with a rather dubious past, sticky fingers and so forth, but who had turned over a new leaf.

Bleeker knew a farmhouse where he got 10 eggs for Mrs. Dijk. Lidia was here. She needed 35 ration cards, but we didn't have any.

July 6, 1944, Thursday

THIS MORNING UP early and on the road with a bike loaded with parcels, clothes for various children, money for them and others, two pairs of clogs for Menno and Annie.

Tante Eef, who is with Mr. Zijlstra is, as always, terribly nervous and depressed. Every night she sleeps in the hiding place, which is fairly good.

I spoke to Leenhouts—he needs a good hiding place. He escaped from the drama at Dedemsvaart in the nick of time, as they were very much after him. We agreed that he would come to Nieuwlande this evening to find somewhere.

I went to Jan Kats, who had just had a meeting with Joop. He had sent him to me, so we just missed each other.

The Landwacht was busy patrolling and carrying out checks. I took every opportunity to avoid them.

Frits and Freddy are very well. I got fifteen eggs from their foster mother as a present. I also got a whole load of material from Mr. Wiegman for Peter and Herman, including a letter box with an ink cushion. I gave him an additional list and he'll do his best to get more things in the future. Loaded with all these precious things, I went unhindered by the Landwacht—who have not been sent to the coast—via byways back to Nieuwlande. Later on, Leenhouts arrived, and he'll sleep at Dijk's tonight.

I saw Joop, who promised to take care of clothes and such. Lately there have been many arrests in Groningen and in Zwolle.

The war news is good. Von Rundstedt has been fired by Hitler.[331]

I was going to Nieuwe Krim with Mia. But not tonight.

July 7, 1944, Friday Evening

WE GOT A shocking message this morning to say that Jan Wildschut had been arrested.[332]

Leenhouts can stay at the Dijk's, but I'll try to find another place for him as it is getting too full.

Yesterday morning Oom Gerrit was again out fishing early and was stung by an insect so that he now has a very swollen face. He now wanders around the whole day looking at himself with a pocket mirror.

Farmer Aasman visited me and asked if I would spare him a few minutes.[333] A woman with her son had arrived [ostensibly] sent by Aasman's brother in Nieuw Buinen. Aasman did not know the woman, and she wasn't carrying a letter of introduction. I went with him and was suspicious. I told the woman that I didn't know any hiding places for her son and had not heard of any organizations in the vicinity. The young man scolded "the rotten lot in Nieuwlande, a nothing organization."

I told Aasman that he needed to find out who they were before we would do anything. Moreover, I said that I could see no reason why he shouldn't hang on to the young man, at least temporarily, but he was not keen on the idea.

I received another letter about Lia and Tineke, but in spite of all the letters and telegrams, I am not prepared to take them to Amsterdam or have them taken there. They are in a good secure place, an excellent boardinghouse with great people.

There was a letter at the post office that Visser did not know what to do with. It was for me from Nel.

Annie is going to take a pair of boots for Herman to Dedemsvaart. I understand she arrived there today.

July 8, 1944, Saturday Evening

LAST NIGHT THERE were ten of us at Mr. Bos's house [Bos is also a schoolteacher], where we held a séance. Those present were Bos and his wife, Dolf and Elly, Henk the journalist, Oom Gerrit, Herman, Mia, Joop, and I. We were given instructions by Henk, who was going to call up the "spirits." No laughing, no talking. On the table was a letter and number board and a cross. In the end the whole thing was nonsense, but we had a bit of fun.

Around 2:15 a.m. a [German] police van passed by.

Around 3:15 a.m. Oom Gerrit and I went home. Everything was locked, but I got in through a tilting window [to open the door], then put on some old clothes and went to our hiding place in the woods, where I had a good sleep.

This morning I heard what had happened the previous evening. There had been raids in Hollandscheveld, Nieuweroord, and Hoogeveen. Headmaster Wiegman had been picked up.[334] Messages came from all directions. From Sister Adema and later from Sister Smid.

I went to Hollandscheveld. At Wiegman's, they had shot through the door and then taken him away. They had also been to Mr. Zijlstra but had found nothing.[335] He had been with his brother and Tante Eef in the hiding place. The thieves [*boeven*] had knocked on the wall; one said, "That sounds hollow, there might be something behind it." Tante Eef was completely overcome by fear.

I had received a message that I had to find places for six people, but it was not that bad. The people hiding at Wiegman's can stay put. Zijstra's son and his wife had gone their own way and that just left Zijstra's brother and Tante Eef.

We decided that he [the brother] could shelter in the attic of the schoolhouse, where Mrs. Wiegman could bring him food. I will take Tante Eef to Bolwijn. I explained the safe route for her to walk to Nieuwlande as she cannot ride a bicycle, but she got lost and ended up back at the school. I went back to fetch her, and we tried again.

Once Tante Eef had been delivered (temporarily) to Dijk I went with Mia to Nieuwe Krim. A heavy thunderstorm threatened, but we arrived still dry. Then I had to return to Nieuwlande with Oom Cor. We prepared quickly but the goodbyes took too long, and as I began to cycle, it began pouring with rain and we got soaking wet. Cor was dead tired from trying to ride the bike in the mud and had to walk for long stretches.

After that I put Tante Eef on the back of my bike and took her to Bolwijn. She caught her leg in the rear wheel and broke a couple of spokes. She was so upset.

At the post office there was a message from Beaver, [asking] if I was coming to Dedemsvaart in the morning.

July 9, 1944, Sunday Evening

CAEN HAS FALLEN.

Last night Herman slept in a farm cart, just for a change.

Jan, the son of Piet Mulder, arrived with a message that if we ever had urgent cases, I could call on him and come and talk.

Hartemink, where Oom Cor had been lodged and where I had suddenly been asked to take him away [because they weren't prepared to have him any more] came to see me and told me that his wife had not slept a wink since he left and that the dominee had preached so beautifully this morning that they had decided that "Oranje" [as they called him] had to be invited back. Miesje had arrived before him and told me that he and Hoogeveen were in the vicinity. We quickly organized a rendezvous in Otten's abandoned house, where Peter also played a part. We explained that Oranje would not return but that we would be happy to use the place for another client. This didn't go down well as Hartemink wanted Oom Cor back. [The negotiations were not easy, but thanks to Peter's good humor and perseverance things worked out OK.]

Oom Cor is happy as he can go outside from time to time. The same can be said for Tante Eef who has calmed down a lot at Bolwijn and finds it wonderful to feel a drop of rain after so many months indoors.

July 10, 1944, Monday

HERMAN IS NOW lodged with the Swiers family (the brother-in-law of the widow), where he had often been before to eat bacon. I found him a new pocket light for the one he lost.

This afternoon, I went to Dedemsvaart via De Krim. The wind and rain were against me, and I got soaking wet. There was a Landwacht checkpoint, but I managed to avoid it.

The ration cards have not yet arrived. [Everyone is asking for them.] We are all on edge.

I arrived in Dedemsvaart and heard that Broenink had gone to Nieuwlande with messages for me. Mrs. Otten had given him my address, which she had no right to do.

The airman who was hiding at Zanting has been picked up.

Seine Otten is also here. He still doesn't have an identity card. I promised to try Gramsbergen for him.

At long last the clothes for "Tante Anny" have arrived. They were brought by two men in a car, one of whom was a Negro. Also clothes for Loekie. Also a letter from Henny that, among other things, says that she will no longer take letters to or from onderduikers anymore.

Sister Scholten had Fl.400 for me.

July 11, 1944, Tuesday

LEENHOUTS IS NOW at Nienhuis, a good hiding place, but . . . at Fl.4 per day . . . scandalous.

July 12, 1944, Wednesday Afternoon

I RECEIVED 100 ration cards with more to follow. I'm trying everywhere to find material and other things for Peter and Herman. The Russians are advancing up to 50 km per day in the Vilna region.

July 12, 1944, Wednesday Evening

JOHAN COMPLAINED THAT his letters don't arrive. I hear the same complaint from every quarter, but there is nothing I can do.

I ordered five boxes of vegetables from Veerman for the onderduikers in Nieuwlande. I'll collect them tomorrow.

This evening I went to see Heerspink. His son-in-law received a message to report to the Sicherheitspolizei in Groningen. Needless to say, he is not going, but it means he has to go underground.

Mrs. Heerspink told me that the Landwacht are very active in and around Zuidwolde where they shoot at onderduikers on the run. One of the Heerspink daughters had found a fleeing onderduiker, unconscious with lead pellets in the back of his head. She took him in.

Found more materials for Peter and Herman in various bookshops.

July 13, 1944, Thursday Evening

ONE OF THE Heerspink daughters brought an NSKK uniform and an identity card that needed to be altered, but it had already been messed with too much, so I gave it back.

In the afternoon, I went to Nieuwlande with the trailer from Stegeman's wood business attached to the back of my bike. First, I went to Veerman's nursery and loaded up four cases of vegetables. I already had suitcases of clothes with me. I fixed the NSKK uniform in a flat box on the underside of the trailer so that it could not be seen. Luckily there were no checkpoints. It was a very difficult trip and took a long time as it rained a lot.

At Dijk's they were amazed to see so many vegetables. I had intended to take the trailer back today, but it didn't happen as too many things got in the way.

In Nieuwlande, the atmosphere was rather tense because of all the stories about raids. Herman had taken Dolf to our hideout in the woods, which I am not happy about. Jo, Eef, and Elly have slept a few nights at Otten's hiding place.

The relationship between Mrs. Dijk and Oom Gerrit is not very good. He was whining about milk, soap, porridge, and all sort of other things. [I'm worried about this.]

Peter now works upstairs, where he has no people looking over his shoulder [*pottenkijkers*]. Herman is back in Bolwijn's peaceful front room.

At last, Tinie Zijstra brought the ration cards. We got 300 although I had asked for 350. They are all KA cards. We'll take the milk and potato coupons off them and send them to the cities, likewise probably those for rye bread.

It is raining almost daily. Everyone asks, "Is there any news?" Everyone is tense. The Russians are marching on toward East Prussia and Warsaw.

Bleeker dropped by and said that he'd had a visit from someone from Amsterdam who could supply Z-cards and *Ausweise*. [Of course, we have to wait in line.] We have reserved a few places for the possibility of mixed marriage couples from Amsterdam.[336]

July 14, 1944, Friday Evening

I HAVE ORDERS for 200 of Herman's cards. I took ration cards round all over the place and gave Tante Eef a letter that made her very happy.

I retrieved Arie Otten's box of building blocks from the empty house and also his rabbits from Norder, which he had asked for.

With every ration card came a printed note: "Hostess, your onderduiker's ration card should be hidden at all times. Onderduiker, the Landwacht is waiting for you, don't wait for the Landwacht."

I took the trailer back to Dedemsvaart with 55 ration cards and two identity cards hidden underneath as well as Herman's cards. The wind was dead against me and I thanked the gods that I finally arrived in Dedemsvaart.

We have two new customers for ration cards. Van der Helm tells me he can help with Z-cards but he needs a list of names and addresses. Mr. de Jong from "Avondrood"[337] also wants some.

In Nieuwlande there has already been a Z-card check.

July 15, 1944, Saturday Evening

I DELIVERED RATION cards all day in the pouring rain. [Good because it meant there were no checkpoints.]

A letter from Cuijk. The distribution office there was emptied.[338]

Last night the Landwacht was busy here in Dedemsvaart.

I have a pamphlet, put together by Peter, I'll get 1,000 copies printed. It is a warning for the onderduikers to be careful and not to go outside.

July 17, 1944, Monday Afternoon

GORTER IN NIEUW-AMSTERDAM has been caught by a Landwacht squad and taken to Assen. A similar squad raided Mary's and searched the house and the garden.

[Only when they had finished did they realize that] they had the wrong address and it was her neighbor they were after (Van der Vinne, from whom I buy gas illegally).

One hundred fifty Landwachters are wandering around Nieuw-Amsterdam [disturbing the peace].

Last night a boy came by who had escaped from a work camp. I found a place for him and took his uniform. I'll take him away this evening.

Mr. de Jong knows a girl who works at the labor exchange and who can put stamps on a batch of *Ausweise*. He gave me a packet of identity cards for alteration [*vervalsing*]. More work for Peter. Near Slagharen, they are busy digging defenses for the Krauts. "Reinforcements."

I'm now off to Nieuwlande with Mrs. Otten and Arie.

July 17, 1944, Monday Evening

ARRIVING IN NIEUWLANDE, some very bad news awaited me. A telegram from Jan Post said that Johannes post was very ill, no details. That means, of course, that he has been arrested. There was also a mass of other messages. Sister Zijlstra came by with the remaining 50 ration cards.

Sister Adema came to say that it was essential to find a place for Zijlstra's brother as the school has become unsafe. Received offers of one or 2 hectoliters [*mud*] of rye from various farmers. [We took them all.]

Also a mass of identity cards that needed altering and loads of requests for *Ausweise* and Z-cards.

Went to Van der Helm for Z-cards but he didn't have them yet.

I need to find another place for Herman as Bolwijn's is too busy, but Jo is happy and settled there.

Nijhof,[339] the local policeman, went to see Bos, the teacher, at my request to warn Dolf and Elly[340] that they should not go out on the streets any more. [This in the name of the 500 or so people whose lives are at risk.] Now the two are cross with Peter, who they think is responsible.

July 18, 1944, Tuesday Evening

FURTHER NEWS ABOUT Johannes: There was a raid planned on the Weteringschans prison in Amsterdam to free, among others, Jan Wildschut. A guard was bribed with Fl.30,000 to help, but it looks like he betrayed the whole enterprise, but in any event, they fell into the trap. There was a shootout and many were killed. Johannes was arrested.

Our hiding place in the woods proved its worth when broom makers came and trampled all over it, cutting branches from the very trees and shrubs I had planted, but didn't uncover anything. These guys [*kerels*] make good money, making brooms for the Krauts.

We got into a row with a neighbor when we hung our blankets and awning over what turned out to be her wash line.

I went to see Hans and Pieterje [Little Peter] with various things I had for them. Pieterje had badly swollen ankles from walking in clogs. I went to ask Dr. Brouwer to see if he would take a look. The lads have built a new hiding place farther into the woods—perfect.

Later I went to Nieuwe Krim. Bobby needs a new place as he is not strong and his mother says he cannot sleep in the hiding place as it is too damp. Recently he has been sleeping in an upstairs bedroom but that is far too dangerous as he has a typically Jewish face. At Nieuwe Krim was someone from Zeeland who told us that several flying bombs[341] had fallen in that region.

Mrs. Otten spent last night with Arie in her old house, which I thought was reckless. Today she was picking peas in her garden and asked Peter to help her. I quickly got Ooms Cor and Gerrit to replace him so that he could go back to his work as he is up to his ears.

Cor and Gerrit are complete opposites. Cor is very modest, and Gerrit sticks his nose into everything. They are always arguing about something.

July 19, 1944, Wednesday Evening

ZIJSTRA'S BROTHER CAN go to Piet Mulder where he will have to do farmwork. I hope that it'll work out as he doesn't strike me as the type who will try anything. I haven't found anything for Bobby yet.

A message from Koekoek: R. de H. has to leave at once and would I come immediately.

Fat Jo, who is at Bolwijn's, can go to the Van Krabbes' next door, where Mrs. Otten and Arie are. If I can put R. de H. in her place, that will be a good solution.

We still know nothing about what has happened to Johannes, but it goes without saying that he is never far from our thoughts.

Oom Gerrit sends messages to his acquaintances in Amsterdam, Groningen, and elsewhere via just about everyone he meets. Ouwe Taai's clothes have finally been dispatched.

Peter is again busy with the rye bread. Sheaves of letters arrive—acknowledgments.

The exchange at Bolwijn's has been agreed.

Tonight, we intend to remove all the house numbers in Nieuwlande.

Bouwe Zijstra and his son dropped in. Bouwe had blank identity cards from the Wisch municipality that needed to be filled in. This gave Peter a whole load more work. Tinie Zijstra also came, as well as Teun de Vries and many others. Herman has moved from Bolwijn's to Dijk's.

July 20, 1944, Thursday Evening

I TOOK JO to Dedemsvaart in Beukema's car. She is happy to be back with Mrs. Otten and Arie. Went back in the car with the Labor Service uniform.

This evening we went round, taking the numbers off the houses. Three groups of two: Herman and I; Teun de Vries with Joop, Bolwijn's servant; and Peter and

Henk Visser. We had a screwdriver and a pot of black paint. Everything went according to plan. Afterward I slept for an hour and half on the couch, Herman in the catacombs.

By this time, smokers' cards could only be acquired with a coupon from the inlay paper, and combined with a distribution card, which are only valid for men over the age of 21. Now that the inlay papers for women over 21 are the same color we can, using the well-known backdoor method, obtain smokers cards. We have to borrow the *stamkaarten* with inlay papers from various women and provide them with food coupons [in return]. We have begun collecting.

Zwart, from 's-Hertogenbosch is underground with his wife and child with Beukema. He is a member of *Vrij Nederland*.[342]

Yesterday, Van der Zwaag came to visit Wieten and thought the plan to remove the house numbers was excellent. This afternoon I went to Koekoek to collect R. de H. She has to be moved as she has been talking with two strange men, who happened to be local NSBers. I gave her one of my "hell and damnation" sermons.

There are many rumors about Johannes Post, but we fear the worst. Nel came with clothes and messages. She was supposed to take Lia and Tineke back with her, but that's not going to happen.

July 21, 1944, Friday

NEL SLEPT IN our hiding place last night. Of course, Oom Gerrit had all manner of errands for her in Amsterdam. I gave her a letter for Lenie. Nel told us a few details about the raid on the Huis van Bewaring in Amsterdam. She thinks Johannes is dead.

I received a hectoliter of rye free from a farmer in Langerak.

There was an attempted bomb attack on Hitler.[343]

July 22, 1944, Saturday

THE DISTRIBUTION OFFICE in Gramsbergen has been raided and completely emptied.

News that Jan Wildschut is dead.[344] He stayed silent even under torture. Many rumors about Germany: something is going on.

I rescued Van der Zwaag's radio from the peat stack. We can use it with a battery if we disconnect the light. I've also acquired a stable lantern (from the municipal fire brigade). "Just take it away" said Frans de Graaf, [before the Landwacht does].

Hammered some nails in to provide coat hooks.

July 23, 1944, Sunday

WANDERED INTO THE woods with Oom Cor to see if he could find the hiding place. He didn't find it, even when we were standing on top of it. He thought it was great, good and safe.

Jan Wildschut. Collection v.d.Sleen.

July 27, 1944, Thursday Afternoon

YESTERDAY I ARRIVED at [De Flochte] Dedemsvaart with Z-cards, copies of *Trouw*, identity cards, *Ausweise*, and Herman's drawings. There were no checkpoints.

This morning up early to visit Melis, whose onderduikers are doing well. He gave me two *mud* (140 Kg) of rye from his new harvest.

Yesterday morning I was called in by Van der Helm. There was an atmosphere of panic. A letter had been received that the wrong people had found out that Van der Helm had onderduikers in his house. Through various expressions I decided that this was a setup. I took the card with me.

I took the Lifeguard and his wife to Dijk's, where they stayed until the evening. They can stay with Piet Mulder for a week.

Because I was going to Dedemsvaart yesterday, I gave Peter and Herman the task of taking them to Mulder.

On Sunday evening, Lidia came with her nephew from Roodeschool.[345] She no longer sleeps at home but at my sister Mary's for safety's sake. She came with a message about Peter Junior's parents, who are safe in Enschede. I went straight to the boy to tell him. He was really pleased. His foot is still swollen and he is not allowed to walk, so the planned rendezvous on Sunday will not take place.

I had a row with Oom Gerrit, but it calmed down. Mrs. Dijk also had a row with him.

I have made an agreement with a number of farmers that I will "steal" some rapeseed from their barns. [This way they do not take any risks and I will pay them for it.]

The business with the Z-cards is still shrouded in mystery. Some say all employers need to have them, others that it only applies to business leaders [*hoofden van zaken*].

[Johannes is dead. He was killed in the dunes near Haarlem and is no longer with us. I feel that it is now a completely different ballgame. While he was alive, I felt that he was somehow nearby and directing me, even though our work was very different. Now that he has gone, I'll never again feel his hand on my shoulder or his cheerful words of encouragement. We have begun a new chapter.

When I mentioned all the things I brought to Dedemsvaart, I forget the most important thing of all—my dirty washing. Dinie Homan has been doing this for me for the last two years.]

July 28, 1944, Friday

I LEFT DEDEMSVAART yesterday afternoon. I wanted to stay another day or so as three nieces were coming from Groningen to stay with Dijk for a couple of days. Peter, Herman, and I all had plans to disappear for a few days. I took 500 printed pamphlets with me and also application forms for Z-cards. These cards are really confusing. [Employers need them], so fictitious businesses and large enterprises that have never existed are now applying for them, for example a large laundry in Meppel that isn't there.

Kwant[346] and Dorgelaar, who were arrested recently, have now been freed again.

The *Ausweise* that Peter had "doctored" and that I had brought to Dedemsvaart were very much admired. Sister Scholten gave me two ideas for Herman to draw and ordered 50 copies on the spot. Two people whisper something to each other while a tree with ears stands nearby. On the second card, there is a man being killed by the Germans as a result of the gossip between the two 'Good' Netherlanders. Bought a whole load more drawing materials.

Came back on a bike packed full of [illegal] materials. No checkpoints on the way in spite of warnings that they were there.

At Moskou I stopped by at Jan van der Helm [a relative of the Nieuwlande Van der Helm] who is married to one of Johannes Post's nieces.[347] They have five Jews in hiding; a married couple, two sons, and a nephew. Two of his [J. van der Helm's] brothers from Diever are also on the run, as is his father, who is now staying with his son.

I was given a pair of slippers by the Jewish couple. They wanted study books for the boys; Geometry, Geography and History. On my travels, I also visited other clients. Everything was fine.

Yesterday Oom Gerrit had a visitor, a plainclothes policeman from Amsterdam. He recognized Johannes Post from a photograph Peter showed him as one of those severely wounded in the prison raid who died soon afterward. He said he would send photos of the fallen [*de gevallenen*].

July 29, 1944, Saturday Afternoon

THE LANDWACHT HAVE been busy with checkpoints in Nieuwlande for the last few nights. One of these idiots had shot a policeman in the leg when he did not get off his bike quickly enough.

The Zijlstra's have been here. Everything will be OK with the ration cards, if a little late. I brought Witske a bottle of peroxide to use on the hair of one of her parents' guests.

At Lunenberg, deep in the heathland, there is a Jewish girl with appendicitis. I went to visit her. Admission to a hospital is not yet necessary. She has to have a great deal of patience as this is a very poor neighborhood.

Went to see Nienhuis. Leenhouts was gone for a few days.

The three nieces are arriving from Groningen tonight. Peter, Herman, and I have decided to bite our tongues and just act normally, but to stay in the background as much as possible.

July 29, 1944, Saturday Evening

THE THREE LADIES have arrived. They are not nearly as bad as we imagined. One is called Lies, and it was her birthday today. All three of them went with me to pick flowers in Post's garden. As we cycled past Bolwijn's I saw Herman and he cocked a snook at me [*een lange neus maakte*]. He came home sometime after 10:00 p.m. and played a bit on his guitar.

July 30, 1944, Sunday Evening

THE THREE GIRLS are called Lies, Tiet, and Ans. Herman played a lot of guitar music, which the girls liked, and we also played games, such as forfeits. I ended up sitting next to Lies, Peter next to Tiet (whom he called Kitty), and Herman next to Ans (whom he called *Wasbeer* [Raccoon]) Lies and I eventually left the scullery to sit outside the back door to enjoy the beautiful evening. All of us; Lies, Kitty, Wasbeer, Peter, Herman, and I with Oom Cor, Oom Gerrit, and Franke all went to our hideout. We held hands and made a long chain through the woods with the flashlights making a nice spectacle.

July 31, 1944, Monday Evening

THE UNBELIEVABLE IS a fact. All three of us have been hit by cupid's arrow. This afternoon we went to the hiding place. Herman and Ans went on ahead "to pick raspberries," but their little tin remained empty. We arrived a little later. It was really nice in the dugout. Peter and Kitty arrived home later than us as they had to "find a handkerchief" that Kitty had lost. Herman had taken his guitar but had not played anything.

In the evening, we went back to the hiding place with a cake I'd baked at baker Bolwijn's. Just us six went and the rest stayed at home, which I thought was really good.

Late last night when we were busy and making a lot of noise, we saw four Landwachters standing in front of the house. There was great consternation. Oom Cor and Oom Gerrit were extremely nervous. The girls remained calm. We smuggled all the clandestine people out through the back garden. Soon afterward, the four took to their bikes and left.

August 2, 1944, Wednesday Morning

YESTERDAY I GOT a message from the Ladies asking me to come. Lia and Tineke's mother had arrived "to collect the children." I was as truthful as I could be with her but pointed out that we were not travel agents, etc. I took the Lifeguard and his wife from Piet Muller's to Padding's.

R. de H. has left Bolwijn again. I had told her that this was her last chance and that if it didn't work out she would be shot. My predictions made little impact on her. Tante Eef was dancing round the room because R. de H. had gone.

Last night we had a bit of trouble. I sat with Lies in the kitchen, Herman with Wasbeer in the lobby, and Peter and Kitty in the parlor when someone walked in. Everything was in uproar. Oom Gerrit and Oom Cor were also still up. Peter flew outside with a knuckle-duster, Herman with a set of tongs, I with a broom. Mrs. Dijk came downstairs in her nightgown, and Mr. Dijk was there too.

It turned out to be Nico, looking for a place to sleep. Peace then returned but the noise returned, this time from inside. Everyone was as thick as thieves and then suddenly came another argument. I have no idea precisely how it started, but Oom Gerrit was certainly involved and it probably concerned some offensive comments he had made. Kitty was in tears. Eventually order was restored.

Mrs. Dijk, Lies, and I went to Dedemsvaart to visit Stegeman this afternoon. There has been little sleep in the last few days. Kitty left for Groningen this morning.

August 3, 1944, Thursday Evening

LIES LEFT THIS morning. She was first going to her sister and brother-in-law, who are in hiding in Amersfoort. I saw her off at the station. On the way back, I visited Kats and Dr. Reijnierse to collect some pills for Peter. Mrs. Reijnierse was worried because Lientje, the little girl lodging with them had been called *Jeude*[348] on the street.

I went to the hiding place and took out the blankets and hung them over the line. It is a bit damp in the dugout. I found Herman and Wasbeer in the woods. She is staying for a couple more days.

August 4, 1944, Friday Evening

I WENT TO and from Dedemsvaart carrying 20 false bargee cards,[349] which I left with Dijselhof.[350] On the return journey I collected 500 pamphlets that had been printed, as well as some drawing materials.

The Dedemsvaart Town Hall was raided during the night by the Germans pursuing their investigations.

Returning to Nieuwlande, I found the Dijk family home very tense. Oom Gerrit stalked back and forth through the house. His jaws were moving—(always a sign that he was nervous). Oom Cor also got some of this. Mrs. Dijk said, "Hai, Hai" every once in a while, [indicating that she had the situation well in hand].

There was a message from Jansje Boer that Herman and I would be picked up by the SD either tonight or tomorrow night. [I don't trust Jansje Boer. He has a low IQ and would probably betray his grandmother for a packet of cigarettes.] I don't have much faith in the warning but in such cases one has to take immediate action.

Peter was busy digging when I arrived, burying all the illegal material in the ground under the hiding place. Oom Gerrit and Oom Cor stayed with us in the woods.

Ans [Wasbeer] is still here. She and Herman seem to have really hit it off.

August 5, 1944, Saturday Evening

WHAT A WRETCHED day. I went to Hoogeveen to meet the first train from the South that Lies could have caught, but she was not on it. Thus, I had to wait in Hoogeveen for other trains. Kitty was also coming, as arranged, so I also kept an eye out for the trains from the North. Nothing came the whole morning. Between the trains, I did various errands. At the hospital, at Pencil's, at the taai-taai man. I ate at his house, where there were 23 at the table.

The 12:30 p.m. train to Groningen had just left Hoogeveen station when it was attacked by a squadron of American fighter planes.[351] I stood on a mound in a meadow and saw everything. The station was also shot-up, as was a nearby small factory that caught fire. There was a lot of shooting and low flying.

When everything was over, as usual, the air raid warning sounded.

I went to the stricken train. Two carriages stood burning and all of them were badly damaged save the one immediately behind the engine, which had had no passengers in it. There were many dead, perhaps 40 in all. A train from Groningen took the wounded to the hospital in Hoogeveen. I took many telegrams from survivors to their families to the post office.

The Americans must have thought it was a military train as there were many Krauts on board at the back. (Once it stopped the train was attacked along its whole length.)

I went to the hospital and spoke briefly to Sister (Tinie) Zijlstra who was busy organizing blood transfusions. I offered my blood and it was tested but was Group A and they wanted lots of Group B. Just bad luck.

I resumed my vigil at the station, but Lies didn't arrive.

Later that evening, Ans and Frouke also came to the station to meet Kitty. The train from Groningen was four and a half hours late and arrived at 11:00 p.m. Kitty was not on board, but there were two aged aunts from Uithuizermeeden. With these two consolation prizes we went back to Nieuwlande.

I was in a bad mood, and it was my task to tell Peter that Kitty hadn't come. There we sat with the 125 dahlias we had bought. I suggested that we cut off all the flowers and just leave the stems, but Mrs. Dijk heard me and said, "I'll cut off your ears first."

August 6, 1944, Sunday Afternoon

LAST NIGHT, PETER, Herman, and I slept in the woods. Oom Gerrit and Oom Cor we farmed out, Gerrit to Mr. Bos's empty house and Cor to Mulder's hiding place.

This morning early, Wasbeer came by to tell us that everything was safe. We heard no more about Herman and I being picked up.

August 7, 1944, Monday Evening

THIS MORNING I went with Frouke to the station where Lies passed by on her way to Groningen. We chatted to her for a minute or two. On the way, we visited a number of onderduikers and took some of Peter's clothes to the tailor.

August 10, 1944, Thursday Evening

IN THE MEANTIME, I have been to Groningen and to Dorkwerd [to my younger brother] to see the baby that my sister Guillette had taken there. All doing well. Also visited a couple of addresses in Pesse.

I spoke to Van der Zwaag, who wanted smokers' cards, but I couldn't help him as we don't have any. He also wants a load of blankets taken to Eerbeek.[352] I told him that I'd do my best to get them there.

When I arrived back in Nieuwlande, I got an unpleasant surprise. De Maa had said that the Dijk residence seemed more like a house of ill repute with all these women. Mrs. Dijk was cross, Peter and Herman were cross, I was cross.

There were masses of tasks to be done; rapeseed, rye, R. de H., twenty students who needed hiding places.

August 11, 1944, Friday Evening

LAST NIGHT OOM Cor slept in the dugout, Peter, Herman, and I near it among the pines. Oom Gerrit was in the catacombs. It was a fine night.

This morning we got a report that the Distribution Office in Dedemsvaart had been raided at 5:45 a.m.[353] Doesburg was also hit.

Message from 's-Hertogenbosch that [brother] Jan has gone underground and that it is far from pleasant [in the city]. I telephoned a policeman I know there and said that Jan should come to Booi [this was my name when I was five years old].

Went to see R. de H. and she seems to be behaving herself.

August 12, 1944, Saturday

THE WORK IS not going as it should. I have to find so many hiding places and it isn't happening. I can't talk to people any more. [They are more scared by the minute.] Peter, Herman, and I are all in a "hell and damnation" mood. We got a bottle of cognac from Klijnsma's Café[354] and finished it. Herman didn't join in as he is teetotal, but Cor and Gerrit did. A stupid thing really. All in all a dreadful day.

August 13, 1944, Sunday

RECEIVED A WARNING that "the Greens" were coming.[355] "They are standing ready to leave in Hoogeveen." I went round with warnings, as did Peter and Herman. In many places I got little thanks, such as, "Oh, you again [stop fooling us]. Nothing will happen."

Miesje came by. We asked her if she wanted to change jobs. We want to put her in the job that Kitty does in Groningen and have Kitty here. We painted a very pretty picture and she'll think about it.

Bleeker came around asking for ration cards, which we can't provide him at the minute.

This morning to church and then with Henk Sweepe to Aasman to drink coffee and to listen to the news in the hiding place in the stable.

August 14, 1944, Monday

LAST NIGHT WE were perishingly cold. Gerrit and Cor were in the hiding place, Peter, Herman, and I outside, but we did not have enough covers.

I went to De Krim and got a packet of bargee-cards back, still unused because they had a printing error on them.

I went to Frans de Graaf, who was looking to get rifle bolts. In the afternoon, we were told that the Green Police were on their way. We went out warning people immediately. Dijk was at Padding's to warn him and had just left when a truck with Greens went through the village. They raided Padding and caught Henk.

The Lifeguard and his wife escaped through the eye of a needle. They had just left Padding's when they ran into the Greens. By sheer chance they were not taken, but 50 meters farther on there were people who were.

They had, following the plan that we had arranged, gone to the woods, where they were greeted by Peter and Herman. Ooms Cor and Gerrit were already there.

The Greens were looking for onderduikers everywhere. Henk got caught through his own stupidity. He had got safely away but went back to fetch his identity card.

In the evening, I went into the woods with food and drink, where the whole group was waiting anxiously for my arrival. I congratulated the couple on their escape, which they did not understand themselves.

The Oostopgaande after the war. Collection v.d.Sleen.

August 15, 1944, Tuesday Evening

LAST NIGHT, PETER, Herman, and I wanted to go back to the house to fetch various work materials. We got close to Kremer's farm when we saw assault trucks [*overvalwagens*] thundering through the village. Krauts jumped out of them. It was a complete mess.

On the Oostopgaande [a sand road that runs on the other side of the canal and runs parallel with our route into the woods], we could see the shadows of some Greens so we soon turned back and then crawled over the fields [to avoid them —translator].

Up early this morning to head home. Peter and Herman remained 100 meters behind me so that I could signal that everything was clear.

Bad news awaited us. Early this morning the Greens had killed two young boys. Evert Post, Jan Post's only son [and nephew of Johannes Post] and Bos, a young man who was hiding with Jan Post. Two boys that I knew well. They got their ration cards from us. These boys had been killed in cold blood having first been wounded in the arms.

Great dismay and fury in the village.

In addition, Dirk, the deserter from the Eastern Front who [at one time] had been hidden under the church with Peter and Herman has been caught. I expect him to get a bullet. Others have also been caught.

[None of "our" onderduikers were caught.]

Peter and Herman eventually came out of the woods. They hadn't seen me waving as they were looking into the sun. We took all the illegal materials from under Dijk's floor to Otten's empty house. There was a lot but the outside world saw nothing of it because we went through the back gardens of Dijk, Griffioen, and Otten.

Everything was stowed away, including the radio. We took another radio into the woods.

I saw Van der Zwaag and his son who had escaped from a raid when bullets were flying round their ears by swimming across two canals.

From Groningen we heard that one of Mrs. Dijk's brothers, who was here for a couple of days last week, had been arrested and seriously beaten up and then taken to the Scholtenhuis in Groningen.[356]

Peter and Herman took a pram full of stuff into the woods. I went to Jan Post to offer my condolences. Once darkness fell, I took a bucket of food and drink, and some blankets into the woods where the whole community was once again waiting anxiously for me.

August 16, 1944, Wednesday Evening

MRS. DIJK, WHO is usually always calm and composed, is now showing some signs of nerves.

This morning, Peter, Herman, and I were coming out of the woods on the way to Dijk's when Kremer came to warn us that things were far from normal.[357] Peter and Herman went back into the woods while I went on to Dijk's.

It wasn't long before assault trucks full of Greens arrived, together with some luxury cars and motorcycles with sidecars. There were also men in overalls who searched through everything at Kleinsma's and Jonker the baker's.

More than a thousand planes came over today. The Greens communicate with each other using lights in the evening.

This morning, I renewed the camouflage on the hiding place, and especially the entrance.

Dirk, the deserter, is free again. Another indication that the various German authorities do not cooperate with each other, as he is listed in the police gazette as highly sought after.[358]

Mrs. Otten has been here, but unfortunately I didn't get to see her.

August 17, 1944, Thursday Evening

AWAKE EARLY THIS morning. Fine weather as it always is now.

Gerrit and Cor have had an almighty row over a piece of soap. I was on my way home and outside the woods when I heard them shouting. Oom Cor's was the loudest. I went back into the woods and found Peter and Herman, who had distanced themselves from the unpleasantness. Oom Cor and Oom Gerrit were literally at loggerheads, but were hindered in their intentions by several gripping arms.

I gave them both a piece of my mind. These people are naturally very nervous and on edge the whole time. Everything was completely at odds today.

Everywhere there were Greens and other riffraff [*gespuis*], some of them in overalls to make carrying out raids easier. The village is in uproar. People are scared and want to be rid of their onderduikers, but I'm not at home. Everyone will have to take care of their own affairs [*zijn eigen boonen te doppen*].

There are also raids taking place in Nieuw Zwinderen and in Hollandscheveld and Schuinesloot, where some onderduikers have been caught. I took some ration cards round.

August 18, 1944, Friday Evening

RUMOR HAS IT that [the Landwacht will] be leaving tomorrow as they have only ordered meat until Saturday.

Peace has been restored in the woods.

Peter is back home. He wants to work and get the rye bread sent out.

Evert Post was buried today. A great procession.

I got a message to say that there were four SD men at the funeral. Peter stood watch to report anything unusual. While the service was taking place (in the school) an assault truck went past.

August 19, 1944, Saturday Evening

IT IS SAID that the Greens have left Hoogeveen, some say to Beilen, others to Emmen.

Peter and Herman have a new headquarters in Otten's empty house. Drawing and illegal work takes place there, as does cursing and laughing. There the radio is cheerful, there the entrance to the hiding place [under the floor] stands open so that one can disappear immediately.

Herman has drawn a new card of the queen. This will be stenciled so that it can be reproduced in quantity and sold. They want to spend the night there too.

I was on my way to the hiding place in the woods with a bucket of baked potatoes and other things when I heard a noise in Griffioen's back garden. I stood still, listened intently and then heard it again. A shuffling of feet. Someone was behind the hedge.

I went back to warn Peter and Herman as they would have to pass by on their way to Otten's house. I found them in Dijk's back garden. We decided to investigate and were about to begin when we heard the sound of someone running away and making a loud noise creeping through the hedge into De Maa's nearby garden and then disappearing. We followed on, each with a flashlight, but found nothing. After that we went into the woods.

This afternoon we searched for two ration cards that the Lifeguard's wife had buried under the floor of the hiding place in a moment of nervous anxiety. The woman was desperate. We turned the whole place upside down but found them eventually.

August 20, 1944, Sunday

THIS MORNING EARLY, Peter, Herman, and I were chased into the hiding place by a rainstorm. After that, we all returned to the civilized world, including the pram. First of all me, then Cor and Gerrit, then the Lifeguard and his wife, and finally Peter and Herman with the pram.

It was a major undertaking to get all the unshaven, unwashed people sorted out at Dijk's. We came out of the woods at 6:00 a.m., and at 10:00 a.m. people were still making themselves presentable. A troop of dirty people, having conquered their nerves, came back to civilization.

Our flight from the rain this morning was amusing. They were all asleep in the hiding place, and we could not wake them. There was no room to get in past them so we just had to wake them up. We also had to bring in all the blankets and I threw them over the sleepers. They were none too pleased.

It is very pleasant at Otten's house. Herman is busy creating cards. Peter and Herman have a bet of two cigarettes that I can sell at least 50 of the new cards in Dedemsvaart. Peter says yes, and Herman no. We have the radio there and listen to all the broadcasts, from Radio Algiers and even from the French partisans.

Peter is busy finishing a circular that we'll distribute from house to house.

The Lifeguard and his wife have found out where their son is hiding, and they've now secretly walked over there. It is not right, but I'm not going to make a big deal out it now that the war is nearly over.

This evening I took a big bundle of circulars to the post office. I stayed to talk to Visser [the postmaster] and before I knew it, it was midnight.

I went to Dijk's house and got in through one of the windows and slept on the divan. Mrs. Dijk, who was going to catch the first train to Groningen, found me at 5:00 a.m. and sent me upstairs, where an empty bed awaited me. "Hai, hai," she said.

August 21, 1944, Monday Afternoon

I AM JUST about to leave for Dedemsvaart. At Otten's house everything is proceeding apace and the radio is broadcasting good news to the world.

August 23, 1944, Wednesday Afternoon

IN DEDEMSVAART. THE fifty cards have long since been sold. Peter won the bet in spectacular fashion and I have orders for many more.

Sister Scholten had been to Maastricht and escaped death there. It had already been rumored that she had been killed in a bombardment.[359] I spoke to her and was given five smoker's cards.

A telegram arrived from Nieuwlande: "Hennie seriously ill, your presence requested." Has she been picked up?

August 23, 1944, Wednesday Evening

BACK TO NIEUWLANDE. Nel has come from Amsterdam. Hennie has indeed been arrested but there are no details. I gave Peter identity cards from Dedemsvaart for alteration, and he has also been to visit Jan Post.

Nel had a nagging message about Lia and Tineke, their parents insist on having them in Amsterdam. I'm going to leave them where they are and where they are safe. The only problem is that they will be given a Christian upbringing.[360]

The French partisans are fighting in Paris.

August 24, 1944, Thursday

LAST NIGHT, THE four of us slept underground at Otten's, Nel included. She left today.

A lady from Gouda had to be taken to the hospital in Coevorden because she had a huge swelling on her shoulder. I primed Beukema to take her in his car and then take Nel to Hoogeveen, but it broke down. I put Nel in a bean truck, but that too broke down and eventually she went on Mrs. Dijk's bicycle. The woman who had the operation was back at home the same evening, as the hospital did not want to keep her and discharged her before she was fully recovered from the anesthetic.

A letter arrived from Sister Zijlstra about smoker's cards. We had advertised the fact that we had not received enough and those we did have were damaged [with some coupons removed].

Peter and Herman are now fully installed in Otten's house. They are mainly printing the [cards showing the] queen's head. They are selling quickly. Albert Nijwening has also sold a lot of them.

August 25, 1944, Friday

RECENTLY, I HAVE been sleeping at the back of the garden and have been busy selling cards. Mr. Bos asked me about overdue payments for board and lodging.

I went to Nieuwe Krim, where everything is fine. I have convinced them that Bobbie will have to stay there and sleep in the hiding place, even though it is not particularly healthy.

August 26, 1944, Saturday

I WENT TO Hoogeveen to buy things for Peter and Herman. I showed a few of Herman's cards and was immediately given new blank ones. At one address I have to come back on Monday to fetch more. Didn't see any checkpoints.

Beukema came to repair our battery-powered radio. I've been to the vegetable-grower to buy leaf vegetables for the woman who had the operation as her doctor says she need to eat lots of them. Also ordered a 20 Kg crate of tomatoes.

At the same time [I encountered] a German soldier who had a few days leave and who had fought in the Balkans. He hoped that Germany would soon collapse so that he would not have to return to the front. I felt a strong urge to offer him a hiding place, but held my tongue.

Herman and I sleep outside in the back garden.

August 27, 1944, Sunday Evening

TO THE CHURCH. The dominee denounced the black market. [A safe topic to talk about from the pulpit.]

Herman is in an awful mood, so is Peter, so am I. Listening to the radio from London we hear some rubbish about the courageous attitude and the backbone of the Dutch people. It makes us angry to hear such twaddle about this supposed backbone.

August 28, 1944, Monday Evening

THE NEW EDITION of *Trouw* is out. It carried a piece about Johannes Post.[361]

I cut 500 cards for Herman from 25 sheets of drawing paper. Mrs. Ham came asking if we could get them a Z-card. They had had a Z-card check.

This evening we heard a volley of machine gun fire not far away. Gerrit was once again very nervous.

August 29, 1944, Tuesday Evening

THIS MORNING I was on my way to Hoogeveen when I was stopped by a girl in the Kerkhoflaan. She warned me not to go on as there were 25 Greens in Hollandscheveld checking everything and they had machine guns.

I went back to warn the people in Nieuwlande and then returned. I didn't see anything unusual in Hollandscheveld. First I went to Kats, who told me that there had been 25 men there; 23 Landwachters and 2 Greens. They had arrested various people who had called the NSB names in public. In one house the head of the family was hiding under the floor and his wife, in a nervous fit, pointed to the hiding place. Another man was shot in the legs.

Dr. Reijnierse, who had come to give first aid, was warned off with the threat of a machine gun but later called back. Then these ghouls [*kerels*] told him that the Netherlands would soon be free and that the Americans were already in Haarlem—all to get him to talk.

Later on these 25 honorary Germans [*Edelgermanen*] had congregated at the house of Benno van der Meer, a filthy NSBer, to have a drink and had put all the lights on. Suddenly a couple of German fighter planes came over and promptly fired a couple of salvos into the building, unfortunately without hitting anyone [although most of the windows were shattered]. This was the shooting we had heard in Nieuwlande.

I went on to Hoogeveen and worked through a long list of errands. I also visited the taai-taai man and talked about Johannes Post. Baker Blanken had taken his death very much to heart.

I went to see Huizinga the bicycle-maker and got 20 batteries from him.

There are still four Greens in Hoogeveen, but their task is to watch the SS.

At Kats's there was a woman from The Hague who said that the 10:30 train from Hoogeveen contained 30 Jews, many of them young girls, being taken to Westerbork. The guard unit consisted of Dutch SS, Greens, and muzzled large dogs.

Visited Miss van Noordt, the schoolteacher, to collect a picture of the three [royal] princesses so that Herman could make a new stencil.

In the evening, I visited the woman who had the operation. She is not very well.

At Dijk's it is a funny situation with all the "aunts" and "uncles" and with Mrs. Dijk swinging her scepter over all of it.

August 30, 1944, Wednesday Evening

WENT TO DEDEMSVAART with 100 Queens,[362] Z-cards, identity cards, copies of *Trouw*, and a few presents for children. Oom Gerrit was afraid that I would be picked up and insisted that I call the post office [in Nieuwlande] as soon as I had arrived. There were checkpoints on the way, but I managed to go around them.

I visited the five Jews at Van der Helm's in Moskou. They are all OK. They had been scared stiff during the last house search, but they have a good hiding place in the hay, with another one behind it. I brought them two identity cards and two *stamkaarten*.

Dropped by Arend Otten's and he had a letter from Mrs. Otten [wife of Seine]. For Frits Stegeman I had all sorts of doctored papers; an identity card, an *Ausweis*, and a permit to show that he is a food controller.

I finally saw Seine Otten and his wife again. I told him that the rumor in Nieuwlande was that he had been shot dead, and that later this changed to say that he was severely wounded and in the hospital with the SD at his bedside.

A girl gave me a bag of sweets and a bunch of flowers for Herman.

[Cards depicting] the Queen's head are being ordered everywhere. Guillette was also there and is also selling the cards.

August 31, 1944, Thursday Afternoon

I WENT TO farmer Melis, who told me he had sent 2 *mud* [140 Kg] of rye on a pallet to baker Nijwening for Peter's rye bread loaves. He wanted no money for it and actually gave me another Fl.10.

Spent the rest of the morning looking for hiding places, but with no success.

Frits nearly walked into a Landwacht trap.

I dug up an old identity card belonging to Johannes Post that I had buried here. We want the photo as there are no pictures of him [except as a child] and this one can be enlarged.

Lenie Zoet, Frits's fiancée and the daughter of the postmaster, came here to tell me that in the area round Zwolle all the telephone lines and underground cables have been cut. The Krauts are furious.

September 1, 1944, Friday Evening

VAN DER ZWAAG came over and was optimistic about the war ending soon. He asked if we could be counted on for "special assignments" if the Allied armies came this way. A superfluous question.

When will we be free? We want it so much.

Albert Nijwening can use 1,000 Queen Wilhelmina cards.

Received 2,000 blank postcards and the promise of a ream of paper, enough for 1,000 cards, from a friend of Peter's in Rotterdam.

September 2, 1944, Saturday Evening

YESTERDAY EVENING THE Landwacht was active in De Krim. Seven men were hunting and shooting at onderduikers. I went there early this morning with one of the identity cards. Everything was OK.

There was a message from Hollandscheveld for me to go to Kats immediately. I went there straight away. Places were needed for four [Jews] from Amsterdam. I said that they should come. Where we will place them we will have to see.

The good policeman (Karelse)[363] was at Kats's house and had a carrier pigeon that was going back to London. He asked me to find information that could be attached to its leg. All this was agreed. There were instructions that I took with me. I got a set of clothes from Kats. He will look out for a new suit, but in the meantime, I can wear this one.

At Nieuwlande we also received a pigeon that arrived last night in a small cage attached to a parachute. Someone else found the instructions that went with it but they were passed to us. I went looking for a better cage and found one at Beukema's and put the bird in Otten's house. There were also five French newspapers with it.[364]

There is activity like never before at the Ottens' house.

I took ration cards round. Many people are very edgy and are "living on their nerves."

The [local] Hitler Youth camp is being dismantled and taken back to Germany on 25 farmer's carts. The camp leader wants to go underground. Bleeker asked me to help him, but I'm not keen and would rather remain healthy.

Tomorrow we are due to receive some French prisoners-of-war.

September 3, 1944, Sunday Evening

THE NEWS REPORTS [from London] are fantastic. We are very optimistic as the Allied advances are astounding. They are approaching our country. At 8:15 this evening there was a radio report that Prins Bernhard had been made commander of all Dutch forces of the interior [Binnenlandse Strijdkrachten][365] under the aegis of Eisenhower as supreme commander.

This morning, Bleeker came and told me a long story, the gist of which was that five officers from the Hitler Youth camp want to go underground and that [in exchange], 100 revolvers, many guns and heaps of blankets would be ours. I'm not going to have anything to do with it. They are Krauts and I don't trust them. I told Bleeker that I'd love to have the weapons but I have no intention of getting involved with these guys.

Everyone, everywhere is very tense. For example, we had a major row over a pair of trousers at Dijk's, where one group thought them long enough, and the other too long. Tante Marie said long enough, and her husband the Lifeguard took her side. They were really cross. The opposition that voted for "too long" consisted of Gerrit and me. Unbelievably laughable.

If we are not very much mistaken, the liberation of our country is at hand. It is almost unbelievable.

This evening we got the Frenchmen, which was fun. We took them to Otten's. Later I took one of them to Mr. Bos, a good place for him. They had had many adventures. One of them had escaped twelve times and been recaptured eleven times, another had escaped seven times and been betrayed by French fascists. One of them is a printer, another a student. We let two of them sleep at Otten's house.

Peter and Herman are very, very busy with drawings and printing. Oom Gerrit, one of the Frenchmen and I went to the hiding place in the woods late last night to fetch all sorts of stuff, especially blankets.

There are storms and rain. By the time we came back, the other Frenchman was helping Peter and Herman with the printing.

September 4, 1944, Monday Evening

THE NEWS REMAINS good but everyone is very tense.

I took the Lifeguard and his wife back to Van der Helm. Two of the Frenchmen are billeted with Piet Muller.

The Allied forces have crossed the Dutch border. Prime Minister Gerbrandy has spoken [on the radio].

Picked up a sack with five blankets from Van der Helm. Snorretje had put them there. They had been stolen from a labor camp.

Prins Berhard spoke on the radio [saying] that only those who were attached to the Dutch Liberation Army of the Interior [Binnenlandse Strijdkrachten] should have an orange armband ready with the word Oranje on it as this will be their temporary uniform.

Now the Dutch public has completely misunderstood this and every Tom, Dick, and Harry is now busy making armbands, even for old ladies and children in prams. It's an insane rage.

The sending of rye bread has ended as packages can no longer be sent through the mail. The baking nevertheless goes on as usual and we'll keep the bread for the Americans, who will perhaps soon be here.

De Maa gave me a letter for Bleeker from Snorretje about the weapons. He (Snorretje) wants them for the Knokploegen [LKP]. I'll believe these weapons exist when I see them.

A collection is being held among the onderduikers for a stone to mark the grave of Evert Post, who was killed by the Greens.

September 5, 1944, Tuesday Evening

RUMORS ARE EVERYWHERE. 100,000 parachutists in Zwolle, Rotterdam liberated, invasion in North Holland, invasion in the German Bight, etc., etc. You cannot believe anything anymore.

In Hoogeveen the children were sent home from school because of the armies advancing from Zwolle. The radio only says that they are in Breda.

We find it difficult to believe that we are close to liberation and that parts of the Netherlands are already free. Why are we not going completely wild and turning cartwheels? [*op onze kop lopen*]

Martial law has been proclaimed in the Netherlands with an 8:00 p.m. curfew and gatherings of no more than five people.

There is a new armband craze: every grandmother and baby is deemed to be a member of the Binnenlandse Strijdkrachten with an orange armband.

[I see it coming. People who wouldn't dream of giving shelter to a Jew because it was far too dangerous will be walking round with orange bands. Only when it safe to do so, of course. That goes without saying.]

Peter and Herman worked all last night on a circular that needs to be distributed tomorrow.

Bouwe Zijlstra and his son came to ask if I wanted to join a group of ten, but I'll wait for instructions from Snorretje.

September 6, 1944, Wednesday Afternoon

THIS MORNING EARLY at sunup we released the carrier pigeon [*duif*]. At first it flew around and then landed on a nearby roof. Later it set off in a westerly direction (luckily not eastward!).

Our motto was again: *Carpe Diem*.

We wrote to the girls that they should listen to London [on the radio].

September 7, 1944, Thursday Evening

NO NEWS ABOUT the Netherlands. Went to Hoogeveen with Frouke to do some shopping.

A train full of fleeing NSBers was used as target practice by the Americans near Assen. In Hoogeveen we saw a long German Red Cross train with wounded come past. The Americans were circling up above and the station personnel fled into the air raid shelter, but nothing happened. There were no newspapers for sale at the station. I had wanted some NSB sheets.

Back to Nieuwlande. I visited onderduikers all over the place, just looking in and then moving on.

I went to Kikkert's [for coffee]. Everything was well with Hoedag (the little three-year-old Jewish boy). Mrs. Kikkert asked me if I knew any way of smuggling people out of Germany, an acquaintance of hers in Aachen. But I had no idea.

In the last few days, there has been a mass flight of NSBers from the Western parts of our country eastward. Trains full of them are passing through Hoogeveen. In Hoogeveen three guys with loaded bicycles and rucksacks asked me the way to the Coevorder Straatweg. I told them the way and thought nothing more of it. Later we saw the same bicycles parked outside the house of a well-known NSBer in the Coevorder Straatweg; thus [they were] also fleeing traitors.

Piet Muller wrote me an angry letter. It had become known that he had Frenchmen in his house. Mr. Bos had been across to his house with a message from one of the other Frenchmen. I wrote back to him to say that I was very sorry, but that there was not much I could do. Mrs. Dijk had probably revealed the address to Mr. Bos.

Henk Sweepe came back from a bicycle trip having seen various things, for example a burning gasoline train.

At Dijk's everyone is in a mood. The advance into Dutch territory seems to have stalled.

Peter has orders from Snorretje to print thousands of pamphlets. The electricity is off so we brought in our battery-powered radio, but it didn't work. Called Beukema in but the battery was dead. We have hired a tandem from Beukema until the end of the war.

We are all down and have established a club, the "Club of the Downhearted."

September 8, 1944, Friday Evening

I WENT TO De Krim this evening. On the way, I met a woman from Nieuwlande, who warned me that it was not safe there. There were Greens everywhere carrying out raids. The woman was a nervous wreck and had only escaped by the skin of her teeth.

When I arrived in De Krim, it appeared that her whole story was a fabrication. There was a single camouflaged bus, filled with ordinary Wehrmacht Krauts, which had apparently broken down. There was no sign of any raids.

I ran my errands. I dropped off 1,000 pamphlets for distribution and got an identity card in return before returning to Nieuwlande. I was stopped everywhere in the village and asked, "What has happened at De Krim." There was a state of total alarm at Nieuwlande, a classic example of how rumors can be created. Piet Mulder was also very scared, [but] I did my best to calm him down.

September 9, 1944, Saturday Evening

I WENT TO Kats's this morning with 500 pamphlets. He will see that they get distributed. I got soaking wet on the way there.

Karelse the policeman was pleased that I had come. He had already tried to telephone me but without success. He had two [escaped] Russian prisoners-of-war,³⁶⁶ did I have somewhere for them to hide? Yes, that would be OK [although I had no idea where].

At Kats's I hung my wet things almost above the stove, had a delicious meal, tickled the maid (which she cannot stand), and read the newspapers. It is nowadays worth the trouble to read the newspapers if only to see how the NSB juggernaut tries to bend over backward to spread syrup over everything.³⁶⁷

Karelse told me that Marechaussee Klein from Hoogeveen was shot dead last night. No further details. He was a good Dutchman.³⁶⁸

After our meal, Kats and I went to fetch the two Russians. It was filthy weather. They had been given new clothes. I took one on my back carrier. Karelse, who was waiting for us, pushed the other one as he could not cycle very well and held him by the shoulders.

In that manner we arrived in Nieuwlande. The people who saw us were all very interested. It was a strange procession. I took them first to Dijk of course. Everything is always possible there [—even the impossible]. Herman thought it was great, two Russians. They are genuine Bolsheviks [one of them is from Ukraine].

At Dijk's we were first given delicious coffee and then something to eat.³⁶⁹ Later we took them to Otten's house where they would sleep in the hiding place underneath. They were so happy when, for the first time in two years, they could listen to the radio from Moscow. We are now learning Russian, but it is not easy. [I know one word—*tovarich*.] Oom Gerrit will be better at it, as he has more time.

Van der Zwaag was also at Dijk's. One of the Frenchmen wants to go to the front. The other has fallen in love with Truusje Muller and so doesn't want to go anywhere.

Bleeker was here with another long story that boiled down to the fact that he had acquired a gun and that the leader of the Hitler Youth camp had gone underground. The Krauts have taken away Harper's tractor.

Peter and Herman are busy printing, so the Queen's heads will have to wait.

September 10, 1944, Sunday Evening

HERMAN IS TICKLED pink with a letter from Wasbeer. The "NV Amor is very much alive," he said.

When the Russians found out that Herman was a Jew in hiding they slapped his back in friendliness so hard that it was bruised. They did the same to me when they heard that I had been in hiding for more than two years.

Two policemen need to go underground. Did we have a place for them? "Of course," we said. One of them will probably come tonight. Arie de Vries, the chief [*opper*] is one of the two. At Otten's, things are busier than ever.

September 11, 1944, Monday Evening

SEARCHING FOR HIDING places, for example at the larger farmers, Van Veen and Elema. No chance. They had all the usual excuses that everyone knows; they don't want to or are too selfish.

I can take the Russians to Lanting and I'll do that tonight. One of them was a tank commander. They told us about the awful things the Krauts had done [in Russia].

I went to Hoogeveen with a huge bundle of pamphlets for Snorretje as well as armbands that Herman had painted. I didn't see him, but left everything with his brother.

I rode to Hoogeveen with Albert Nijwening. The station was deserted. I returned laden with drawing materials. At Hollandscheveld I collected my bicycle (I had gone to Hoogeveen on Kats's bike). He had given me a large carrier for the back of my bike as a present. He also knew someone who could give Mrs. Dijk a slaughtered pig and two bottles of oil also as a present.

I have now heard the story that an onderduiker hiding in a haystack at Daling's in Pesse had been burned alive.

Dijk and I, each with a Russian behind us, cycled to Lanting.

September 12, 1944, Thursday Evening

I MADE A visit to our Russian friends. They were pleased to see me, but I had to leave quickly. Lanting would like me to find somewhere else for them. He finds it very weird, to have two escaped prisoners of war—and communists at that.

I took all sorts of packages to Dedemsvaart—all neatly wrapped by Peter; pamphlets for various people, ration cards, and rye bread loaves for anyone who wanted them.

In Elim I was warned that there was a checkpoint. I cycled back and went via Schuine Sloot. Everything was quiet.

From Bleeker I got an address where a motorbike can be found.

September 13, 1944, Wednesday Noon

IN DEDEMSVAART. THERE were letters waiting for me there. There is one that I do not understand. Also Fl.1,000. A carrier pigeon was caught here, sat on the street half-conscious with an English ring on its leg. I take it with me.

Prins Bernhard broadcast and said there needed to be more cooperation between the various resistance groups.

September 14, 1944, Thursday Morning

STILL IN DEDEMSVAART. I wanted to be away yesterday, but it didn't happen. I went around to various people with ration cards and pamphlets.

Saw Fat Jo, who wants to do something useful for the cause. She gave me a letter for Herman. She listens to the broadcasts from London every morning at 6:45 a.m. Yesterday morning early, she brought me the news that the Allies had broken through the Gothic Line in Italy.[370] I ventured to point out that this had been news three days ago, but she did have other, real, news. She also had money from the sale of the Queen's head cards.

I went to see Veerman where Johan also had money from the sale of cards. He is doing very well, both in selling the cards and in vegetable growing. I ordered a crate of carrots for delivery to De Krim.

Masses of bombers and fighters flew over, not as usual in formation, but spread out.

I acquired a stencil machine from Oom Freek for as long as it is needed. I'd like to see the faces of Herman and Peter when they see it.

I got word that we should be careful with carrier pigeons as London have not sent any out recently, and that all the recent ones have been Kraut ones. I'll take this one with me to Nieuwlande and let it fly, without any names or addresses.

Guillette also had money from the sale of the Queen cards. She says that they are not so easy to sell now as people say, "It's not necessary any more as the onderduikers will be able to resurface before too long." We can only hope.

With great difficulty, I got my hands of 2,000 sheets of paper and a small quantity of stencil paper, which is becoming increasingly scarce.

Seine Otten, his wife, and Arie came for a while yesterday. That was fun. They had all sorts of questions and why I hadn't come last Saturday as arranged. (It seems to be my fate either to forget or not to be able to keep appointments.)

Melis also came with card money and had a roll of paper for me.

There were also lovely letters from Lia and Tineke for their parents, which I'll now send on.

Sister Scholten gave me three tins of sardines for Peter and Herman. Nice.

Here in Dedemsvaart there are a couple of rotten Krauts [*rotmoffen*] who shoot at anyone out on the street after 8:00 p.m. Even the doctors are afraid to be out after curfew. I'm about to go to Nieuwlande. I have never been so loaded up before. The stencil machine is the largest thing.

September 15, 1944, Friday Evening

IT IS IN reality September 29, and I am sitting here with a couple of pages of notes from September 15 onward. I am in Otten's house in Nieuwlande. I have acquired a new notebook as I haven't been to Dedemsvaart to write in my other book which is safely hidden in the ground there. I am sitting here in the upper room [*opkamertje*] because the kitchen is full of people.

Peter, Herman, Johan (the Belgian), Thijs (Karel's brother), Anjo Muller and one of his sisters, and Frouke Dijk are all busy writing addresses on pamphlets printed by Peter that have to be sent to Hollandscheveld, Nieuwlande, Hoogeveen, etc., etc.

The radio is also busy. Every now and then we hear, "Hello, hello, hello" and then news items or messages in code. The news reports are thankfully a little better.

It is 5:30 p.m. in the afternoon.

Yesterday afternoon [September 14] I left Dedemsvaart fully loaded. I had the stencil machine, the carrier pigeon that had to go back to England, stencil paper, apples, clothing, drawing materials, paint, etc., and a lot of money. Guillette came part of the way with me, about halfway, and we agreed that she should come to Nieuwlande the following Sunday.

Peter told me that the Frenchmen wanted to get back to France or Belgium, but luckily the urgency has passed. Peter is over the moon with the stencil machine.

In Otten's house there is feverish activity and "auxiliary troops" [hulptroepen] have arrived; Truusje and Anjo Muller and Johan the Belgian are writing and printing addresses. Herman was depressed, this happens more and more often, but this time it was more noticeable.

Last night we worked until 5:00 a.m. This morning I cleaned the house. It was high time. Straw, peel, dirty dishes, scraps of paper, mud. Now it is tidy, at least for the time being.

Maastricht is in Allied hands. We heard a report about the reception of the troops there. The people were mad with joy.

We got an interesting letter from Nel. She talked about the flight of the NSBers that took place in Amsterdam last week. They were gripped by panic. A train load of those scum [schorum] was shot at by the Americans. Nel could tell me nothing about what had happened to Henny. She did tell me that the Krauts were emptying all the prisons in Amsterdam and taking the victims [slachtoffers] elsewhere.

So-called emergency ration cards are being issued by the local distribution offices, which are only valid in the locality. This inevitably brings more problems.

Yesterday evening I got a message asking me to come to the post office immediately. Mrs. Kikkert was there and needed to speak to me urgently. She was very nervous and told me a rambling tale that amounted to the following: There was a young man who had come to their neighbors saying he was an onderduiker looking for a place to stay. The neighbors took this stranger in but now want rid of him and came to ask the Kikkerts if they would have him. The stranger had seen the onderduikers at Kikkert's and they do not trust him. They are afraid that he's a Gestapo agent. I told her that the onderduikers and the little boy should spend a few nights sleeping in the woods, under a tarpaulin or something, and then see which way the wind blows.

Herman has spent the last few nights sleeping at Bolwijn's.

September 16, 1944, Saturday Evening

EARLY THIS MORNING to De Krim. The identity card that was "risky" is now OK and only needs a fingerprint. We have agreed that the person concerned will come for that himself.

On the way back I went through the countryside and past the Sloten farm, where there are two onderduikers. I had a letter from Sister Scholten for one of them. Mrs. Sloten told me stories about the Labor Service [*Arbeidsdienst*] in De Krim, where all 110 young men there decided to escape en masse. She herself had four of them under her roof, but they wanted to move on, in spite of warnings from her and her husband. They did not get farther than Zwolle before they were picked up, although one of them escaped again.

There is all sorts of trouble over the new emergency ration cards. Everyone wants to know how it is supposed to work. We find it easier to get ration coupons in Oosterhesselen than in Hoogeveen. They don't ask to see *stamkaarten* there, but only to hand in voucher 271 from the old cards. In Hoogeveen they insist on seeing the *stamkaarten*.

In Hoogeveen there are huge posters saying that farmers' horses are to be requisitioned and that the farmers should bring them in. Peter is now busy printing posters saying that the requisition has been canceled [with] the signature of the mayor underneath.

I took a bundle of these things to Kats for distribution, and in the evening Peter, Herman, and I put others up in strategic points in the village.

I fetched a radio from Schuiling's and took it to the dominee, who was very happy with it. At Schuiling's, I ate wonderful bacon, smoked a prewar cigar, and was given some tobacco leaves and a new cap, the latter will be good for some onderduiker or other.

Went to see Tante Marie, the wife of the Lifeguard, who is lodged at Van der Helm's house to get her to repair my old coat. Mrs. Dijk wants me to take all the onderduikers' sewing and clothing repairs to her, but Mrs. van der Helm vetoed the idea.

I went to Hollandscheveld via the Oostopgaande and stopped at Kikkert's where I was told that the stranger who had been at the neighbors and whom they had christened the "SS-man" had gone.

I met Leenhouts and his fiancée in Hollandscheveld. Went also to Big [Wiegman] and Zijlstra. Everything is OK with the onderduikers.

Later on I cycled to Hoogeveen with 20,000 pamphlets, which I took to Snorretje's brother's farm. Snorretje himself was not there. In Hoogeveen the situation was better than I expected. There had been rumors that it was no longer peaceful there. In the main canal, there were 30 barges loaded with [stolen] copper heading for Germany. Today American planes shot at a car full of SS men; two dead and five injured.

There are all sorts of uniforms in the streets [some I have never seen before].

It is said that all men in the municipality between the ages of 17 and 55 will be called up to help with defense works.

I took a bottle of rapeseed oil that I had promised to Duiker the photographer. At Pet the bookshop, I was still able to buy some materials for Peter and Herman.[371]

At some of Schuiling's acquaintances I attempted to get my hands on an electric hand lamp with 300 hours for the hiding place in the woods. Outcome uncertain.

On the way back went to Kats, who gave me a huge joint of meat and a pound of butter. When I got to Dijk's, Bleeker was waiting for me to talk about *Ausweise* that needed preparation.

Zwart came to me and asked if I would go with him to Marienburg to blow up the railway line. We have agreed that he'll let me know when. There was also a letter from Bep, [asking] if I would take her fingerprints.

The Siegfried Line has nearly been breached.[372] In the distance, we can hear the rumbling of gunfire.

September 17, 1944, Sunday Evening

LAST NIGHT, PETER, Herman, and I went around with the printed announcements telling the people that the horse requisitioning in Oosterhesselen had been postponed for the time being.

Late in the evening, we ended up at Wietske's for some of the famous delicious coffee and six packs of Consi-cigarettes.[373] Real smokes are nowhere to be had now.

This morning early, I was on the bike again to put up a few more of our "horse-bulletins." The reaction of Joe Public was great to hear, for example when they came out of church where there were many winks and meaningful glances exchanged.

Oom Cor came to church this morning. After the service Guillette arrived and came to greet us. She was healthy and well.

After eating, I collected the two Russians to take them for a walk. They were elated and happy as children. Dijk, Oom Cor, Guillette, the two Russians, Peter, Herman, and I went into the woods and looked at the hiding place. Herman had his inseparable guitar with him and played many songs, including one Russian death march [*treurmars*]. Dijk, Ivan, Michael, and Guillette were full of praise for the hiding place that was completely undetectable. In honor of the Russians, Guillette had sewn a Russian flag onto her dress.

On the way back, Corrie came looking for us to say that we had to hurry as food was on the table. She kept on asking us to go faster, but it was no good as we sauntered at a snail's pace. Suddenly she said that there was important news on the radio, what, she didn't know. That helped. We shot like arrows from bows at top speed back to the house where we discovered that paratroopers had landed close to our great rivers. There was no question of eating as we just sat and listened. One thousand planes had delivered the paratroopers as well as gliders with men and materials. Our government has ordered a railway strike.

Guillette and I brought the Russians back. They want a different hiding place, with simple people. Of course, they don't realize that there are virtually no places at all. They don't know that the majority of our people have no concern for our compatriots.

Guillette came to visit the Ottens' house, where "business" was in full swing. She stayed here tonight to sleep. Having heard the big news, she wanted to leave this evening, but that wasn't possible.

Herman and I slept outside last night. The weather is perfect. There is lots of noise from aircraft and there is fire to the South West. Over the last few nights there has been a lot of gunfire in the distance.

September 18, 1944, Monday Evening

SLEPT IN DIJK's back garden. I was on the divan and Herman on a packing case for glass. At 5:00 a.m. we were woken by Peter who had worked through the night. I took Guillette part of the way [home]. It was still dark when we left. On my way back I noticed a troop of Landwachters. I hid in a thicket until I was absolutely sure it was the Landwachters approaching.

Mr. Bos [the schoolmaster] came to me to demand that the Frenchman lodged at his house had to leave immediately. A relationship had developed between him and Elly, and they are talking about marriage and so forth. He has made her completely crazy. Dolf (her husband) had found out and was extremely angry, etc., etc. Mr. Bos talked about the good name of the village, etc., etc. [and went as far as accusing me of trying to be a matchmaker]. The upshot was our French friend had to have a new hiding place. I told him (recalling Nico's phrase) that the man was not a biscuit that one could swallow, but an escaped prisoner-of-war of the Krauts and that hotels for these types of men are not thick on the ground. I went to Lanting and brokered a solution whereby he swapped the two Russians for a Frenchman, but Bos refuses to have the two Russians in his house.

I then went to Padding to sound him out, first of all to see if he would take the two Russians. He asked if they were Bolsheviks. I confirmed this, "but" I said in passing, "they don't have tails and there are no horns on their heads." They seem to be ordinary good-natured souls who would not hurt a fly, except kill Krauts. But no, Padding will not contaminate his house with Russians.

Then I asked if he would at least take a Frenchman, just the one. He remained intransigent even though I played with his young son, a latecomer after six daughters, of whom he was inordinately proud. Although I praised the intelligence of the young chap, it did no good. Padding was not to be persuaded.

Bleeker, the illegal oil presser, came over and gave me addresses in De Krim, where we could take away a car and a motorcycle.

Went to see Schuiling and was given a cigar, but no places for Russians or Frenchmen.

At the horse-requisitioning in Hoogeveen, there were [only] twelve horses, so the inspection committee were discharged and these twelve were also sent home.

I went to see Bos and told him he would have to wait another day. He was unimpressed. Elly sat in the parlor with the expression of a naughty sinner on her face.

Mrs. Snorretje was in the village. I went to Wietske and drank real coffee and smoked a real cigar. She had a pair of shoes for Peter. He needed to come over to see if they would fit.

The radio had a report about the Allied arrival in Valkenswaard.

I hauled water from Elema's channel for Mrs. Dijk using milk cans so that she can do the washing. Water is a problem here.

September 19, 1944, Tuesday Evening

THIS MORNING I went to Padding with a new solution. The Russians would stay at his house during the day and sleep at night in a hiding place we would construct a little way behind his property. This he had to think about, and I would have to come back. When people have to think about it, it is usually all right, as it was this time.

The Frenchman from Bos is now at Dijk's as Bos wouldn't have him any longer. I'll now try to swap him for John, the Belgian who is with Piet Muller. John wants to come to Dijk's so that he can help Peter with the printing.

The mayor of Oosterhesselen has been lured into a car by the Krauts and murdered on the road between Oosterhesselen and Zweeloo.[374]

The electricity supply was cut off today. Our battery radio wasn't working so I went off in search of another one. After several attempts, I managed to get one.

I owed Nienhuis Fl.220, which I paid.

The news is really good. Nijmegen has been taken and there is fighting near Arnhem.[375] I wonder how things are in Cuijk and 's-Hertogenbosch?

We had a pleasant evening. The new kindergarten teacher [*Freubeljuf*] was there with one of Kremer's girls and also Toon Kwant and Jan de Maa. There was singing and guitar playing.

I collected a bale of straw to replace the flooring in our hiding place from a threshing machine that has begun work again on orders from London.[376]

Reports came in of arson attacks by the Krauts. The houses of railway workers and other onderduikers seemed to be the main targets.

September 20, 1944, Wednesday Evening

THIS MORNING THE whole village was in turmoil. The Greens were coming. The farmers hadn't delivered up their horses and so the Greens were coming to fetch the animals. We were kept informed about their progress. Then we were told that they were also searching ordinary houses, looking for onderduikers and radios, and they were close by.

Herman and I went straight to Otten's house and took all the illicit material below. Peter and John, who had been working all night, were sleeping there. Stencil machine, pamphlets, everything was put down there. Hatch closed with some rubbish strewn on top and we were away.

We wanted to go to our hiding place in the woods, but we had to change our plans because we saw two of the Green *kerels* walking along the Oostopgaande.

We went through some gardens to the post office and then along the way a little further and across a meadow and toward the woods. We went around the edge of the woods and surprised a group of onderduikers who were bivouacked there. We frightened the life out of them as, for a moment, they thought they were lost.

We got bread and milk from a farmer's wife and finally came to "our" wood. We didn't stay there long, but went back home. We heard a couple of shots. We learned later that they had shot at a couple of fleeing onderduikers in the vicinity of the Kerkhoflaan without hitting them or catching them.

They had acquired seven horses, all the other animals had "gone underground," just like the men. No one saw horses any more, they were all gone.

Tante Marie, who is staying at Van der Helm's had walked across to Dijk's. They felt safer there, *de kaffers*.[377] She asked me if she looked like a horse.

This morning Van Ekelenburg from Nieuw-Amsterdam arrived. He had to go to Hoogeveen and had money for Peter. He said he hadn't seen any checkpoints.

We sent the carrier pigeon that we still had here to Snorretje.

Joop from Groningen arrived by bicycle in the early evening. He was in a hurry as he had to get to Vroomshoop to fetch a motorbike. He'd had no problems with checkpoints on the way, but had traveled via the byways. He'll drop by tomorrow to collect a letter I have for Lies. He told me that a whole load of Krauts had arrived in Groningen and that the house of a railway worker who had gone underground had been burned down.

We received a railway worker who had gone into hiding and found him a safe place. I collected blankets and Fl.35 that I had paid in advance for the Frenchman from Mr. Bos. He and the journalist spent the day in the woods.

More [Allied] paratroopers have landed in the Netherlands [Arnhem].

September 21, 1944, Thursday Evening

I WENT IN search of gas cans. I got a couple from Dijk, one from Bleeker, one from a farmer in Langerak, and two from Schuiling. Teun de Vries and I then went to addresses that Bleeker had given us. The first was a shopkeeper who had hidden a Citroën. He told us a story about two Germans, or at least two men in German uniforms, who had already requisitioned the car. Of course, he wanted to help but we were too late (*visten achter het net*). Teun and I had our own ideas about all this and decided to investigate a little further. The man seemed to be a prototypical self-centered, egotistical bourgeois type, like Babbit in Upton Sinclair's book.[378]

In the meantime, we had found out where the car was hidden, but our friend Babbit has the ignition key. I had already agreed with Herman and Peter that I'd drive it along the Kremer path and hide it somewhere in the woods.

At another address we had better luck, finding a DKW motorbike.[379] It is currently in bits but will be put back together by an expert.

There were again many Krauts at the threshing machine, but Piet, the operator, was notable by his absence. The Krauts have also been to farmer Haspers and drove away on his tractor.

The Frenchmen have left as they want to reach France. The railway worker wants an identity card. His wife and daughter are coming here too. There is also a 17-year-old lad, again a railway worker.

The news from the French is good. In the evening, Dijk, Oom Cor, Oom Gerrit, Peter, Herman, and I are bent over the map of the Netherlands.

Last night an onderduiker was shot dead at Mans Meyer's, a farm on the corner of the Coevorder Straatweg and Elim Fietspad. It was said that he was an SS man in hiding.

September 22, 1944, Friday Evening

OOM COR AND I went to the woods today with a bale of straw to make the hiding place habitable again. I completely recamouflaged the entrance with shrubs, grass, leaves, and dead branches.

The wife and daughter of the railway worker and the 17-year-old were meant to arrive today. No one came.

News about the fighting round Arnhem is not good.

In Hoogeveen, all the houses of railway workers are being robbed clean.

I took ration cards to distant farms.

September 23, 1944, Saturday Evening

THIS MORNING THERE was pouring rain. There are 100 rye bread loaves getting old, but no means of sending them, not even to Hoogeveen.

Mans Meyer, at whose farm the shooting took place, has gone underground with his entire family, as well as his servant and his family. His brother, Boele Meyer, who lives in the Kerkhoflaan has also gone underground with his family. His little daughter was taken in by a neighbor [Kreeft]. The SS have taken possession of both farms. They steal and plunder, shoot at chickens, eat eggs, and stop anyone who passes by. The SS also visited Kreeft and, through the innocence of the girl herself, discovered that she was Meyer's daughter. She is now being used as a hostage and Kreeft will be shot if she disappears. Her father is hiding at Van der Helm's.

I had a strange dream about Oom Gerrit. He was cross because I had not found him a hiding place where there were young girls in the vicinity.

We have plans to take the young girl away from Kreeft's.

September 24, 1944, Sunday Evening

THIS MORNING I cycled to Hoogeveen to fetch clothes for the railway man. One of Meyer's sisters was at Bakker's [Pencil]. At Hollandscheveld, one of Kreeft's sons asked me if I knew where Boele Meyer was, but of course I didn't know. Zwart and his wife and daughter were also at the Pencils'. Zwart and I went looking for tobacco and came back with cigarettes and some pipe tobacco.

We went to an address to ask about the wife and daughter of the railway man. They are staying in Hoogeveen and have a safe address at night, but live in their own house during the day as we think this is the least risky. Empty houses are the first to be plundered.

Coming home, I heard that Karelse the policeman from Hollandscheveld who lives at Kats's had been looking for me with ideas about setting up a resistance group.

September 25, 1944, Monday Evening

THIS MORNING EARLY I went to De Krim with Teun de Vries to fetch the DKW motorbike. There were plenty of Krauts there but they did not trouble us.

Then I went to Hollandscheveld via Van der Helm to sort out some errand or other before arriving in the village and going to Kats's. A right collection was waiting for me there [and a visit I will never forget].

I walked completely unsuspecting into Kats's kitchen. The whole kitchen was full of SS-riffraff. Offeringa[380] the patrolman from Elim and Seller, the be-whiskered patrolman from Hollandscheveld, were also there, but obviously not of their own volition. Also sitting there as captives were Paulien Zijlstra, the nurse and daughter of Bouwe, and another woman whom I did not know. Kats wasn't there and neither was Mrs. Kats, who was "searching for her husband."

It scared me a bit as I had all manner of illegal things in my pockets [and even more in my bicycle panniers, including ration cards, *Ausweise*, some altered identity cards, some Wilhelmina cards, other Herman cards, five copies of *Trouw*, and 100 or so pamphlets that Peter had printed]. Paulien behaved splendidly and gave no indication whatsoever that we were friends, or that she had ever seen me before. Both the patrolmen also acted as though they didn't know me.

I was questioned by the "gentlemen"; why I had come, where I lived, but they didn't ask for my identity card. I told them that my bicycle was broken and asked what was happening, but received no reply. Griet, the maid, was very busy making coffee for the "gentlemen." I asked her if she had a cup for me and then prepared to drink it. I went to sit next to the connecting door between the kitchen and the living room.

With some pretext about "what a draft there is here, I'll shut the door," I made my escape and left via the front door. Paulien had already made eye contact with me saying, "Make sure you get out of here."

I cycled away as fast as I could and attracted the attention of the Schonewille brothers, who were committed NSBers and Kats's arch enemies.

I went to Wiegman's and Mrs. Wiegman warned me not to go to Kats's, because it wasn't safe there. I said, "Yes, I know, as I've just been there." They didn't understand. Neither did I.

In the meantime, it was also unsafe in Hoogeveen. From various quarters, I was warned that major raids were taking place. I went home via the Oostopgaande.

When I returned home, Peter and Herman had been worrying about me. There had been a message from Hollandscheveld five minutes after I left telling me not to go to Kats's. They assumed that I had been picked up.

There were worrying reports from Dedemsvaart that a Kraut had been shot and that reprisals would be taken.

In Hoogeveen there are many ships laden with copper for Germany, but the skipper of the first ship saw an opportunity to ram his vessel into a bridge and nothing can now get in or out.

There were many visitors today, too many to list in detail. Among them was the father-in-law of Mans Meyer's servant. He asked for a place for his daughter and son-in-law. There are rumors that Boele Meyer has been picked up, but luckily these are false, as he is at Van der Helm's.

Lots of people are being picked up by the SD, SS, Greens, and Landwacht. There is also a new sight in the Drentsche landscape, of groups of NSBers, fully laden, heading eastward.

Vondel was here today with the same purpose at Karelse yesterday, to talk about forming a resistance group. He was meant to come back at 8:00 p.m. but didn't arrive.

It is said that the whole male population of Beilen has gone underground. Mussert has gone with his aunt to the eastern border.[381]

We [now] smoke only home grown [tobacco] that we acquire here and there, mainly from Teun de Vries.

September 26, 1944, Tuesday Evening

TODAY IS FROUKE Dijk's birthday. I decorated the house with flowers and greenery. Bouwe Zijstra, who is being sought as a "terrorist," will, if he is caught, be shot, as will Karelse, and maybe Kats as well.

Nijhof came with Karelse's brother, who needs somewhere to hide. We put him with Ham for the time being. Mrs. Karelse has given herself up to the Krauts!

This afternoon, Bouwe Zijlstra, four of his sons and two members of the *Knokploeg*—all but two of them well-armed—arrived by bike. Three of the sons needed somewhere to hide. They stayed at Dijk's but the others moved on, but not before eating. Mrs. Dijk moves through the house, muttering, "Hai hai, my dear people, hai hai." She cooks delicious pancakes, her specialty in times of need and speed. All the rooms, kitchen, and WCs are full at Dijk's.

Later I took two of the sons to Piet Muller as this is a great hiding place. Piet Muller is very scared, but in spite of that he helps a lot. He has had a Jewish girl under his roof since 1942 and gradually acquired more onderduikers.

The third Zijstra I took to Mr. Scholten late in the evening. I said, "Please, can you look after him yourself or give him to Hartemink, soon there will be another one."

I received word that there was a railway worker in the area needing somewhere to hide for his whole family. Mrs. Faber was also there, as was Kats's servant, who had also gone underground. Teun de Vries brought a motorcycle inner tube that I'll take to De Krim tomorrow so that we can acquire another motorcycle.

We had a delightful evening in honor of Frouke. Two-thirds of the company were onderduikers. There were, as usual, guitars and much singing. Oom Cor had dressed himself as Ouwe Taai, the lady who had given us so much trouble. Oom Cor knows her through-and-through as he had to spend three months in her company. She is a real witch [heks]. He impersonated her perfectly. I had pains in my stomach from laughing.

Bleeker has pressed oil for Mrs. Dijk gratis. Jan Zijstra came and warned us to be alert, as his sister had been picked up.

The nursery school teacher was also here this evening. She told Peter and me that she'd like to help with this and that, but Kremer, with whom she is staying, will have none of it.

The news is not good. The Krauts have retaken Elst.[382]

The SD is becoming more and more active.

I received a great drawing in the post from Herman. "Flower-waterers exempt" it said, with a whole screed about the importance of people who water flowers and who are exempt from any duties for the German army. Signed Rauter. This was on account of me having gone to water Mrs. Otten's garden last week as a sort of camouflage when the Greens were nearby.

Herman is busy with cards depicting Prins Bernhard in front of a map of the Netherlands with a red white and blue flag. After the liberation, this card will be given to all those who have understood their duty and have sheltered onderduikers in their houses.

We have taken the key to the Ottens' house to a blacksmith to make copies, so we now have to get in through a window.

September 27, 1944, Wednesday Evening

I RECEIVED THE following letter from Piet Muller:

> Dear Friends,
> I am forced to write this letter to you about the lodgers we have. I had thought that this was a matter [strictly] between us, but someone [else] came to see them this afternoon. This I think is wrong, that someone else knows what is going on in our house. These people are not normal onderduikers, there is more to it than that [as they have a price on their heads], and it's not good that someone else knows because if one knows then others will find out. This cannot be right, can it? On those grounds, I would prefer it if someone else had them if it cannot be kept secret.
> Hoping to hear your reply. In expectation, your friend.

What had happened was this:

Mr. Bos, who also had a Frenchman in his house, had a letter for the other Frenchman and went to Mrs. Dijk, who directed him to Muller. In the evening when I heard this I was annoyed and pleaded with her never to give away a hiding place to anyone ever again. Mulder had been right and I went over there to calm things down.

The following letter was given to me for Hendrik Bleeker:

Dear Sir,
With regard to our meeting yesterday morning about the things you though you could get, the following: You should try to get hold of them personally and then notify Arnold. You will ensure that they do not fall into the hands of civilians. You remain responsible for these things. Consider this an order from the provincial commander of the resistance movement.
    Furthermore, stay silent about it to everyone.
This related to the weapons that Bleeker thought he could get from the Hitler Youth camp.

A note from Bep:

Arnold,
Wietske has asked you three or four times for the things needed for fingerprints. Have you forgotten or do you not want to do it? Please let her know, so that at least I'll know where I stand.
Bep

A letter from the "journalist":

Dear "Oom Gerrit,"
I believe that Arnold visits you on many occasions. Will you please ask him during his next visit about my identity card, which I think he has.
Henk

One of Peter's writings, which we put in all the latest ration cards [we distributed]:

In Paris, those who were underground do not have to hide their ration cards any more. Here you can still be arrested. Prevent this. Hide your card!

A letter from the distribution clerk in Dedemsvaart:

Herewith the coupons returned, which cannot be cashed because they are too different from the originals. The letter D on these sits under the line, while on the originals the letter D stands directly under the 4. Very careless of the organization, especially where these things can confuse an entire process.

Another note:

Dear Sister Smid,
The postcards that I had to buy for L I have bought, but now my question is, because they are children's cards, whether I can hold onto these and that Arnold will give L some others. Because I got these things from him quite late, I sometimes get into difficulties.
    It was very stormy here last week. There were house-searches at the four Lubbers' families on the Zwarte Pad. Nothing was found. Booty consisted of a live pig and two bicycles.

This morning I went to De Krim with the inner tube. Rode on to Slagharen and was given 5,000 sheets of stencil paper at a bookshop. I also bought a book, *De Schepping*,[383] for Guillette's birthday, which was some time ago.

I heard some details about the events in Dedemsvaart. There was shooting on a boat with Krauts. One Kraut was wounded in the jaw, which must have happened near the Balkbrug. As a result, the Krauts arrested everyone on the street, including the son of one of Dedemsvaart's doctors. This young man had a revolver on him. They shot him dead on the spot and left his body at the side of the road with a placard, "Terrorist." Another boy, who was by chance cycling with him, they [arrested], tied his hands, and then drowned him. A third boy cycled to the doctor's house to report, but he stayed too long and the Krauts arrived, found him, and after first maltreating him, shot him. Then they beat up the locum doctor (the regular doctor had already been taken and was somewhere in Germany). They wrecked the house from top to bottom, reduced the dispensary to rubble, down to the last bottle. Finally, they took all the clothes, linen, and foodstuffs with them.

Piet Muller has a new onderduiker.

I took Karelse's brother to Doornbos in Nieuw Zwinderen. I had to do a whole lot of talking before he was eventually allowed to stay. I thought it lucky that at least I could still persuade people (because it is far too busy at Dijk's), and then this evening, long after the curfew, he stood at the door again. Doornbos had sent him away because it had become unsafe as the SS had arrived in Nieuw Zwinderen.

Peter and I went to see Dominee van der Bos to talk over various things. We had three items on the agenda:

1. Cooperation between different groups
2. The new police chief
3. Blankets for onderduikers

Mrs. van der Bos came in and added a fourth point, namely her garden. Would I lay it out? Not going to happen. After the war, perhaps.

Yesterday, I went looking for the railway worker's family that needed a place to hide. I discovered that the man was still working at Coevorden Station, the ass. He only wanted to bring his family to safety, so I was no longer interested.

The news about Arnhem is very bad. The last paratroopers have retreated back over the Rhine.

September 28, 1944, Thursday Evening

THIS MORNING THERE was much traffic, for example Bouwe Zijstra and his son, and Karelse. Also another, to whom we have given the alias "Cupido" [Cupid]. He is the man who guided us during the raids on the distribution offices last year.

The case of Kats is very puzzling. He was seen yesterday cycling with a Kraut. Yesterday evening he went with the Kraut to see "Cupid," in whose house there was someone else who was being sought. This other person went away with them. This morning Kats was seen cycling between two Krauts in and around Hoogeveen. Paulien Zijlstra is free again, as is Mrs. Kats.

In Hoogeveen only 20 of the 400 men who were called up have reported. In Oosterhesselen everyone between the ages of 17 and 55 has to report.

Albert Nijwening asked for a place for an entire family. "Let them come," I said.

Our neighbors, Kwant the barber and his family, are very worried about the new regulations. Once again, there was a Kraut at the threshing machine. Piet, the boss of the enterprise was, as usual with such an occurrence, absent.

Mrs. Dijk has been to Hoogeveen and returned with, among other things, a pair of new shoes for me.

Peter and I have been to Wieten and Van der Helm. At Wietens we agreed measures for feeding the onderduikers as there will not be enough ration cards this time.

In the news this evening, Cuijk was listed among the places liberated, and Elst is once again in Allied hands.

I took blankets to Piet Muller for the youngsters.

September 29, 1944, Friday Evening

LAST NIGHT A burning plane came over our heads and crashed near the Kanaaltje. I went there. It was a fighter. Two dead.[384]

Went out with Henk Sweepe looking for hiding places. We did a whole lot of traipsing about, talking and preaching (from Henk), which would have filled three books.

We also went to the distribution office in Hollandscheveld where a group from Hoogeveen was busy delivering the distribution records. We spoke to one of the clerks who promised us 100 ration cards. They'll be delivered to Nieuwlande.

I went to see Jonkman, Bouwe Zijlstra's son-in-law. He is supposed to report to the SD in Hoogeveen on Saturday. He says he is going.

I have ordered blankets for Zijlstra's sons, which will be given to a carrier [for delivery].

Recently there was someone here from Bennekom, who gave us an eyewitness account of the airborne landings there.

I wanted to visit Mrs. Kats, but I was strongly discouraged because the SS were often still at the house. On the way, we met Dr. Reijnierse. "So," he said, "I've heard that you're now having coffee with the SS." He also told us that his nine-year-old son had been arrested and searched by a local NSBer.

In the afternoon, there was much to-ing and fro-ing. Mrs. Dijk called me even when I had retreated [*uitgeweken*] to the WC.

The dominee came to see Oom Cor.

Wieten gave us tobacco and cigarettes.

For a while there were two Krauts busy with a checkpoint about 100 m from our house. We were all taken by a report via Radio London that all the NSBers in Zeeuws Vlaanderen were being given first class treatment in a concentration camp.[385]

September 30, 1944, Saturday Evening

OOM GERRIT AND Oom Cor are complete opposites. Gerrit cannot get along with the children. Mrs. Dijk doesn't mind him as he is really not so bad. On the other hand, she is fond of Oom Cor, and the children like him too. Oom Gerrit meddles in things that don't concern him.

For these reasons, we thought it better that Oom Gerrit was found another place. Now I had a place for him with the evangelist in Nieuwe Krim.[386] It so happened that Oom Gerrit asked me for another [hiding] place of his own volition. He sees all sorts of dangers here, which are indeed present, and ones that we have also exaggerated a little to make it easy for him to make up his mind.

Our problem had been: how do we get Oom Gerrit to leave of his own free will. This has turned out wonderfully well. Tomorrow I'll take him to the other place.

But now, Oom Cor has become very afraid. So much so that he has taken it upon himself to nose around and has secured a place for himself at Kremer's. He has gone there this evening already, complete with blankets. Thus, he has left before Oom Gerrit, for whom the fear campaign was originally intended. Oom Cor wanted to leave straightaway as otherwise he would have to spend another night with Oom Gerrit, who would ask him all sorts of questions, for example, where he was going, and this he did not want to say.

Oom Cor has gone, but now Mrs. Dijk is angry because she wanted to keep him. She blames me for having cajoled "her" Oom Cor [into leaving] with the intention of bringing the Russians back to her. Nothing is further from the truth.

It is a real hassle, and the atmosphere has not been improved.

October 1, 1944, Sunday Evening

KATS HAS BEEN released and is back at home. It is a murky affair.

Mrs. Dijk is still annoyed and says that we can all scram if we don't ensure that Oom Cor comes back.

The Krauts have been patrolling Nieuwlande the last few days and nights.

This afternoon I took Oom Gerrit to Nieuwe Krim, where we arrived during a church service, so that I had to take him to the "harem," that is, the Hoogeveen family's, where Tante Louise, Mia, and Tante Annie are living.

Later on, we went to the evangelist, who was not expecting us. In the end, it was all fine, but a hiding place had to be constructed. After much searching and endeavor, we decided that the best place was probably under the pulpit in the church. I will get in touch with Norder [the carpenter] to make a hatch. It seems to me to be a suitable address for Gerrit. He is spoiled and difficult to adapt to.

I had hoped to attend the five o'clock church service at Nieuwlande, but it didn't happen. (The dominee was going to say something about sheltering onderduikers.) I was far too late because there was too much to talk about at the "harem" and I also called in on Hartemink.

Coming back, it was very difficult cycling with two bikes. It was raining and the roads were muddy. On the main road near Nieuwlande there were two Krauts cycling in front of me. They had a dog with them. They didn't leave me enough room to pass and I hit the dog with the second bicycle. The animal started and leapt at one of the Krauts' bikes with the result that the other Kraut fell by the side of the road, close to the water, floundering. I had considerable momentum, so could not stop to watch. I saw a Kraut in a heap, arms legs and bicycle wheels all caught up with the barrel of a gun. There was a great deal of cursing and roaring.

Kats had been and gone with his wife. He said that he had gambled and won. He had bribed the whole lot and had probably saved Hollandscheveld from more disasters. There were more on the list.

We got, via Kats, 100 pounds of pork.

October 2, 1944, Monday Evening

LAST NIGHT AT about 2:30 a.m. we heard two heavy thumps and there were signs of fire. I looked out of the window to the West and saw something white falling in the moonlight. Thinking it was a parachute, I went looking along the Oostopgaande and nearby. Found nothing. Two patrolling Krauts came by but they didn't see me because I hid in the shadow of the woods.

I went to see Lanting who has now decided he wants to be rid of the Russians. "It is no longer safe with us," he says. The Krauts had visited Lanting, namely, an officer who began to speak to one of the Russians when he saw him. The Russian referred him in broken German to the farmer. Lanting assumed there were more of them, but the Kraut had come alone to hunt up eggs and didn't realize that he had a Russian in front of him.

We have hidden the motorbike from De Krim under the hop barn at Kremer's.

In the municipality of Dalen, a loudspeaker van has been going around telling the male population that they have to work for the Krauts. Tomorrow they have to assemble on the marketplace, each with a shovel and blankets.

In Oosterhesselen there is a new mayor, an NSBer who has come [fled] from Zeeuws Vlaanderen. He is called Schipper. All men under the age of 55 have to report.

Norder has arranged the hiding place for Oom Gerrit. His judgment is good: A first-rate shelter.

Kats came; he brought eggs and butter. The pig was coming as well, he said.

This morning I was [up] early, on account of my nighttime hunt for the parachutist. I began to clean the Dijks' kitchen. When Mrs. Dijk came downstairs at 7:00 a.m., the first thing she saw through the window was all the kitchen furniture standing outside and though that the Krauts were clearing out [*leegroven*] the house.

Mrs. Dijk is easier to talk to today. She had decided not to be angry today, with anything or anyone, but she does want Oom Cor back, and that we have to arrange, otherwise you can all beat it [*hoepel je allemaal op*], she says.

There was a request from Visser for me to visit him. Peter and I went there. He spoke of his great unrest over the situation and asked us, as a matter of urgency, to advise the people to go to work for the Krauts. This would save a great deal of trouble.

October 3, 1944, Tuesday Afternoon

THE VILLAGE WAS on edge [*op stelten*] today. Thirty Landwachters and SD were haunting the place. At 10:00 p.m. last night they were round at Ham's, 15 of them. Why him, we have no idea, but perhaps because they think he is a soft touch [*sukkel*].

Peter, Herman, and John had gone to bed early and had just shut the trapdoor of the hiding place at Otten's when the thieves arrived and encircled the house. The boys assumed that they had come for them. The [Krauts] had interrogated Ham to find out where all the Gereformeeden [Orthodox Calvinists] lived. Ham spoke properly to them, according to Thijs, Karelse's brother, who had spent three full days under his roof but was now back on the road.

Mrs. Ham came around very early this morning, very nervous. They were all going to be arrested and we should immediately clear out Otten's house and all the stuff there, and the radio and so on. (Ham and Otten's houses shared a single roof). I told her that we were not thinking of leaving and that I had Otten's permission to be in his house for as long as I wanted.

"And Thijs must leave immediately, Mrs. Dijk must look after him in the future," she said.

The gentlemen of the SD had also visited Beukema for information as well as the dominee, whom they probably wanted as a hostage. Dominee van den Bos was just showing Sister Adema out and they were standing in the hallway when the bell rang. The dominee knew to crawl into a hiding place. He is now underground, as is his wife.

Many of their belongings were taken to safety.

Teun de Vries and I visited the parsonage this morning and she had not yet left.

The little EDS steam tram has also now finally stopped running.

In Langerak many have registered.

In Nieuwlande, almost nobody.

Ham and Arend Westra, and a few others from this heroic elite are going to register.

I spoke to Albert Nijwening, who said that he would soon have to stop selling bread. He could get an exemption [from labor service] as a baker but will not do so, which I think is the only proper course of action.

Today was a day full of annoyances and stress. How will it turn out? We will have to wait and see, and in the meantime, take all [necessary] measures.

Hendrik Bleeker stopped me and said he could get 200 *mud* of rye at half price, that is Fl.5 per *mud*, from the Krauts who are stealing the harvest from Mans Meyer's farm. What do I think about it? He knows all too well. I won't consider it and wouldn't buy for one cent from the Krauts.

October 3, 1944, Tuesday Evening

OOM COR IS back, he was evicted [by Kremer]. I very much expected that.

The whole group is currently in the woods. Karelse and his neighbors Thijs, Peter, Herman, John, and Oom Cor. All six went out, each with a bundle of blankets under their arm, taking the stable light with them. Mrs. Dijk is now content as Oom Cor has returned.

I'll look for a place for Karelse's brother in the morning.

Peter and I went to Arend Westra to hear again if he was talking nonsense, which seemed to be somewhat better than expected. Later Ham and Westra came here to say that we shouldn't go into Otten's house any more. They threatened betrayal if we went back there.

In Zwolle, houses have been taken over directly by the Germans in tandem with their clearance, so that the onderduikers hiding under the floor have had no opportunity to escape.

October 4, 1944, Wednesday Evening

YESTERDAY EVENING THE Landwacht came by delivering summonses to work on Kraut fortifications [*stellingen*]. Dijk also got one of these. Me they seem to have overlooked, although I am registered (under the name of Henrikus Marinus van der Vegt). The whole village is on edge but virtually no one goes.

Masses of people come who want to be rid of their onderduikers, but we are "not at home" to all of them because we can't start doing that.

It seems to be that case that the whole village is going underground.

Here below is the summons that Dijk received:

S. Dijk Esq.
H. 60 1
Nieuwlande
   On Wednesday morning October 4 you must take the 9:30 a.m. tram to Assen, from where you will be given further instructions. You should bring with you; two blankets, cutlery, a drinking mug, shovel or spade, and warm clothing. The wages will be Fl.5 per day and Sunday working Fl.10. Ration cards do not need to be brought. People should take heed of my instructions.
   The Mayor
   A Schipper

Here follows a letter from an onderduiker, who had tricked us and was trying to fool us again:

> Dear Arnold or Nico,
> I'm writing to you again in the hope that you'll receive it. You are aware that I left the Mol family of my own volition. You were against this and I didn't want to leave without asking you first, but couldn't reach you so decided to act, which I [now] very much regret.
> But now to the purpose of my letter. You know that I am at v. B te E. This man and his sons fall into the age category [17–55 for labor service] and thus have to leave. They are not going [to report] but have to go underground. I therefore also have to disappear. v. B has often said: I wish you had another place [to hide], but that is more easily said than done. Can you help me?
> Hoping that you won't disappoint me,
> Cor

*Lies: In a letter to his father he had said "Arnold and Nico know nothing about this so please don't speak to them about it." That was a couple of days before he moved to the new address.

We got the following epistle from Lucas Snoek, the radio technician in Langerak who has a really bad stutter.

> Dear Friends,
> From well-informed sources I have heard the following:
> The NSB mayor of Oosterhesselen has said that he will make the infamous Nieuwlande pay. He'll allow the whole place to burn if people don't report [for work], so that it will be impossible for onderduikers to remain there. He specifically referred to Jewish onderduikers, which makes it all the more clear to me that we are facing treason here. I am handing you this note underlining that you truly have to be on your guard and please be invisible, you know to whom I refer.
> Dan Dijk, I do not know whether you have been called upon as well, I find it very irresponsible not to go. With a few exceptions, everyone here in Langerak has left. We did not yet receive a call up ourselves. Anyway, you have to decide yourself, but if they set the house on fire, and you will agree with me upon this, I think it is better than one man, rather than a handful of people, is sacrificed.[387]

I had intended to get the boys out of the woods this morning, but it didn't happen as there was always something [to deal with]. One stopped me in the street, another came on foot, and all with the same questions: What shall we do? Where can we hide? Where are we with our onderduikers?

Eventually Frouke fetched the boys as unless someone comes for them, they don't know if it is safe.

Miesje came during the day with, among other things, a request from Oom Gerrit, mainly about his clothes.

Mrs. Lanting came to say that the Russians had to go immediately. I went to fetch them. They'll have to go into the woods for the time being.

The dominee came, camouflaged in overalls which fitted him well. He is fine these days.

Kremer's daughter came to summon us to take the motorbike away that we'd hidden under their haystack. Her father had said it was too dangerous. We put it under Griffioen's hedge, a thick, wide, and unpruned hedge. It was well camouflaged with a covering to keep the rain off.

At Dijk's it was more than usually busy. We ate in three sittings at the table, Mrs. Dijk holds together well in these times. Peter and I have laid in supplies from Wieten for the woods. Plenty of food in tins and other nonperishable things. We are going to make a much bigger hole, where perhaps 80 people can get in.

Cupid came by with tobacco, which was very welcome.

Went to Norder, who doesn't know what he should do. He has also been called up. He doesn't want to go but has two old people in his house and doesn't want to risk them being found. I have tried to find [another] place for them but that's no longer possible. Finally, I advised Norder to go and report.

At Johannes Post's farm, I picked up the covering, the stable lantern and digging tools.

Ham's behavior is more than sad. He threatens to betray us if we go to Otten's house again.

I have been searching for materials for our hole; nails and so forth, as well as asphalt. We had a comical trip to the woods where we brought everything in on various wheelbarrows.

The whole village shows signs of having gone underground.

October 5, 1944, Thursday

WENT EARLY THIS morning into the woods. Everything was quiet.

Jan Post has gone to see the mayor, "to have a chat." His Excellency had uttered all kinds of profanities about Nieuwlande. Nothing good came out to the village. Horses were not handed in, the people did not report [for work], etc., etc., but the consequences were inevitable.

I got a 300-hour electric lamp from Schuiling. He himself has gone underground, so it was his wife who handed it over.

John, the Belgian, is delighted by life in the woods. "Dass ist leben" [this is the life], he shouts. We have a rifle and two revolvers, as well as some blackjacks and truncheons.

Toon Kwant, the son of our neighbor, the barber, has also gone underground, against the wishes of his parents and is with us in the woods. We are going to dig a big new hole, and I have already found the place. It has to be large enough to accommodate 100 people in an emergency. There were eight of us digging. The

Russians were also meant to be there, but they had a new place in Nieuwe Krim. We started the digging, but this was not work for those unused to heavy work.

Oom Cor is suffering from nerves. He wants to go back to Nieuwe Krim, where he says it is safer. We try to talk him out of it:

1. It isn't safer there; there are no woods.
2. The people there won't have him as they already have two onderduikers.
3. As soon as he is there, he'll want to come back here.

The dominee has asked to reserve places for [his] wife and children in the woods.

There are reports of billeting in Hollandscheveld and in Elim.

October 6, 1944, Friday Evening

MASSES OF PLANES in the sky. Droning in the distance, shooting nearby.

Recently we had a nice joke with the Russians. Mrs. Dijk gave each of them a tomato. "Ah Apfel" [Oh an apple], said Ivan and bit a large mouthful out, with the result that the insides went in all directions.

Henk Sweepe was witness to a house being blown up in Beilen, a reprisal action.

Oom Cor is our *corvee*[388] in the woods. He has got this name because his real surname begins with the letter V, hence Cor V.

In Nieuwlande there is an atmosphere of panic. At Dijk's the door is being knocked down by people who want to be rid of their onderduikers. They ask for me, but I'm not there.

Today we were given three bales of straw and three rolls of asphalt. Peter is responsible for the provisions and came today with everything, including cigars.

Frouke came with a big bucket of food and soup.

There was a Kraut who came along the edge of the wood, but he didn't see us. He can get the Ram-Bam (?),[389] the whole world can get the Ram-Bam. This has become our expletive. Herman started it.

October 7, 1944, Saturday

BUSY WITH WORK in the woods. The weather is with us, unusually nice. The boys are washed out in the evenings. They're not used to the heavy work.

The whole day we heard the booming of guns. There are rumors that the Allies have a bridgehead over the Rhine at Wageningen. Leenhouts told us that he had been to Wageningen by bike and that terrible things had happened there. Most of the resistance groups had been massacred.

John told us about being a prisoner-of-war in Hamburg and Bremen. Initially he had been in Hamburg and lived through the massive bombardment there. "That was the life," he said. Then he was in Bremen and saw the whole thing repeated.

Our work is going well, in spite of the blistered hands of most of the participants. It's a huge task. Our Cor V is in action. It's great to see him busy when we are sitting on the ground and taking turns to get a sandwich from him.

October 8, 1944, Sunday

TODAY WE HAVE violated the Sabbath and carried on working. We have too few excavators. The ground is rock hard and difficult to shift, but ideal for a hole.

Frouke came with coffee, just like every other morning. She always comes bounding along, frolics with this and that, pours our coffee and then flutters away like a butterfly.

In the afternoon, Mr. and Mrs. Dijk came to look. The comments from Mrs. Dijk were priceless: "That is no life, living in the woods, etc., etc." She also crawled into our old hiding place, accompanied by many shrieks.

Henk Sweepe held two services today for the dominee, who has gone underground. The dominee held a service for onderduikers in a private house.

There were five shots fired on the bridge in Nieuwlande last night.

Mrs. Dijk will see if we can get Sliekers to come to the woods to help with the digging. Herman was too washed out and too tired to eat this evening.

Peter and Oom Cor went to Dijk. Peter stayed there to falsify *Ausweise* and Cor returned alone.

We need to cover a proportion of the hole as soon as possible as it is threatening to rain for a while.

In Nieuwlande, many people and whole families have been expelled.

Dijk is back at home, he has decided to chance it. He was with us in the woods for one day and then at De Krim. My collar and clothes are filthy, but the hole has to be finished first. I wrote a letter to Nico, asking him if he wanted to come to the woods. Oom Cor also wants to help digging. This provided some extremely comical situations. Every time he took a shovelful of earth, he looked like someone trying to lift a ball with a walking stick. However, in any case he did his best.

We had an issue with him over the loaded Kraut rifle that we had with us at all times. He wanted to get rid of it, because, "it was forbidden by the Krauts."

The hole is beginning to take shape and most of the digging is now done.

October 9, 1944, Monday Evening

SLIEKERS, WHO HAD been summoned by Mrs. Dijk, came to the woods today to help with the work. Mrs. Dijk had promised me: "He's happy to help, he is strong and will give you plenty of help." Well, he came, I gave him a spade, and he went to work. After less than an hour of this, he remembered that he had "things to do" and left.

Later we heard from Frouke, who came with the food, that he had said, "It is not for me, they want me there dead, a respectable person could not stand it there."

Today Cupid arrived at our camp. I think the work we have done is worthwhile.

We now sleep four-strong outside the hole, namely, John, Herman, Karelse and I. The others sleep inside.

We only learn gradually what is happening in our country nowadays.

October 10, 1944, Tuesday Evening

WE HAVE BEEN given a new guest in our little community. He's called Sylvester Rambam, a small field mouse who has his hole close to our bivouac. He is becoming ever tamer.

We work with feverish haste and the weather is still with us.

Dijk came today with the food instead of Frouke.

Herman got a letter from Wasbeer, which had taken ten days [to reach him].

The Russians are advancing 50 km per day in Hungary. What is happening in our country?

October 11, 1944, Wednesday Evening

LAST NIGHT WE were overtaken by rain. We crawled under the awning, but it guttered and then came through. Herman gave a roar of laughter. John said very indignantly, "Herman has no feelings." We fled into our hole and spent the rest of the night there, lying in between the others. Our blankets had got awfully wet.

In the hole, there was much confusion: pushing, laughter, swearing, and grunting.

This morning we got a message from Peter to say that a 330 lb pig had arrived. Mrs. Dijk had almost fainted.

We have yet another newcomer, an acquaintance of Cupid, he calls himself "Nightowl."

The weather remained good today. A proportion of the hole is now covered over but not ready to be lived in yet; for example, there is no straw in there.

We sleep outside again as it will stay dry. According to Nightowl there won't be any rain. "Impossible," he says.

We went to bed immediately after eating and smoked a pipe of homegrown. The others sleeping in the hole then lie around us telling stories and jokes.

There was a German car with a trailer in Nieuwlande today.

October 12, 1944, Thursday Evening

MY BEARD IS taking on alarming dimensions.

Herman and I went to see Dijk at 5:00 a.m. I had a wonderful wash and shave, and now feel like a new man.

I sought out the dominee, who wants to go back to the parsonage and also wants to preach next Sunday. He's never at home at night.

This morning we made the new hole partially habitable.

Ham has carried out some pretty ugly sabotage, throwing all our things from under Otten's house and nailing the hatch shut, although under pressure from Peter he has opened it again.

October 15, 1944, Sunday Evening

I GOT THE following letter from Peter:

> Dear Arnold,
> I can get a first-rate new workplace. We can have a room at Jan Post's and sleep in a hiding place in the shed. The only problem with this place is that no one must know that we are working there so there can be no coming and going. It is therefore necessary that you are at Dijk's at least two hours every day to receive people. This is essential as otherwise Mrs. Dijk will not be able to continue with her work.
> Can you give me your opinion verbally, as I will hear today and will have to make a decision?
> P.P.

For me, it seems far too dangerous there. When our hole is finished, this seems to be a much better place [to hide].

Friday 13, I went to Dedemsvaart to try to obtain asphalt and nails.

On the way, I visited Van Wimmenhoven where I got two and a half rolls [of asphalt]. He was not at home, and the women there did not know me and as a result did not trust me. I persuaded them enough that his daughter would take me to him. He was busy shoring up a hole for onderduikers, not that they told me this, but I divined it from the general situation. He is one of the few "good" Dutchmen who does everything possible to sabotage and generally frustrate the Krauts. His daughter is cut from the same cloth and has already had a Kraut revolver pointed at her chest but refused to say where her father was.

She brought me to a small farm where only a girl was at home. The menfolk had all gone underground. She disappeared into the woods and returned ten minutes later with Van Wimmenhoven. He'll set out the two and a half rolls for me.

In Dedemsvaart I found the situation was peaceful—too peaceful. Many had registered [for work] and had left for Hasselt with shovel on shoulder to help with the defense works.

Stegeman helped me to round up the asphalt: nine rolls in all and an abundance of nails in all sizes (which were now almost unobtainable). The asphalt will be brought to De Krim tomorrow by Broenink using a goat and others who are traveling on to Coevorden to fetch peat.

I slept in Dedemsvaart on Friday and Saturday night. I had no ration cards with me and was overwhelmed by requests. I was given an example of a [certificate of] exemption from labor (for the Krauts) from Zuidwolde and took it back for Peter to imitate.

I got complaints about Jo. She was too indiscreet in what she said and was out on the street after 8:00 p.m. [curfew]. Jo gave me a letter for Herman. Hauw, one of the onderduikers with Heerspink was at Stegeman's because it wasn't safe at Linde.

Back at Nieuwlande I found the situation anything but peaceful. The Landwachters were marching through the village. In my absence, a number of things had gone wrong with the construction of our hole. At least I was happy to be back. Jo had wanted to come back with me to Nieuwlande.

Four Jews from Hoogeveen had been arrested on the Balkbrug. They had moved hiding places a week ago.

I acquired ammonia and pepper to use against bloodhounds.

Last night, Nightowl had a visit from his wife, Roosje. I don't like that sort of thing. I went home yesterday evening as I had no desire to sleep in the same hiding place as Roosje. At Dijk's everyone was already in bed, so I climbed in through the window in the shed. Mrs. Dijk got a scare.

This morning to church. After the service Guillette arrived. Herman was busy writing a letter to Jo.

The onderduiker at Thalen's came asking for another hiding place. Thalen had said it was too dangerous. I told him to tell Thalen that, as an elder of the church, he should have more confidence. I also told him to go back soon and tell Mr. Thalen that I will send him three more onderduikers.

Tonight there were Landwachters haunting the village. They shot through the windows at Kamphuis's, but the entire family was already underground.

There are strange rumors in the village about a family that I have always completely trusted, and continue to trust. It is said that many Krauts come to their house and that the wife had been to the mayor and committed treason. I don't believe a word of it.

Today I went with Guillette to the hole. The Visser girls and To also came along. Dijk has influenza.

October 16, 1944, Monday Evening

THIS MORNING I went with "Little Owl [Uiltje] to De Krim to collect the asphalt. Nine rolls was a heavy weight. I had Beukema's trailer on the back of my bike.

Teun de Vries came again with tobacco and said that we could collect some each week.

Elly (at Mr. Bos's) has a birthday today. There was a party and Herman went along.

The Landwacht is again in the village. I hear shooting and see lights on the road.

Karelse has hit himself on the foot while chopping trees for our hole and has to lie down for a while. It was not easy to get him out of the woods. I put an emergency dressing on it and called the doctor [Reijnierse].

October 17, 1944, Tuesday Evening

YESTERDAY EVENING I waited at Dijk's for Herman, who had gone to Elly's birthday party. I thought he'd come back about midnight. I had dozed off and was rudely awakened at 5:00 a.m. by a hammering on the window. It was Herman. He told me that there had been a Landwacht raid in the middle of the birthday party at Mr. Bos's. Herman, Hillie Bolwijn, and Bolwijn's servant had escaped in the nick of time. Elly and Dolf, the "journalist," and Hans also all escaped. Hans had gone to Van der Helm's, crawling on his belly. Herman had been wandering around with the other two all night.

I immediately took a bicycle and started to look around. I found a ship's captain who had gone "underground" with his boat in a place between the woods and the canal. There I discovered the journalist, Mrs. Bos's maid, and another girl from Limburg who was also underground. They had spent the whole night in the woods under a raincoat. It was by no means warm as it was cold, wet weather.

We drank a cup of coffee with the captain in the wheelhouse and then went to Dijk's. Elly and Dolf had been looking for me according to the journalist. We found them both at Dijk's, where they were warming themselves behind the stove, and we learned a bit of their story. The house was full of onderduikers; 13, including Dickie Dijk, who had been ordered with all the other schoolchildren to lift potatoes, but had refused.

Mr. Bos has been caught.

I entrusted Freek, Karelse's brother, with a letter for Dedemsvaart. This was one less, and he did not come back, but it should be OK. I had written to Stegeman, asking him to find a place [for Freek] at the Moerheim nursery or on a farm.

I went to see Mrs. Bos and saw bullet holes in the windows and floor. Mrs. Bos was ill in bed, but very calm. The dominee was there as well. Mr. Bos had probably been taken to Assen, or perhaps Oosterhesselen.

I took all the clothes belonging to Dolf, Elly, Hans, the journalist, and Hillie, the maid out of the house. It took a long time. As soon as I had taken the last suitcase out, a troop of Krauts and Landwachters arrived at Bos's house and elsewhere in the village, where they poked about a bit, for example, at Kamphuis's empty house as he and his family have all gone underground. They stole a good many things, and an NSBer lives in the house now.

The Dijk house is full of onderduikers who would need to be in the hiding place. The hatch stood open so that all of them could get in quickly. It looked for a minute as though Dijk was going to get a visit as well. Eight of the troop came toward the house. All the onderduikers were hidden, save Herman and I, and we went out the back and hid in a ditch. They went next door to Kwant the barber's and picked on someone who was just being shaved.

Later a motorcycle and sidecar with two Krauts stopped outside Dijk's. The result was panic. Oom Cor, who saw no chance to get into the hiding place in time, ran—as hard as his short legs and corpulent body would allow—into the back garden and out the back. It was a false alarm. The "gentlemen" were just looking for the post office.

Van der Zwaag was here and very optimistic about the course of the war. "Inside a month, we'll be free," he said.

In the evening, everyone, including the girls, went to our hiding place [in the woods] to spend the night there. I had tried to find an alternative place for the women, but it hadn't worked out. Peter even went to "Flipje," the evangelist,[390] but had no success there.

October 18, 1944, Wednesday Morning

I FOUND A place for the girls at the Bethesda Hospital in Hoogeveen. What they have to do there I have no idea, but the main thing is that they can go there. After a lot of fuss, they left on a tandem. Mrs. Kats, who was here by chance, went in front of them to warn of any dangers.

Everyone had slept well in our hole and was very complimentary.

Lidia and Suze arrived and are still here. Everything has been very quiet in Nieuw-Amsterdam for the last few days.

We had many visitors. Hillie Marissen's uncle [the girl from Limburg] came storming in demanding to know where she was staying. Naturally, I didn't tell him, except to say she was with good people in a very good hiding place. He was angry and insisted to know where she was, which of course I did not do.

This is where my diary ends. The following day I was arrested.

NOTES

1. Here and elsewhere in the diary, Douwes uses the derogatory term *mof* or *moffen* (best translated as Krauts) to describe the Germans rather than the more usual Dutch term *Duitsers*.

2. Douwes's later writings make reference to the German parachutists arriving in disguise, although his original notes make no mention of this. This story, while current during the invasion and subsequently, has not been authenticated (L. de Jong, *The German Fifth Column in the Second World War* [London: Routledge & Kegan Paul, 1956]).

3. This was Bertha Douwes, who lived with her husband, Pastor Herman Stegeman, at the parsonage in the Grotestraat in Cuijk aan de Maas.

4. Pastor Jan Douwes (1900–1976) was married to Nicoline (Niek) van Doesburgh (1903–1985). They lived in the Gereformeerde parsonage at Zuidwillemsvaart 18.

5. The mayor of Gorinchem from 1939 until 1971 was Louis Rudolph Jules (Rolly) Ridder van Rappard (1906–1943). He was active in the resistance and arrested by the NSB in 1943. He subsequently became a well-known politician in the postwar period.

6. The mayor of Capellen between 1934 and 1944 was Adrianus Prins. He was a member of the ARP and during the war was attached to the André resistance group, which organized hiding places for around 900 people during the occupation.

7. This is a reference to the men of the Koninklijke Marechaussee, a section of the armed national police charged with guarding borders, main roads, strategic locations, and the royal palaces in peacetime. They were also employed as a military police force. The Koninklijke (Royal) was dropped when the occupation began.

8. Generaal Henri Gerard Winkelman (1876–1952). Nominated as supreme commander of all Dutch forces on August 28, 1939, he was forced to surrender on the evening of May 14, 1940, and signed the capitulation a day later. Refusing to declare not to resist German forces in any way, he was interned for the remainder of the war.

9. Precisely the opposite direction.

10. This was Robert Paul Belinfante (1905–1940) and his wife, Marianne (1902–1944). They were discovered, but he died in the hospital soon afterward. She survived but lost her unborn child and died suddenly on January 10, 1944, while in hiding at the house of Janke Nooitgedagt. Robert's sister, Frieda Belinfante (1904–1995), a well-known cellist and female conductor also became involved in resistance activity and helped falsify identity cards and arrange hiding places. At the end of 1943, she fled to Switzerland and later immigrated to the United States.

11. Salomon (Sam) Jacobs (1903–1941) owned a butcher's shop at Dorpstraat 41 in Laag Keppel. The later English version explains that Douwes learned about Jewish religious and family traditions through his friendship with the Jacobs family when he was growing up and before the occupation. He learned about the Jewish National Fund and Zionism from them and subsequently encountered a group of Palestine-Pioneers (Chalutsim) from Germany in hiding in Het Oude Huis in the Rijksstraatweg. Of the twenty-one young men at Laag-Keppel, only two survived the war. See Sjoerd Laansma, *De joden van de Kleine Haar te Gorssel—een groep Palastina-pioniers* (Zutphen: Delta, 1986).

12. This was the home of the noble Van Pallandt family.

13. His father, Petrus Arnoldus Conradus Douwes (1871–1935), was from 1902 until his death Reformed minister in Hummelo and Laag-Keppel.

14. This was, in fact, October 8, 1941. The German *Ordnungspolizei* (uniformed order police) was often referred to as the Grüne Polizei (Green Police, or just Greens).

15. *Overvalwagen.*

16. Jacobs was among the first Jews deported from the Netherlands as a punishment. His official date of death was October 31, 1941, so sometime later than Douwes credits here.

17. German sources suggest that the cables were cut in 21 places. The guards were threatened with severe punishments if the cable was damaged in their area. One group carved "Kabelwacht 1941" in a tree on the Tolstraat in Laag-Keppel, which can still be seen today. The English version also notes the wholesale (national) registration of workers in the summer of 1941.

18. This was Graaf Adolph Sweder Hubertus van Rechteren-Limpurg, Heer van Enkhuizen and owner of the castle in Hummelo that bore his name. He was married to Eleonore, Prinzessin zur Lippe-Weissenfeld (1913–1964, divorced 1944). She was a distant relation to Bernhard zur Lippe-Biesterfeld, the consort of the future Queen Juliana of the Netherlands.

19. According to Geert Hovingh in discussion with the editors, this was probably a Stirling bomber of the Seventh RAF Bomber Squadron that had taken off from RAF Leeming in North Yorkshire to raid the Potsdammer Bahnhof in Berlin.

20. Bertha Stegeman-Douwes in Cuijck.

21. Almost certainly the cells behind the police station at Roggestraat 9–13, now De Roode Toren Museum.

22. Sicherheitsdienst (German Security Police).

23. This was probably Jacobus Smit (1880–1943), a teacher and resistance worker.

24. Kool was head waiter at Hotel-Restaurant Den Boogerd in Zaltbommel. He was active in the local resistance, specializing in the hiding and onward transmission of Allied aircrew. He survived the occupation.

25. The *Jodenster* [Jewish star] had been introduced across the country by the German authorities on April 29, 1942. In protest, some non-Jews had also worn the star in solidarity with their Jewish neighbors.

26. *Fout* refers to the binary division used in the Netherlands to distinguish those who had acted against the national interest in siding with the Germans, as opposed to *goed*, who encompassed the resistance, and by implication also the majority of the Dutch population. This rather simplistic formulation has now been replaced by a more nuanced analysis of Dutch behavior—at least in academic circles.

27. "NSBer": Shorthand for an individual member of the NSB.

28. This was the Protestants Christelijke School voor Lager Onderwijs in the Spoorstraat in Boxmeer.

29. Cedar trees.

30. The Imperial Agricultural High School, now Wageningen University.

31. Frederik Stegeman (1887–1984) was the younger brother of Herman Stegeman, the husband of Douwes's sister Bertha.

32. Hendrik Heerspink Jnr (1887–1955).

33. Dr.Willem Volger (1904–1980) was reformed minister in Hollandscheveld between 1939 and 1944. He was married to Anna Kurpershoek (1907–1999).

34. Members or followers of the Nationaal-Socialistiche Beweging (NSB), the Dutch National Socialist Party led by Anton Mussert.

35. Johannes Post (1904–1944) was the youngest son of peasant farmer Jan Wolters Post (1863–1942) and Trijntje Tempen (1865–1937). He was born on the family farm in Moscou. In 1929 he married Dina Salomons (1903–1991), the daughter of Geert Salomons (1865–1918) and Hilligje "Oma" Salomons-Huizingh (1875–1950). Just before the marriage, Johannes had been able to acquire a farm on the Nieuwlander Straatweg, and eight of his nine children were born there.

36. The Bouvier des Flandres is a herding dog breed originating in Flanders.

37. Willem Roffel and his wife, Ritske Roffel-Blaak, lived next to the church and were awarded the title of Righteous Among the Nations by Yad Vashem in 1983 for their help in hiding Jews in Nieuwlande, not least in hiding Ish Davids (Peter) and Lou Gans (Herman) in the undercroft of the church.

38. Under the regulations, children under 15 years old were not required to carry identity cards.

39. *Onderduiker* (literally someone who has "dived under"), a term used to denote anyone who had to go into hiding. There is no direct English translation and the word has therefore been left in the original throughout.

40. Jan Wildschut became a member of the armed resistance in the region. He was ultimately captured and taken to KZ Sachsenhausen from where he was sent to an Aussenkommando of KZ Natzweiler and died on or around January 1, 1945.

41. Celina Johanna Kuyper (1923–1943) alias "Thea" was Johannes Post's friend and first courier. She was engaged to Ish Davids, alias "Peter."

42. The English text explains that this was often done by the so-called Knok-ploegen, armed squads that raided local government offices. This was a better source of supply than stealing cards from individuals, not least because the authorities had nominal lists of those that had been "lost" or "stolen."

43. A corruption of the Dutch word *razzia* (a raid).

44. This was the Eerste Drentsche Stoomtramweg-Maatschappij that ran trams and bus services in Eastern Drenthe.

45. Koninklijke Marechaussee, an element of the Rijkspolitie (National Police) responsible for security and border control. During the occupation, it was referred to as the Marechaussee and in this text also refers to individuals.

46. A reference to Princess Juliana and her husband, Prince Bernhard.

47. The term *oranje* (orange) is used extensively as a symbol of Dutch nationalism and as an epithet for the Royal Family.

48. *Gewestelijke bureauhouder*.

49. German local commander.

50. The implication being that some element of the resistance had removed all the files from under the noses of the Germans.

51. WA (Weerafdeling) The paramilitary section of the Dutch National Socialist Movement (NSB).

52. A reference to the assassination of Opperluitenant van Politie Pieter Kaay, who had been shot early on Saturday morning. He was well known for being pro-German and had a reputation for hunting down Jews in hiding.

53. "Peter," whose real name was Isidor Joseph Davids, and had specialized in forging identity cards, was engaged to Thea.

54. Douwes and many other rescuers would often refer to their charges as looking Jewish or, in Dutch, as *rasecht-Joods* because it made a material difference as to how easily they could travel and if they had to remain in hiding all the time.

55. This might possibly be better expressed as "Hear no evil, see no evil, speak no evil."

56. This followed from an attempt by the Germans to coordinate the medical profession into a single National Socialist organization (Artsenkamer). Most doctors chose to avoid this by removing their titles from the doors and offices after March 24, 1943. A clandestine alternative, Medisch Contact, was created to circulate information between practitioners.

57. Presumably a euphemism for an onderduiker.

58. This is a peculiarly Dutch term to differentiate individuals who were loyal to Dutch interests (*goed*) and those who sided completely with the Germans and National Socialism and collaborated (*fout*).

59. "K.K.": Ostensibly a shortened form of the NSKK, the Nationalsozialisches Kraftfahrkorps (National Socialist Motor Corps).

60. Ds. Dirk van Ekelenburg (1917–1945), who was assistant Reformed pastor in Nieuw-Amsterdam from 1941 to 1945 and died that year in the Landeskrankenhaus Neustadt (Oldenburg-Holstein).

61. These are references to the bombers that crossed Dutch territory on their way to raids on German cities in the Ruhr and elsewhere.

62. Ds. Klaus Eduard Henri Oppenheimer (1905–1986).

63. This presumably refers to milk acquired on the black market.

64. Ds. Hielke Willem Hielkema (1904–1991), who was Reformed minister in Schoonebeek from 1940 to 1944.

65. The latter two were often referred to by the initial letters of their first names NV—which is also the abbreviation of *Naamloze Vennootschap*—literally a limited liability company—but also the name given to a resistance organization during the occupation. "Nico" was Jan Naber (1923–1957) and "Victor," Albert Jan Rozeman (1922–1984).

66. Landwachters were uniformed rural policemen.

67. Jan Dekker (1901–1981) was married to Arendina Zwiers and (1901–1987) and lived on the corner of the Kerkhoflaan and the Nieuwlander Straatweg, almost opposite Johannes Post's farm.

68. In the original, Douwes refers to him erroneously as "Wigman" throughout. Wiegman was the headmaster of the Reformed School voor Christelijke Volksonderwijs in Hollandscheveld. He was close friends with Ds Volger (who was chairman of the Reformed School Association). Wiegman's house became the local center of operations for the Landelijke Organisatie voor Hulp aan Onderduikers (LO).

69. This was presumably Ds. Louwrens Seinhorst (1895–1986) who was Reformed minister in Pesse from 1929 to 1947.

70. Hendrik Julius André Douwes (1914–1991), who was Reformed minister in Dorkwerd from 1942 and married to Wilhelmina Koning (1916–2016).

71. This was presumably a reference to the German bombing of Rotterdam on May 14, 1940, that flattened areas of the city. The excuse of being an evacuee from the city was also widely used by onderduikers to explain their accents and presence in rural areas of the Netherlands.

72. Guillette Agathe Douwes (1915–1996).

73. This was the so-called eerste distributiestamkaart, introduced when rationing began in 1939. This document entitled the holder to receive ration coupons in accordance with the regulations then in force. It also included interleafing (*inlegvellen*) that indicated when coupons could be collected. It was later replaced by a tweede distributiestamkaart, introduced at the behest of the Germans to flush out onderduikers. In this system, individuals had to present their identity papers and new *stamkaart* to verify their identities with the officials before receiving their coupons.

74. Doeks was the alias of Mrs. Frida Jeanne de Clercq Zubli (1902–1985), a writer and novelist living in Groningen. She was married to Jaap Mulder, a doctor at the Academisch Ziekenhuis in Groningen. Both were involved in rescuing Jewish children and arrested on a number of occasions.

75. H. de Kruyff (1903–1974).

76. Ds. Klaus Eduard Henri Oppenheimer (1905–1986).

77. SA (Sturmabteilung): The paramilitary section of the German Nazi Party (NSDAP).

78. This was probably Hendrik van Ekelenburg. Then 21 years old, he was killed in an accident soon afterward.

79. Mokum is the Dutch Jewish name for Amsterdam and taken from the phrase "*Mokum en Mediene*," referring to the city on the one hand, and the areas beyond the city on the other.

80. Klaas Blanken Jzn (1892–1964), who ran a bakery at Grote Kerkstraat 3 in Hoogeveen.

81. Gerrit Post (1898–1976).

82. Ds. Rients Ypma (1914–1996), Orthodox pastor in Pesse from 1940 to 1944.

83. The King James Version of the Bible renders this as: "every one with one of his hands wrought in the work, and with the other hand held a weapon."

84. Albert Meekof, a farmer who lived on the Oostering in Pesse. (Douwes misspells his name as Mekof.) He was a well-known NSBer, and two of his sons were even more infamous. One died serving on the eastern front while another, Jan, was a member of an execution squad in Friesland. After the war, the latter was sentenced to death, but this was commuted and he remained in prison until 1960.

85. This was Jan Coenraadts (1896–1944), a Calvinist *opperwachtmeester* in the state police who had contacts with the Knokploegen (KP) in Meppel. He was mortally wounded in a gunfight on April 14 and died twelve days later in a Groningen hospital. Wolter Post's farm, Eben Haëzer, was Postweg 2, Staphorstermaten.

86. This had occurred when two members of the Knokploeg in De Krim traveled to Oud-Schoonbeek by motorcycle to examine the possibilities of raiding the government offices and

destroying the records that were being used to call up young men for labor service in Germany. Tipped off about their arrival, the newly arrived NSB burgemeester Geert Bisschop ordered their arrest and while examining their papers was shot dead, as was Roelof Jan Oostindiën, another NSB civil servant, and a loyal colleague, P. J. de Boer. The local policeman, Johannes Kippers, claimed to have fired at the assailants, but both his guns jammed. He was accused of complicity and executed on April 14, 1944. Five other people also lost their lives, shot as reprisal.

87. The only official concentration camp in the Netherlands, KZ Vught, was a short distance from 's-Hertogenbosch in Brabant.

88. Jan Post was the sixth child and second son of Jan Wolter Post and Trijntje Tempen. Married to Jantje (Janke) Schuiling (1897–1968), he lived on a large farm, H24 on the Dwarsgut (now Brugstraat 7). He was an elder of the orthodox Calvinist church in the village.

89. Ambt Vollenhove was the district surrounding the municipality of Vollenhove. It was formally incorporated into the town in 1942.

90. *Trouw* was one of the most prominent underground newspapers during the latter stages of the occupation. It had its origins within the Dutch Calvinist community and began publication in January 1943.

91. This is a genuine location in Drenthe and the founding of these villages dates from the time when the Netherlands was occupied by Napoleon's armies and men were conscripted to fight in the Russian campaign.

92. Dutch: *Overvalwagens*.

93. Jantina Zwiers-Dekker.

94. Jan Albert Rozeman (1914–1944).

95. Johannes Mulder (1887–1943), notary; Adriaan Baas (1913–1943), teacher and resister; Jonkheer Marinus Cornelis Willem de Jonge (1881–1943), director of the Drentse Kanaal Maatschappij and resister.

96. The actual term used here was *duikelaars*, literally, "those who had dived under," or gone underground.

97. An underground organization based around the illegal newspaper *Trouw*.

98. Blokzijl was the propaganda chief of the Dutch NSB.

99. The notation in the diary indicated that Douwes had forgotten what "Jack's" real name was.

100. The name given to S. Norden-Davids.

101. Kornelis (Kees) de Maa, whose shop was in the Dwarsgat in Nieuwlande and used by Johannes Post as a temporary hiding place while he handed over his operations to Douwes and others.

102. "Herman" Scholten (1899–1960).

103. *Knokploegen* was the term used to describe the armed resistance groups spread across the country. Usually abbreviated to KP or LKP, for *Landelijk Knokploegen*.

104. Ds. Hendrikus Albertus (Henny) Visser (1911–2006) was Reformed minister in Raalte from 1940 to 1944. After the war, he became nationally known as the minister of the Westerkerk in Amsterdam and as a broadcaster on the NCRV radio station.

105. Johannes's brother.

106. This card, dated August 10, 1943, was found in the attic of Jacoba (Tante Koos) Thijs-Compagner's house in Hoogeveen in 1981. Post had hidden there for some time in October 1943.

107. The term used here is *duikelaar*.

108. Ration cards were time-limited, but by exchanging it with a retailer, Douwes could get ones with longer expiry dates. Bakkerij Troost had been founded by Jan Troot's grandfather

in the nineteenth century and was on the corner of the Zuidopgaande and Hoekje in Hollandscheveld.

109. *Gemeentesecretaris*.

110. Douwes notes that the population registers for the municipality had disappeared and were actually buried under the burgemeester's house, but luckily the Germans did not find them.

111. This was Bouwe Weima (1897–1990). This daughter married the Orthodox Calvinist minister and resister Hendrik (Henk) Sweepe (1917–2001) after the war. The mayor Cornelis Kock (1907–1944) was also an active resister and probably knew about Weima's disappearance. He was shot dead outside his house by the so-called Silbertanne Sonderkommando on September 18, 1944.

112. The Nederlandse Arbeids Dienst (NAD).

113. This was Albert Moes (1889–1982), who was married to Hendrikje Post, one of Johannes Post's elder sisters. They had a farm on the Gedempte Wijde Wijk in Hollandscheveld.

114. This refers to NSBer Hendrik Oosterveen and his wife, Aaltje Kist. They were both committed Nazis, and it surprised no one that their farmhouse at Wijkbrug was set on fire. Not long after, they were attacked by the resistance. Oosterveen was shot and killed, but Aaltje Kist was severely wounded and taken to hospital.

115. Jantina Gerritdina (Janny) Raak (1922–1957) lived at her parents' house called the "Hoekje" in Hollandscheveld until 1947 and worked as civil servant in the distribution office in Hoogeveen. Through her brother Hendrik (Henk) Raak (1920–1944), she became involved in the work of the LO. After the war, she married Jan Naber ("Nico"). Both died in a motor accident at Orvelte in 1957.

116. Ds. Jacobus Arnoldus Steenbakker Moriljon Loijsen (1893–1983), who was Reformed minister in Erica from 1927 until 1946.

117. The Wilhelmus. Banned by the Germans.

118. Although unknown to Douwes, "Zwaantje" was Allard Lambertus Oosterhuis (1902–1967), a doctor in Delfzijl, and "Winchester" was Harm Koning, a wireless operator. Oosterhuis had been in the army and after demobilization built an espionage line, the so-called Zweedse Weg, that worked with the British SIS.

119. Unknown to Douwes at the time, Thea had been sent on a transport to Auschwitz some three days earlier.

120. The card was dated August 24, 1943.

121. Frederika van der Zwaag had already been working as a courier. Her husband's alias was Arie de Boer, so she may be the person referred to as Annie de Boer.

122. This was the so-called Zeemanspot, a fund set up in 1940 to help the families of seamen serving the Allied cause who would otherwise have had no means of support. Founded by Abraham Phillippo, it was originally sustained by donations but, with the permission of the Dutch government-in-exile, was also subvented by bankers such as Walraven and Gijsbert van Hall. This also allowed funds to be channeled to the resistance, something that Phillippo objected to, but it later gave rise to the Nationaal Steunfonds.

123. This was Jan Zijlstra, who, like his father, worked for the Crisis Controle Dienst, which meant he could travel freely and undertake resistance work.

124. Ds. Jan Dirk Stegeman (1875–1970) and his wife, Hendrika Stegeman van Dorp (1873–1948). Stegeman had been Reformed minister in Aalten until his retirement in 1940.

125. The English text also includes the self-reflexive "No, not that. Oh my God, no, not that." Presumably an allusion to the possibility that she would have to be murdered in the interests of safety.

126. The raid was carried out by the Meppel Knokploeg on the night of September 8–9 and yielded at least 8,500 ration cards and 127,000 ration stamps, which, until the raid on a printer in Groningen on May 17, 1944, was the most successful raid of all time.

127. This was introduced from January 23, 1942, onward.

128. This was not, in fact, the case. The Jewish partners in mixed marriages had an open red J stamped on their identity cards and half-Jews and quarter-Jews had their cards stamped with GI and GII respectively. Peter Tammes, "Het belang van Jodenregistratie voor de vernietiging van joden tijdens de Tweede Wereldoorlog," *Tijdschrift voor sociale en economische geschiedenis* 6, no. 2 (2009): 34–62.

129. Literally "evening light." Ostensibly an old people's home.

130. The English version contains an additional note from Douwes. "I did not have to be afraid of that, they would never have said that."

131. Gerbrandy was the minister-president (prime minister) of the Dutch government-in-exile in London.

132. This was Hendrik Lips (1892–September 24, 1943). He is buried in the cemetery at Osterhesselen.

133. Orange Hotel: Name given to the jail in Scheveningen used by the Germans to house political prisoners and suspected resisters.

134. A euphemism for cat.

135. The Dutch text here refers to Mokum, the Jewish term for Amsterdam.

136. The later English version provides a detailed description of the hiding place and how it was created in a disused ditch.

137. SS and Police Second Lieutenant Jannes Doppenburg had been "liquidated" by local resistance fighter Joop Abbink (1916–2013) outside Apeldoorn station. He was a product of the Schalkhaar Academy, which had trained a new cohort of policemen along National Socialist lines. His funeral took place with full military honors. Abbink was caught by the SiPo (Sicherheitspolizei) on October 10, 1944, but survived camps in Amersfoort and Sandbostel.

138. This was Johannes Albertus Matthijs van Oorschot (1885–1974).

139. He was therefore among the first hostages taken by the Germans after the Februaristaking or after the sabotage in the summer of 1941, and who all met their end in KZ Mauthausen soon after their arrival there.

140. Mussert had been required to obtain special permission to marry one of his aunts.

141. Cornelis van Geelkerken was the cofounder of the Dutch National Socialist Movement and had been appointed as inspector general of the Landwacht.

142. This last section exists only in the later English edition but reflects on his views about some of the people who had offered hiding places.

143. Now called Weiteveen.

144. This is a direct reference to the Antirevolutionaire Partij (ARP), a prewar Orthodox Calvinist political party.

145. "Herman" was Louis (Lou) Gans (1925–2008), born in Amsterdam, the son of Zadok Gans, typesetter, and Rachel Bos. Both his parents were murdered in Sobibor on April 2, 1943, and neither of his elder brothers survived the war.

146. This was probably the edition from mid-November that included an article by J. A. H. J. Sieuwert Bruins Slot, "Onze christelijke plicht" [Our Christian duty].

147. "Nico" was Max "Nico" Léons, born in Rotterdam in 1921, the son of Nathan (Nico) Léons (1887–1960) and Rosetta Souget (1898–1978). He went underground against his parents' wishes and ended up in Nieuwlande, where he worked alongside Arnold Douwes.

148. Albert van Dijk (1917–2001), a hairdresser in Nieuwlande, and his wife, Roelofje van Dijk Kraal (1923–). Both were recognized as Righteous Among the Nations in 1983.

149. This is given as Johannes Post in the later English edition.
150. The later English edition refers to Hollandscheveld and Nieuw-Amsterdam.
151. It is unclear what a summer farm was.
152. This is a translation of "Die Gedanken sind frei," a German protest song against censorship and control that seems to have emerged around 1815. Both German and Dutch versions are known to have been sung by concentration camp inmates during the Second World War.
153. Actually in the Friedhof at Ugchelen.
154. Lord Wanhoop had appeared as a character in three novels in the 1930s. He was a loser who was clueless in any given situation. Lord Haw-Haw was the name adopted by William Joyce, who made regular propaganda broadcasts to Britain via German radio stations throughout the war.
155. The later English edition tells a much longer story about how the girl with jet-black hair was made less conspicuous and more like the family Zwiers—who all had red hair.
156. The feast of St. Nicholas, which is the traditional time for present-giving in the Netherlands.
157. Taai-taai is a type of biscuit traditionally baked for the feast of St. Nicholas. It is similar to *speculaas* (cinnamon, cloves, nutmeg, and ginger) but chewier and with the added taste of aniseed. Often made in human shape, they could be equated to gingerbread men.
158. The later English edition suggests that he was an assistant pastor (*onderpastoor*), but during the war he was still a theological student and went underground at Johannes Post's farm. When the Orthodox Calvinist minister was forced to retire on health grounds, Sweepe took over unofficially at Post's suggestion, but he was never formally an assistant pastor. He later hid with Seine Otten in Nieuwlande and married Annie Weima, the daughter of the municipal secretary in Oosterhesselen, in 1946.
159. *Volk en Vaderland* was the Dutch National Socialist newspaper.
160. A Dutch daily newspaper.
161. Described as doughnuts without the hole. Usually made around Sinterklaas and the New Year.
162. Jan Pieter Strijbos (1891–1983) was a Dutch naturalist, filmmaker, photographer, journalist, writer, and proponent of the nature protection movement.
163. Carl Denig's shop was in the Weteringschans 113–117 in Amsterdam but sold tents. It still exists to this day.
164. Her husband, Jaap Mulder, was a doctor at the University Hospital.
165. Julius was the Calvinist pastor in Dorkwerd.
166. The later English edition speaks of many more presents and help from Bep, the girl in hiding with the Ladies.
167. The *Vliegende Hollander* (Flying Dutchman) was a series of Dutch-language leaflets in the form of newspapers dropped by Allied forces over the occupied Netherlands during the Second World War.
168. Literally, "the one who dives."
169. The English edition reflects on her earlier refusals and Nico's "fountains of eloquence" in persuading her this time.
170. Kasteel Middachten dates from the end of the 12th century but was rebuilt at the end of the 17th century as a country house, although it retained it moat and other defensive features. This was in fact the home of the noble Van Aldenburg-Bentinck family, so Arnold and Nico may have encountered Adriana Vegelin van Claerbergen, the wife of Willem Frederik Karel Hendrik; Graaf van Aldenburg Bentinck; and his daughter Isabella Adriana Bentinck.

Alternatively, they went to the nearby Huis Rhederoord where the antirevolutionary politician Alexander, Baron van Heeckeren (1871–1945), lived with his wife.

171. "Frightened as rabbits" might have been a less literal translation.

172. Martinus Johannes van Ginhoven (1908–1995) and his wife, Bertha Antonia van Ginhoven-Jongenotter (1913–2013), who had taken in a young Jewish neighbor, Ursula Zimak. They were both recognized at Righteous Among the Nations in 1978.

173. The "Aunts" were the three unmarried sisters of Douwes's father's second wife, Cornelia Charlotta Knake (1888–1972), whom he had married in 1926, namely, Hermina (Mies) Knake, Maria (Let) Knake, and Gezina (Sina) Knake, who lived at Huis Aurora. Their father had been head gardener at Ulenpas Manor in Hoog-Keppel.

174. Literally, "divers delight."

175. Rigardus Rijnhout (1922–1959) was known as the giant of Rotterdam (de Reus van Rotterdam) because of his height of 229.87 cm (7 ft., 6.5 in.). He was the second-tallest Dutchman ever, after Albert Jan Kramer.

176. Arend Jan van der Kerk (d. 1970) was a manufacturer originally from Meppel who was active in the resistance and, among other things, helped Allied pilots on the run.

177. Take it.

178. Mien Ruys (1904–1999) was a well-known garden designer and the daughter of Bonne Ruys, who had established the Moerheim nursery in 1888 (now De Tuinen van Mies Ruys). She was active in the resistance. Mikie was her sister, Marie Christina Henrica Ruys (b. 1911).

179. Douwes uses the term *Aryan* rather than non-Jewish here.

180. This is broken text and annotations in the later English version indicate that Douwes could also not remember what all the names and places referred to.

181. This is code where the first *m* refers to a man; the *j* to a *jongen*, or young man; and the second *m* to a *meisje* or young girl. The concept of "looking good" refers to their appearance and that they could pass for non-Jewish.

182. This was probably Wilko Emmens (1890–1945), baker and resister who was executed along with 116 others at Woeste Hoeve in reprisal for the attack there on Höhere SS- und Polizeiführer, SS-Obergruppenführer Hanns Albin Rauter.

183. Mr. A. M. P. Thomason (1887–1969), member of the NSB and mayor from October 30, 1943, until October 28, 1944, when the city was in Allied hands. He was formally dismissed on December 12, 1945, while imprisoned in Kamp Vught. He was the father-in-law of the equally Nazi-oriented regional chief of police, N. J. van Leeuwen.

184. This was a further reference to the onderduiker in hospital in Groningen who had been accused of saying too much. The Christmas cards were ration cards—and there was a comment about the "detestable" black market in cards that had sprung up.

185. This was probably Ds. Bastiaan Jan Ader (1909–1944), who was Reformed minister in Nieuw-Beerta from 1938 to 1944. He was married to Johanna Adriaan Appels (1906–1994). They were active in finding hiding places for Jews—and were recognized as Righteous Among the Nations in 1967. His idea was to drive a train into Westerbork (he had previously been trained as a train driver) and collect Jews "for transport" then drive the train to Groningen where they would be spirited away to hiding places in the city. He also reputedly had contacts with Ds. Johan Willem Siertsma (1890–1953), who worked closely with Corrie ten Boom in Haarlem. The plan collapsed when Ader himself had to go into hiding in Amsterdam in 1944. He was arrested in Haarlem on July 22, 1944, and executed near Rhenen on November 20 of that year.

186. This was a series of fortifications based around defending the line formed by the Rhine, Waal, and Ijssel Rivers. Begun in the sixteenth century, it had been regularly updated

as a defense of the provinces of Holland against attack and was still part of the defensive plan in 1940.

187. This was Dutch language newssheet dropped by the RAF. *Wervelwinden* means "tornados."

188. A German ordinance of May 1943 had offered Jews in mixed marriages the option of sterilization instead of deportation, but there was some confusion about its application. In this case, the debate may have been prompted by the call-up of Jews in mixed marriage for labor service in December 1943.

189. "Snorretje" was van der Zwaag's underground alias.

190. The word used here was *landverraad*.

191. This is an unusual story insofar as enlisting in the Dutch SS was not thought to be compulsory. The later English edition claims that the rescuers did not entirely trust him.

192. These and subsequent references to appearance relate to how Jewish the individuals looked and whether they could pass for non-Jews at the door or in public places.

193. Limburg province borders Germany, and his accent would be seen as normal given the patois spoken in the region.

194. In Dutch, a *woonwagenbewoner*. It is possible that he was regarded by the Germans as a gypsy and treated accordingly.

195. Licht en Kracht, literally "light and power." This was the General Psychiatric Hospital, an institution for the mentally ill. The director sheltered Jewish patients until March 3, 1943, when he was ordered to hand them over but refused and was arrested. Three police detectives from Assen also refused to locate them and were dismissed without pensions and sent to KZ Vught. The work was ultimately carried out by WA and NSB policemen. See *Trouw*, April 6, 1943.

196. This list is reproduced in H. van Riessen et al., *Het Grote Gebod*, 2 vols. (Kampen: Kok, 1951), 111 and 114.

197. Anyone staying at a hotel needed to register, which meant their existence was automatically reported to the police. With no registration, Ata could come and go without arousing any suspicion from the authorities.

198. This was a Gereformeede institution for the mentally ill. Its director, Ds. Arie Ringnalda (1895–1945), was responsible for finding a hiding pace for at least one onderduiker. A hidden radio was discovered in his house in 1943, and he was taken to a camp at Mühlbergen (attached to KZ Neuengamme) and died in crossfire the day before it was liberated.

199. This was Huibert Cornelis Johannes van Ginhoven (1892–1942) from Castricum, who had been shot on March 17, 1942, at Laren for being a member of the Orde Dienst resistance group.

200. This was almost certainly "Bep," real name Ursula Zimak (1919–2000), who had come to the Netherlands as a refugee from Hamburg in 1938. She stayed there for two and a half years. After the war, she married an American serviceman and moved to the United States.

201. This is almost certainly a reference to *kniepertjes*, a type of biscuit baked in the locality around New Year. Normally baked round and flat to symbolize the old year, they are baked in a roll in the New Year, to symbolize the time yet to come.

202. Only a sample of these has been translated and included here.

203. Arnold and Nico were to have been responsible for spiriting those freed from Westerbork away into the countryside. His later recollections state that he was warned from entering Elim by a member of the Salvation Army and thus walked on by. He was also able to warn Nico before he walked into the trap.

204. Klaas Gorter (1905–1945) ran an electrical business and was a member of the resistance. He was arrested on July 14, 1944, in Nieuwlande and eventually transported to KZ

Neuengamme. He was killed when camp inmates on board the ships *Cap Arcona* and *Thielbeck* were bombed by the RAF in Lübeck Bay.

205. The term used in the Dutch version was *arische*.
206. *Nuphar lutea* or *Gele plomp*, a type of water lily.
207. These were people removed from the coastal parts of the city to build the Stützpunkt Scheveningen-Clingendael—part of the Atlantic Wall. Some 135,000 people were affected.
208. Carolina Cornelia van Ginhoven-Feij.
209. This was the Hamelakkers district of Wageningen. It was heavily bombed by the US Eighth Army Airforce on September 17, 1944.
210. Maria Theodora Leenderz-Hoog. In 1985, she was recognized as Righteous Among the Nations by Yad Vashem.
211. There is a Dutch tradition of buying cake for friends and relatives on your own birthday.
212. In the later English version, Douwes refers to the KK men as Dutch uniformed traitors charged by their German bosses to find Jews and others. He does not know what KK stands for. The description fits the various bounty hunters active in the Netherlands hunting Jews, the most famous being the Henneicke-Kolonne. KK is generally understood to refer to a shortened form of the NSKK, the Nationalsozialistisches Kraftfahrkorps (National Socialist Motor Corps).
213. Hillechien Bolwijn (1927–).
214. Douwes subsequently renders "Big" as Jacobus Wiegman, the headmaster of the Reformed Junior School in Hollandscheveld—although Johannes Post was often referred to as "Big" or the "Big Man."
215. This was the so-called tweede distributiestamkaart introduced to flush out all those hiding underground by stopping them gaining access to food. To obtain a control stamp, you needed to show a valid identity card, although even this system was sabotaged by civil servants and by resistance raids on government offices and printers.
216. Douwes describes the vehicle as running on beech wood and having a huge balloon on the roof to provide the fuel.
217. The later version describes one as having an SS uniform and the other in civilian clothes.
218. This raid did take place in early 1944, led by a certain "Joop" who turned out to be an informer. All 19 involved were captured and executed save one of three brothers, who was spared because he shared his birthday with Adolf Hitler. The fact that Douwes knew about the plans says much for the lack of security involved.
219. Evidence suggests that while the story Post told Douwes was substantially accurate, the shooting on January 17, 1944, in Rijnsburg was actually carried out by Jan Wildschut.
220. Douwes seems to have plucked this story from thin air—or at least believed what he was told. There were plans in 1943 for the airfield to be a base for night fighters, but nothing came of them.
221. De Bijenkorf was a famous department store opposite the royal palace on the Dam in Amsterdam.
222. This valedictory was originally in English.
223. This was a plea for ration cards.
224. The term *canary* was used as a euphemism for a pistol or revolver, while *seed* was ammunition.
225. *Arbeitseinsatz*.
226. On February 21, 1944, 34 B-17 bombers of the US Eighth Army Air Force returning from a raid on the Third Reich and thinking they were still over German territory, dropped

their remaining bombs. A wood-gas generator factory was completely destroyed, killing seven workers and injuring 12, as well as damaging to the potato flour plant, several houses, two farms, and three ships.

227. The Rijks Middelbare Tuinbouwschool, 1918–1987.

228. Christiaan Johannes Hermanus Wilhelmus Stakenborg (1903–1987), who was burgemeester of Cuijk and Sint Agatha in 1943–44 before transferring to Waddinxveen. After the war he was purged and dismissed from government service.

229. Dutch pancakes made with raisins.

230. Het Tehuis voor Bejaarden "Avondlicht" stood in the Molstraat in Dedemsvaart.

231. Douwes asserts that she was one of the "remarkable creatures" who went out at night with food and other provisions for those hiding in the nearby woods and forests.

232. From the Dutch *zes en een kwart*.

233. The English text implies that the onderduiker smith was Jewish, but the Dutch version makes no mention of this.

234. Douwes uses the term *duikelaars*, literally divers.

235. Frederik Jacobsz Eppinga (1890–1975) was a Reformed evangelist based at the Bethel chapel in the then Dwargat in Nieuwlande between 1930 and 1946.

236. Padding is a person rather than a place.

237. The English version gives a much longer and slightly different account of what took place.

238. Ds. Jan Simon van den Bos was installed as minister at the Gereformeerde Kerk in Nieuwlande on February 27, 1944.

239. This was the Bethesda Hospital on the Hoogeveense Vaart in Hoogeveen, established in 1910 by the Landelijke Vereniging voor Gereformeerde Ziekenverpleging.

240. Referred to by Douwes as *hoge Pieten*.

241. The raid took place on February 22 and was carried out by US B-24 Liberators of the 446th Bombardment Group. Their target was the airplane manufactory at the Gothaer Waggonfabriek in Gotha, but bad weather prevented them getting there, and so Nijmegen, Arnhem, and Enschede were hit instead. In Nijmegen a good deal of the old city was destroyed, including the Stevenskerk. More than 800 civilians were killed, and only 771 were ever identified.

242. That day, two German Focke Wulf 190 were shot down in the vicinity. One of the pilots, Feldwebel Werner Dietrich Dotzauer, was killed.

243. The name may be a reference to a blues musician born in Dallas who played with, among others, the better-known Whistlin' Alex Moore.

244. The English version notes that Roberts was able to escape via Eindhoven and the Ardennes to England.

245. This was Sally Appel, who had been rescued by Hester van Lennep from the crèche next to the Hollandsche Schouwburg, the holding center for Jews in Amsterdam.

246. Douwes suggests they were (non-Jewish) evacuees from the inundations in that province but must have been in hiding there to require sheltering in Drenthe.

247. A reference to the idea that downed pilots could best be disguised in workers' overalls before being taken to a place of safety.

248. Presumably as part of a disguise.

249. Ouwe Taaie. Literally "old rope" but possibly better rendered as "old bag."

250. "Tante Koos" was Jacoba Thijs Compagner (1891–1983), who lived at Bentinckslaan 50, where Johannes Post hid for a short time at the end of 1943.

251. Jan van der Helm (1911–1945) was married to Johanna (Jo) Moes (1918–2008), a niece of Johannes Post (as the daughter of Post's sister). Jan and Jo took over the grandparents' farm when they died and ran it mainly as an arable enterprise. They sheltered a number of onderduikers, including Szaya Reiner, Lea Goldberg, and their two sons, Avraham and Marco, until February 7, when the farm was raided by the Landwacht. Jan was shot and Szaya was beaten so badly that he died soon afterward. His wife and sons were taken to Westerbork, but as transports had stopped, they survived the remaining months of the occupation in the camp.

252. The English version mentions a postwar telephone conversation with Otten in which he remembered arriving in the street to be told that a raid had taken place and was able to make his escape unnoticed.

253. Jacobus Jonker (1880–1977) and husband of Catherina van der Veen. Since 1921 he had run a bakery next to the café in Nieuwlande.

254. Wiepke van der Zee (1918–1944) was in charge of employment and benefits in the Oosterhesselen municipality. He was an active resister, sabotaging the confiscation of radios and issuing false identity cards. This was made possible because the town clerk, Douwe Weima, had hidden the population register, which made checking impossible. He was a member of the Orde Dienst and worked closely with the LO/LKP. Arrested on March 22, he was shot on the dunes near Overveen on June 6, 1944.

255. Janny Raak worked at the municipal offices in Hoogeveen and was heavily involved in illegal work.

256. Ds. Hendrikus van der Wey (1910–1983) was the Calvinist pastor in Dedemsvaart from 1942 until 1945, when he went to the Dutch East Indies as an army chaplain.

257. This was an RAF Lancaster bomber from 635 Squadron. All six crew died in the crash and were buried in the local cemetery at Hollandscheveld. The Wilfred Stillweg there is named after the pilot.

258. The Dutch version has the location as Het Loo, on the outskirts of Apeldoorn and the site a Royal Palace.

259. Paleis Het Loo, one of the royal residences.

260. Homme de Groot (1903–), who was married to Martje Nienhuis. They were both recognized as Righteous Among the Nations by Yad Vashem in 1983.

261. There is no direct translation of this, save to say that "pip" is a respiratory disease found in poultry.

262. Otto Herz, born in 1881 and his wife, Frieda Liebenstein (1880–1968). After the war they immigrated to the United States.

263. Herman Scholten was born in 1899 and was a teacher at the Christelijke Lagere School in Nieuwe Krim.

264. The later English text suggests that her first job would be to find more hiding places.

265. This took place on March 28, 1944.

266. Ds. Maarten Post (1885–1978) was the Calvinist pastor in Bunschoten-Spakenburg from 1921–1946 but had previously served in parishes in Drenthe.

267. See note 159.

268. He was christened "Oom Gerrit" (Uncle Gerrit) and was reportedly an educated man.

269. Oom Gerrit was Abraham Gompert Verdoner, who had founded an ironmongery business in Amsterdam with Leman Alexander Velleman. During the 1920s, they built a bicycle factory and sold Magneet bicycles. During the war, the company was designated as a

Jewish business. Velleman had already left the company and was murdered in Sobibor, while Verdoner survived underground but died of cancer in 1947.

270. Douwes makes reference to all three daughters having immigrated to the United States after the war, where they subsequently published the letters sent to them by their mother in Westerbork.

271. Joost Pieter Bos (1910–1979) who was a teacher at the Hervormde School in Nieuwlande. He sheltered at least three Jews, Elly Kappers, S. H. (Hans) de Lelie, and Henk Bonewit, as well as a French pilot. His house was raided on October 16, 1944, but the fugitives were not found. He was arrested and brutally beaten by the Sicherheitspolizei in Assen before being sent to an Organisation Todt labor camp from which he later escaped. He and his wife, Goverdina Bos-Schermers, were both posthumously awarded the title Righteous Among the Nations in 1983.

272. This makes no sense and was excluded from the later English version.

273. This enterprise had begun in 1904, importing bicycles from England and bought the rights to use the name Magneet. It was also famous for having sponsored the first professional cycle team in the Netherlands in the 1930s. In 1969, it was taken over by Batavus NV.

274. Jacob (Job) van der Vinne (1908–1980) was married to Geesje Bergmeester (1909–2001).

275. Zetten was the site of the Heldringsstichting established by Ottho Gerhard Heldring (1804–1876) as a refuge for (former) prostitutes that grew into a complex of large and small houses with a mission to help vulnerable and neglected young woman and girls.

276. This could be a reference to *Trouw*, the illegal newspaper, or to the Trouw-groep, the resistance organization that engaged in direct action but was also involved in sheltering onderduikers.

277. This is a reference to a game of some description.

278. Albert (Ab) van Aalderen was an estate agent in Hoogeveen but also very active in the resistance, running a distribution network for Vrij Nederland and Trouw, and became provincial leader of the LO and a member of its national council. He and his wife, Jantje van Aalderen-Koster, sheltered Rivka Vleeschhouwer, a four-year-old Jewish girl, in their house and were recognized as Righteous Among the Nations.

279. Menno was Menachem Philipson, the son of the Jacob Philipson, the secretary of the Jewish orphanage in Leiden. Menno was sheltered in the house of Headmaster Wiegman and his sister also survived underground. They were niece and nephew of Isaac Philipson, the last rabbi in Hoogeveen.

280. Pieter Germen Muller (1888–1945) married to Itje Muller-Norg and had a farm in Nieuwlande. They sheltered Hanna Catharina (Hannie) Blein. She and her parents survived the war in hiding, and the Mullers were recognized as Righteous Among the Nations.

281. In the English manuscript, Douwes says that he does not remember if the father and son were Jewish or not and that in the case of non-Jews his interest was "not great," arguing that places for non-Jews were not difficult to find and that others who, up to now, had done nothing take up the task.

282. Again, Douwes notes that everyone is on edge and that they are all waiting for the invasion.

283. House and apartments where Jews were arrested were then sealed by the authorities to prevent looting (and so that the contents could be cataloged by the Hausraterfassungsstelle [Office for the Registration of Household Effects], the German department charged with collection of Jewish assets).

284. Probably Johannes Bos and Geertje Bos-Doze, who gave shelter to Jewish onderduikers and were subsequently recognized as Righteous Among the Nations.

285. Hendrikus van Veen (1901–1982), who, with his future wife, Margje Corba, gave shelter to Jewish onderduikers. They were recognized as Righteous Among the Nations in 1983.

286. The Afsluitdijk was the barrier constructed across what had been the entrance to Zuider Zee between Noord Holland and Friesland to create the Ijsselmeer, a freshwater lake and facilitate future land reclamation.

287. A reference to Zeeuwse Mosselen. Zeeland Mussels.

288. *Drie verzopen katten.*

289. A reference to the German orders disconnecting most private phone lines.

290. Literally, the Vinery Pension or Hotel.

291. This whole letter is in code, where NSBers are presumably Jews and the CDK is probably the Centrale Distributie Kantoor. The reference to bridge is impossible to decipher and even Douwes could not subsequently remember what it was about.

292. This was a system for identifying genuine underground resistance workers.

293. Gerrit Snippe (1892–1972) lived in Elim and worked as a traveling slaughterer.

294. Willem Koert Slik (1886–1967) was a teacher and married to Derkje Slik-Stikker (1891–1973). Both were recognized as Righteous Among the Nations in 1983.

295. English text refers to Wieten, the shopkeeper.

296. Douwes then uses a racially derogatory term to describe the police (*Kaffirs*).

297. Slomp was a founder of the Landelijk Organisatie and had previously been the pastor at Nieuwlande. He was freed from the Koepel prison in Arnhem by a resistance group on May 11, 1944.

298. A reference to the arrest of Willem Slik.

299. Jan van der Helm (1897–1988) and his wife, Annechien van der Helm-Boels (1894–1971), lived on the Hoop der Toekomst (Hope for the Future) farm in Nieuwlande and kept an open house for Jewish and other onderduikers, including Louis Levie and Mietje Levie-Rabbie; the Groningen lawyer Maurits Levie (1885–1957), who had defended the murderer IJe Wiekstra, who had shot dead four veldwachters at Doezem in 1929; and Andries van Grondelle (1921–1970), who later married a daughter of the house, Stientje van der Helm. Another daughter, Coba van der Helm married the rescuer and later Calvinist pastor Arend ten Hoeve (1922–2010) who had been hidden in the parsonage of Ds. van den Bos in Nieuwlande. Maurits Levie was a keen amateur filmmaker and after the war made a film of an imagined raid on the farm, where Douwes and van den Bos played themselves as rescuers.

300. Dirk Jan de Geer had been appointed as minister president (prime minister) in August 1939. When the Germans attacked the Netherlands on May 10, 1940, the deteriorating military situation forced the government to flee to London. While in London, De Geer advocated negotiating a separate peace between the Netherlands and the Third Reich. He damaged Dutch morale by openly stating that the war could never be won and was removed from office in September 1940 and replaced by P. S. Gerbrandy. Sent on a mission to the Dutch East Indies, he jumped ship in Lisbon and returned to the Netherlands, with the permission of the German authorities.

301. Ds. Rickert Arnoldus Hoogkamp (1909–1996) was Calvinist assistant pastor in Bunschoten-Spakenburg (1940), Hollandscheveld (1941), and Elim (1941–1942). From 1942 to 1945, he was pastor in Elim and stand-in pastor in Nieuwlande when the incumbent fell ill. A good friend of Johannes Post, he was also active in resistance.

302. Havelte was the projected site of an airfield for German night-fighters. The building work was controlled by the Operation Todt/Einsatzgruppe-West with German and Dutch contractors involved. Some 5,600 men worked on the project, some voluntarily and others, including many Jews, as forced laborers. The Jews were given separate barracks. The airfield was operational from October 1944 but was rarely used and was heavily bombed in the last phase of the war.

303. A euphemism for sleeping in the open.

304. Mia Davidson, who, after the war trained as a social worker and family therapist and also became a writer.

305. Arnold Schonewille (1903–1955) married to Roelofje Schonewille-Ham. He was a pig-dealer and gave shelter to both Jews and non-Jews.

306. What Douwes did not know was that on May 17, 1944, around 10 members of the LKP under the command of Johannes Post raided the strongly guarded Hoitsma printers, where ration cards were known to be printed. Post had recruited the best people from the local LKP to carry out this highly successful raid that yielded at least 133,450 ration cards, which were taken by car to Zuidlaren and then taken by couriers across the whole country. This raid reinforced Post's reputation as a successful resistance leader.

307. Apart from generally annoying the Landwacht, this tactic also served to slow them down and thus possibly prevented others on the train from being interrogated and having their papers closely inspected.

308. Not entirely clear what this is. Ostensibly a shipment of (blank) *Ausweise*.

309. Hendrik Bleeker (1904–2001) allowed his premises on the Coevorder Straatweg to be used for illegal milling and also sheltered Franz Strobel, a German deserter from the nearby Hitler-Jugend Camp at Geesburg. Theunis Homme (Teun) de Vries (1922–1945) worked at his father's smithy and was active in the resistance. Arrested in November 1944 in Beerze in Overijssel, he died in KZ Neuengamme shortly before the end of the war.

310. Nel was Nelly van den Akker, who lived in Hygeiaplein in Amsterdam. She had known Lou Gans (Herman) as a child as her brother had worked at Gans's father's printing firm. She worked initially for the Westerweel Group and then for Post and Douwes. She brought Herman under a false name to Nieuwlande. In 1946, she married Ernst Asscher, who had been hidden by her parents. He had tried to escape to Switzerland, was caught, and survived KZ Buchenwald and KZ Dora-Mittelbau. She was awarded the title of Righteous Among the Nations in 1964 but refused to attend the ceremonies for others in 1988 because she "disagreed with the political stance of the State of Israel."

311. Trijntje (Tine or Tinie) Zijlstra was the daughter of Bouwe Zijlstra and Dina Post and worked as a nurse at the Bethesda Hospital in Hoogeveen. Like her parents, she was active in escorting and supporting onderduikers, and also helping wounded resistance workers. After the war she married Anne van der Wal, whom she had nursed after being severely wounded in a raid. They immigrated to Canada and their granddaughter wrote a memoir of her life. Paulina Rustenberg-Bootsma, *A Mighty Fortress in the Storm* (Neerlandia, Alberta: Inheritance, 1992).

312. Probably an orthodontic brace.

313. Albert Jan Rozeman (1914–1944), Wiepke van der Zee (1918–1944), and Hendrik Raak (1920–1944), brother of Janny Raak who later married Jan "Nico" Naber. These three with others were condemned by a police court and shot on the dunes near Overveen on June 6, 1944.

314. The raid on the Huis van Bewaring in Rotterdam took place on June 6 and was carried out by the LKP, led by Samuel "Paul" Esmeijer to free 17 prisoners from the Je Maintiendrai

group, four of whom had been sentenced to death. Those rescued included Ds. Jacob Dirk van Ginhoven (1902–1975), who was the Calvinist pastor at Vledder/Nijensleek from 1930 to 1946 and active in the resistance. Five days later, on June 11, there was a raid on the Huis van Bewaring in Arnhem, led by Johannes ter Horst (1913–1944) but planned by Post and others where 54 political prisoners were freed. Douwes later included Frits Slomp, cofounder of the Landelijk Organisatie voor Hulp aan Onderduikers among those rescued, but in fact Frits de Zwerver had been freed in an earlier raid on the Koepelgevangenis on May 11 of that year.

315. In fact, a reference to Rahab (not Rachab) the Whore, who was spared by the Israelites after their conquest of Jericho because she had sheltered their spies. Book of Joshua 6:25.

316. They were from the camp at Geesburg which had been established as a work-creation project in 1940. From January 1942, it was used as a Jewish labor camp for agriculture and drainage work. On October 3, the camp was cleared and the inmates taken to Westerbork. Then used as a temporary camp for evacuees from the West, it was given over to the Hitler Youth. After the war, it was used to house conscientious objectors and finally Moluccans from the East Indies.

317. Frederik "Frits" Stegeman (1887–1984)

318. This was Tunnis Buursma, Heerbancommandant der WA en Districtskommandeur van de Landwacht, in Drenthe, who had been shot dead on the night of June 16–17 during an attempt to arrest Dirk de Ruiter (1920–1944), a resistance worker who had been a member of the Marechaussee before the war and had tried to help people in Westerbork before being dismissed from the service. Later de Ruiter had joined the armed resistance and was involved with the LKP in carrying out raids on government offices. He died in a firefight with the Landwacht near Onswedde on June 13, 1944. Buursma was buried with full military honors and the funeral was attended by Mussert, Rauter, Feldmeyer, and Van Geelkerken. He was posthumously awarded the *Kriegsverdienstkreuz IIe Klasse* for "his devotion to the Germanic community."

319. Z-maps—assumed to be folding maps.

320. The Mannerheim line was named after Field Marshal Carl Gustaf, Baron Mannerheim, and was a defensive line built by the Finns across Karelia in the 1920s and 1930s to forestall invasion from the USSR. It had been breached first in 1940, but definitively in 1944.

321. *Ons Volk* was an illegal monthly newspaper produced in large quantities between October 7, 1943, and May 1945. It had been started by students and graduates and was the first newspaper to print photographs and also contained much inside information from government circles.

322. On June 20, 1944, the KP–Noord Drenthe led by Catharinus "Kees" Veldman raided the distribution office in the Wilhelmina School. The security guard Johannes Prins was shot and the cashier Jan Frowijn (who was in on the plot) knocked senseless (presumably for his own protection). The whole office was emptied. Two of the perpetrators escaped by bicycle but were overhauled by four pursuers in a car. In the subsequent firefight, it emerged that the raiders had more ammunition than their pursuers and the latter were forced to retreat, "to the loud cheers of the assembled public."

323. Jan de Boer was arrested toward the end of 1944, he was sent to a Todt Organisation work camp in Western Germany but returned home unscathed.

324. Hermannus (Mans) van Goor (1904–2000) and his wife, Femmina Roelina van Goorten Buur, lived in the farm adjacent to that of Johannes Post. When Post and his family had to underground in July 1943, he asked the Van Goors' to take in his youngest daughter, Hermien, and register her as their own daughter, which they duly did.

325. This was Mietje (Mima, Mimi) Lelie-Rabbie (1899–1945), the wife of Levie (Louis) Lelie (1902–1989), whom Douwes referred to as the "Lifeguard." This couple were sheltered by Jan and Annechien van der Helm, while their son Salomon Hans Lelie was in hiding with three others at Meester Bos's house.

326. Probably a reference to contractor Wilhelm Sliekers, who lived in the village.

327. This is given as Slijkers in the original but is assumed to be the same family as indicated in the entry for June 24.

328. Jacobus (Koos) Koekoek (1888–1983), who had a farm at Langerak and was married to Roelofje Koekoek-Euving (1888–1970). He was a good friend of Johannes Post and "Dinie" (Dina Johanna) Post was with them from July 1943 onward.

329. This presumably refers to the members of the Landelijk Organisatie (LO) in Dedemsvaart.

330. Johannes Lanting had an arable farm on the Nieuwlande Straatweg, not far from Post's farm. In mid-1943 he gave a shelter to a number of escaped Russian soldiers. At the beginning of 1945, the whole family had to go underground and the farm was taken over by an NSBer named Snijder.

331. A reference to General Field Marshal Gerd von Rundstedt being dismissed from his command by Hitler in the aftermath of the Allied landings in Normandy.

332. Wildschut was arrested after an abortive raid on a distribution office in Haarlem. He had been recommended to join the group by Post because of his experience as an armed resister. This may explain Post's eagerness to raid the prison in the Weteringschans where Wildschut was held as he felt guilty for persuading him, against other advice, to participate.

333. Hendrik Aasman (1885–1958), an arable farmer in Nieuwlande.

334. The raid on Wiegman's house took place on July 8, 1944. At that time, there were two onderduikers there, Kitty and Grietje Hoepelman, who rushed back to their hiding place and were not found. Wiegman was arrested and spent eight weeks working for the Todt Organisation at Havelte before he was released.

335. Johannes Zijlstra, a teacher at the Reformed School who lived on the Riegshoogtendijk in Hollandscheveld.

336. This relates to the possibility that Jews in mixed marriages might no longer be protected from arrest and deportation—a rumor presumably doing the rounds in underground circles.

337. This is probably Avondlicht, the old people's home.

338. The office was raided and all the ration cards stolen by the resistance.

339. Johannes Nijhoff, the Marechaussee in Nieuwlande, was a "good" policeman and lived in the police house on the corner of the Nieuwlandse Straatweg and the Dwarsgat/Oostopgaande.

340. Dolf Kool and Elly Kapper were a Jewish married couple hidden at the house of Headmaster Bos.

341. Presumably V1 rockets as the V2 versions were not deployed until September 1944.

342. This was the resistance group associated with the underground newspaper of the same name.

343. A reference to the Stauffenberg bomb plot that took place the day before on July 20, 1944.

344. In fact he was still alive and died in an Aussenkommando at Leonberg near Stuttgart around January 1, 1945.

345. A small municipality in the northeast of Groningen Province near Eemshaven.

346. Toon Kwant was a barber in Nieuwlande.

347. Jan van der Helm (1911–) was married to Johanna (Jo) Moes (1908–2008), the daughter of Albert Moes and Hendrika Post, Johannes Post's sister. They took over her grandparents' farm in Nieuw-Moscou and had many onderduikers under their roof.

348. Drents dialect for "Jew."

349. These were probably cards that certified the holder as working on the inland waterways and thus exempted from labor service.

350. Probably Egbert Dijsselhof (1900–1971).

351. This raid was probably carried out by P-47 Thunderbolts of the US 61st Fighter Squadron. Thirty-four Dutch and 9 German passengers were killed and a further 113 wounded, 33 of them seriously. At the site there is a memorial with the epithet: *Hier vloeiden vriend en vijand in het dodelijk vuur, 5 Augustus 1944—hartje zomer rond één uur.* [Here fell friend and foe in the lethal fire, 5 August 1944—in the middle of summer around one o'clock.]

352. Douwes later comments that he thinks Van der Zwaag was, by that stage, in hiding in or near Eerbeek.

353. This was carried out by the LKP led by Marinus, Post's elder brother. Some of the booty from the raid was hidden in a shed at his brother Jan's farm in Nieuwlande. When he came back to fetch it on August 15, he found the whole family in deep mourning. That morning there had been a raid in the village and his only son and Bastiaan Bos, who was hiding at their house, had decided to flee into the nearby cornfield. Unfortunately, they were seen by a German patrol, severely wounded, and then finished off by a German officer. They were both nineteen years old. The whole village turned out to walk behind the funeral cortège.

354. On the corner of the Nieuwlander Straatweg and the Oostopgaande.

355. Gruene Polizei. German Order Police.

356. The Scholtenhuis in the city center was one of six German regional headquarters [*Aussenstelle*] in the Netherlands during the occupation and also the headquarters of the Sicherheitsdienst. Many resistance workers were imprisoned and tortured there, either dying in the process or then being sent to concentration camps elsewhere.

357. Farmer Kremer lived on the Dwarsgat, and onderduikers had dug a camouflaged hole behind the farmhouse in case of raids.

358. The later edition sees this as one of two possibilities, the second being that he has bought his life in exchange for becoming a spy and should therefore not be trusted.

359. On August 18, 1944, Maastricht was bombed by US B17 bombers targeting the bridges over the River Maas. The railway bridge was hit but not destroyed, and the other bombs fell on factories and houses; 103 people were killed.

360. In the later version, Douwes refers to this as brainwashing.

361. *Trouw*, end August 1944.

362. These were copies of Herman's drawings of Queen Wilhelmina.

363. Piet Karelse, who later was a member of the Binnenlandse Strijdkrachten, the Dutch forces of the Interior for the liberated Netherlands.

364. Douwes's later comments suggest that he was suspicious about the arrival of these carrier pigeons in different cages from ones seen before, but intimated that "we must take a chance."

365. Appointed by Queen Wilhelmina to coordinate and control the various resistance organizations inside the Netherlands in the expectation of a rapid Allied liberation of the whole country.

366. There is no means of knowing precisely who these men were. Russian POWs were used extensively as slave labor by the Nazi regime in the latter stages of the war, but others were

persuaded to join German military formations and could be found in large numbers in Wehrmacht uniforms, especially in the Netherlands.

367. A convoluted reference to attempts by the NSB press to put a positive gloss on the situation.

368. Willem Klein, the Wachtmeester [watch commander] at Hoogeveen who with two colleagues had been arrested for catching two *moffenmeiden* [girls who associated with Germans] and giving them a hard time. One night they were taken out and shot outside Beilen. Two died at the scene, but the third, Arie de Vries, survived.

369. The later version goes on at length about the Mrs. Dijk's meal—of large pancakes 30–35 cm in diameter and filled with bacon. "One of those pancakes is enough for one man, even an escaping Russian POW, to live on for two or three days."

370. This was the German defensive line that stretched from Pisa on the Mediterranean coast to Pesaro on the Adriatic.

371. Boekhandel en boekdrukkerij Pet. Established in 1857, it specialized in newspapers and advertising sheets, but had to stop in 1942 due to the paper shortage. It still exists today in its original premises at Hoofdstraat 122–126, Hoogeveen.

372. The German defensive line from Kleve to Basel.

373. The so-called Consi-cigaretten were ersatz cigarettes named as a joke *Cigaretten onder Nationaal-socialistische Invloed* [Cigarettes under National Socialist Influence] and were produced by (among others) Mignot and De Block, a major tobacco company based in the Kanaalstraat in Eindhoven.

374. Cornelis de Kock (1907–1944) had been mayor of Oosterhesselen since 1937 and had worked closely with Johannes Post as wethouder [alderman]. He worked to exempt people from Arbeitseinsatz [forced labor] and undoubtedly knew about the plan for the council secretary to disappear with the local population register. He was taken away by a death-squad as part of Aktion Silbertanne and shot by the side of the road near Meppen. There is now a monument on the site.

375. This refers to the beginning of Operation Market Garden, the unsuccessful Allied attempt to cross the major rivers into the northern Netherlands.

376. There had been a general shutdown in addition to the railway strike ordered by the government-in-exile in London to hinder the Germans as the Allies advanced, but as there was no immediate breakthrough, businesses were advised to carry on working in order to keep supplying the country. The railway strike led to severe sanctions against railway personnel by the Germans, and they shut down all civilian traffic as a punishment for the remainder of the occupation, using German personnel to keep the network running purely for military purposes.

377. Literally, "the kaffirs."

378. This is in fact a reference to Sinclair Lewis, *Babbitt* (New York: Harcourt, Brace and Co., 1922), a satirical novel about American culture and society that critiques the vacuity of middle-class life and the social pressure toward conformity. The controversy it provoked helped Lewis win the Nobel Prize for literature in 1930.

379. DKW (Dampf-Kraft-Wagen) was a German car and motorcycle manufacturer based in Saxony. In the 1930s, it was the world's largest producers of motorcycles.

380. Ibele Offeringa (1904–1980) was a policeman in Elim and lived in the Zuideropgaande in Hollandscheveld.

381. Anton Mussert, the leader of the NSB, had obtained special permission to marry his aunt (his mother's sister), who was 18 years his senior, in 1917.

382. Elst was finally liberated on September 25 by the Seventh Somerset Light Infantry Regiment, First Worcester Regiment, and the 4/7th Royal Dragoon Guards.

383. The only book with that precise title is Hugo Visscher, *De Schepping: bijdrage tot de bevestiging der christelijke wereldbeschouwing* (Zwolle: La Rivière & Voorhoeve, 1930). As this author evinced sympathy for National Socialism in the 1930s and became an adviser on teaching and worship to Anton Mussert, this seems unlikely. More likely, because she had some sympathy for Roman Catholicism, Dr. Herman Robbers SJ, *Menschelijk weten over God en Schepping* (Utrecht: Spectrum, 1937).

384. A De Havilland Mosquito NF-XIX of 157th Squadron from Swannington, Norfolk. Flying Officers P. W. Fry and H. Smith were both killed when their aircraft was attacked by a German night fighter.

385. Zeeuws Vlaanderen is the Dutch territory in the far south west, below the Scheldt estuary and bordering on Belgium.

386. This was Hendrik Jan Nijen Twilhaar (1901–1966), who was an evangelist with the Hervormde Evangelisatie in Dalerpeel and active in the resistance. He was in close contact with resistance man Hendrik Kikkert, who was married to the daughter of Nijen Twilhaar's predecessor.

387. This was written in poor Dutch and almost untranslatable in places, which may help to explain why the English version also makes little sense.

388. Literally, one who does fatigue duties in the armed forces.

389. The question mark in the original text suggests that Douwes had no idea of its provenance or meaning. It can mean "drop dead" or "get lost" or "it gets on my nerves." However, it is also a shortening of Rabbi Moshe Ben Maimon, the world-renowned doctor and intellectual Maimonides. Thus Rambam can also indicate an illness.

390. Almost certainly a reference to Eppinga the evangelist from Nieuwlande. The name comes from a newspaper cartoon character from 1935 to 1953 and was also the mascot of De Betuwe Jam factory in Tiel.

Aftermath

THIS WAS THE end of my diary, but now let me tell you what happened afterward.

That evening, before I was "lifted" out of my bed, I felt very tired and in spite of Mrs. Dijk's warnings I decided to take a chance. There was an empty bed upstairs, and this was far too enticing. I was stupid not to listen to sound advice.

When I was roughly awakened at night, I saw Mrs. Dijk in the room and with her, a dozen men, half of them Landwacht and the others German Secret Service [SD]. It was about 1:00 a.m. if I remember correctly. I could have escaped. It would not have been too difficult. I knew all the ins and outs. Because it was night, I would have been able to get out of the house and disappear into the darkness.

However, I thought better of it. If I had escaped, the men would have been furious and would have been bent on revenge. They would have turned the whole Dijk house upside down. They would have stolen all the foodstuffs I had brought in the day before. Many baskets of potatoes, cabbages, onions, leeks, and all sorts of others. It would all had been stolen, and what is much more important, they could just, maybe, have found the seven Jews in the hiding place under the floor.

No, I couldn't flee, I had to give up.

I was brought to the Marechaussee police post in Oosterhesselen. I expected to be able to escape from there because I knew the man in charge. He was a "good" Dutchman and there were not many like him. But this was not to be. He had been arrested by the SS just the day before. His wife told me this when she came to my cell at great risk to herself and told me about a plan she had devised to free me. I told her: "No way. You'll get into terrible trouble and your husband may suffer because of it as well." I thanked her for her good intentions and said, "Don't worry about me. I'll be all right. I feel it in my bones." I have never seen that lady again.

I was in a cell, one of a row that bordered on to a corridor. The policemen there were all the wrong sort. The good ones had been replaced. My mind was bent on escaping. Above the door of my cell was a tilting window the same width as the door. It could be closed with a clip, but it was open and hanging on two hinges. In front of the window were two iron bars embedded in an oak frame. Now, if I could get one of these bars loose? Only loose on one end, the lower end, that would be enough. I could then bend it upward. I would need a knife or other sharp tool to get the wood out from around the bottom end of the bar. Trouble was, I did not have a knife or other sharp instrument. My eyes alighted on the two hinges holding the window. There was my tool! One of these hinges had to come off.

When I stood on the barrel that was my toilet I could reach one of these hinges. It was only fastened with two little wood screws. I started working on it. In less time than you can say "come out" they came out. I pick them up carefully and put them in my pocket. This meant that the hinge now was fastened on only one side. I closed the window, which made the hinge come down, so I got a good grip of it. A few movements did the trick. The two little screws on the windows side came loose, and the hinge was mine. I quickly opened the window again. It now hung on one hinge only. If my jailers had been in any way inquisitive, they would have seen it, but they didn't.

I got to work. I was in luck because the policemen were listening to the radio. Well, I don't know if they were actually listening, but in any case, the radio blared these horrible songs that the Germans were always singing into the air. Songs like "Lili Marlene." That radio now served a very good purpose because I made a noise and they didn't hear it. My instrument was as sharp as a knife, but only the blunt side of a knife, if you know what I mean. In other words, it was as thick as the chief of the Landwacht.

Oak is a hardwood, but after three days of onerous work, I got one of the two bars loose on the bottom side. This meant that I would only have to pull the bar toward me upward and there would be room to stick my head through, but one bar was not enough. I had to do the other one the same way.

With new hope and fresh energy I started on the second bar. It was not easy, not only because of the "knife" that I had, my one and only tool, but also the noise it made when scratching. On the other hand, the ever-blaring radio helped a lot, although that same radio prevented me from hearing someone coming. More than once I nearly got caught. Only through very quick action was I able to prevent this. I had to make my knife disappear as well as all the woodchips and flakes that had fluttered down onto myself and the floor. I had to make them disappear under my mattress with one sweep of my arm, no time for two sweeps.

When the policeman came to investigate, I pretended I was sound asleep and that they had woken me up. When they asked me what the noise was that they'd heard, I started to laugh and told them I was famous for talking loudly in my sleep. Thus far, these nincompoops had not noticed one of the hinges that held the window wasn't there, so I'd started full speed on my second bar. Then disaster struck. My jailers were honored by a visit from some SS VIPs. They were talking in German, and about me. I did not feel particularly flattered. One of the visitors noticed that my cell window was supported by only one hinge. That was the beginning of the end. They put me in a cell. They spoke to me in German: "So you wanted to escape," etc., etc.

I was then put in a straitjacket. The next day, it was removed, and I was taken by car to the prison in Assen. I was put in cell 7. That evening, I heard the "V" sign tapped [in Morse code] onto the pipe of the heating system. I placed my ear on the pipe and answered. I heard a voice: "Welcome 7, here is a message from 5 for 9. 5 has been under interrogation and has told them that he does not know you, has never seen you, and never heard of you. End of message. Pass it on to 8." This was a telephone. I got quickly used to my new surroundings. I found out that in cell 8, next to me, was schoolmaster Zijlstra.[1]

I tried a new approach, pretending that I was not all there and that I was slightly crazy. You should try this. Pretend to be crazy when you're not. I can tell you that it is extremely difficult. I kept it up for a full week. After that I was examined by psychologists in the presence of some high-ranking German. The verdict of this expert was that "this man is just as sane as any of you," which I did not regard as a compliment. Then one of these guys, I think he was the chief of this outfit, sat down at the other side of the table and offered me a cigarette, which I accepted. "Now," he said, "we must talk because you are not crazy." He spoke in Dutch with a German accent.

"OK," he said "Shoot: Tell me."

"What should I tell you?"

"Everything. What is your name?"

"Hendrikus Marinus van der Vegt."

"Are you sure that is your name."

"Quite sure."

He said in German to the others, "Gentlemen, did you hear this? He knows for sure that that is his name. Please give me those papers." They gave him some papers, I presume from the SS or SD in Arnhem, or perhaps from the *Police Gazette*, where I knew I was listed.

He started to read: Petrus Arnoldus Conradus Douwes. And in German "Stimmt das?" [Is that correct?] I said, "Yes, correct."

"You and I must talk," he said once more. "And this time no nonsense."

"Tell me," he said, "where did you get that false identity card?"

"From Annie."

"Annie who?" he asked.

"I don't know," I said. "I didn't know her, never saw her before, never seen her since."

"Where did you meet this Annie?" He asked. I am sure he knew I was lying, but he remained civilized.

"In Cuijk, in Brabant." This was where my sister lives and was [by this time] liberated territory.

I fed him more and more lies, altogether a nice fat slice of them.

I never saw that first interrogator again. After that first time, the work was taken over by less civilized human beings or in any case ones without an outward veneer of civilization. The interrogators were mainly lackeys of the Germans, our own traitors, and there was nothing genteel or civil about them. They were a degenerate bunch.

I was lucky; in my cell was a spider. We became friendly.

I was in Assen prison for two months, and then IT happened.

Monday morning, December 11, 1944, a morning never to forget. Daylight had not yet arrived, but I was already awake. My cell door opened wide. A German soldier with a revolver in hand stood in the doorway, looked at me, and passed on. For a moment I thought, the Americans have parachuted in nearby and the Germans are going shoot all of us before they flee, but lo and behold, he didn't shoot, but just laughed and moved on.

Now it dawned on me. This was a liberation raid. They had come to free us! This must be the North Drenthe Knokploeg. We had heard, via the grapevine, that many friends had been liberated from the prison in Leeuwarden a week earlier, which must have been the work of the Friesian Knokploeg. And now this!

They put on a beautiful performance. They had borrowed, especially for this occasion, two German assault cars, German uniforms, and German speech. Not a shot was fired and everything went off according to plan. Thirty-one of us were loaded into these two German cars. Near the city center, one of them went left and the other right. They put me in the second one and I was the last one to get in. I'd been under interrogation the day before, and because of that, I had to be helped in and out of the car. We stopped in the village of Veenhuizen. One of the raiders got out there and said: "I can take one person along, who wants to come? There was silence. "Well," he said to me, "will you come with me?" Of course I did. I had been sitting at the back of the second vehicle, which was open and where two of our liberators were sitting each with a machine gun, each in a German uniform. When we passed Germans on the road, they gave the Hitler salute. One of our sham-Germans took me with him. He was Hendrick Woering from Veenhuizen.[2]

I was then witness to the reunion with his fiancée. One of those little things that remain firmly imprinted on my memory. The girl had been terribly worried about her hero, and there he was back alive and well, and with him one of those he had saved. I was cordially received by the Meyer's, the young lady's parents. I knew that in this house at least one American airman was in hiding. To this day, I don't understand how it was that I knew. After the war I found out that there were not one but two Yanks hiding there. How did I know? I have no idea. Perhaps an American word was used, an idiom, something I subconsciously picked up? Or was it some form of telepathy? My life is full, and has been full of such cases of contact with others, mostly with my own mother, but also with others and even persons unknown to me.

I did not stay at the Meyer household that night but was taken after dark to another family a few hundred meters away. That same night the Green Police carried out a raid and took Mr. Meyer away. They did not find the Americans.

I stayed only one night at that second address but was moved in the evening to a third address in Veenhuizen. I slept well there but in the morning heard that the man from my second address had also been taken into custody that night. A large force had come and ransacked the house: broke vases and mirrors, tore the wallpaper, and took away the head of the household.

The lady where I was now, my third address in Veenhuizen, had a nervous breakdown. In a house only 200 m away, the Germans were at it. We could hear them shouting and understood what they said sometimes. We also heard shooting nearby. I realized that I could not stay there, and I said so to the man of the house. He said, "Yes, you're right, but I don't know of any place where you can go. My wife has become hysterical." I asked him about some little wooden sheds I had seen in the distance. It was a swimming pool with locker rooms. Not in use because it was winter. I said, "I'll go there and sooner or later we'll think of something." When darkness came, I walked over to the swimming pool. With me I had a lot of goodies the man had given me: apples, bread, cooked beans, a pillow, and a blanket.

Veenhuizen was a village dedicated to the rehabilitation of men who had committed minor offenses: smugglers, gamblers, petty thieves and so forth. They were usually sentenced to short-terms living on the work farms in the village. Most of the prisoners loved the life there. When the Germans occupied our country in May 1940, nothing much happened in Veenhuizen as they considered the village to be a prison and were happy for it to remain so. This status quo continued until shortly before I was liberated from prison. The Germans had found weapons dropped by the Allies in or near Veenhuizen. If I remember well, that ended the status quo, but in any case, the Krauts were raving mad.[3] Two raids on two prisons in a short space of time had done nothing to pacify them.[4]

[At the swimming pool] I found the little rooms were unlocked. The pool itself was empty and I installed myself in one of the huts and closed the door from the inside. There was plenty of shooting nearby. The Germans are very trigger-happy people, I said to myself. I felt pain from some of the places where the Germans had burned me with cigarettes. I believe that they did this to all the prisoners under interrogation. They also stood with a revolver against my head when they asked questions. Funny thing though: before I was in that interrogation room, I was scared, but once there, the fear left me, as if by magic. On the way over I was full of dread and terror, but once inside this was completely gone.

I was thinking of all this while in my cubbyhole, half dozing off on a sort of bench. I was happy with a pillow and the blanket. For December the weather was not cold. [Although I had promised to stay there,] I decided to break my promise and instead try and reach Nieuwlande, trusting in my sense of direction which was not at all bad, and hoping for the chance to steal a bicycle somewhere along the way. Just as I was about to set out on my hike, I heard a voice: "Here is a bike, follow me. Watch out, small path, deep water next to it." I followed. It was pitch dark. After a few stops and a whispered explanation, my new friend brought me to Mr. Pastoor's farm. (The name I found out after the war.)

I saw my guide for the first (and the last) time in the light of the living room of my new hosts. This man was doing the same kind of work that I had been doing, so, I was thinking, he must be very busy. Never a dull moment. My guardian angel had a cup of coffee and left. I have never seen him since. My new host, the farmer,[5] told me the situation was very tense. I slept that night in the hay above the cows. A good sleep. It was the first and last time I slept there in the hay. That night the Germans came very close to us, and Mr. Pastoor expected them to come back one day and look through everything, turn the whole farm upside down, including the hayloft. They had done this in many other places, he said. "But," he continued, "I have thought of another place that is much less dangerous. Would you mind very much sharing a pigsty with five gentile pigs?" "Of course not," I said. And so it came to pass that my next home was a pigsty, a bit away from the farm buildings and in a field. They were illegal pigs, not registered with the authorities, but as Mr. Pastoor said, "The Germans that we have to deal with here are not looking for pigs, legal or otherwise. They want to find men, and they'll not look under the pig dung."

I spent three days in the company of these five pigs. There were very pleasant animals, friendly and sociable. I never had to crawl under the dung because there was plenty of straw to hide under. Only once did the Germans come looking into our parlor. They were greeted by friendly grunting and left within seconds.

After three days, a farmer came and I went with him to his farm, just over the provincial border in Friesland, a place called Donkerbroek.[6] This had been my brother's first placement as a minister in the church. I had a foolproof hiding place where I slept every night. Sometimes, when necessary, I was also there during the day. No more activity for me. It was all over.

My consolation was that there were no more Jews being deported because of the railway strike. If Jews were caught they were brought to Westerbork by car, but there were no more transports from Westerbork to the death camps. The German commander there was now behaving "nicely," knowing that the time of reckoning was at hand.

When I finally got a new identity, as Jan van den Toren who had fled from the city of Arnhem, I "borrowed" a very good quality bicycle from an NSBer who had been pointed out to me by my benefactor, Piet de Boer, and set out for Nieuwlande. I got there safe and sound. On the way over I heard two German soldiers talking (although they did not see me), and I heard one say, "We'll live to see a nice end here."

I met Nico again and together we went to Coevorden, which had [by this stage] been freed by a Polish armored division.[7] The Germans were scared stiff of the

Poles because they took no prisoners. "Too much trouble," they said. We, Nico and I, met the Poles in Coevorden and followed them to Oosterhesselen, which had in the meantime been freed by the Americans.

I will stop with my story here.

NOTES

1. Hendrik Zijlstra (1914–2005), a teacher in Hollandscheveld.
2. Hendrik "Bill" Woering (1918–2002) was a member of the LKP and charged with taking some of those freed to Friesland. His father, Koop Woering (1890–1945), died in KZ Neuengamme.
3. Hendrik Egberts (1907–1945) had been arrested and, after being severely tortured by the Bloedgroep Norg, gave up the names of resistance men in the village. Eleven of them were arrested and a further 14 joined them when the weapons were found. All of them were sent to KZ Neuengamme, and none of them returned.
4. There had been an attack on the prison at Leeuwarden on the evening of December 8, 1944, carried out by 30 resistance workers led by Piet Oberman [Piet Kramer]. Five of them gained entry to the prison masquerading as two policemen and three prisoners. This allowed the other resisters in, and using skeleton keys, they were able to liberate 51 inmates, many of them leaders of the Frisian resistance and including Jurjen Dreeuws, the former inspector of police. All those freed were spread over the city, and all but one survived the war. The events were later made into a film, *De Overval* (1962). The raid that freed Douwes took place some three days later and was led by Catharinus "Kees" Veldman (1918–1996) with the Noord Drenthe LKP—all dressed in German uniforms. It freed 31 inmates, including Douwes and Veldman's brother Jan "Guus" Veldman (1922–1998). The planners had discovered that the prison was lightly guarded at certain times of the day. They used the arrival of the first relief guard to storm the doors and gain access. All those inside were freed and the guards locked up.
5. Mr. Klooster, who had a farm between Veenhuizen and Oosterwolde.
6. This was Petrus "Peet" de Boer, whose farm, Ter Haule, was a center of resistance activity in Haulerwijk. He had four Dutchmen who had deserted from the NSKK and brought with them uniforms, weapons, and a car. Three of the four were later caught and shot. His farm was raided on February 8–9, 1945. He and his wife escaped, but a sister-in-law and the maid were arrested. On March 3, his brother, Wiebe Gerrit de Boer (1924–1945), was shot by a Landwachter.
7. The majority of the Allied forces that liberated Coevorden on April 6, 1945, were Canadian, the Argyll and Sutherland Highlanders of Canada [part of the Fourth Canadian Tank Division], but the liberating forces in the area also included Polish units under the command of General Stanislaw Maczek.

Epilogue

AFTER DOUWES HAD been freed from prison, he went underground again. Like a "hunted deer" (*opgejaagd hert*) he felt safe nowhere, not least because the Germans had located the house of one of the resistance fighters involved in the raid on the prison. Another of them, Freek Datema, was killed in a shootout with Germans. During his stay in a farm in Haulerwijk with the De Boer family, Douwes slowly regained his peace of mind.[1] He was not arrested again and, against all the odds, survived the Nazi occupation.

In 1946 Douwes, at that time 40 years old, married Jet Reichenberger (1926–2004). They had gotten to know each other during the occupation. She was twenty years his junior and, like her sister Miep, had been saved by Arnold and survived in hiding with the Otten family in Nieuwlande.[2] Within months of the marriage ceremony, they immigrated to South Africa, where their three daughters, Henny, Jenny, and Irit, were born. Jet Reichenberger also gave birth to a son who died very young. In South Africa, Douwes found it difficult to make a decent living as a gardener because he always quarreled with everybody he worked with, and thus the family moved house 15 times in nine years.[3] Obviously, this was not beneficial for the children. On returning to the Netherlands in 1956, Douwes gave an interview to the national daily newspaper, the *Algemeen Dagblad*, where he forcefully criticized the racial divide in South Africa and claimed that this was why he did not want to return.[4]

In April of that year, the whole family immigrated to Israel via the Netherlands at Arnold's behest. His wife joined him, although she wanted "peace and quiet." She had a brother and a sister living there. Time did nothing to mellow Douwes. He remained very difficult to work with, and he, his wife, and his family lived in poverty. As a father, his personality was far from easygoing and often intemperate. His daughters were no longer allowed to speak Dutch, nor were they allowed to listen to the radio, go to the movies, or attend school parties. They had

Arnold Douwes and Max Léons outside van der Vinne's cafe in Nieuwlande, c. 1983. Collection Hovingh.

to spend time with their dictatorial father, who talked about the war a lot. The marriage turned into "a tragedy," because his wife, Jet, slowly but surely realized how difficult he was to live with. In the mid-1960s, Jet told him that she intended to leave him at her earliest opportunity. Douwes could not believe she would leave him like his father had been left by his mother until she actually did so two years later, having by that stage qualified as a nurse and therefore being financially independent. Formally, their marriage was never dissolved. This was not even necessary because as a gentile, Douwes had no rights in Israel whatsoever, and their Dutch civil marriage had no standing or validity there. The spiteful Douwes never paid any money for his children's maintenance.[5] He moved to a wooden shack of some 16 square meters, filled with books, about 50 meters from his former home.[6] Sometimes his daughters were able to steer clear of him for months on end.[7]

In 1983, Douwes returned to the Netherlands. He was then 77 years old, and his niece Joke Stegeman, who was much younger than he was, took him into her home in Utrecht. She took extremely good care of him until he died in 1999, as a born-again and re-baptized Christian, aged 93.[8]

NOTES

1. Letter by P. de Boer to Arnold Douwes, October 1, 1974, Yad Vashem File: Douwes, p. 175–76.
2. Letter by Lou Gans to Yad Vashem, February, 1973, ibid., p. 105; first conversation with the daughters, October 28, 2016.
3. First and second conversations with the daughters, October 28 and December 2, 2016.
4. Editorial in the *Friese Koerier*, March 29, 1956.
5. First and second conversations with the daughters, October 28 and December 2, 2016. Municipality of Utrecht, Uittreksel uit een overlijdensakte, February 8, 1999, Aktenummer 200328.
6. Conversation with Chaim Roet, October 22, 2016.
7. First conversation with the daughters, October 28, 2016.
8. Second conversation with the daughters, December 2, 2016. Municipality of Utrecht, Uittreksel uit een overlijdensakte, February 8, 1999, Yad Vashem File: Douwes, p. 267.

Glossary

Foreign words, but not proper nouns, are in italics. Likewise for newspapers and publications.

Afsluitdijk	dyke finished in 1932 that links Noord-Holland with Friesland, effectively turning the Zuiderzee into an inland lake (Ijsselmeer)
Amersfoort	a town in central Netherlands but here refers to a camp were political prisoners were held
Anti-Revolutionaire Partij (ARP)	the Anti-Revolutionary Party formed by Abraham Kuyper in 1879 to represent the interests of Orthodox Calvinism in the Dutch parliament
Arbeidsdienst	See Nederlandse Arbeids Dienst
Arbeitseinsatz	Dutch: *arbeidsinzet*; compulsory labor service in Germany
Artsenkamer	(Dutch) National Socialist doctors organization
Aryan attestation	Dutch: *Ariërverklaring*; form issued to all Dutch civil servants in the autumn of 1940 to attest that they had no Jewish forebears
Ata	a brand of scouring powder
Ausweis	German identity papers
Avondlicht	Dedemsvaart nursing home; also referenced incorrectly as Avondrood
Bijenkorf	the leading department store in Amsterdam, situated on the Dam opposite the Royal Palace
Binnenlandse Strijdkrachten (BS)	the umbrella organization that coordinated the various resistance organizations in the Netherlands in the final stages of occupation and liberation; commander-in-chief was Prins Bernhard
blanco	a blank identity or ration card
boerenboter	Euphemism for a revolver (literally: farmer's butter)
bonkaarten	ration coupons or cards; these could be for specific foodstuffs or goods such as meat, butter, bread, tobacco, or textiles
Bureauhouders	see Plaatselijke Bureauhouders
Burgelijke Stand	population registry
Centraal Distributiekantoor (CDK)	municipal office for the distribution of ration cards
Centrale Crisis-Controle-Dienst (CCCD)	service charged with combating the black market

Glossary

citronella	oil used to deter mosquitoes
Consi	A type of cigarette (cigaretten onder Nationaal-socialistische invloed; cigarettes produced under National Socialist influence)
dakhaas	literally, "a roof hare"; slang for "cat"
distributiestamkaart	originally an identity card introduced in 1939 to indicate inclusion in the population register; possession of such a card entitled the holder to a monthly card and coupons for rationed goods.
distributietransport	the transfer of *distributiestamkaarten* and coupons
dominee	generic term for a (protestant) minister of religion; abbreviation "Ds."
duikboot	euphemism for an *onderduiker*
De Duikelaar	illegal newspaper produced in Nieuwlande by Peter and Herman
Duikelaar	literally, a diver; see *onderduiker*
Eerste Drentsche Stoomtramweg-Maatschappij (EDS)	the First Drenthe Steam-Tram Company, which operated a steam tram serving the towns and villages in the district
Februaristaking	National Strike on February 25–26, 1941, protesting the German actions in Amsterdam against the Jews and others.
Fl.	Dutch guilders
Flying Fortress	American long-range heavy bomber B-17
fokvergunning	permit for animal-husbandry
fout	term used to describe a collaborator
führer	Adolf Hitler
Gereformeerde Kerk	the Orthodox Calvinist Church
Gestapo	German Political Police, by this time combined with the Sicherheitsdienst (SD)
goed	a term coined to describe a patriot who opposed Dutch National Socialism and Nazi Germany,
Groenen	Greens; see Grüne Polizei
groepsleider	local leader of the Dutch NSB
Grüne Polizei	German Ordnungspolizei, so called because of their green uniforms
Haagsche Post	liberal Dutch weekly newspaper
Hausraterfassung	organization charged with collecting the property of Jews deported from the Netherlands
Henneicke Kolonne	a group of Jew hunters that operated in Amsterdam and elsewhere.

herrenvolk	tongue-in-cheek term used to describe the "racially superior" Germans
Hervormde Kerk	Dutch Reformed Church
Het Joodsche Weekblad	Jewish newspaper published by the Amsterdam Jewish Council
Het Nationale Dagblad	daily newspaper of the Dutch National Socialist NSB
Hitler Youth	German National Socialist Youth Organization
Hollandsche Schouwburg	collection point for Jews arrested in Amsterdam
Huis van Bewaring	prison
inlegvel-bonnen	insert in ration cards which could be exchanged for goods
Jan Hagel	Euphemism for the Landwacht because they carried shotguns (*hagelgeweer*); Jan Hagel was also a type of (Christmas) biscuits
Jeude	Jew (Drents dialect)
Jewish star	yellow star with the word *Jood* (Jew), which was introduced on April 29, 1942; Jews above a certain age had to wear these on their clothing
KK	See NSKK
Knokploeg (KP/LKP)	Landelijk Knokploeg; an armed resistance group
Kraut	slang Dutch term
Lancaster	British heavy bomber
Landelijke Organisatie (LO)	national organization that provided help to *onderduikers*, created by the pastor Frederik Slomp and Helena Kuipers-Rietberg in mid-1942
Landwacht	militia created by the Germans in November 1943 largely from NSB members.
Leider	"the Leader" Anton A. Mussert, as leader of the NSB
Liberator	American long-range heavy bomber B-24
Licht en Kracht	psychiatric hospital in Assen
LO	see Landelijke Organisatie
London	used to describe the broadcasts emanating from the United Kingdom via the BBC; this included some broadcasts in Dutch as well as those in English
Mannerheim-Line	Finnish defense fortification line
Marechaussee	formerly the Koninklijke Marechaussee until reorganized by the Germans in 1940 to carry out policing tasks and frontier duties; in the diary, the term is used to describe individual members as well as the organization itself
Mauthausen	concentration camp in Austria famous in the Netherlands for the first deaths of deported Jews in 1941

mixed marriage	marriage between a Jew and a non-Jew
moffen	slang Dutch term used to describe Germans
Mokum	Amsterdam
mossel	a mussel, euphemism to describe an *onderduiker* from Zeeland
mud	local measure equivalent to 100 liters or 70 kilograms (potatoes/rye)
Naamloze Venootschap (NV)	a resistance organization
Nederlandsch Algemeen Politieblad	Dutch Police gazette
Nederlandse Arbeids Dienst (NAD)	Voluntary and later compulsory labour scheme
De Nieuwsflits	illegal newspaper produced in Nieuweland
NSB	Nationaal-Socialistische Beweging (the Dutch National Socialist Party)
NSKK	National-sozialistisches Kraftfahrkorps, a motorized German police service
oliebollen	a type of doughnut with currents, raisons, and apple
onderduiker/onderduikster	literally, someone who had dived under—in other words, who had gone into hiding; included both Jews and those evading compulsory labor service
onderpastoor	assistant pastor
Ons Volk	resistance newspaper
oom	uncle
oranje	generic term to describe patriots
Oranjehotel	the prison in Scheveningen that was used to hold resistance workers caught by the Germans
Ortskommandant	local German military commander
Overvalwagen	assault truck used by Germans for raids
persoonsbewijs (PB)	personal identity card; carrying such cards was compulsory throughout the occupation for all those over 15 years of age
Plaatselijke Bureauhouders (PBH)	local representatives of the Provinciale Voedselcommssarissen (provincial food commissioners) who had oversight of food production and distribution; they controlled slaughtering and the movement of animals and also had some control on who could be sent for work in Germany by identifying essential workers who could not be spared
RAF	Royal Air Force
Ranja	a type of orangeade drink

razzia	a raid carried out either by the Germans or by the collaborating Dutch organizations
Reichskristallnacht	pogrom against the Jews in Germany on November 9–10, 1938
Reichssicherheitshauptamt (RSHA)	Reich Security Main Office in Berlin
Scholtenshuis	headquarters of the German Police in Groningen
Sicherheitsdienst (SD)	German Security Service
Sicherheitspolizei (SiPo)	German Security Police
Sinterklaas	the feast of St Nicholas (December 6)
speculaas	a type of seasonal biscuit produced around the feast of St. Nicholas
Spoorwegstaking	the railway strike ordered by the Dutch government-in-exile in London in November 1944 to hinder German reinforcements being moved to oppose Operation Market Garden
stamkaart	identity card that allowed the holder to receive ration cards; see also Tweede Distributiestamkaart
Sturmabteilung (SA)	paramilitary organization of the German NSDAP
taai-taai	a type of seasonal biscuit
tante	aunt
Tommy, Tommies	British soldiers, but also used to describe British aircraft
Trouw	illegal protestant newspaper
tweede distributiestamkaart	a new *distributiestamkaart*, introduced in 1944 primarily to make it difficult for individuals to remain underground
Vliegende Hollander	(Flying Dutchman) Dutch-language newssheet produced in London and dropped over the Netherlands by the RAF
Vlugschrift	illegal newspaper
Volk en Vaderland	NSB newspaper
Vrij Nederland	illegal newspaper
Vught	concentration camp in Noord-Brabant used to imprison both Jews and political opponents
De Waarheid	Communist illegal newspaper
Waffen-SS	The military wing of the SS
Weer Afdeling (WA)	paramilitary organization of the NSB
Wehrmacht	the German armed forces
De Wervelwind	newssheet produced in London and dropped over the occupied Netherlands during the occupation.
Westerbork	transit camp used to house Jews before their deportation to the East

Wilhelmus	The Dutch national anthem; singing or playing the anthem was illegal during the occupation
Winterhulp	National Socialist welfare organization in the Netherlands
woonwagenbewoner	caravan dweller, Roma, or gypsy
Yankee Doodle	American folk song
Zes-en-een-kwart	"6¼": a play on the surname of the Reich commissioner for the occupied Netherlands, Arthur Seyss-Inquart
Z-kaart	A permit indicating that the holder was an essential worker and thus not liable for labor service in Germany

Biographical Sketches

This list of biographical sketches is incomplete but as comprehensive as possible given the available literature. Douwes himself was not sure of some of the names, and others have been misspelled throughout, but what follows is an attempt to identify and give further details on some of the main personalities mentioned in the diary. Also included are details of family members where the relationship establishes links within and between communities.

Aalderen, Albert (Ab) van (1892–1982). Realtor in Hoogeveen who was very active in the resistance (*Vrij Nederland, Trouw*, and the LO). Married to Jantje Koster (1896–1967). Both were recognized as Righteous Among the Nations by Yad Vashem in 1983.

"Aaltje, Tante." Alias of a Jewish *onderduikster*, S. Norden-Davids, who quarreled with whoever she was hidden by. She was also a kleptomaniac. She stayed with the Pennings family, then with Riek van der Veen, and finally went back to the Deesker family, where she had started out.

Aardema. See Hoogeveen-Aardema.

Aasman, Arend. Farmer in Nieuw Buinen and half-brother of Jan Aasman.

Aasman, Jan (1912–1972). Farmer in Nieuw Zwinderen married to Renske Aasman-van de Maar (1914–1982).

Adema, Sister.

Adler, Nanci. Historian.

Aken, van. A retired missionary from South Africa.

Akker, Nelly van den (1917–). Under the alias Nel, rescued Jews and in 1964 was designated Righteous Among the Nations by Yad Vashem.

Alting, Andries. Watch commander of the police in Hoogeveen.

"Ammi/Ammy, Tante." Jewish *onderduikster* and mother of "Bobby."

Anne(n), Evert. He lived in the Krakeelsewijk with his brother and sheltered Manfred and Frits Cohen.

"Annie, Tante." Jewish *onderduikster*.

Annie. A rescuer of Jews in Amsterdam.

Ans. A friend of Lou Gans (Herman) and also known as Wasbeer (Raccoon).

Appel, Sally. Little Jewish boy who was known as "broertje" and hidden with Albert Nijwening and his wife. His parents were murdered by the Nazis, and he went to his grandparents in Paris after the war.

Asscher, Abraham (1880–1950). Amsterdam diamond dealer and politician, he was also cochairman of the Amsterdam Jewish Council.

Ata. "Baron" was underground with Jan Douwes, Arnold's brother. [Ata was a well-known brand of abrasive powder.] With Elly, he planned a raid on the Westerbork transit camp to liberate Jews who were held there as prisoners, usually Jews arrested while in hiding. Arnold also discussed this with Geert Schonewille. The plan folded because Ata and Elly were arrested in Amsterdam.

Baanders. A friend of Arnold Douwes from his time at the Horticultural College in Boskoop.

305

306 | Biographical Sketches

Baas, Adriaan (1913–1943). Schoolmaster of the Gereformeerde School in Hoogeveen who was executed by the German police.

Bastiaanse, Cor. Rescuer of Jews.

Bejski, Moshe (1921–2007). Judge and Head of the Commission for Righteous among the Nations (1970–1995).

Belinfante, Robert Paul (1905–1940). A doctor married to Marianne Belinfante-Lisser who committed suicide.

"Bep." German Jewish kindergarten teacher whose real name was Ursula Zimak (1919–2002). She was hidden by, among others, the Nieuwboer sisters. After the war she married an American soldier, Fred (Ephraïm) Auerbach, and moved to the United States.

Berends. Shopkeeper in Nieuw-Amsterdam.

Berenschot, Derk Willem (1893–1979). Marechaussee First Class in Laag-Keppel.

Bergh-van Teyn, Mrs. J van den. The mother of Octavie van Vloten-van den Bergh (1898–1944) of Wageningen.

Bernhard, Prins von Lippe-Biesterfeld (1911–2004). Prince of the Netherlands, the husband of (then) Princess Juliana.

Bert. An associate of Mien Ruys.

Bertha. Jewish Onderduiker in Stadskanaal.

Beukema. See Buikema.

"Big." See Wiegman.

"Big Shot." A nick-name for Johannes Post.

"Bijenkorf, De." A Jewish *onderduikster* named after the famous Amsterdam Department Store.

Bisschop, Miesje. Johannes Post family domestic servant.

Bisschop, Roelof (1899–1989). A farmer in Hollandscheveld and father of Miesje.

Blanken, Klaas Yzn (1892–1964). An owner of farmland and baker in Hoogeveen who was often referred to as the "taai-taai man" by Douwes after his efforts to produce this particular type of biscuit for the feast of St. Nicholas on December 5, 1943. When Douwes came to Hoogeveen to pick up Jewish fugitives from the train station and move them to a safe location, he often stopped off at the Blanken bakery on the Kerkstraat in Hoogeveen. The Blankens, who lived about a seven-minute walk from the station, had 13 children of their own but nonetheless welcomed five fugitives into their home. At their home, the new arrivals, inevitably needing to recuperate from their anxiety-laden train journey, were welcomed with a cup of coffee and Drenthe spice cake. Klaas and his wife, Albertha Blanken-Stoit (1896–1988), were always supportive and deeply involved in the rescue efforts of the resistance. In 1983 Klaas and Aaltje were designated Righteous Among the Nations by Yad Vashem.

Bleeker, Hendrik (1904–2001). Wagonmaker in the Coevorder Straatweg in Geesburg.

Bloemink. One of Douwes' helpers.

Blok. Family in Nieuw-Amsterdam that hid Tante Ammi.

Blokzijl, Max (1884–1946). Notorious radio propagandist for the Dutch Nazi Movement (NSB).

Bobby. A young Jewish onderduiker and son of Tante Ammy.

Boer, Annie de. A schoolteacher in Nieuw-Amsterdam.

"Boer, Arie de." See Zwaag, Hemke van der.

Boer, Jan de. Shoemaker in Nieuwlande.

Boer, Jansje. A man suspected of being a traitor in Nieuwlande.

Boer, Piet de. Sheltered Arnold Douwes after his escape from Assen Prison.

Boertien. A member of the resistance.
Boertje, Aaltje. The domestic servant employed by Willem Volger.
Bogaard, Johannes (1881–1974). Rescuer of Jews in Nieuw-Vennep.
Bolle-Levie, Mirjam (1917–). Secretary, Writer and Translator.
Bolwijn, Engel (1903–1988). Baker in Nieuwlande and married to Sieuwke Bolwijn-Witteveen. They had 10 children but also sheltered onderduikers Lou Gans and Jet Reichenberger. Both were recognized as Righteous Among the Nations in 1979.
Bolwijn, Hillechien (1927–). Daughter of Engel and Sieuwke and ran the family home when her mother was ill. Also recognized as Righteous Among the Nations in 1979.
Bonsius. Bicycle-maker in Dedemsvaart.
Boom, Corrie ten (1892–1983), and Willem ten Boom (1886–1946). Sister and brother who were rescuers of Jews in Haarlem.
Bos, Bastiaan (1924–1944). Onderduiker in Nieuwlande who was shot and killed by the German police.
Bos, Jan Simon van den (1901–1966), and Petra Suzanna Wilhelmina Van den Bos-Verhave (1911–1971). Calvinist minister in Nieuwlande, 1944–1953. Before the war, he had worked as an assistant pastor in Rijnsburg, where he had been succeeded by Hendrik Post in 1939. On June 9, 1983, both of them were posthumously designated as Righteous Among the Nations by Yad Vashem.
Bos, Johannes, and Geertje Bos-Doze. Lived in Nieuwlande and in 1983 were designated as Righteous Among the Nations by Yad Vashem.
Bos, Joost Pieter (1910–1979), and Goverdina Bos-Schermers (1909–1957). He was a teacher in Nieuwlande. They sheltered a number of onderduikers and were recognized as Righteous Among the Nations in 1983.
Bos, Willem. Teacher in Hollandscheveld who helped Jewish onderduikers there.
Bosch, Hendrik. Half brother of Arnold Douwes and resident of the United States.
Broenink, Harmen (1916–1995), and Aaltje Broenink-Strijker. Neighbors of Arnold Douwes in Nieuwlande. In 1983 they were designated as Righteous Among the Nations by Yad Vashem.
Broenink-Homan, Gerdijna "Dinie/Dien" J. G.(1919–1994). When the war broke out, Frederik Stegeman and his sister, Berendina (Dien) Homan-Stegeman, lived in Dedemsvaart, Overijssel. The Stegeman household became a way station for Jews on their way to permanent hiding places. Dien's daughter, Gerdijna (also called Dien, later Broenink), took charge of running the household and of caring for the fugitives. In 1983 Dinie was designated as Righteous Among the Nations by Yad Vashem.
Broenink, Jannes. The fiancé of Dinie Homan.
Broertje. See Appel, Sally.
Brouwer, Dr. Hendrik A. (1914–2003), and Gertha Hermien Brouwer-Swieringa (1914–2014). Medical doctor from Elim who treated Jewish patients without asking any questions and his wife. On June 9, 1983, Hendrik and Gertha were awarded Righteous Among the Nations by Yad Vashem.
Bruin or **Bruyn, Mrs de.** One of Douwes's contacts in Amsterdam.
Buikema, Hiddo (1903–), and Antje Buikema-van der Woude. Garage owner in Nieuwlande who regularly transported fugitives in his car. Also the bicycle repairman in Nieuwlande who gave Léons a bicycle, indispensable for transportation. Léons misspells his name as (Bernard) Beukema. On June 9, 1983, Hiddo and Antje were recognized as Righteous Among the Nations by Yad Vashem.
Burema. A doctor.

Burgers. A member of the NSB in Dedemsvaart.
Buursma, Tonnis (1909–1944). Head of the WA in Drenthe and assassinated by resistance worker Dirk de Ruiter.
Churchill, Winston S. (1874–1965). British statesman, prime minister and writer.
Clercq Zubli, D. de. Known as "Doeks," a resistance fighter in Groningen.
Cohen. A Jewish couple from Hooogeveen who were onderduikers.
Cohen, David (1882–1967). Classicist and professor at the University of Amsterdam and cochairman of the Amsterdam Jewish Council.
Cohen, Frits. A young Jewish onderduiker from Leiden.
Cohen, Manfred. A young Jewish onderduiker from Leiden whose alias was "Freddy."
"Cor, Oom." The alias of an onderduiker also known as "Oranje."
"Cupido." The alias of a guide involved in raids on distribution offices.
Dalen, Pieter van. Municipal Policeman in Laag-Keppel.
Daling. A farmer in Pesse and neighbor of Gerrit Post.
Dam, Prof. dr. J. van (1896–1979). Secretary general of the Department of Education, Science, and Culture during the occupation period.
Datema, Freerk (1922–1944). Resistance fighter who was killed in the attack on Assen prison.
Davids, Isidor Joseph, alias "Peter" (1918–1996). Born in Amsterdam, lived in Rotterdam, where he worked as a typographer, engaged to C. J. Kuyper (Thea). Davids had stayed at 30 different hiding places, until Post picked him up in Amsterdam and brought him to Nieuwlande, to the house of Wolter Padding. While in hiding in Nieuwlande, Davids became the specialist in forging identity papers in the network run by Post and Douwes. For more than six months, Peter and Lou Gans (Herman) hid under the floor of the Gereformeerde Kerk in Nieuwlande and subsequently with the Dijk family. Using candlelight, they wrote and edited *De Duikelaar*, a magazine for the fugitives in Nieuwlande, handwritten by Peter and illustrated by Herman. After the war Davids calculated that 104 members of his and Thea's families had not survived the Nazi occupation.
Davidson, Mia. Daughter of Jewish *onderduikster* "Tante Loes."
Deesker, Anthony (1882–?), and Aleida Deesker-Rökker (1892–?). Deesker, originally from Lochem, and his wife, born in Binnenborg, owned a bakery in Nieuw-Amsterdam. They hid Jewish fugitives in their home, among them Tante Aaltje, her son Ruben, and Henk Roet. In 1983 Anthony and Aleida were designated by Yad Vashem as Righteous Among the Nations.
Dekker, Jan Hzn (1901–1994), and Arendina Dekker-Zwiers. A postman, and near neighbor of Johannes Post. Armed resistance fighter and involved in the liberation of resistance men from camp Amersfoort. Among others they hid Lou Gans (Herman) in their home. On June 30, 1974, Jan and Arendina were awarded Righteous Among the Nations by Yad Vashem.
Denig, Carl (1892–1975). Shopkeeper in the Weteringschans in Amsterdam.
Derk or Deik, Jan. Assistant pastor in Nieuw Amsterdam.
Dick. Onderduiker hidden by Hilbrand Veenstra's father.
Dickie. A schoolchild.
Dijk, Albert van (1921–). Hairdresser in Nieuwlande.
Dijk, Ans van (1905–1948). Jewess executed postwar by the Dutch state for betraying hidden Jews to the Germans.
Dijk, Corrie. One of Douwes' helpers.
Dijk, Simon (1900–1988), Ida Dijk-Mos (1903–2000), and Frouke Dijk. Simon Dijk was a housepainter in Nieuwlande. The Dijks were devout Calvinists. The Dijks' home

became the center of Douwes's activities, and there were always about six Jews in hiding there, as well as resistance workers. Max Léons (alias Nico) was sheltered by the Dijks from the time he first arrived in Nieuwlande. On October 19, 1944, however, Douwes was arrested at the Dijks' home, and the whole family immediately went into hiding themselves. The Jews who had been hidden at their home had to flee to the woods, where Frouke continued to supply them with food. The family emigrated to Canada in 1953. On June 30, 1974, Ida and Frouke were awarded Righteous Among the Nations by Yad Vashem.

Dijkema. Farmer in Nieuwlande.

Dijken, van. A farmer in Nieuwlande who hid onderduikers.

Dijsselhof, Egbert (1900–1971). Helped Arnold Douwes in Dedemsvaart.

Dirk. A Dutch Waffen-SS deserter who had gone underground and was hidden for a time underneath the church in Nieuwlande.

"Dirk, Oom." A Jewish onderduiker.

"Doeks." The alias of Frida Jeanne de Clerq Zubli.

Doornbos, Douwe. A farmer in Nieuw Zwinderen.

Doppenberg, Jannes (1892–1943). Born in Putten, worked as a Dutch policeman in Apeldoorn with the rank of *hoofdwachtmeester* but later cooperated with the German Security Police in Arnhem. He was said to have been involved in the arrest of more than 60 Jews and resistance workers. He was "liquidated" by the resistance on October 20, 1943, as Douwes noted in his diary.

Dorgelaar. Member of the resistance.

Douwes, Albertha (Bertha) Arnolda Catharina (1898–). A sister of Arnold Douwes and married to pastor Herman Stegeman (1878–). She was recognized as Righteous Among the Nations by Yad Vashem on June 9, 1983.

Douwes, Guillette Agatha (1915–1996). Sister or half sister of Arnold Douwes who also hid Jewish fugitives. In 1983, she was designated Righteous Among the Nations by Yad Vashem.

Douwes, Hendrik Julius André (1914–1991), and Wilhelmina (Mimi) Douwes-Koning (1916–2016). Younger brother of Arnold Douwes, Dutch Reformed pastor in Dorkwerd, 1942–1949, and his wife. Both were awarded the title Righteous Among the Nations by Yad Vashem on June 9, 1983.

Douwes, Henny (1950–). Daughter of Arnold Douwes.

Douwes, Irit (1948–). Daughter of Arnold Douwes.

Douwes, Jan (1900–1976), and Nicoline (Niek) Henriëtte Douwes-van Doesburg (1903–1985). Oldest brother of Arnold Douwes and pastor of the Dutch Reformed church in Den Bosch and his wife. During the occupation, he was held as a hostage in camp St. Michielsgestel and as a prisoner in Schoorl and in Amerfoort. Because they hid five Jews in their private home, while raising nine children of their own, Jan—posthumously—and Niek were awarded Righteous Among the Nations by Yad Vashem on June 9, 1983.

Douwes, Jenny (1947–). Daughter of Arnold Douwes.

Douwes, Juliana Anna Louise (1909–1999). Sister of Arnold Douwes who converted to Roman Catholicism and became a nun.

Douwes, Mathilda Maria Cornelia (Mary) (1902–1986). Unmarried sister of Arnold Douwes who hid Jewish fugitives. It is said that she once refused to take in a Jewish man because he was ill. He subsequently killed himself. Arnold held her responsible and could not forgive her.

310 | Biographical Sketches

Douwes, Petrus Arnoldus Conradus Cornelius (1871–1935). Father of Arnold Douwes, born in Leens (Groningen). He worked as candidate pastor in Anloo and as pastor in Zuidwolde. His marriage with Johanna Adriana Willleumier (1875–1938) was dissolved by the District Court of Arnhem on March 29, 1917. She remarried the local doctor Hendrik J. Bosch (1863–1933), who fathered Arnold's half-brother Hendrik Willeumier and Guillette Douwes, formally his sister. Douwes stayed on in Laag-Keppel as the pastor of the Hervormde Kerk until 1925, when he left for Stevensweert. There he married Cornelia Charlotta Knake (1888–1972) in 1926; this marriage was without children.

Drogt, H. Shot by the Gestapo in Meppel in 1943.

Drukker. Associate of Arnold Douwes.

Duiker. Photographer in Hoogeveen.

Edith. Onderduiker.

"Eef, Tante." Jewish Onderduiker.

Egberts, Hendrik (1907–1945). Member of the resistance who died in KZ Neuengamme.

Eichmann, Adolf (1906–1962).

Eisenhower, Dwight D. (1890–1969). American General and later President of the United States.

Ekelenburg, Dirk van (1917–1945), and Lientje van Ekelenburg-an der Mast (1914–1988). Dutch Reformed assistant pastor in Nieuw-Amsterdam. Dirk was arrested by the Germans because he was involved in the distribution of an illegal paper. He died in KZ Neuengamme. Because of their help to Jews they were awarded Righteous Among the Nations by Yad Vashem, on June 9, 1983.

Elema. Farmer in Nieuwlande.

Elly. A resistance contact in Groningen. See also Ata.

Elzenga [Elsinga], Anne Jannes (1908–1943). Policeman from Groningen who collaborated with the Germans.

Emmens, Wilko (1890–1945). Baker in Nieuwlande and married to Diepke Emmens-de Groot (1889–?) They were recognized as Righteous Among the Nations in 1983.

Eppinga, Frederik Jacobsz (1890–1975). Dutch Reformed minister in Nieuwlande and married to Klazina Eppinga- van der Togt (1896–?) Both were recognized as Righteous Among the Nations in 1983.

Faber, (1901–?). Baker in Hoogeveen known as "Pencil," named after the famous German pencil company Faber-Castell.

Flim, Bert Jan (1957–). Historian.

Frank, Anne (1929–1945).

Frank, Otto (1889–1980). Businessman and father of Anne Frank.

Gans, Lou (1925–2008). Jewish onderduiker alias "Herman" who worked closely with "Peter" (Isidor Davids) falsifying identity papers and ration cards, and also made cartoons that were sold to fund resistance work.

Geelkerken, Cornelis (Kees) van (1901–1976). Deputy leader of the Dutch Nazi Movement (NSB).

"Geer, Minister de." Alias of an onderduiker who bore a resemblance to the Dutch prime minister of that name.

Gerbrandy, Pieter Sjoerds (1885–1961). Prime minister of the Dutch government-in-exile in London, 1940–1945.

"Gerrit, Oom." Alias of Abraham Gompert Verdoner (1870–1947), Jewish director of the Magneet bicycle factory in Weesp.

Gijp. Baker and helper.
Ginhoven, H. C. J. van (1896–1942). Accountant in Castricum.
Ginhoven, J. D. van (1902–1975). Orthodox Calvinist minister in Vledder who was active in the resistance.
Ginhoven, Martinus Johannes van (1908–1995). Worked at a fertilizer factory in De Steeg. Married to Bertha Antonia van Ginhoven-Jongenotter (1913–2017); they were both recognized as Righteous Among the Nations in 1978, not least for having helped Bep (Ursula Zimak).
Goor, Hermannus (Mans) van (1904–1945). Farmer in Nieuwlande and friend of Johannes Post.
Gorter, Klaas (1905–1945). Director of the electricity company in Nieuw-Amsterdam and married to Titia Egberdina Jacoba Gorter-Schonewille (1906–1994); they were both recognized as Righteous Among the Nations in 1983.
Goudoever. Headmaster of the lower school in Boxmeer.
Graaf, Frans de (1912–1990), and Antje de Graaf-Deuring (1913–1949). Frans de Graaf, born in Gramsbergen, and his wife, Antje, originally from Vlagtwedde, had a farm in Nieuwlande. Frans was active in the local Knokploeg (LO-LKP) led by Hemke van der Zwaag. Hemke was the brother-in-law of Frans de Graaf. In December 1944, Frans and his brother Ake were arrested for not having reported for forced labor. They were sent to Assen prison, where the Reverend Jan van den Bos interceded on their behalf and succeeded in freeing them. In the meantime, the SS had commandeered de Graaf's farm and established their Nieuwlande headquarters there. However, the family continued living on the farm despite the appalling interrogations that were carried out there. Frans did not get arrested again because he supplied the German authorities with potatoes. Although he and Antje could not actually hide people in their home, Frans was involved in caring for Jews. Because of their help to Jews they were recognized as Righteous Among the Nations by Yad Vashem, on June 9, 1983.
Griet. Domestic Servant employed by Jan Kats.
Griffioen, Agatha (1927–1987). Daughter of Rijk and Ellsje Griffioen who was wounded during a German police raid.
Griffioen, Rijk (1892–1951), and Elsje Griffioen-Kraay (1893–1954). Rijk Griffioen was a school principal in Nieuwlande, He and his wife, Elsje, hid two Jewish girls in their home, thereby helping them survive the war. Because of their help to Jews, they were recognized as Righteous Among the Nations by Yad Vashem, on June 9, 1983.
Groenendijk, Ad. Rescuer of Jews.
Groot, Homme de (1903–). Married to Martje Nienhuis.
Haak, Jur (1891–1945). Rescuer of Jews.
Hagen. Widow and one of Douwes' helpers.
Haitjema. A man from De Krim.
Ham, Gerrit. Grocer in Nieuwlande and neighbor of Seine Otten.
"Hannie." A Jewish onderduiker hidden by Sister Scholten.
Harry. One year-old hidden Jewish child.
Harry. Onderduiker hidden by Hendrik Heerspink in Zuidwolde.
Harster, Wilhelm (1904–1991). Gruppenführer and Chief of the Gestapo/SD in the Occupied Netherlands between July 1940 and August 1943.
Hartemink, Albert Jan (1916–1945), and Hendrika Johanna Hartemink-Schierbeek (1917–). Albert Hartemink, born in Dalen, and his wife, Hendrika, originally from Coevorden, lived in Nieuwlande. Albert was arrested at his parents' farm on January 11, 1945 and

he and his brother Bernard were executed with 115 other prisoners at Woeste Hoeve on March 8, 1945 in reprisal for the resistance attack on Hanns Albin Rauter. Because of their help to Jews, Albert (posthumously) and Hendrika were recognized as Righteous Among the Nations by Yad Vashem, on June 9, 1983.

Haspers. Farmer.

Heeckeren van Kell, Alexander, Baron van (1871–1945). Resident of De Steeg.

Heerspink, Hendrik (1885–1955). A farmer in Zuidwolde.

Helm, Arend van der (1880–1949). Father of Jan van der Helm.

Helm, Jan van der (1897–1988). Farmer in Nieuwlande and married to **Annechien van der Helm-Boels (1894–1971)**. They gave shelter to four onderduikers. Recognized as Righteous Among the Nations in 1983.

Helm, Jan van der (1911–1945). Farmer in Hollandscheveld and married to Johanna (Jo) van der Helm-Moes who gave shelter to the Reiner family. Recognized as Righteous Among the Nations in 1983.

Helm, Krijn van den (1913–1944), and Johanna Cornelia van den Helm-Logtenberg (1905–1994). One of the most important leaders of the LKP in Friesland and his wife. A Baptist and civil servant employed by the tax office in Leeuwarden. Started by helping Jews and Allied airmen but was later active in the armed resistance. Was shot and killed in Amersfoort on August 25, 1944, at the age of 31 by the Dutch policeman P. J. Faber. On January 28, 1982, Krijn and Johanna were designated as Righteous Among the Nations by Yad Vashem.

Henk. Journalist.

Henneicke, Wim (1909–1944). Leader of a group hunting hidden Jews in Amsterdam.

Hennie. See Winkel, Hendrika.

"Herman." See Gans, Lou.

Hertz, Otto (1881–?), and Frieda Hertz-Liebestein (1880–1968). Jewish onderduikers in Nieuwlande.

Hielkema, Hielke Willem (1914–1991). Pastor in Schoonebeek.

Himmler, Heinrich (1900–1945). Reichsführer SS and Chief of the German Police.

"Hoedag." Nickname of a hidden Jewish child.

Hoepelman, Grietje. Jewish *onderduikster*.

Hoogeveen, Jacob (1909–1988), and Bontje Hoogeveen-Aardema (1912–1988). Very active in the underground movement, they ran a grocery store in Nieuwe Krim. They were far from wealthy and had three young children, but were willing to hide Jews in their home. Their situation was incredibly precarious. While Jacob and Bontje were hiding Mrs. Anholt, Henriette Verveer, and her seven-year-old son, their neighbors were caught hiding a Jew and some armaments, and the father of the family was executed. Around the same time, another neighbor was hiding a Jewish woman who went mad and became a danger to her hosts and to the other fugitives in the village whom she knew about. Bontje and Jacob managed to arrange for the woman to be hospitalized in an asylum. In November 1944, Bontje's family in Veenoord was caught hiding a Jewish girl and both the girl and Bontje's two brothers, Meindert and Jacob Aardema, were deported to concentration camps, although they managed to survive the war. The Hoogeveens therefore decided that it was too dangerous to continue sheltering people in their home, but while their guests left temporarily, they soon returned and remained with the Hoogeveens until the liberation. On May 24, 1979, Jacob and Bontje were recognized as Righteous Among the Nations by Yad Vashem.

Hoogkamp, Rikkert Arnoldus (1909–1996). Orthodox Calvinist minister in Elim between 1940 and 1946 and leader of the LO there. Married to Fenny Hoogkamp-Wolting (1908–1990). They were both recognized as Righteous Among the Nations in 1987.
Hoogkamp, Tjeerd (1855–1953). Director of a dairy in Bunschoten and married to Lubbertje Hoogkamp-Los (1884–1965). The parents of Rikkert Hoogkamp.
Houweningen, Mrs. Onderduiker.
Hovink, Dr. Doctor in Nieuw Amsterdam.
Hovingh, Geert C. Pastor and Historian.
Huizinga. Bicycle maker.
Ivan and Michael. Also known as "the Russians" who were escaped prisoners-of-war.
Jack. Onderduiker.
Jacobs, Salomon (Sam) (1903–1941). Sam Jacobs, a butcher, was the head of the only Jewish family in Douwes's hometown, Laag-Keppel. He was deported to the Austrian concentration camp KZ Mauthausen in Austria in 1941 and was killed there. His wife, Betje Jacobs-Goldsteen (1902–1943), was also deported from the Netherlands and murdered.
Jan. Onderduiker who was caught.
Jan. Ten-month-old onderduiker.
Jansen. Onderduiker hidden by Jacobus Wiegman.
Jansen, G. Shot dead by the Gestapo in Meppel in 1943.
Jo. Onderduiker.
Job. Douwes' helper in Nieuw-Amsterdam.
Johan. Jewish onderduiker hidden by Sister Scholten.
Johan or John the Belgian. Onderduiker.
"Johanna, Tante." Onderduiker also known as "Rachab the Whore."
Jong, de. Headmaster in Zweeloo.
Jong, de. Director of the old people's home Avondlicht.
Jonge, Jhr. Marinus W. C. de (1881–1943). Murdered by the German police.
Jonker. Teacher in Zweeloo who hid "De Bijenkorf."
Jonker, Jacobus (Kobus) (1880–1977). Baker in Nieuwlande and married to Catharina van der Veen (1885–).
Joop. Servant employed by Bolwijn, the baker, and active in helping Douwes.
Juliana (1909–2004). Crown princess and later queen of the Netherlands, 1948–1980.
Kaay, Pieter (1904–1943). Opperluitenant in the Dutch police in Enschede who was liquidated by members of the CS-6 resistance group on July 3, 1943.
Kamphuis. Family of onderduikers.
Kapper, Elly.
Karelse, Pieter J. Dutch policeman who went underground after being rescued from "Camp Erica" near Ommen by Bouwe and Jan Zijstra.
Karelse, Thijs (Freek). Brother of Pieter Karelse and onderduiker.
Kats, Jan (1905–), and Geesje Kats-Booy (1908–). During the war, Jan and Geesje Kats lived in Hollandscheveld, where he ran a bicycle and a car rental business. Jan, who had a telephone, was involved in the Nieuwlande-based underground network with the codename "Vondel," and deceived the Germans into believing he was a Nazi sympathizer. Consequently, he was able to secure a permit allowing him to keep his car, in which he clandestinely drove many fugitives to their hideouts and also delivered food and clothing. Jan also participated in a surprise attack on a transport carrying a shipment of ration cards. Ultimately, the Germans arrested him and on December 1, 1944, Jan suffered a severe beating. Despite the torture, Jan did not divulge any information to his

314 | Biographical Sketches

captors. Eventually, he managed to escape by jumping off a train bound for a concentration camp in Germany. By doing so, he succeeded in surviving the war. On June 10, 1987, Jan and Geesje were recognized as Righteous Among the Nations by Yad Vashem.

Kees. Onderduiker who was arrested.

Kerk, Arend Jan van der (?–1970). Member of the resistance in Hoogeveen who helped downed Allied aircrew. Mayor of the town after the war.

Kessel, Monique van.

Kikkert, Hendrik (1915–2001), and Griet Kikkert-Pol (1920–2002). Hendrik and Griet Kikkert were farmers in Nieuwlande. Lou Gans was hidden by Hendrik and Griet Kikkert after being hidden by the Dekkers and before being relocated to the Ottens'. The Kikkerts eventually had to go into hiding themselves after learning that the Gestapo was searching for them. Hendrik was related to the other Hendrik Kikkert, who was also active in the Nieuwlande-based underground movement. On August 15, 1974, Hendrik and Griet were recognized as Righteous Among the Nations by Yad Vashem.

Kikkert, Hendrik (1912–1988), and Maria Kikkert-Veldmeyer (1910–1991). Hendrik and Maria Kikkert were farmers in Nieuwlande, Drenthe. Hendrik was active in the resistance and during the war they hid Lou Gans under the name "Herman" and a young Jewish boy who survived the war in their home. Hendrik later became a member of the Dutch parliament, representing the Christelijk Historische Unie (CHU). Hendrik was related to the other Hendrik Kikkert, who was also active in the Nieuwlande-based underground movement. On June 9, 1983, Hendrik and Maria were recognized as Righteous Among the Nations by Yad Vashem.

Kist, Jan (1888–1969). Farmer and NSB member in Hollandscheveld married to Berendina Kist-Koopman (1890–1969).

Kitty (Tiet). Friend of Isidor Davids.

Klaas. Onderduiker hidden by Farmer Elema in Nieuwlande.

Klein, Willem Hendrik (1919–1944). Police watch commander in Hoogeveen.

Klijnsma. Café

Klooster. Farmer who hid Douwes after his escape from prison in Assen.

Knake, Cornelia Charlotta (1888–1972). Second wife of Arnold Douwes' father.

Knake, Gezina Berendina (1879–1952). Known as Tante Sina, the sister of Douwes' father's second wife.

Knake, Maria Magdalena (1877–1949). Known as Tante Iet, the sister of Douwes' father's second wife.

Kock, Cornelis de (1908–1944). Mayor of Oosterhesselen who was murdered by the Germans on September 18, 1944.

Koekoek, Jacobus (1888–1983), and Roelofje Koekoek-Euving (1888–1970). Had a farm in 't Langerak and gave shelter to many onderduikers, including the Levie family from Hoogeveen. They were both recognized as Righteous Among the Nations in 1983.

"Koenraad." See Raad, Klaas de.

Koning. A friend of Julius Douwes.

Koning, Harm (1894–1945). Resistance worker whose alias was "Winchester." He died in KZ Neuengamme.

Kool, Dolf. Jewish onderduiker in Nieuwlande and married to Elly Kapper who was also hidden in the village.

Kool, Eddy. Head waiter at the Hotel-Retaurant Den Boogerd in Zaltbommel and resistance worker.

"Koos, Tante." Alias of Jacoba Thijs-Compagner (1891–1983), who helped many fugitives in Hoogeveen, including Johannes Post.

Krabbe. Two sisters who ran a small shop in Nieuwlande.

Kreeft, Joop. Associate of Arnold Douwes.

Kremer. Farmer in Nieuwlande who had a telephone.

Kruyff, Hendrik de. Dutch police detective and traitor living in Assen, the capital of Drenthe, and employed by the German Security Police. In 1934, De Kruyff had been fired from the Dutch force but was later reinstated. De Kruyff was responsible for more than 20 arrests of resistance fighters in Oosterhesselen and Hollandscheveld. On July 16, 1943, De Kruyff was shot while walking his dog, by Victor and Nico. He was hit by as many as five bullets but survived. Traumatized, he almost completely stopped working for the Germans, but in 1947, he was sentenced to a prison term of 20 years, convicted for, among other things, having confiscated Fl.100, 000 from Jews, some of which he had kept for himself.

Kurpershoek, Mrs. Mother of Anna Volger-Kurpershoek.

Kuyper, Abraham (1837–1920). Orthodox-Calvinist theologian, politician and Minister-President of the Netherlands between 1901 and 1905.

Kuyper, Celina Johanna (1923–1943). Alias "Thea," fiancée of I. J. Davids and Johannes Post's first courier. She was arrested together with Johannes Post in Ugchelen on July 16, 1943, in a trap set by the German police. They were brought to the police station in Apeldoorn by Doppenberg and another Dutch policeman. Post was freed from the station, but Thea was taken to the Westerbork transit camp. From there she sent three postcards to the Post family. In her last card she wrote, from the departing train: "I am in good spirits and firmly believe everything will turn out fine. . . . I will be back soon." She was murdered upon arrival in Auschwitz-Birkenau on August 27, 1943.

Kwaat. Baker in Dedemsvaart.

Kwant, Toon. Hairdresser in Nieuwlande.

"Ladies, the." See Nieuwboer, Tjitske (1901–1988), and Hendrika Evelina Nieuwboer (1898–1991).

Lages, Willy Paul Franz (1901–1971). Chief of the German police in Amsterdam.

Lanting, Johannes. Farmer with extensive lands in Nieuwlande.

Leendertz-Hoog, Mrs.M.Th. (1892–1945).

Leenhouts, T. Population registry clerk in Dedemsvaart from 1941.

"Lekkere Liebe Lutschie" (LLL). A Jewish onderduiker named after the way he addressed letters to his mistress in Amsterdam.

Lelie, Levie/Louis (1902–1989). Jewish onderduiker who was nicknamed "the Lifeguard" by Douwes. Married to Mietje Lelie-Rabbie (1899–1945) whose alias was "Tante Marie."

Lelie, Salomon Hans (1926–). The son of Louis Levie (1902–1989), "the Lifeguard," and Mietje Levie-Rabbie (1899–1945).

"Lenie" and "Piet." Two people who provided material help to Douwes, for example by giving a revolver and ration cards to Léons. Piet may have been Piet Meerburg.

Lennep, Hester van (1916–2000). Rescuer of Jews in Amsterdam.

Léons, Chelly. Sister of Max Léons.

Léons, Max (Nico) (1921–). Born in Rotterdam as the son of a sugar merchant. He refused a job with the Jewish Council in The Hague. The entire family—his father, mother, two sons, and one daughter went into hiding in July 1942. All survived the occupation. After the war, Léons became a very successful real estate entrepreneur in Amsterdam, where he still lives.

Léons, Nathan. Married to Rosetta Léons-Souget. The parents of Max and Chelly Léons.
Lia. Jewish onderduiker and sister of Tineke.
"Lidia." See Lier, Klaartje van.
Lientje. Young Jewish onderduiker and sister of Liesje.
Lier, Klaartje van. Alias "Lidia," daughter of Peter's mother's second husband.
Lies. Friend of Arnold Douwes.
"Lies, Tante." Jewish *onderduikster*.
Liesje. Five-year-old Jewish onderduiker and sister of Lientje.
"Lifeguard." See Lelie.
Lips, Hendrik (1892–1943). Onderduiker who was shot dead.
Loekie. Onderduiker.
"Louise, Tante." Jewish onderduiker and mother of Mia Davidson.
Lubbers. Family who lived on the Zwarte Pad.
Lunenberg. Gave shelter to a young Jewish girl.
Luten. Manufacturer.
Luth. Associate of Arnold Douwes.
Maa, Kornelis, or Cees de (1900–1971). Owner of the Nieuwlande haberdashery.
Mannerheim, Carl Gustaf, Baron (1867–1957). Finnish Field Marshal.
"Marie." Jewish *onderduikster* (a widow with two children).
Marissen, Hillie. Domestic servant from Limburg.
Marlijn, Mrs. Relation of Arnold's brother Jan.
Mars. Garage owner in Dedemsvaart.
Meekof, Albert (1897–1987). Farmer and NSB member in Pesse whose farmhouse was burned down.
Meer, Benno van der. NSB member in Nieuwlande.
Meerburg, Piet (1919–2011). Rescuer of Jews in Amsterdam and the founder of the Amsterdamse Studentengroep that specialized in hiding Jewish children.
Melis. Farmer.
Metselaar, Albert. Historian.
Meulenbelt, Jan (1921–2011). Rescuer of Jews and founder of the Utrechts Kindercomité that specialized in hiding Jewish children.
Meyer, Boele. Farmer in Nieuwlande.
Meyer, Mans. Farmer in Nieuwlande.
Michman, Jozeph (1914–2009). Historian.
Moes, Albert (1890–1982). Resistance fighter, married to Hendrikje Post (1889–1966), the sister of Marinus and Johannes Post.
Mol. Family that helped Arnold Douwes.
Molen, Gezina van der (1892–1978). Lawyer and journalist who worked with underground newspapers *Vrij Nederland* and later *Trouw*, and also helped to hide Jews.
Mooi, Frederik (Frits) (1921–2008). Younger brother of Herman's Mooi. He was the assistant pastor in Zuidwolde.
Mooi, Hermannus Gerardus (1905–1983). His uncle, Herman Stegeman, was married to Albertha (Bertha) Douwes, one of Arnold's sisters. Mooi was Dutch Reformed pastor in Koekange.
Moore, Bob. Historian
Mulder, Jan (1901–1980). Farmer in Diever who was married to Trijntje Post (1904–1991). On March 4, 1985, Jan and Trijntje were recognized as Righteous Among the Nations by Yad Vashem because they had hidden Jewish fugitives during the occupation.

Mulder, Johannes J. (1887–1943). Notary public who was killed by the German police.
Muller, Anjo. Onderduiker.
Muller, Jan. Son of Piet Muller.
Muller, Pieter Germen (1888–1945). Farmer in Nieuwlande married to Itje Muller-Norg (1887–?) recognized as Righteous Among the Nations by Yad Vashem in 1983 because they had hidden Jewish fugitives during the occupation.
Muller, Truusje.
Musch, Gerard. Brother of Jacob (Jaap) Musch who worked with Pastor Constant Sikkel and the so-called Naamloze Vennootschap (NV) hiding Jews, primarily in Limburg.
Musch, Jaap. Brother of Gerard Musch who worked with Pastor Constant Sikkel and the so-called Naamloze Vennootschap (NV) hiding Jews, primarily in Limburg.
Mussert, ir. Anton Adriaan (1894–1946). Leader of the Dutch Nazi movement. He was married to his aunt. Hence the song, popular in circles of the resistance: "If you want to build a new country, it is better not to marry your auntie."
Naber, Jan (1923–1957), and Jantina Gerritdina Naber-Raak (1922–1957). Jan Naber, born in Hoogeveen, lived in Nieuwlande and worked in the distribution office in Hoogeveen, alias "Nico de Roo." Together with Albert Rozeman (Victor), Jan was active in the local Knokploeg, which conducted raids on food distribution and population registration offices, stealing food coupons and blank identity cards. Jan's wife, Jantina, supported him in his underground work. Jan and Albert called themselves "de N.V."—a play on words, N.V. meaning "limited company" in Dutch. They had no connection with the big organization run by Jaap Musch that had the same name. Jan and Albert undertook a mission to free a Jewish woman, Thea Kuyper, from Westerbork. However, the mission failed, and she later perished in Auschwitz. The N.V. also shot H. de Kruyff in Assen, the Dutch policemen who worked for the Nazis. Jan survived the war; he and his wife died in a traffic accident in 1957. On June 9, 1983, they were posthumously designated as Righteous Among the Nations by Yad Vashem.
Nachuil. Also known as Uiltje and an associate of Cupido.
"Nel." The alias of Nelly van den Akker (1917–), a courier and rescuer who was recognized as Righteous Among the Nations by Yad Vashem in 1964.
Neutel-Zomer, Hilligje (1889–1970). A widow in Nieuwlande who, with her two sons, Harm (1917–) and Wolter (1912–), hid onderduikers and the resistance worker Gerben Ypma in their home before the latter was arrested and shot.
"Nico." See Léons, Max.
Nie, Johannes Arnoldus van (1893–1979). Reformed minister in Hoogeveen and active in the resistance.
Nienhuis, Klaas (1872–1963), and Jantje Nienhuis-Belhuizen (1889–?). Lived in Nieuwlande and were recognized as Righteous Among the Nations by Yad Vashem in 1983.
Nieuwboer, Tjitske (1901–1988), and Hendrika Evelina Nieuwboer (1898–1991). The Nieuwboer sisters, both born in Bunschoten, lived in Nieuwlande. Tjitske (Tjits) was a teacher and lived with Hendrika (Riek), who was responsible for the household. Together they ran an underground center from their home next door to Wietske and Hilbrand Veenstra, where they hid onderduikers and resistance workers. The sisters also harbored a fugitive, 19-year-old German Jewish Ursula Zimek (later Auerbach). Ursula, alias Bep, was taken to the Nieuwboers in November 1942, where she remained until May 1945. Toward the end of the war, in August 1944, Nico was also afforded shelter in the Nieuwboers' home. In addition to Ursula and Nico, the sisters sheltered three other fugitives. Nico later recalled the feast of St. Nicolas, December 5, when Tjits

and Riek prepared a celebration for about 100 children hidden in the Nieuwlande area. Known as "the Ladies" by Douwes and his group, on April 16, 1978, the sisters were awarded as Righteous Among the Nations by Yad Vashem.

Nijen Twilhaar, Hendrik Jan (1901–1966). Evangelist in Nieuwlande.

Nijhof, Johannes. Policeman in Nieuwlande.

Nijwening, Albert, and Jacoba Nijwening-Sikkema. Thanks to his creative talents, Albert Nijwening managed to use his job as a bread delivery man to serve the resistance. Based in Nieuwlande, where his family lived, he began working at his brother Jan Nijwening's bakery in Hoogeveen before the war. When he married in December 1942, he moved to Hoogeveen, but continued his work in Nieuwlande. His wife, Jacoba, was his partner in all these activities, hiding members of the resistance and Jews as well as others in need. They hid Sally Appel, a Jewish boy, for two years. Toward the end of the war, Albert joined the Rieks group, which was based in Alteveer, Drenthe. He helped the group in its attempt to free two Resistance members, Dr. van de Velde and Dirk van Trouw (an alias), by storming the local prison, which was housed in a private home in Hoogeveen. Also, at the end of March 1945, Albert received a quick lesson in weaponry and was sent out with a group that included his brother Jan to retrieve arms dropped by the Allies in Mantingerzand. In April 1945, the arms were supplied to resistance fighters, who used them to arrest about 100 German soldiers and SS men as well as Nazi collaborators in the area. On June 18, 1972, Albert and Jacoba were recognized as Righteous Among the Nations by Yad Vashem.

Nijwening, Jan (1900–?), and Hermina Nijwening-Zeldenrust (1904–?). Jan Nijwening, born in Ruinen and working as a baker in Hoogeveen, employed his brother Albert as the bread deliveryman. Jan was active in the resistance and was hiding two Jews in his home in a hiding place so well camouflaged that the Germans never discovered it. At one point, Jan was arrested and interrogated by the police in nearby Hollandscheveld, who were mainly concerned with the whereabouts of his brother. Jan was forced to admit that he had a brother named Albert and that Albert lived in Hoogeveen, but the Hoogeveen population registration office had been "relieved" of its files on the Nijwening family, and Albert was not found. Jan's wife, Hermina, then managed to get her husband out of the Hollandscheveld prison by telling the prison commander that her husband had a contagious skin disease. She knew that the authorities were terrified of catching diseases from prisoners. Jan did, in fact, have a skin disease that he had contracted from fugitives from Limburg whom he and his wife took in in addition to the Jews. Toward the end of the war, Jan joined the local LKP headed by Albert, which was affiliated with the Rieks group and picked up weapons dropped by the Allies in an attempt to arm the population against the retreating German army. In 1983 Jan and Hermina were designated as Righteous Among the Nations by Yad Vashem.

Nolet, Wim. Friend of Arnold Douwes from the Horticultural College at Boskoop.

Noordt, Miss. Teacher.

Norden, Robert. Alias "Ruby" or "Henk." The son of A. Norden-Davids, alias "Tante Aaltje."

Norden-Davids, S. Also known as Tante Aaltje, she caused trouble wherever she was placed. She spent time with Pennings Family and then with Riek van der Veen before returning to the baker Deesker, where she had been initially.

Norder, Johannes (1897–1959), and Jantje Norder-Eilander (1905–1984). Lived in Nieuwlande, where Johannes was the village carpenter. He carried out many commissions for Arnold Douwes in constructing or adapting hiding places. Toward the end of the war, he was called up, along with many others, to build defenses for the retreating German army. Unlike many others, Johannes reported for work, which surprised the community. They were even more surprised when, after the liberation, Otto and Frieda Hertz emerged from the Norder home, where they had been hiding in an attic room for more than two years. In 1983 they were posthumously designated as Righteous Among the Nations by Yad Vashem.

"**Nuphar.**" See Plomp.

Offeringa, Ibele (1904–1980). A "good" policeman from Elim.

Oorchot, J. A. M. van (1893–1959). Mayor of Hardenberg.

Oosterhuis, A. L. (1902–1967). Resistance worker from Delfzijl whose alias was "Zwaantje."

Oppenheimer, Dr. Klaus E. H. (1905–1986). Dutch Reformed pastor at Nieuw-Dordrecht, 1939–1946.

Otten, Arend. Brother of Seine Otten.

Otten, Arie. Son of Seine and Jo Otten.

Otten, Seine (1910–1993), and Dirkje Jantje Otten-Bovendorp (1905–1988). Schoolmaster at the protestant school in Nieuwlande, known as "Beaver." He cooperated closely with his neighbor Johannes Post. At various moments Arnold Douwes hid in his house, and so did numerous Jews. In their two-bedroom house and in hiding places under and above their house this nonaffluent couple hid up to 12 fugitives. Seine was also involved in raids by the local Knokploeg and eventually took over its leadership from Hemke van der Zwaag. On June 30, 1974, Seine and Jantje were recognized as Righteous Among the Nations by Yad Vashem.

"**Ouwe Taaie.**" Jewish *onderduikster*.

Padding, Wolter (1906–1953), and Grietje Padding-Nijwening (1904–1960). On June 9, 1983, Yad Vashem recognized Wolter Padding and his wife, Grietje Padding-Nijwening, as Righteous Among the Nations. Wolter Padding was the son of Berend Padding and Metje Post, a younger sister of Jan Wolters-Post. Jan Post, the father of Johannes, adopted Wolter as his stepson and raised him as a twin brother of Johannes Post. The Padding family hid Peter (I. J. Davids) for a couple of months and at least 12 other Jews as well.

Paldiel, Mordecai (1937–). Director of the Department of th Righteous at Yad Vashem, 1982–2007.

Pallandt Family.

Pastoor. Gave shelter to Arnold Douwes after his escape from Assen prison.

Pattist, Auke (1920–2001). Leader of the Dutch SS men in Hollandscheveld, nicknamed "the executioner of Drenthe." Originally an Amsterdam policeman, he volunteered for the Waffen-SS and did service at the front. In 1944, he returned from there and went to Hollandscheveld, where he was responsible for the torture of the prisoners in his charge, albeit not personally. He was arrested in 1946 but managed to escape and fled to Germany (which had granted all SS volunteers German nationality in 1943). He then went to Spain, which refused to extradite him. In the meantime, he had been convicted and sentenced to life in prison in Holland in absentia.

"**Pencil.**" Alias of Dirk Faber the baker in Hoogeveen.

Pennings, Pieter Jan (1894–1975), and Johanna Bernardine Pennings-de Rooij (1909–1979). Headmaster in Moscou. On June 9, 1983, Yad Vashem recognized Pieter Jan and his wife, Johanna, as Righteous Among the Nations.

Pet, Claas (1846–1916). Founder of the bookshop in Hoogeveen.

"**Peter.**" See Davids, I. J.

Petertje. A young Jewish onderduiker in hiding in Pesse and nephew of Hans Lelie, not to be confused with Peter (I. J. Davids).

Philipson, Menachem (Menno). Young Jewish onderduiker who lived with Jacobus Wiegman and his family in Hollandscheveld.
Piek, Carel. Director of the Dutch National Socialist Winter Help from 1940 to 1943.
Pijl, Miss. Housing inspector in Emmen.
Plomp. Alias "Nuphar"—one of Douwes's female relations who lived in Wageningen.
Pol. Director of the Distribution Office in Nieuwlande.
Pontier, Gerard (1888–1976). Pastor and rescuer of Jews based in Heerlen, Limburg.
Post, Evert Egge (1925–1944). The son of Jan Post and Jantje Post-Schuiling who was shot dead by the German police on August 15, 1944.
Post, Gerrit (1898–1976). Seventh child of the Post family, married Geesje Guichelaar (1903–1993) in 1924. He rented a large farm from baker Blanken in Pesse in 1942 where he hid his brother Johannes. On June 9, 1983, Yad Vashem recognized Gerrit and Geesje as Righteous Among the Nations.
Post, (Hendrik) Henk JWzn. (1900–1982), and Harmina Aaltina Salomons (1904–1969). Eighth child of the Post family, studied theology at the Free University in Amsterdam, and was pastor of the Calvinist Gereformeerde church in Ambt-Vollenhove, 1930–1939, and in Rijnsburg near Leiden, 1939–1965. Henk Post found hiding places for Jews among his flock in Rijnsburg and handed out forged identity papers. He hid fugitives in his own house—among others, his brother Johannes. Like Johannes, he also was a talented businessman; he traded in typewriters and furniture. Henk was close friends with the local doctor, Edzard E. van der Laan (1910–1983), the son of a Gereformeerde pastor, who also was active in the resistance. In 1983 Henk and Harmina were posthumously designated as Righteous Among the Nations by Yad Vashem.
Post, Hennie (1938–). The daughter of Marinus Post.
Post, Hermine. Youngest daughter of Johannes Post and Dina Post-Salomons.
Post, Hilda. Eldest daughter of Johannes Post and Dina Post-Salomons.
Post, Hillegienus (1929–2007). Son of Marinus Post and Hannechien Post-Salomons.
Post, Jan. Farmer in Nieuwlande married to Jantje Schuiling (1897–1968), who were the parents of Evert Egge Post.
Post, Johannes (1906–1944). Alias "Bigshot" and married to Dina (Dien) Post-Salomons (1903–1991), Farmer and community leader in Nieuwlande who began the resistance in the village and engaged in direct actions against the occupier. He introduced Douwes to illegal work before having to go underground himself, later being involved in national resistance organisations before he was arrested by the Germans and shot.
Post, Maarten (1885–1978). Orthodox Calvinist minister in Bunschoten-Spakenburg.
Post, Marinus (1902–1944). Ninth child of the Post family, a farmer. In 1943, all Dutch policemen were instructed to look out for Marinus. His face was on the cover of the *Nederlandsch Buitengewoon Politieblad* of August 2, 1943. Marinus Post was shot and killed in Amsterdam on November 17, 1944, by the German police because of his activities in the resistance. His wife, Annie (1909–1980), survived KZ Vught and KZ Ravensbrück. On May 23, 1979, Yad Vashem recognized Marinus Post as Righteous Among the Nations.
Post, Trijn. Daughter of Gerrit Post.
Post, Wolter JWzn. (1892–1969), and Rika Post-Kamphuis (1896–1970). Third child of the Post family, farmer in Staphorstermaten.
Post Mzn, Jan (1926–2014). Son of Marinus and Annie Post who survived KZ Dachau.
Post Mzn, Wolter (1929–). Son of Marinus and Annie Post.
Post-Salomons, Dien (1903–1991). Married Johannes Post in 1929. She gave birth to her last child on April 18, 1945, after Johannes Post had been executed. She named him Johannes

Marinus Evert, after her husband, her brother-in-law Marinus, and her nephew Evert, all of whom had been killed by the Germans. However, she refused to cry over Johannes, who had, when discussing possible misfortune, often quoted Psalms 68, verse 6: "God is a father of orphans and a judge of widows" (*God is een Vader der wezen, en een Rechter der weduwen*). The theme of her funeral service was that this strong and courageous woman had not found her strength and her courage in herself but that they were God's gift to her.

Pronk, Catrien. Nurse from Groningen who was a friend of Guillette Douwes.

Raad, Klaas de (1904-1945). Alias "Koenraad," taught mathematics at the Gereformeerde MULO (secondary school) attended by Johannes Post. He was born in Oude Pekela and was a resistance fighter who was active in the LO, in the Vrij Nederland and Trouw groups, and in helping Allied airmen. He was arrested by the German police in Amsterdam on May 8, 1944, and sent to the German concentration camp of Neuengamme, where he died on January 15, 1945.

Raak, Hendrik (1920-1944). Resistance workers and brother of Jannie Raak.

Raak, Jantina Gerritdina (Jannie) (1922-1957). See Jan Naber.

"R(achab) de H(oere)." (Rachab the Whore) also known as Tante Johanna. The biblical alias given to this onderduiker came about because of her friendliness with local Germans.

Rauter, Hanns Albin (1895-1949). German SS and Police Leader in the occupied Netherlands.

Rechteren Limpurg, Graaf van (1909-1962). Adolph Reinhardt Zeyger, Graaf van Rechteren Limpurg.

Reichenberger, Jet (1926-2004). Jewish girl who with her sister Miep was first hidden by the Van Ginhoven family in De Steeg and then was brought to Nieuwlande by Arnold and Léons. Miep was hidden in Wageningen, as household help. Arnold Douwes and Jet married in the Netherlands in 1946. She left him twenty years later.

Reichenberger, Miep. Sister of Jet Reichenberger.

Reijnierse, Jozias (1904-1981). Reijnierse was a doctor in Hollandscheveld who used a motorcycle to visit his patients. He treated fugitives discreetly and often at no charge, often pretending that he did not know he was treating Jewish children or those underground. He—posthumously—and his wife, Suze Reijnierse–van Zanten (1906-1984), were awarded the title of Righteous Among the Nations by Yad Vashem on June 9, 1983.

Reine, Klaas. Member of the NSB.

Reiner, Szaya (Jozef) (1897-1945). Jewish manufacturer married to Lea Reiner-Goldberg. They had two sons, Avraham (Ab Rinat) and Marco, and a stepson, Sal Kimmel.

Ridder van Rappard, Louis Rudolph Jules (1906-1996). Mayor of Gorinchem.

"Riek." Herman's sister who was also in hiding in Nieuwlande.

Riek. Jewish onderduiker hidden by Seine Otten.

Rinsema, Thijs. Historian.

Roberts. American pilot; see Texas Slim.

Roet, Barend (1916-1983). Jewish onderduiker in Niewlande. After the war, he married Rebecca Roet-Blitz (1921-). Both had been caught by the Germans but too late to be sent to the East. After the liberation they immigrated to Canada.

Roet, Henk later Chaïm (1932-). Young Jewish boy hidden by baker Deesker and his family. He immigrated to Israel and made a career in international finance, becoming Israel's representative at the World Bank. He lives in Jerusalem.

Roffel, Willem (1902-). Farmer in Nieuwlande and sexton of the Gereformeerde Kerk whose identity papers were used by Douwes.

Romijn, Peter. Historian.

Rost van Tonningen, mr. Meinhoud Marinus (1894–1945). Dutch National Socialist and editor in chief of its newspaper *Het Nationale Dagblad*. As a leading member of the NSB, he was appointed secretary general of the Department of Finance and president of the Nederlandsche Bank, 1941–1945.

Rotterdam, Reus van. Real name Rigardus Rijnhout (1922–1959), the tallest man in the Netherlands, at 2.42 meters high, weighing 230 kilograms, and with a shoe size of 62.

Rozeman, Albert (1922–1984). Resistance fighter, see Naber, Jan. Albert was awarded the title of Righteous Among the Nations on June 9, 1983.

Rozeman, Albert Jan (1914–1944). During the war, Albert Jan Rozeman played an important role in the rescue of many Jews and was among the initiators of the LO in Drenthe and an advisor to the KP in Hoogeveen. He worked closely with Johannes Post. Albert Jan was also responsible for the distribution of illegal newspapers and a leading figure in the resistance carried out by civil servants. He was arrested with his father, Steven Rozeman (1882–1945), on March 20, 1944. Albert Jan was executed in the dunes of Overveen on June 6, 1944. His father was deported to KZ Oranienburg, where he perished in January 1945. The Dutch government awarded Albert Jan posthumously the Dutch Resistance Cross. In 1985 Albert Jan was designated as Righteous Among the Nations by Yad Vashem.

Rozeman, Steven (1882–1945). The father of Albert Jan Rozeman and resistance worker who died in camp Henkel. He and his daughter Geesje were awarded the title of Righteous Among the Nations on June 9, 1983.

Rundstedt, Gerd von (1875–1953). German Field Marshal.

Ruys, Mien. Gardener and garden designer.

Salomons-Huisingh, Hillighe (1875–1950). Mother-in-law of Johannes Post, nickname "Oma."

Schindler, Oskar (1908–1974). Industrialist.

Schipper, A. NSB mayor of Oosterhesselen.

Scholten, Herman (1899–1960). Headmaster of the Dutch Reformed School in Nieuwe Krim.

Scholten, Jo, and Bep Scholten. Two sisters from Dedemsvaart, Overijssel, who worked at a religious medical and welfare center and took care of a number of Jews in hiding. Jo Scholten worked as a district nurse (Sister), and Bep was the administrative manager of the health cooperative Het Oranje Groene Kruis (The Orange Green Cross). The sisters, who shared a house, ran a two-person resistance organization, which took in the fugitives for whom Douwes and Léons could not find places in Nieuwlande. They found hiding places for Jewish children and adults and supplied them with food coupons, forged identity papers, and other necessities. The two little sisters, Mery and Emmi Freibraun, were taken into hiding thanks to the Scholten sisters. Jo and Bep also sheltered two Jews in their own home for a long period. In October 1944, the Scholtens were arrested by the Germans and imprisoned in Westerbork camp. They were liberated on April 12, 1945, and were awarded the title Righteous Among the Nations by Yad Vashem on February 28, 1967.

Schonewille, Arend (1903–1955). Pig dealer who hid fugitives in his home.

Schonewille, Geert (1913–1988), and Hendrika Annechina Schonewille-Nijzing (1914–1978). Lived in Nieuw-Zwinderen. Geert was involved in underground activities, and among other things, he found a hiding place in Nieuw-Zwinderen for a young woman in the last stages of her pregnancy. Once the baby was born, it was taken to Geert and Hendrika's own doorstep and left there as if it were a foundling. The Schonewilles took the child in and registered him under the name "Frits Schonewille." Geert and Hendrika were arrested a few months later and taken to the Assen prison. Although they were only detained for one day, the baby had already been snatched by the German police and sent to Theresienstadt. The baby survived the camp, but his mother perished. After the war, the child ended up with the Schonewilles once again but was later found by surviving relatives who took him in and raised him in the United States. During the war, Geert also acted as an escort for the de Groot family, taking them to a safe haven in the Ottens' household. In the summer of 1944, Geert was again arrested and taken to Kamp Erika near Ommen, Overijssel, and from there to De Koepel, the prison at Arnhem. There, he was incarcerated for five weeks before being transferred to the Oranjehotel in Scheveningen, where he spent another month before unexpectedly being released. Toward the end of the war, he was once again rounded up in a wave of arrests precipitated by the imminent defeat of the Germans. In 1954, Schonewille immigrated to Canada and was recognized as Righteous Among the Nations by Yad Vashem in 1983. Two years later, he was struck by dementia and was taken in by a man who had been saved by him during the war.

Schonewille, Piet (1896–1963). Also known as "Bonen Piet," he was group leader of the local NSB in Hollandscheveld and stand-in mayor.

Schouten. One of Douwes's contacts in Utrecht.

Schuiling, Jantje Post- (1897–1968). Married Jan Post (the sixth child) in 1921. On August 15, 1944, their only son, Evert Egge Post, was brutally murdered by the German Police. He was 19 years old.

Schwegman, Marjan. Historian.

Seinhorst, L. Dutch Reformed pastor in Pesse.

Seller, H. C. Member of the Marechaussee in Nieuwlande and Hollandscheveld, nickname "Snorrebaard."

Seyss-Inquart, Dr. Arthur (1892–1946). Reich commissioner for the occupied Netherlands.

Shackleton, Ernest (1874–1922). British explorer most famous for his journeys to the South Pole.

Sikkel, Constant (1895–1967). Pastor in Amsterdam and rescuer of Jews.

Sleen, Jan van der.

Sliekers, Willem.

Slijkhuis (Sliekers).

Slik, Willem Koert (1886–1967). A teacher in Elim and married to Derktje Slik-Stikker (1891–1973) who hid Jewish onderduikers. Both were recognized as Righteous Among the Nations by Yad Vashem in 1983.

Slik, Willem (1921–). The son of Willem Koert Slik, a member of the NSB and SS.

Slikker, Bram. Friend of Arnold Douwes from the Horticultural School in Boskoop.

Slomp, Frits Jzn. (1898–1978), alias "Frits de Zwerver," and Tjaltje Slomp-Ten Kate (1896–1988). Calvinist pastor in Nieuwlande 1927–1930, and responsible, with Mrs. Helena Kuipers-Rietberg (1893–1944), for the creation of the Landelijke Organisatie voor Hulp aan Onderduikers (LO) in 1942. On April 28, 2014, both were designated as Righteous Among the Nations by Yad Vashem.

Sloten. Family who helped Arnold Douwes.

Sluys, Pieter van der (1887–1973). Dutch Reformed pastor in Dedemsvaart, 1923–1952, who was held for 16 months as a hostage at the camp at St. Michielsgestel.

Smid, Sister.

Smit, Adrianus (1899–1963). Mayor of Sprang-Capelle and member of the André resistance group.

Smit, Jacobus (1880–1943). English teacher and resistance worker.

Snippe, Gerrit (1892–1972). Butcher in Elim.
Snoek, Lucas. Radio technician in Langerak.
"Snorrebaard." See Seller, H. C.
"Snorretje." See Zwaag, Hemke van der.
Soet (or Zoet), Lenie. Fiancee of Frits Stegeman.
Stakenborg, C. J. H. W. (1903–1987). NSB mayor of Cuijk/St. Agatha.
Steenbakker Moriljon Loijsen, J. A. (1898–1983). Dutch Reformed minister in Erica.
Stegeman, Frederik (1887–1984), and Berendina Homan-Stegeman (1879–1955). Frederik Stegeman and his widowed sister, Berendina (Dien) Homan-Stegeman, lived in Dedemsvaart, Overijssel. The Stegeman home became a temporary home for Jews on their way to permanent hiding places and also acted as a refuge for Arnold Douwes. Some elements of his diary were buried in their back garden. Dien's daughter, Gerdijna (also called Dien, later Broenink), took charge of running the household and of caring for the fugitives. All three were awarded the title of Righteous Among the Nations by Yad Vashem on June 9, 1983.
Stegeman, Frits. Onderduiker from Doorn.
Stegeman, Herman (1877–1961). Dutch Reformed pastor at Cuijk aan de Maas, 1931–1943, was married to Albertha (Bertha) A. C. Douwes, a sister of Arnold Douwes. With three brothers and brothers-in-law, the Stegemans were awarded the title of Righteous Among the Nations by Yad Vashem for their help to Jews in hiding in 1983.
Stegeman, Jan Derk (1875–1970). Pastor, born in Avereest.
Stegeman, Joke.
Strijbos, Jan P. (1891–1983). Well-known Dutch naturalist and ornithologist.
Süskind, Walter (1906–1945). Responsible for helping to save Jewish children from the crèche attached to the Joodse Schouwburg detention center in Amsterdam.
Suzy. Jewish onderduiker in Nieuw-Amsterdam.
Sweepe, Henk or Hendrik (1917–2001). Assistant pastor who was in hiding with Dominee van den Bos in Nieuwlande. After the war, Hendrik finished his study of theology and became a Calvinist pastor. On June 9, 1983, Hendrik Sweepe was recognized as Righteous Among the Nations by Yad Vashem because of his help for Jews during the occupation.
Taai-taai man. See Blanken
"Texas Slim." Nickname of the American pilot of the Flying Fortress A. D. Roberts, originally from Fort Worth, Texas, who crashed in Nieuwe Krim on March 6, 1944, and was rescued by Douwes and Léons.
Thalen, Jacob (1877–1960). Married to Reina Kreeft (1893–1962), from Langewijk, traded in cattle, and was and elder of the church in Elim. He hid Jewish fugitives in his home, among them the Cohen family from Hoogeveen, a former competitor of his in the cattle trade who had become his favorite enemy. When the Cohens entered their room in Thalen's house, they found a table with a huge leather-bound Bible on it. That was his revenge. Later, Thalen was arrested and detained for a time at Kamp Erica in Ommen but was ultimately released.
"Thea." See Kuyper, Celina Johanna.
"Thea, Tante." Jewish onderduikster.
Thijs-Compagner, Jacoba (1891–1983). See Koos, Tante.
Thomassen, mr. A. M. P. NSB mayor of 's-Hertogenbosch.
Tineke. Jewish onderduiker and sister of Lia.
Tjalma, Jetze (1893–1986). Mayor of Hoogeveen and later hostage of the Germans. After the war, he resumed his office.

Toet, J. Shot dead by the Gestapo in Meppel.
Toren, Jan van de. Alias used by Arnold Douwes.
Troost. Baker in Hollandscheveld.
Veen, Gerrit van der (1902–1944). Artist and resistance leader in Amsterdam responsible for the mass production of false identity cards. Awarded the title of Righteous Among the Nations by Yad Vashem on March 9, 2002.
Veen, Hendrikus van der (1901–1982). Married to Margje van der Veen-Corba (1907–2002). Both were recognized as Righteous Among the Nations by Yad Vashem for their help to Jews in hiding in 1983.
Veenstra, Hilbrand (1919–1986), and Wietske Veenstra-Dekker (1919–). When the war broke out, Hilbrand Veenstra, born in Oosterhesselen, and his wife, Wietske, originally from Hoogeveen, lived in Nieuwlande. The Veenstras shared a semidetached property with the Nieuwboer sisters, Tjits and Riek, who were very active in the resistance. Fugitives sheltered by the sisters, such as Ursula Zimek, alias "Bep" (later Auerbach), and "Nico" (Max) Léons, were also helped by the Veenstras. The Veenstras shared the responsibility of caring for these charges and three others with the Nieuwboer sisters. During the war, Hilbrand also belonged to the Rieks group, which operated from Alteveer-Kerkenveld, not far from Nieuwlande. This group had a cache of arms and latterly collected weapons that were dropped by the Allies with the intention of fighting the Germans, but in the end, this was rendered irrelevant by the speed of the Allied advance. In 1978 Hilbrand and Wietske were recognized as Righteous Among the Nations by Yad Vashem.
Veenstra, Johannes (1890–), and Roolfje Veenstra-Gringhuis (1891–). Hid Jewish fugitives in Nieuwlande and were designated as Righteous Among the Nations by Yad Vashem in 1983.
Veerman. Vegetable grower.
Vegt, Hendrikus Marinus van der. Alias used by Arnold Douwes.
Veldman, Catharinus "Kees" (1918–1996). Commander of the KP Noord-Drenthe.
Veltman, mgr Petrus Johannes (1885–1974).
Venhuis. Headmaster in Nieuw-Amsterdam.
Verdoner, Abraham G. Onderduiker known as "Oom Gerrit." Jewish director of the Magneet-rijwielen-fabriek in Weesp.
Versteeg. Associate of Arnold Douwes.
"Victor." See Rozeman, Albert.
Vinne, Jacob (Job) van der (1908–1980).
Vinne, Jitse van der (1876–1951), and Albertje van der Vinne-Plaggenborg (1887–1963). Jitse, known by locals as "Olle Jitse"; his wife; and their son, Ake, managed the grocery store that was located on the main square, adjacent to the church. The store had a café and a telephone, and these facilities gave it a prominent place in the village's illegal activities. Jitse and Albertje were a vital link in the resistance's communication network. The telephone in their store was used to relay messages from Amsterdam and other places about the arrival of more fugitives. The messages were sent in code, reporting the imminent arrival of new "goods," of type A, BC (referring to the degree to which the new arrivals were distinguishable as Jews). The telephone in the Van der Vinnes' store was also used to arrange rendezvous points—usually the Hoogeveen railway station but sometimes Dedemsvaart or Nieuw-Amsterdam. Warnings of imminent raids were also given to the underground via this phone line. In 1983, both were designated as Righteous Among the Nations by Yad Vashem.

Visser, Hendrik (1906–1962), and Annechien Visser-Huttinga (1893–1981). Sheltered Jews in hiding. With others from Nieuwlande, Hendrik was responsible for removing the house numbers from buildings in order to make it difficult for the German police to locate Jews and others in hiding. On June 9, 1983, Hendrik and Annechien were awarded as Righteous Among the Nations by Yad Vashem.

Visser, Henk. Pastor in Raalte.

Visser, Jan. Journalist, active in hiding Jewish children near Leiden and worked together with his sister Lenie Visser.

Visser, Miss. Postmistress.

Vlesman, Léon. Asssociate of Arnold Douwes.

Vloten, Heinrich van (1895–1964), and Octavie van Vloten-van den Bergh (1898–1944). Helped hide Jews in Nieuwlande. On June 9, 1983, Heinrich and Octavie were awarded Righteous Among the Nations by Yad Vashem.

Volger, Pim. Youngest son of Willem Volger.

Volger, Dr. Willem (1904–1980), and Anna Volger-Kurpershoek (1907–1999). Volger, who had originally been a Calvinist pastor, was Dutch Reformed pastor, first in Nieuw-Amsterdam, where Arnold's sister Mathilda (Mary) Douwes (1902–1986) lived in his house, and subsequently in Hollandscheveld. Arnold Douwes went into hiding with Volger from May 1942 onward. Volger cooperated with Johannes Post. In the final months of the war, two of Henk Post's daughters went into hiding with the Volger family. Because they had hidden Jews on June 9, 1983, Willem—posthumously—and Anna were designated as Righteous Among the Nations by Yad Vashem.

"Vondel." See Kats, Jan.

Vree, Frank van. Historian.

Vries, Anne de (1904–1964). Writer.

Vries, Arie de (1895–1962). Police-adjutant in Hoogeveen.

Vries, Theunis Homme de. Resistance fighter and helper of fugitives who was arrested on November, 4, 1944, and deported to the German camp of Neuengamme (or died during a shipwreck according to Huizing). After his death, his wife gave birth to a daughter and named her after him: Teuna Hommina.

Vries de. Policeman in Nieuw-Amsterdam.

Vries de. Teacher.

Warendorf, Hans.

"Wasbeer." See Ans.

Weij, Hendrikus van der (1910–1983). Orthodox Calvinist pastor in Dedemsvaart.

Weima, Douwe (1897–1990). Employed in Oosterhesselen town hall.

Westra, Arend. Framer in Nieuwlande.

Wiegman (Wigman), Jacobus (1905–), and Aikina Wiegman-Hensums (1908–). Jacobus was schoolmaster in Hollandscheveld and was also known as "Big." The couple was neighbors of the Zijlstra family. They hid a Jewish couple and continued to take care of their baby after the parents fled to Belgium and France. The parents did not survive. Because they had hidden Jews, Jacobus and Aikina were awarded as Righteous Among the Nations by Yad Vashem on June 9, 1983.

Wieren, Bernardus Carolinus van (1892–1965). Bookseller in Nieuw-Amsterdam.

Wieren, Bernardus Carolinus Bzn. van (1924–1945). Son of Bernardus snr. and died in KZ Lüneberg.

Wieten. Grocer in Nieuwlande.

Wiggerink, H. J. Farmer in Nieuw-Amsterdam.

Wijk, Levie (1878–1943), and Manus van der (1881–1943). Jewish onderduikers who were shot by the Germans after their arrest on August 3, 1943.

Wildschut, Johannes Wilhelmus (Jan) (1913–1945). Originally from North Brabant and a Roman Catholic, he had worked for Philips in Eindhoven and had been a sergeant in the Dutch air force before the war. He moved from Leeuwarden to Nieuwlande in May 1943. He was very active in the resistance alongside Johannes Post and participated in many raids on distribution offices. The testimonies of Douwes and Léons confirm the important role that he played in the rescue of many Jews in the Nieuwlande area. Wildschut moved to Rijnsburg, after Post had gone there, and participated in the raid on the Gemeentehuis in Leiderdorp on January 4, 1944, and in other raids. Wildschut was arrested and incarcerated in the Weteringschans prison in Amsterdam. Johannes Post, who felt guilty about this arrest, organized the attempt to rescue, but this failed, with fatal consequences for Post. Jan Wildschut was subsequently deported to several camps and died in a German concentration camp on New Year's Day 1945. On June 9, 1983, he was posthumously recognized as Righteous Among the Nations by Yad Vashem.

Wilhelmina (1880–1963). Queen of the Netherlands.

Willeumier, Hendrik J. (1917–2006). Douwes's half-brother who lived in the United States.

Willeumier, Johanna Adriana. First wife of Petrus Arnoldus Conradus Douwes, Arnold's mother.

"Willie/Willy." Another name given to the Jewish onderduikster known as "De Bijenkorf."

Willie. Jewish girl hidden by the baker in Hollandscheveld.

Wim. Onderduiker.

Wimmenhove (Wemmenhove), Harm (1908–1975). Shopkeeper in Elim who was head of the LO there alongside Minister Hoogkamp and who became commander of the Binnenlandse Strijdkrachten in the village.

"Winchester." Alias of Harm Koning (1894–1945), a resistance worker who died in KZ Neuengamme.

Winkel, Hendrik Johannes (1888–), and Reina Gezina Winkel-Krabben (1892–). The Winkel family, originally from Amsterdam, owned a farm in Nieuwlande next door to the Van der Zwaag family. During the occupation, they hid Jewish friends and later also others whom their daughter Hennie needed to place, but had no alternative accommodation. On June 9, 1983, Hendrik Johannes andhis wife, were designated as Righteous Among the Nations by Yad Vashem.

Winkel, Hendrika Johanna (1922–), or "Hennie." The daughter of Hendrik and Reina Winkel, she was one of Post's and Douwes's contacts in Amsterdam who sent Jewish fugitives to Nieuwlande. She had a shop and a house on the Zuider-Amstellaan 98 in Amsterdam, owned by her parents. Usually Hennie brought the Jews to Hoogeveen by train. She also saved the lives of Max Léons's parents, who were hiding in The Hague. On June 9, 1983, Hendrika was designated as Righteous Among the Nations by Yad Vashem.

Winkel, Kitty (1916–). Daughter of Hendrik and Reina Winkel. She lived in the Michaelangelostraat in Amsterdam and helped Jews. She was designated as Righteous Among the Nations by Yad Vashem on December 20, 1983.

Woering, Henk/Hendrik (Bill). Resistance worker in Veenhuizen and member of the KP Noord Drenthe.

Ypma, Rienks (1914–1996). Minister of the Orthodox Calvinist church in Pesse between 1940 and 1944.

Zanting. A farmer in Nieuwlande.

Zee, Wiepke van der (1918–1944). Member of the resistance who worked in the town hall at Oosterhesselen.

Zijlstra, A. P. Trainee notary in Nieuwlande.

Zijlstra, Bouwe (1887–1975), and Diena Zijlstra-Post (1888–1975). Bouwe Zijlstra was a farmer who lived in Noordscheschut, between Hoogeveen and Coevorden, and who had married a sister of Johannes Post. They were always willing to take fugitives into their home. After Arnold Douwes and Max Léons had rescued the American pilot Texas Slim, whose plane had crashed, they brought him to the home of the Zijlstra family. They organized an escape route for the American, who posed as a big dumb and deaf woman, accompanied by Tinie Zijlstra, their daughter, who worked as a nurse in Bethesda Hospital in Hoogeveen. The pilot was escorted to Eindhoven, from there to Maastricht and Belgium, and eventually returned to his base in England, safe and sound. On June 9, 1983, the Zijlstras were designated as Righteous Among the Nations by Yad Vashem for their work in helping Jews.

Zijlstra, Hendrik (1914–2005), and Hendrikje Zijlstra-van der Leij (1915–1999). He was a teacher in Nieuwlande and the family hid Jewish fugitives in Nieuwlande. On June 9, 1983, the Zijlstras were recognized as Righteous Among the Nations by Yad Vashem.

Zijlstra, Jan. The son of Bouwe Zijlstra who was active in the resistance and sheltered Jews. He was recognized as Righteous Among the Nations by Yad Vashem in 1983.

Zijlstra, Jantina (Tine, Tinie). The daughter of Bouwe Zijlstra and Dina Post, she was a nurse and married to Anne van der Wal, who was also a member of the resistance. They were recognized as Righteous Among the Nations by Yad Vashem in 1983.

Zijlstra, Paulien. Daughter of Bouwe Zijlstra and active in the resistance.

Zimak, Ursula (1919–2002). Used "Bep" as an alias, she was a kindergarten teacher and onderduiker sheltered by the sisters Nieuwboer. After the war she married an American serviceman, Fred (Ephraïm) Auerbach and went to live in the United States.

Zomer, Tien. Refugee and resistance worker.

Zwaag, Bote van der. Father of Hemke van der Zwaag.

Zwaag, Hemke van der (1899–1990), and Frederika van der Zwaag-de Graaf (1901–1992), alias "Arie de Boer." This farmer and his wife in Nieuwlande, originally from Friesland, were the *achterbuurman* (back neighbor) whose property backed onto that of Johannes Post. He grew into one of the most important resistance men in the region. He was involved in a raid with Johannes Post and Arnold Douwes, and when Post left Nieuwlande, he appointed Van der Zwaag as his successor as leader of the regional armed resistance. After a narrow escape during a German raid on the house they were hiding in, Hemke was active as the collector and distributor of arms that had been dropped by the Allies. During the final months of the war, he slept with a loaded revolver under his pillow. He survived the occupation but was seriously traumatized. In 1983 Hemke and Frederika were designated as Righteous Among the Nations by Yad Vashem.

"Zwaantje." Alias of A. L. Oosterhuis, a member of the resistance in Delfzijl.

Zwart. Resistance worker and associate of Arnold Douwes.

Zwiers, Jantina Margaretha (1907–1992). She was the widow of Jan Zwiers (1906–1941) in Hollandscheveld who frequently helped Arnold Douwes. She was a sister-in-law of postman Jan Dekker and lived next door to him. (Douwes misspells her name as Swiers.) She was recognized as Righteous Among the Nations by Yad Vashem in 1979.

SOURCES

Hovingh, G. C. *Johannes Post: Exponent van het verzet. Een biografie.* Kampen: Kok, 1995.
Huizing, Lammert. *Zij konden niet anders. Herinneringen aan het verzet in Nieuwlande [1940-1945].* Zuidwolde: Stichting Het Dretse Boek, 1985.
Huizing, Lammert, and Jan Braker (eds), *Gedenkboek Hoogeveen 1940-1945.* Hoogeveen: Historisch Kring Hoogeveen, 1999.
Léons, Max, and Arnold Douwes. *Mitswa en Christenplicht. Bescheiden helden uit de illegaliteit.* s'-Gravenhage: Bzztôh, 2000.
Michman, Jozeph, and Bert Jan Flim, with the assistance of Conny Kristel. *The Encyclopedia of the Righteous Among the Nations.* Jerusalem/Amsterdam: Yad Vashem/NIOD, 2004-2005.
Schonewille, J., J. Engels, and J. van der Sleen. *Nieuwlande 1940-'45, een dorp dat zweeg.* Nieuwlande: Private Publication, 1993. The list of Protestant ministers who helped Jews published by G. C. Hovingh. www.hdc.vu.nl/nl/Images/Predikanten_die_joden_hielpen _IV_tcm215-460512.pdf.

Index

Aalderen, Albert (Ab) van (1892–1982), 177
"Aaltje, Tante," 85, 89–93, 98, 100, 102, 112, 134, 139
Aasman, Arend, 211
Aasman, Jan (1912–1972), 140, 211, 225
Adema, Sister, 212, 216, 255
Adler, Nanci, xiii
Aken, van, 186
Akker, Nelly van den (1917–), 105–7, 110, 118, 120, 131, 136, 142, 155–56, 177, 180, 196, 207, 212, 218, 230, 240
Alting, Andries, 237
"Ammi/Ammy, Tante," 139, 148, 156, 163, 171–72, 174, 208
Anne(n), Evert, 146
Annie, 121, 139, 210
"Annie, Tante," 140, 211
Ans, 221–24, 237, 261
Appel, Sally, 159, 164–65, 173, 189, 203, 207, 210
Ata, 129–30, 132, 133–36, 139, 147

Baanders, 145, 149
Baas, Adriaan (1913–1943), 81, 162
Bastiaanse, Cor, 23
Bejski, Moshe (1921–2007), viii
Belinfante, Robert Paul (1905–1940), 50
"Bep," 114, 116, 137, 138, 164, 177, 181, 189, 242, 250
Berends, 85, 92, 171
Berenschot, Derk Willem (1893–1979), 57
Bergh-van Teyn, Mrs, J van den, 141, 143, 175
Berkelaar, Wim, xiii
Bernhard, Prins von Lippe-Biesterfeld (1911–2004), 65, 233–34, 238, 249
Bert, 128
Bertha, 121
"Big." See Post, Johannes; Wiegman, Jacobus
"Big Shot." See Post, Johannes

"Bijenkorf, De," 145–47, 152, 154, 160, 179, 181–82, 202
Bisschop, Miesje, 72, 89, 92, 145, 172, 213, 225, 257
Bisschop, Roelof (1899–1989), 145
Blanken, Klaas Yzn (1892–1964), 75, 78, 88, 105, 112, 117, 120–22, 125, 130, 137, 141, 144–46, 150, 152–54, 160, 162, 172, 180, 185–86, 223, 231
Bleeker, Hendrik (1904–2001), 196, 200, 209–10, 215, 225, 234, 237–38, 242–43, 245, 249, 250, 256
Bloemink, 262
Blok, 171
Blokzijl, Max (1884–1946), 82–83
Bobby, 138–39, 156, 172, 185, 209, 217, 230
Boer, Annie de, 92, 94
"Boer, Arie de." See Zwaag, Hemke van der
Boer, Gerrit de, 28
Boer, Jan de, 204
Boer, Jansje, 193, 200, 223
Boer, Piet de, 292, 295
Boers, André, xiii
Boertien, 95
Boertje, Aaltje, 38, 69, 78, 87, 92, 97
Bogaard, Johannes (1881–1974), 21–22
Bolle-Levie, Mirjam (1917–), xv
Bolwijn, Engel (1903–1988), 117, 151, 153, 155, 196, 198, 200, 204, 209, 212–14, 216–17, 221–22, 240
Bolwijn, Hillechien (1927–), 151, 194, 264
Bonsius, 210
Boom, Corrie ten (1892–1983), 21–22
Boom, Willem ten (1886–1946), 21–22
Bos, Bastiaan (1924–1944), 226
Bos, Jan Simon van den (1901–1966), 154, 173, 206, 251, 255, 258, 264
Bos, Johannes, 179–80
Bos, Joost Pieter (1910–1979), 173, 212, 216, 224, 230, 234, 243–45, 249, 263–64

331

Bosch, Hendrik, 36–37
Bos-Doze, Geertje, 179–80
Bos-Schermers, Goverdina (1909–1957), 173, 212, 216, 224, 230, 234, 243–45, 249, 263–64
Bos-Verhave, Petra Suzanna Wilhelmina Van den (1911–1971), 154, 173, 206, 251, 255, 258, 264
Broenink, Harmen (1916–1995), 84, 91, 98, 106, 108, 145, 165, 167, 213
Broenink, Jannes, 68, 73, 75, 88
Broenink-Homan, Gerdijna "Dinie/Dien" J. G. (1919–1994), 56 -7, 64, 68, 73, 75, 88, 93, 181–182, 186, 199
Broenink-Strijker, Aaltje, 84, 91, 98, 106, 108, 145, 165, 167, 213
"Broertje." *See* Appel, Sally
Brouwer, Dr. Hendrik A. (1914–2003), 135, 157, 189, 197, 204, 217
Brouwer-Swieringa, Gertha Hermien (1914–2014), 135, 157, 189, 197, 204, 217
Bruin or Bruyn, Mrs de, 121, 132, 144
Buikema, Hiddo (1903–), 99, 119, 120, 181–82, 192–93, 217, 230, 233, 236, 255, 263
Buikema-van der Woude, Antje, 99, 119, 120, 181–82, 192–93, 217, 230, 233, 236, 255, 263
Burema, 135
Burgers, 62, 72
Buursma, Tonnis (1909–1944), 203–4

Churchill, Winston S., (1874–1965), 169
Clercq Zubli, D. de, 73, 96, 122, 126, 129, 130, 134
Cohen, 156, 160–62, 166–67
Cohen, Frits, 211
Cohen, Manfred, 197, 211
"Cor, Oom," 156, 159, 208–9, 212–13, 217–18, 221–25, 227–28, 229, 242, 246, 249, 252–53, 255–56, 259–61, 264
"Cupido," 251, 258, 264

Dalen, Pieter van, 51, 55, 124
Daling, 132, 135, 238
Datema, Freerk (1922–1944), 295
Davids, Isidor Joseph, alias "Peter" (1918–1996), xi, 10, 71–72, 80, 86, 89–90, 92–95, 97–102, 105–6, 111, 117, 123, 131, 152–54, 156, 158–59, 162, 164–66, 170, 173, 176–78, 180–86, 187–93, 196–201, 203, 205–8, 209–11, 214–32, 234, 236–46, 248–52, 255–56, 258–62, 265
Davidson, Mia, 112, 126–27, 138, 143, 151, 155, 172, 184, 186, 194–96, 208–9, 211–12, 253
Deesker, Anthony (1882–?), 112
Deesker-Rökker, Aleida (1892–?), 112
Dekker, Jan Hzn (1901–1994), 72, 75, 81–82, 89–92, 94–95, 97, 99, 102–3, 111, 114, 118, 126, 129, 138, 152, 165, 178–79, 187
Dekker-Zwiers, Arendina, 72, 75, 81–82, 89–92, 94–95, 97, 99, 102–3, 111, 114, 118, 126, 129, 138, 152, 165, 178–79, 187
Denig, Carl (1892–1975), 121
Dick, 138, 183
Dickie, 264
Dijk, Corrie, 207, 242
Dijk, Frouke, 112, 174, 189–93, 195–96, 199–201, 204–6, 210–12, 214, 217–20, 222–30, 232, 234, 236–38, 241–46, 248–49, 251–53, 255–64, 287
Dijk, Simon (1900–1988), 112, 174, 189–93, 195–96, 199–201, 204–6, 210–12, 214, 217–20, 222–30, 232, 234, 236–38, 241–46, 248–49, 251–53, 255–64, 287
Dijkema, 31
Dijken, van, 129, 210
Dijk-Mos, Ida (1903–2000), 112, 174, 189–93, 195–96, 199–201, 204–6, 210–12, 214, 217–20, 222–30, 232, 234, 236–38, 241–46, 248–49, 251–53, 255–64, 287
Dijsselhof, Egbert (1900–1971), 223
Dirk, 131, 205, 226–27
"Dirk, Oom," 164, 168, 189, 196
"Doeks." *See* Clercq-Zubli, Frida Jeanne de
Doornbos, Douwe, 171, 183, 187–88, 191–92, 200–201, 251
Doppenberg, Jannes (1892–1943), 107, 116
Dorgelaar, 220
Douwes, Albertha (Bertha) Arnolda Catharina (1898–), 38, 54, 60, 150
Douwes, Guillette Agatha (1915–1996), 73, 96, 99, 122, 126–27, 133, 186, 224, 232, 239–40, 242–43, 251, 263
Douwes, Hendrik Julius André (1914–1991), 37, 73, 96, 122, 126, 159, 184
Douwes, Henny (1950–), xiii, 36, 295, 297
Douwes, Irit (1948–), xiii, 36, 295, 297

Index | 333

Douwes, Jan (1900–1976), 37, 47–48, 124, 128–29, 142, 224, 292
Douwes, Jenny (1947–), xiii, 36, 295, 297
Douwes, Juliana Anna Louise (1909–1999), 37
Douwes, Mathilda Maria Cornelia (Mary) (1902–1986), 75, 89, 142, 215, 219
Douwes, Petrus Arnoldus Conradus Cornelius (1871–1935), 8, 36–37, 124
Douwes-Koning, Wilhelmina (Mimi) (1916–2016), 37, 73, 96, 122, 126, 159, 184
Douwes-van Doesburg, Nicoline (Niek) Henriëtte (1903–1985), 37, 47–48, 124, 128–29, 142, 224, 292
Drogt, H., 87
Drukker, 195
Duiker, 82, 241

Edith, 131, 138
"Eef, Tante," 168, 178, 197, 211, 212–15, 222
Egberts, Hendrik (1907–1945), 291
Eisenhower, Dwight D., (1890–1969), 233
Ekelenburg, Dirk van (1917–1945), 70–71, 74, 89, 94–95, 99, 126–27, 154, 171, 179, 245
Ekelenburg-an der Mast, Lientje van (1914–1988), 70–71, 74, 89, 94–95, 99, 126–27, 154, 171, 179, 245
Elema, 119–20, 160, 204, 238, 244
Elly, 130, 132–34, 139, 147
Elzenga [Elsinga], Anne Jannes (1908–1943), 130
Emmens, Wilko (1890–1945), 128, 139
Eppinga, Frederik Jacobsz (1890–1975), 107, 172, 265

Faber, (1901–?), 107, 125, 147, 152, 177, 223, 246
Flim, Bert Jan (1957–), xiii, 30
Frank, Anne (1929–1945), 18
Frank, Otto (1889–1980), 18, 19

Gans, Lou (1925–2008), vii, xi, 10, 18, 111–12, 114, 117–19, 123, 130–31, 141, 143, 152–54, 156, 158–59, 162–66, 173–75, 177–93, 201, 203–8, 210–34, 237–45, 247–49, 255–56, 259–61, 263–64
Geelkerken, Cornelis (Kees) van (1901–1976), 108
"Geer, Minister de," 192, 195–96, 201

Gerbrandy, Pieter Sjoerds (1885–1961), 102, 234
Gerding, Michiel, 26
"Gerrit, Oom." See Verdoner, Abraham Gompert
Gijp, 127
Ginhoven, H. C. J. van (1896–1942), 137, 141
Ginhoven, J. D. van (1902–1975), 201
Ginhoven, Martinus Johannes van (1908–1995), 124, 136–37, 201
Goor, Hermannus (Mans) van (1904–1945), 165, 204
Gorter, Klaas (1905–1945), 112, 139, 171, 204, 215
Goudoever, 56
Graaf, Frans de (1912–1990), 184, 205, 208, 218, 225
Graaf-Deuring, Antje de (1913–1949), 184, 205, 208, 218, 225
Griet, 247
Griffioen, Agatha (1927–1987), 189, 191
Griffioen, Rijk (1892–1951), 151–52, 156, 158, 169–70, 188–89, 191, 199, 227–28, 258
Griffioen-Kraay, Elsje (1893–1954), 151–52, 156, 158, 169–70, 188–89, 191, 199, 227–28, 258
Groenendijk, Ad, 23
Groot, Homme de (1903–), 169

Haak, Jur (1891–1945), 23
Hagen, 91, 98, 101, 103
Haitjema, 198
Ham, Gerrit, 175, 180, 191–92, 231, 248, 255–56, 258, 262
"Hannie," 143
Harry, 131, 263
Harster, Wilhelm (1904–1991), 38
Hartemink, Albert Jan (1916–1945), 156, 159, 172, 213, 248, 254
Hartemink-Schierbeek, Hendrika Johanna (1917–), 156, 159, 172, 213, 248, 254
Haspers, 156
Heeckeren van Kell, Alexander, Baron van (1871–1945), 116, 124
Heerspink, Hendrik (1885–1955), 57, 98, 101, 140, 214, 263
Helm, Arend van der (1880–1949), 220

Helm, Jan van der (1897–1988), 120, 163, 172, 192, 195–96, 201, 204, 206
Helm, Jan van der (1911–1945), 215, 219–20, 234, 241, 245–48, 252, 264
Henk, 173, 212, 245, 250, 264
"Herman." *See* Gans, Lou
Hertz, Otto (1881–?), 170
Hertz-Liebestein, Frieda (1880–1968), 170
Hielkema, Hielke Willem (1914–1991), 71
"Hoedag," 151, 170, 235
Homan-Stegeman, Berendina (1879–1955), 9, 38, 39, 56–57, 60, 64, 67–68, 84, 88, 91, 108, 136, 167, 181, 186–87, 202, 222, 232, 263–64
Hoogeveen, Jacob (1909–1988), 126, 156, 160, 194, 208, 213, 253
Hoogeveen-Aardema, Bontje (1912–1988), 126, 156, 160, 194, 208, 213, 253
Hoogkamp, Rikkert Arnoldus (1909–1996), 192
Hoogkamp, Tjeerd (1855–1953), 192
Houweningen van, Mrs., 197–98
Hovingh, Geert C., xiii, xvi, 36
Hovink, Dr., 134
Hurk, Peter van den, 28

Ivan and Michael, 237–38, 242, 253–54, 258–59

Jack, 84–86
Jacobs, Salomon (Sam) (1903–1941), 9, 52
Jan, 131, 138, 207
Jansen, 73
Jansen, G., 87
Jo, 137, 145, 263
Job, 122
Johan, 114, 169, 200, 202, 214, 239
Johan or John the Belgian, 239–40, 244, 255–56, 258–59, 261
"Johanna, Tante." *See* Rachab the Whore
Jong, de (headmaster), 146, 216
Jong, de (director), 101, 106, 108, 150, 165, 199, 215
Jonge, Jhr. Marinus W. C. de (1881–1943), 81
Jonker, 152, 179, 181
Jonker, Jacobus (Kobus) (1880–1977), 123, 165, 209, 227
Joop, 217
Juliana (1909–2004), 65, 182

Kaay, Pieter (1904–1943), 66
Kamphuis, 263–64
Kapper, Elly, 212, 214, 216, 243, 263–64
Karelse, Pieter, J., 98, 233, 237, 247–48, 251, 256, 261, 263
Karelse, Thijs (Freek), 239, 248, 251, 255–56, 264
Kats, Jan (1905–), 9, 64, 67–68, 73, 75–76, 83–85, 88–92, 94–95, 98–100, 102, 104–6, 117, 125, 135, 152, 154, 156–57, 181, 195, 211, 222, 231–33, 237–38, 241–42, 247–48, 251–54, 265
Kats-Booy, Geesje (1908–), 9, 64, 67–68, 73, 75–76, 83–85, 88–92, 94–95, 98–100, 102, 104–6, 117, 125, 135, 152, 154, 156–57, 181, 195, 211, 222, 231–33, 237–38, 241–42, 247–48, 251–54, 265
Kees, 138, 207
Kerk, Arend Jan van der (?–1970), 207
Kessel, Monique van, xiii
Kikkert, Hendrik (1915–2001), 114, 118, 130, 145–46, 151, 153, 162–63, 166, 170, 177, 189, 191–93, 235–36, 240–41
Kikkert-Pol, Griet (1920–2002), 114, 118, 130, 145–46, 151, 153, 162–63, 166, 170, 177, 189, 191–93, 235–36, 240–41
Kist, Jan (1888–1969), 91
Kitty (Tiet), 221–25
Klaas, 120
Klein, Willem Hendrik (1919–1944), 237
Klijnsma, 225, 227
Klooster, 292
Knake, Cornelia Charlotta (1888–1972), 37, 124
Knake, Gezina Berendina (1879–1952), 124
Knake, Maria Magdalena (1877–1949), 124
Kock, Cornelis de (1908–1944), 90, 244
Koekoek, Jacobus (1888–1983), 207–8, 217–18
Koekoek-Euving, Roelofje (1888–1970), 207–8, 217–18
"Koenraad." *See* Raad, Klaas de
Koning, Harm (1894–1945), 94–95
Kool, Dolf, 212, 214, 216, 243, 264
Kool, Eddy, 54
"Koos, Tante," 153, 163, 175
Krabbe, 202, 217
Kreeft, Joop, 159, 246
Kremer, 189, 226–27, 244–45, 249, 253–54, 258

Kruyff, Hendrik de, 28, 72, 74, 139
Kurpershoek, Mrs., 83
Kuyper, Abraham (1837–1920), 33
Kuyper, Celina Johanna (1923–1943), 35, 62–63, 70, 72, 75–76, 78, 80, 89, 94, 193
Kwaat, 210
Kwant, Toon, 220, 244, 252, 259, 264

"Ladies, the." *See* Nieuwboer
Lanting, Johannes, 210, 238, 243, 254, 258
Leendertz-Hoog, Mrs.M.Th. (1892–1945), 141, 143
Leenhouts, T., 98, 101, 202, 209, 211, 214, 221, 241, 259
"Lekkere Liebe Lutschie" (LLL), 170, 173
Lelie, Levie/Louis (1902–1989), 152–53, 160, 162–63, 177, 204, 219, 222, 225, 228–29, 234, 241, 245
Lelie, Salomon Hans (1926–), 110, 152, 160, 170, 177, 204, 217, 264
Lennep, Hester van (1916–2000), 23–24
Léons, Chelly, 130, 143
Léons, Max (Nico) (1921–), vii, viii, xi, 10, 110, 112–17, 121–26, 127, 130–32, 133–37, 139–46, 149–59, 161–64, 166, 168–69, 172–81, 184, 189–91, 193, 196, 203–4, 222, 243, 257, 260, 292–93, 296
Léons, Nathan, 123–24, 130
Lia, 139, 147, 151–52, 161, 171, 199, 212, 218, 222, 230, 239
"Lidia." *See* Lier, Klaartje van
Lientje, 155, 181, 222
Lier, Klaartje van, 71, 85, 89–90, 92, 94–95, 99, 134, 139, 171, 184, 204, 210, 265
Lies, 221–24, 245
"Lies, Tante," 179
Liesje, 131, 155, 196, 201
Lips, Hendrik (1892–1943), 104
Loekie, 139, 150–51, 178, 213
"Louise, Tante," 120–21, 126, 138–39, 143, 151, 155–56, 172, 185, 208, 253
Lubbers, 250
Lunenberg, 187, 221
Luten, 183
Luth, 202

Maa, Kornelis, or Cees de (1900–1971), 86–87, 99, 105, 119, 224, 228

Mannerheim, Carl Gustaf, Baron (1867–1957), 203
Marissen, Hillie, 264–65
Marlijn, Mrs., 142
Mars, 108
Meekof, Albert (1897–1987), 76, 78, 94, 103
Meer, Benno van der, 231
Meerburg, Piet (1919–2011), 23
Melis, 75, 219, 232
Metselaar, Albert, xiii
Meulenbelt, Jan (1921–2011), 23
Meyer, Boele, 246, 248
Meyer, Mans, 246, 248, 256
Michman, Jozeph (1914–2009), viii
"Mirjam," 127, 140–41, 143–44, 155, 175, 179
Moes, Albert (1890–1982), 91, 93–94
Mol, 257
Molen, Gezina van der (1892–1978), 24
Mooi, Frederik (Frits) (1921–2008), 80, 84
Mooi, Hermannus Gerardus (1905–1983), 80
Mulder, Jan (1901–1980), 95
Mulder, Johannes J., (1887–1943), 81, 85, 173
Muller, Anjo, 239–40
Muller, Jan, 213
Muller, Pieter Germen (1888–1945), 179, 213, 217, 219, 222, 224, 234, 236, 244, 248–49, 251–52
Muller, Truusje, 237, 239–40
Musch, Gerard, 23
Musch, Jaap, 23
Mussert, ir. Anton Adriaan (1894–1946), 68, 94, 108, 178, 199, 201, 248

Naber, Jan (1923–1957), 34, 72, 74, 78, 80–82, 86, 112, 140, 142, 165
Naber-Raak, Jantina Gerritdina (1922–1957), 34, 72, 74, 78, 80–82, 86, 112, 140, 142, 165
Nachtuil, 261, 263
"Nel." *See* Akker, Nellie van den
Neutel-Zomer, Hilligje (1889–1970), 137, 145, 166, 168
"Nico." *See* Léons, Max
Nie, Johannes Arnoldus van (1893–1979), 81
Nienhuis, Klaas (1872–1963), 153–54, 160, 162, 192, 214, 221, 244
Nienhuis-Belhuizen, Jantje (1889–?), 153–54, 160, 162, 192, 214, 221, 244

Nieuwboer, Hendrika Evelina (1898–1991), 114–17, 125, 127, 134, 137, 140, 147, 151–52, 155–56, 159, 161, 163, 165, 167–69, 181, 193, 203, 222
Nieuwboer, Tjitske (1901–1988), 114–17, 125, 127, 134, 137, 140, 147, 151–52, 155–56, 159, 161, 163, 165, 167–69, 181, 193, 203, 222
Nijen Twilhaar, Hendrik Jan (1901–1966), 253
Nijhof, Johannes, 185, 216, 248
Nijwening, Albert, 120, 159, 173, 175, 196, 209, 230, 232–33, 238, 252, 255
Nijwening, Jan (1900–?), 184, 187, 232
Nijwening-Sikkema, Jacoba, 120, 159, 173, 175, 196, 209, 230, 232–33, 238, 252, 255
Nijwening-Zeldenrust, Hermina (1904–?), 184, 187, 232
Nolet, Wim, 149
Noordt, Miss, 232
Norden, Robert, 86, 90
Norden-Davids, S., 86, 90–93, 98–100, 102, 112, 134, 139
Norder, Johannes (1897–1959), 166, 170, 173, 183, 185, 191, 193–94, 201, 215, 253–54, 258
Norder-Eilander, Jantje (1905–1984), 166, 170, 173, 183, 185, 191, 193–94, 201, 215, 253–54, 258
"Nuphar." *See* Plomp

Offeringa, Ibele (1904–1980), 247
Oorchot, J. A. M. van (1893–1959), 107
Oosterhuis, A. L. (1902–1967), 94–95
Oppenheimer, Dr. Klaus E. H. (1905–1986), 71, 74
Otten, Arend, 191, 232
Otten, Arie, 99, 106, 166, 169, 176, 181–83, 188–92, 200, 202–3, 215–17, 239
Otten, Seine (1910–1993), 111, 120
Otten-Bovendorp, Dirkje Jantje (1905–1988), 111, 120
"Ouwe Taaie," 160–62, 171–72, 174, 208, 217, 249

Padding, Wolter (1906–1953), 145, 153, 163, 170, 173, 178, 196, 201, 222, 225, 243–44
Padding-Nijwening, Grietje (1904–1960), 145, 153, 163, 170, 173, 178, 196, 201, 222, 225, 243–44

Paldiel, Mordecai (1937–), xiii, 39
Pallandt Family, 51
Pastoor, 292
"Pencil." *See* Faber
Pennings, Pieter Jan (1894–1975), 89–90, 94, 98, 102, 141, 170
Pennings-de Rooij, Johanna Bernardine (1909–1979), 89–90, 94, 98, 102, 141, 170
Pet, Claas (1846–1916), 241
Petertje, 132, 135, 148, 160, 163, 170, 177, 204, 217, 219
Philipson, Menachem (Menno), 178, 211
Piek, Carel, 71
Pijl, Miss, 74–75
Plomp, 140, 155
Pol, 183, 207
Pontier, Gerard (1888–1976), 23
Post, Evert Egge (1925–1944), 226, 228, 235
Post, Gerrit (1898–1976), 59, 75–76, 78, 135
Post, (Hendrik) Henk JWzn. (1900–1982), 35, 75–77, 81
Post, Hennie (1938–), 94
Post, Hermien, 58–59
Post, Hilda, 58–59, 100, 102
Post, Hillegienus (1929–2007), 77
Post, Jan, 78, 91, 97, 100, 126, 191, 196, 216, 226–27, 230, 258, 262
Post, Johannes (1906–1944), vii, xi, 7, 9, 26–28, 30, 32–36, 38, 58–59, 60, 62–63, 66–67, 69, 71, 74–78, 80, 82, 85–87, 91–92, 95, 97, 100, 102–3, 107, 129, 133, 144–45, 153–54, 158–59, 165, 172–73, 178, 184–85, 193, 198, 207–8, 216–18, 221, 226, 231–32, 258
Post, Maarten (1885–1978), 172
Post, Marinus (1902–1944), 34, 35, 81, 76–77, 88, 94
Post, Trijn, 100
Post, Wolter JWzn. (1892–1969), 77
Post-Kamphuis, Rika (1896–1970), 77
Post Mzn, Wolter (1929–), 77
Post-Salomons, Dien (1903–1991), 38, 58–59, 62, 71, 75, 78, 85–86, 95, 100, 103–4, 183
Pronk, Catrien, 73

Raad, Klaas de (1904–1945), 82, 84, 93, 198
Raak, Hendrick (1920–1944), 166, 199
Raak, Jantina Gerritdina (Jannie) (1922–1957), 87, 92, 99, 101–2, 106, 166

"R(achab) de H(oere)," 138, 182, 200–201, 203–8, 210, 217–18, 222, 224
Rauter, Hanns Albin (1895–1949), 249
Rechteren Limpurg, Graaf van (1909–1962), 53
Reichenberger, Jet (1926–2004), 295, 297
Reichenberger, Miep, 295
Reijnierse, Jozias (1904–1981), 66, 117–18, 158, 161–62, 188, 195, 198, 222, 231, 252, 263
Reine, Klaas, 199
Reiner, Szaya (Jozef) (1897–1945), 220
"Riek," 180, 185
Riek, 129, 134, 139, 210
Rinsema, Thijs, 30
Roberts. *See* Texas Slim
Roet, Henk later Chaïm (1932–), vii, viii, 112
Roffel, Willem (1902–), 58, 60, 68, 96, 103, 119
Romijn, Peter, xiii
Rotterdam, Reus van, 124–128
Rozeman, Albert (1922–1984), 28, 34, 72, 74, 78, 85–86, 100–102, 112, 140, 142, 165
Rozeman, Albert Jan (1914–1944), 28, 79, 81, 86, 101, 104, 114, 165, 170, 175, 199
Rozeman, Steven (1882–1945), 79, 114, 165
Rundstedt, Gerd von (1875–1953), 211
Ruys, Mien, 127

Salomons, Harmina Aaltina (1904–1969), 35, 75–77, 81
Salomons-Huisingh, Hillighe (1875–1950), 69, 72, 100
Schipper, A., 254, 256
Scholten, Bep, 60, 64, 66–67, 72, 75, 93, 95, 98, 101, 103, 105, 108, 114, 127, 137, 140, 143, 150, 161, 167, 182, 194, 197, 200, 202, 210, 214, 220, 229, 239, 241
Scholten, Herman (1899–1960), 9, 86, 94, 151, 156–57, 172, 194, 209, 248
Scholten, Jo, 60, 64, 66–67, 72, 75, 93, 95, 98, 101, 103, 105, 108, 114, 127, 137, 140, 143, 150, 161, 167, 182, 194, 197, 200, 202, 210, 214, 220, 229, 239, 241
Schonewille, Arend (1903–1955), 195
Schonewille, Geert (1913–1988), 104, 131–34, 136, 139, 147, 151, 195, 210
Schonewille, Piet (1896–1963), 88, 195

Schonewille-Nijzing, Hendrika Annechina (1914–1978), 104, 131–34, 136, 139, 147, 151, 195, 210
Schouten, 131, 134, 139
Schuiling, Jantje Post- (1897–1968), 165, 210, 241–42, 243–45, 258
Schwegman, Marjan, xiii
Seinhorst, L., 76
Seller, H. C., 81, 102, 104, 117
Seyss-Inquart, Dr. Arthur (1892–1946), 30
Shackleton, Ernest (1874–1922), 121
Sikkel, Constant (1895–1967), 23
Sleen, Jan van der, xiii
Sliekers, Willem, 260
Slijkhuis (Sliekers), 206
Slik, Willem Koert (1886–1967), 189, 197
Slikker, Bram, 149
Slomp, Frits Jzn, (1898–1978), alias "Frits de Zwerver," 34, 191
Slomp-Ten Kate, Tjaltje (1896–1988), 34, 191
Sloten, 241
Sluys, Pieter van der (1887–1973), 65
Smid, Sister, 209, 212, 250
Smit, Adrianus (1899–1963), 49
Smit, Jacobus (1880–1943), 54
Snippe, Gerrit (1892–1972), 188
Snoek, Lucas, 257
"Snorrebaard." *See* Seller H. C.
"Snorretje." *See* Zwaag, Hemke van der
Soet (or Zoet), Lenie, 232
Stakenborg, C. J. H. W. (1903–1987), 150
Steenbakker Moriljon Loijsen, J. A. (1898–1983), 92
Stegeman, Frederik (1887–1984), 9, 38, 39, 56–57, 60, 64, 67–68, 84, 88, 91, 108, 136, 167, 181, 186–87, 202, 222, 232, 263–64
Stegeman, Frits, 84, 98, 101, 107, 108, 138, 142–43, 149, 171, 181–82, 199, 232
Stegeman, Herman (1877–1961), 38, 54–56, 149–50
Stegeman, Jan Derk (1875–1970), 98
Strijbos, Jan P. (1891–1983), 121
Süskind, Walter (1906–1945), 24
Suzy, 131, 142
Sweepe, Henk or Hendrik (1917–2001), 118–19, 136, 166, 169, 201, 203, 225, 236, 252, 259–60

Taai-taai man. *See* Blanken, Klaas
"Texas Slim," 157–62, 181
Thalen, Jacob (1877–1960), 160, 263
"Thea." *See* Kuyper, Celina Johanna
"Thea, Tante," 175
Thijs-Compagner, Jacoba (1891–1983). *See* "Koos, Tante"
Thomassen, mr. A. M. P., 128–29
Tineke, 128–129, 147, 151–52, 161, 181, 199, 212, 218, 222, 230, 239
Tjalma, Jetze (1893–1986), 150
Toet, J., 87
Toren, Jan van de, 292
Troost, 90

Veen, Hendrikus van der (1901–1982), 165, 180, 185, 239
Veenstra, Hilbrand (1919–1986), 158, 163–64, 181, 183
Veenstra, Johannes (1890–), 164, 183
Veenstra-Dekker, Wietske (1919–), 158, 163–64, 181, 183
Veenstra-Gringhuis, Roolfje (1891–), 164, 183
Veerman, 214, 239
Vegt, Hendrikus Marinus van der, 202, 256, 289
Veltman, mgr Petrus Johannes (1885–1974), 109
Venhuis, 102
Verdoner, Abraham G., 173–75, 177, 179, 180, 187, 191, 201, 206, 208–9, 211–12, 215, 217, 225, 227, 229, 231–34, 237, 246, 250, 253–54, 257
Versteeg, 175
Vinne, Jacob (Job) van der (1908–1980), 175
Vinne, Jitse van der (1876–1951), 69, 90, 160, 167, 175, 177
Vinne-Plaggenborg, Albertje van der (1887–1963), 69, 90, 160, 167, 175, 177
Visser, Hendrik (1906–1962), 174, 193–94, 201, 203, 210, 212, 218, 229, 255
Visser, Henk, 85, 127
Visser, Jan, 85
Visser, Miss, 195
Visser-Huttinga, Annechien (1893–1981), 174, 193–94, 201, 203, 210, 212, 218, 229, 255
Vlesman, Léon, 127

Vloten, Heinrich van (1895–1964), 56, 60, 141, 143, 155
Vloten-van den Bergh, Octavie van (1898–1944), 56, 60, 141, 143, 155
Volger, Pim, 82
Volger, Dr. Willem (1904–1980), 9, 38
Volger-Kurpershoek, Anna (1907–1999), 9, 38
Vree, Frank van, xiii
Vries, Anne de (1904–1964), 36
Vries, Arie de (1895–1962), 238
Vries, Theunis Homme de, 196, 200, 217, 245, 247–48, 255, 263
Vries de, 102

"Wasbeer." *See* Ans
Weij, Hendrikus van der (1910–1983), 167
Weima, Douwe (1897–1990), 90
Westra, Arend, 256
Wiegman (Wigman), Jacobus (1905–), 142, 144–46, 162, 168, 178, 197, 212, 241
Wiegman-Hensums, Aikina (1908–), 142, 144–46, 162, 168, 178, 197, 212, 241
Wieren, Bernardus Carolinus van (1892–1965), 134, 178
Wieren, Bernardus Carolinus Bzn. van (1924–1945), 178
Wieten, 174, 196, 208, 218, 252, 258
Wiggerink, H. J., 103
Wijk, Levie (1878–1943), 84
Wildschut, Johannes Wilhelmus (Jan) (1913–1945), 34–35
Wilhelmina (1880–1963), 34
Willeumier, Hendrik J. (1917–2006), 36
Willeumier, Johanna Adriana, 36
Willie, 81, 91, 100, 102
"Willie/Willy." *See* "Bijenkorf de"
Wim, 107
Wimmenhove (Wemmenhove), Harm (1908–1975), 262
"Winchester." *See* Koning, Harm
Winkel, Hendrik Johannes (1888–), 121, 143–46
Winkel, Hendrika Johanna (1922–), or "Hennie," 107–8, 118–19, 121, 127, 130, 134, 143, 145, 147–49, 150–54, 159, 162, 165–67, 171–72, 174–75, 179–82, 184, 186, 194, 196–98, 207, 214, 229–30, 240
Winkel, Kitty (1916–), 130, 143, 145

Winkel-Krabben, Reina Gezina (1892–), 121, 143–46
Woering, Henk/Hendrik (Bill), 290

Ypma, Rienks (1914–1996), 73, 103, 106

Zanting, 133, 213
Zee, Wiepke van der (1918–1944), 166, 168–70, 183
Zijlstra, A. P., 71, 103
Zijlstra, Bouwe (1887–1975), 75, 95, 100, 102, 104–5, 107, 126, 135, 154, 156–59, 162–63, 174, 178–80, 193, 195–96, 199–200, 205, 209, 217, 235, 241, 248, 251–52
Zijlstra, Hendrik (1914–2005), 87, 92, 98, 102, 105, 117, 125, 142, 145, 168, 178, 197, 211–12, 216, 221, 241, 289
Zijlstra, Jan, 95, 176, 205, 217, 235, 248
Zijlstra, Jantina (Tine, Tinie), 122, 154, 158, 174, 196, 200, 204–5, 207, 215–17, 223, 230
Zijlstra, Paulien, 199, 247, 252
Zijlstra-Post, Diena (1888–1975), 75, 95, 100, 102, 104–5, 107, 126, 135, 154, 156–59, 162–63, 174, 178–80, 193, 195–96, 199–200, 205, 209, 217, 235, 241, 248, 251–52
Zijlstra-van der Leij, Hendrikje (1915–1999), 87, 92, 98, 102, 105, 117, 125, 142, 145, 168, 178, 197, 211–12, 216, 221, 241, 289
Zimak, Ursula (1919–2002), 177, 181, 189, 242
Zomer, Tien, 100
Zwaag, Bote van der, 132
Zwaag, Hemke van der (1899–1990), alias "Arie de Boer," 28, 35, 61–62, 76, 82, 90–93, 95, 97, 99–100, 102, 104, 106, 112, 116–17, 119, 126, 131–32, 134, 156, 161, 165–66, 193, 205, 218, 224, 227, 233–38, 241, 244–45, 265
Zwaag-de Graaf, Frederika van der (1901–1992), 28, 35, 61–62, 76, 82, 90–93, 95, 97, 99–100, 102, 104, 106, 112, 116–17, 119, 126, 131–32, 134, 156, 161, 165–66, 193, 205, 218, 224, 227, 233–38, 241, 244–45, 265
Zwart, 177–178, 28, 242, 246
Zwiers, Jantina Margaretha (1907–1992), 80, 82, 84, 86–87, 89–90, 94–95, 102, 117–19, 131, 177, 196, 201, 213

Arnold Douwes (1906–1999) was an itinerant Dutch horticulturalist who spent time in the United States as well as his native Netherlands and ran a rescue network during the German occupation. He was designated as Righteous Among the Nations by Yad Vashem in 1965.

Bob Moore is Professor of Twentieth-Century European History at the University of Sheffield. He has published extensively on the history of Western Europe in the mid-twentieth century, including *Victims and Survivors: The Nazi Persecution of the Jews in the Netherlands, 1940–1945*; *Resistance in Western Europe*; (with Frank Caestecker) *Refugees from Nazi Germany and the Liberal European States*; and *Survivors: Jewish Self-Help and Rescue in Nazi-Occupied Western Europe*.

Johannes Houwink ten Cate is Professor Emeritus of Holocaust and Genocide Studies at the University of Amsterdam. He has published extensively on the Nazi occupation of the Netherlands and the persecution of the Jews. His many publications include an introduction (with Dan Michman) to an edition of the war diary letters of Mirjam Bolle-Levie.

Printed and bound by CPI Group (UK) Ltd, Croydon, CR0 4YY
31/07/2025

14711786-0001